Combating Proliferation

Combating Proliferation

Strategic Intelligence and Security Policy

Jason D. Ellis and Geoffrey D. Kiefer

The Johns Hopkins University Press

Baltimore and London

Preface © 2004 The Johns Hopkins University Press
All rights reserved. Published 2004
Printed in the United States of America on acid-free paper

Johns Hopkins Paperbacks edition, 2007
9 8 7 6 5 4 3 2 1

The Johns Hopkins University Press
2715 North Charles Street
Baltimore, Maryland 21218-4363
www.press.jhu.edu

The Library of Congress has cataloged the hardcover edition of this book as follows:

Ellis, Jason D.
    Combating proliferation : strategic intelligence and security policy / Jason D. Ellis and Geoffrey D. Kiefer.
        p.   cm.
Includes bibliographical references and index.
ISBN 0-8018-7958-2 (hardcover : alk. paper)
1. Military intelligence—United States.   2. National security—United States.   3. United States—Military policy.   4. Weapons of mass destruction.   5. World politics—1989–   I. Kiefer, Geoffrey D., 1974–   II. Title.
    UB251.U5E43 2004
    358′.3′0973—dc22

                                        2003025936

ISBN 10: 0-8018-8626-0 (pbk. : alk. paper)
ISBN 13: 978-0-8018-8626-3

A catalog record for this book is available from the British Library.

Contents

Figures and Tables

Acronyms and Abbreviations

AFRL	Air Force Research Laboratory
BJP	Bharatiya Janata Party (India)
BW	Biological warfare
BWC	Biological and Toxin Weapons Convention
CDISS	Centre for Defence and International Security Studies
CENTAF	US Central Command Air Forces
CENTCOM	US Central Command
CIA	Central Intelligence Agency
CTR	Cooperative Threat Reduction
CW	Chemical warfare
CWC	Chemical Weapons Convention
DCI	Director of central intelligence
DIA	Defense Intelligence Agency
DOD	Department of Defense
DPRK	Democratic People's Republic of Korea
DTRA	Defense Threat Reduction Agency
EMPTA	O-ethyl methylphosphonothic acid
FAA	Foreign Assistance Act
FBIS	Foreign Broadcast Information Service
HUMINT	Human intelligence
IAEA	International Atomic Energy Agency
IAU	Information Assessment Unit (UNSCOM)
IMINT	Imagery intelligence
INR	Bureau of Intelligence and Research (US Department of State)
IRBM	Intermediate-range ballistic missile
ISG	Iraq Survey Group
KGB	Soviet Committee for State Security
MASINT	Measurement and signature intelligence
MEL	Mobile erector launcher

Minatom	Ministry of Atomic Energy (Russia)
MRBM	Medium-range ballistic missile
MSE	Muthanna State Establishment (Iraq)
MTCR	Missile Technology Control Regime
MWe	Megawatt electric
NATO	North Atlantic Treaty Organization
NIC	National Intelligence Council
NIE	National Intelligence Estimate
NIF	National Islamic Front (Sudan)
NPT	Treaty on the Nonproliferation of Nuclear Weapons
OPCW	Organization for the Prohibition of Chemical Weapons
PRC	People's Republic of China
RSA	Russian Space Agency
SIGINT	Signals intelligence
SNIE	Special National Intelligence Estimate
SOF	Special operations forces
SRBM	Short-range ballistic missile
TD-1	Taepodong-1
TD-2	Taepodong-2
TEL	Transporter erector launcher
TsAGI	Central Aerohydrodynamic Institute (Russia)
UNMOVIC	United Nations Monitoring, Verification, and Inspection Commission
UNSCOM	United Nations Special Commission
WHO	World Health Organization
WMD	Weapons of mass destruction

Preface

It was an extraordinary moment in American diplomacy when Secretary of State Colin Powell briefed the UN Security Council in a last-ditch diplomatic effort to avoid war. In a once-in-a-lifetime presentation on February 5, 2003—one reminiscent of that given by his predecessor, Adlai Stevenson, in the context of the Cuban Missile Crisis—Powell charged that the Iraqi government was in "material breach" of a decade's worth of Security Council resolutions, presented substantial intelligence data to make the case, and charged that Iraq's recalcitrance had moved it "closer to the day when it will face serious consequences for its continued defiance of this Council."[1] President George W. Bush had addressed the United Nations in September 2002, warning that Saddam Hussein's regime posed a "grave and gathering danger" and throwing down the gauntlet to the assembled body: "The conduct of the Iraqi regime is a threat to the authority of the United Nations, and a threat to peace. Iraq has answered a decade of U.N. demands with a decade of defiance. All the world now faces a test, and the United Nations a difficult and defining moment. Are Security Council resolutions to be honored and enforced, or cast aside without consequence? Will the United Nations serve the purpose of its founding, or will it be irrelevant?"[2]

Set against the backdrop of the post–September 11, 2001, security landscape, this was a defining moment for American foreign policy. The administration's just-released national-security strategy was quite pointed in its appraisal of the twin challenges posed by weapons of mass destruction (WMD) and terrorism to US national security: "The gravest danger our Nation faces lies at the crossroads of radicalism and technology. Our enemies have openly declared that they are seeking weapons of mass destruction, and evidence indicates that they are doing so with determination. The United States will not allow these efforts to proceed. . . . History will judge harshly those who saw the coming danger but failed to act. In the new world we have entered, the only path to peace and security is the path of action."[3] In this context the intelligence community assessed, among other things, that:

- "Iraq has continued its WMD programs in defiance of UN resolutions and restrictions."
- "Since inspections ended in 1998, Iraq has maintained its chemical weapons effort, energized its missile program, and invested more heavily in biological weapons; in the view of most agencies, Baghdad is reconstituting its nuclear weapons program."
- "We have low confidence in our ability to assess when Saddam would use WMD."
- "Baghdad *for now* appears to be drawing a line short of conducting terrorist attacks with conventional or [chemical or biological weapons] against the United States, fearing that exposure of Iraqi involvement would provide Washington a stronger case for making war."
- "Saddam, if sufficiently desperate, might decide that only an organization such as al-Qa'ida—with worldwide reach and extensive terrorist infrastructure, and already engaged in a life-or-death struggle against the United States—could perpetrate the type of terrorist attack that he would hope to conduct. . . . In such circumstances, he might decide that the extreme step of assisting the Islamic terrorists in conducting a CBW attack against the United States would be his last chance to exact vengeance by taking a large number of victims with him."[4]

The "high confidence" intelligence judgments that Iraqi WMD programs were continuing and, in some areas, expanding were paired with "low confidence" judgments relating to when the Iraqi leadership would use WMD, whether they would engage in clandestine attacks against the US homeland, and whether they would ultimately share chemical or biological weapons with al-Qaeda, the organization responsible for widespread, high-impact acts of terror against the United States at home and abroad. In the context of such uncertainty the policy calculus adopted by senior White House officials was straightforward: the risks of inaction would outweigh the risks of action. Subsequent to what would eventually be known as Operation Iraqi Freedom, Vice President Dick Cheney argued that failing to confront the government of Saddam Hussein would have been "irresponsible in the extreme" since the "safety of the American people was at stake."[5]

In the five-month period following President Bush's challenge to the United

Nations and Secretary Powell's final diplomatic full-court press, the United Nations Monitoring, Verification, and Inspection Commission (UNMOVIC), a body that had been created in 1999 to replace the United Nations Special Commission on Iraq (UNSCOM) but that had not been allowed to conduct even a single inspection, was energized. UN Security Council Resolution 1441 charged that Iraq was in violation of its post–Gulf War obligations and offered a "final opportunity" to comply. The government of Iraq was required to provide within thirty days a "currently accurate, full, and complete declaration" of *all aspects* of WMD programs, ballistic missiles, and other delivery systems; any holdings and precise locations of such weapons, components, or constituent materials; and the locations and work of its research, development, and production facilities, including any that the state claimed were for unrelated purposes. Failure to adhere to the resolution or to cooperate fully in its implementation, including any false statements or omissions in the materials submitted, would constitute a further material breach and be reported immediately to the Security Council for appropriate action.

UNMOVIC's executive chairman, Hans Blix, reported back to the Security Council in December 2002 that Iraq "continues to state" that there had been no WMD in Iraq when inspectors left at the end of 1998 and that "none have been designed, procured, produced or stored in the period since then." At the same time, he noted that particular governments—including, although not mentioned by name, the United States—had indicated that they possessed convincing evidence to the contrary. UNMOVIC, he argued, "at this point is neither in a position to confirm Iraq's statements, nor in possession of evidence to disprove it." But Blix's "overall impression" was telling: "Not much new significant information has been provided . . . nor has much supporting documentation or other evidence been submitted."[6] Thus, the information gaps identified previously by UNSCOM remained.

Nor would they be resolved by January 2003, when Blix reported once again. A consummate diplomat, Blix walked a fine line in his eagerly anticipated report, on the one hand not asserting that proscribed items or activities existed in Iraq, on the other suggesting that "if they do, Iraq should present them and then eliminate them in our presence." While this was not the condemnation sought by some member states, it was a clear warning to Iraq that "if evidence is not presented, which gives a high degree of assurance, there is no way the inspectors can close a file by simply invoking a precept that Iraq cannot prove the negative." In other words, unless Iraq provided evidence that it no longer had any prohibited weapons—for example, documentation, testimony by individuals who had taken part in the purported destruction activities, and/or physical evidence—UNMOVIC would be unable to offer a clean bill of health.

The permanent UN Security Council members remained fundamentally divided in their assessments of the urgency of the problem and how best to resolve it. The United States, together with the United Kingdom, generally argued that the Iraqi programs continued, that Baghdad remained in noncompliance, that inspections were not likely to yield satisfactory results, and that military action might ultimately be required to remedy the problems identified. In contrast, a coalition of France, Russia, and China agreed that Iraq might not be in compliance with its disarmament obligations but fought for a continued inspections process in an effort to minimize the prospects for further military confrontation. The United States and the United Kingdom intimated that any new Iraqi revelations would be evidence of Iraqi noncompliance and therefore would require punitive action, while the absence of evidence would suggest continued Iraqi defiance of UN resolutions and indicate that inspections were not working. The French, Russian, and Chinese position suggested implicitly that any new Iraqi revelations would prove the efficacy of inspections, while the absence of any new information would highlight the need to offer Baghdad incentives to comply and perhaps strengthen the inspection mechanism.

When Blix reported in late January that Iraq's twelve-thousand-page declaration contained little that "would eliminate the [outstanding disarmament] questions or reduce their number," the insolvable diplomatic conundrum came to a head.[7] A paralyzed Security Council, given one final opportunity to engage by Secretary Powell's February presentation, would ultimately sit on the sidelines while the United States and the United Kingdom undertook joint military action outside the confines of a specific UN resolution authorizing the use of force in this instance but within the context of a material breach of UN resolutions, some of which arguably allowed the use of force in the context of Iraqi noncompliance.

Operation Iraqi Freedom and Beyond

The war that ensued was short, and the Iraqi regime's downfall quick. During the conflict Iraq did not employ WMD; and neither during combat operations nor in the months immediately following their termination did coalition forces uncover a "smoking gun" proving the extensive prewar WMD allegations. Surely, there were a number of early indicators of Iraqi noncompliance, such as the discovery of a proscribed Scud ballistic missile, revelations of a handful of warheads apparently designed for bulk-fill with chemical agents, and the recovery of two tractor-trailers that the Central Intelligence Agency (CIA) and the Defense Intelligence Agency (DIA) jointly assessed to be among the eight mobile biological-weapons production facilities reportedly in the Iraqi arsenal and about which Secretary Powell had briefed the UN Security Council.[8]

Moreover, as the approximately fourteen-hundred-member Iraq Survey Group (ISG) conducted its extensive postwar investigation into Iraq's WMD-related programs, plans, and intentions, further information came to light. Under Saddam Hussein Iraq had evidently continued, among other things, to experiment with the toxin ricin, to engage in ballistic missile research disallowed by UN Security Council Resolution 1441, and, clearly, not to "come clean" as required by that or preceding resolutions. Yet, discerning the status and achievements of specific programs would prove beyond the pale for analysts in many areas. Deliberate Iraqi concealment measures, coupled with the immediate postwar looting of several suspect sites, such as the Al Tuwaitha nuclear facility, and the loss of key Iraqi program personnel in combat or in its aftermath resulted in what ISG head David Kay would eventually call an "unresolvable ambiguity."[9]

In general, however, postwar information developed (or, in many cases, *not* developed) by the ISG called into question the accuracy of both prior intelligence assessments and policy judgments in key areas. For example, subsequent reevaluation of the supposed BW-related mobile trailers more heavily weighed their putative non-weapons-related applications. Similarly, little evidence was uncovered to support the 2002 National Intelligence Estimate (NIE) majority view or other judgments by senior administration officials—including the president—that Iraq had reconstituted its nuclear weapons program. While Kay ultimately concluded that "we have to understand why reality turned out to be different from expectations and estimates," it is also the case that not *all* prewar estimation was inaccurate. In Kay's view, Iraq had retained a "weapons program . . . designed to allow future production," presumably a WMD reconstitution capability geared toward an eventual postsanctions era.[10]

The absence of substantial evidence proving clandestine prewar Iraqi WMD-related activities led, not surprisingly, to widespread criticism of the US-UK military action. Some critics questioned whether this constituted a substantial intelligence failure, while others queried whether the Bush administration's actions were better characterized as a failure of policy: how could Iraq present an "imminent threat" when its purported WMD capabilities could not even be found? Administration critics were quick to raise the specter of politicized intelligence, charging that senior administration officials had manipulated intelligence data, either making use of data that only supported the policy agenda (and ignoring those that did not) or pressuring the intelligence community to produce products that would support the administration's already developed policy positions. In this vein, critics disputed administration claims that Iraq possessed WMD and challenged administration interpretations of scarce data relating to Iraqi WMD capabilities and intentions.[11] Nor was the Bush administration the only target of this criticism; for many of the same reasons, British Prime Minister Tony Blair found his government under siege by opposition parliamentarians and other domestic critics.[12] In each state critics called for inquiries into both the manifest large-scale intelligence failure and the allegations that policy officials had "cooked the books" along the way.[13]

Missing in this latter line of criticism, though, was the obvious: that for more than a decade there had been widespread agreement, both domestically and internationally, that Iraq had successfully developed particular WMD, that it had not met the requirements of successive Security Council resolutions, and that it retained the clear capacity to reconstitute its programs—a task that would only become easier once international sanctions were lifted. The historical record reveals that there was *limited* disagreement on the current status and specific scope of the Iraqi WMD and ballistic missile programs from the mid-1990s through Operation Iraqi Freedom and *substantial* disagreement both on how best to achieve the stated disarmament objective and on its prospective achievability. But the proposition that Iraq had likely continued its weapons programs resonated among the vast majority of the US political elite on a bipartisan basis over three successive presidencies and a dozen congressional sessions. This was a bedrock policy and planning assumption and a fundamental point of departure for discussions of the post–Cold War international-security landscape, the regional-security consequences of the continuing spread of WMD, and the impact of that spread on the US defense posture and US foreign policy more generally.

For his part, Kay concluded that with respect to assessments of Iraqi WMD capabilities "we were all wrong." "If you read the total body of intelligence in the last 12 to 15 years that flowed on Iraq," he argued, "it would be hard to come to a conclusion other than Iraq was a gathering, serious threat to the world with regard to WMD."[14] Independent postwar investigations by both the House Permanent Select Committee on Intelligence and the Senate Select Committee on Intelligence substantially echoed this critical finding, concluding that the United States had experienced severe collection and analytic failures in this area.[15] Similarly, former Deputy CIA Director Ronald Kerr, who had led the agency's own postwar inquiry into the subject, both rejected charges of politicized intelligence and found that "it is very hard to see [prewar assessments] as anything but a failure in terms of the specifics that we provided to policymakers."[16]

The Iraqi arms-assessment and arms-inspection sagas may never come to full, final, and complete closure. Prewar Iraqi deception tactics, wartime Iraqi and coalition actions, and postwar looting constrained how much ultimately could be discovered and verified. As important as any of these program specifics, though, was the preconflict analytic deficit that missed an apparent breakdown in the command structure for Iraqi WMD programs. Even as UNSCOM inspectors departed the country in 1998 this "vortex of corruption" engulfed many residual program elements and opened a sizable rift between leadership and scientific perspectives on when, whether, and how rapidly prior programs could be reconstituted once sanctions had been lifted. David Kay has postulated that Saddam Hussein deliberately chose not to publicly declare the de facto Iraqi disarmament posture in an effort both to enhance his (and Iraq's) standing in the region and to retain his power base in the context of key domestic critics.[17] In hindsight Hans Blix does not "think it's so improbable that [Hussein] Kamal, who defected in 1995 to Jordan, was telling the truth when he said that he had ordered the destruction of all [stockpiles] in 1991. This is also what Amer Al Sa'adi said to us—that it was destroyed in 1991" in the absence of inspectors.[18]

Ironically, it appears that both the US-UK and French-German-Russian prewar Security Council positions were partially vindicated by postwar ISG inspection data derived from those most critical to unraveling the Iraqi WMD enigma: the program officials and scientists themselves. On the one hand, prewar international inspections apparently contributed more significantly to the prevention of effective breakout or reconstitution of sought-after capabilities than inspections skeptics had predicted. On the other, many knowledgeable Iraqis reportedly did not, and by their own account would not have, come clean to international inspectors on Saddam's watch.[19]

While definitive, final answers to at least some of these questions should become more clear over time, substantial evidentiary shortfalls highlight the intrinsic collection and analytic challenges the issue of WMD poses to the intelligence community, the complex and difficult policy trade-offs it demands of policymakers, and the risk-laden operational requirements it presents to the military. Certainly, one tangible implication of these difficulties is Secretary Powell's own reassessment, about one year after his UN Security Council address, concerning whether he would have recommended war absent WMD. Even while defending the go-to-war decision, he acknowledged in a January 2004 press conference that the administration's prevailing judgment that Iraq was WMD-capable had made the case much more compelling in January 2003: "The stockpile presented the final little piece that made it more of a real and present danger and threat to the region and to the world." The "absence of a stockpile changes the political calculus; it changes the answer you get."[20] The lessons herein clearly transcend the most recent Iraqi case. Developing tailored policies and appropriate operational capabilities to effectively counter WMD is a core security challenge for twenty-first-century US foreign and defense policy and for international security more broadly.

This book provides a candid assessment of the inherent intelligence challenges, policy trade-offs, and operational considerations central to America's longstanding quest to prevent and ultimately manage WMD proliferation and to defend against an adversary's use of such weapons. This comprehensive review of the available open-source data suggests a security conundrum: intelligence collection and analysis are becoming more difficult, the trade-offs inherent in policy toward both rogue states and regional allies remain acute, and the operational challenges to warfighting in a WMD context are only modestly more solvable today than during the Gulf War—more than a decade ago. As WMD-related capabilities continue to proliferate to key regions, the challenge of fashioning a cogent and effective national strategy to combat WMD arguably has never been greater; at once, it is both prone to failure and critical to advancing US national security in the years ahead.

Considerable research and analysis have been conducted over the years on the intelligence process, producer-consumer relations, and the role of intelligence in the making of policy more generally. Similarly, ample literature exists on the nature and dimensions of the WMD threat, actual or recommended US and international policies in this area, and various procedures for implementing US non- and counterproliferation policies. However, to date comparatively little systematic study has been devoted to the intersection of the separate literatures on intelligence and WMD proliferation.[21]

As a result, the relationship between the US policy and intelligence communities, the notable intelligence difficulties in the WMD area, and the challenge to design and implement effective policy responses are not generally well understood. At best, select journal articles or book-length studies illuminate, say, the prospects for a nuclear arms competition on the Indian subcontinent, the role of inspections and the potential implications of a post-UNSCOM Iraq, the purported status of the Russian biological warfare (BW) program, or the rationale for China's arms transfers. At worst, significant WMD-related issues are not systematically explored or rely on fragmentary and sometimes unreliable information, the difficulties faced by and prospects for improving intelligence are simply assumed rather than analyzed, and the appropriateness or effectiveness of policy tools is not scrutinized or key lessons go unlearned.

This book is designed to help fill these evident gaps in the literature, to improve our understanding in each area, and, as far as possible, to recommend appropriate improvements for the intelligence and policy communities as they tackle these vexing problems. It is built on a set of case studies designed to cover a range of WMD-related issues, at different time intervals over the past two decades, involving both Republican and Democratic administrations and congressional leadership, and relating to a substantial number of proliferant states. Each case has a lengthy open-source paper trail and was chosen on the basis of both the sufficiency of information and its fit within the context of the larger work.

While each case yields particular insights, together they provide an improved understanding of the substance and process of the WMD issue area as a whole. Clearly, the cases chosen for discussion may raise questions of case-selection bias, especially since many of these have been labeled intelligence "failures." However, the cases were selected principally on the basis of sufficient and accessible open-source information; and, of course, intelligence successes are, by definition, seldom recounted in the public domain.

Chapter 1 outlines the dynamic WMD issue area and discusses the corresponding post–Cold War evolution of US policy. Chapter 2 focuses on standards of evidence for strategic intelligence. Based on analyses of both Chinese technology transfers to Pakistan and the often contentious annual US certification process relating to Pakistani efforts to develop nuclear weapons, this chapter examines the relationship between information inputs and policy determinations in the context of broader foreign-policy concerns and a divided domestic political arena. Chapter 3 deals with estimative uncertainties, situations in which the intelligence and policy communities deal with sometimes important information gaps. The uncertain status of the North Korean nuclear weapons program and the assessment of Soviet (and possibly Russian) BW efforts before and after the defector revelations of the early 1990s are examples of such uncertainties. Chapter 4 examines the prospects for strategic surprise in the WMD arena. The practice and implications of improved and widespread deception and denial practices, the pursuit of alternative technological pathways, and the growing use of underground facilities are assessed in the context of the 1998 Indian nuclear tests and the North Korean effort to develop ballistic missiles.

Chapter 5 explores the potential benefits and evident risks of intelligence sharing. Sensitive information provided both to help stem Russia's missile assistance to Iran and to support UNSCOM's Iraqi disarmament activities yielded notable intelligence gains and posed considerable risks to important collection sources and methods. Chapter 6 examines intelligence in an operational context. The military was called on to interdict the Chinese vessel *Yin He* and to strike the Sudanese al-Shifa facility, actions with considerable political fallout. Chapter 7 deals with intelligence in an operational context, looking at support to military counterforce operations in a wartime context. The efforts of coalition forces to hunt down and destroy Iraqi Scud missile launchers during the 1991 Gulf War and the Operation Desert Fox air strikes on Iraq in December 1998 illustrate the critical importance and common limitations of intelligence support in such operations. Finally, chapter 8 concludes with a set of lessons learned from the broader study and implications for the emergent national counterproliferation strategy.

Acknowledgments

While research on sensitive subjects can sometimes be difficult, the degree to which both intelligence and policy considerations relating to WMD proliferation have been publicly discussed, especially over the past decade, only underscores the extent to which the subject has emerged as a central post–Cold War security concern. All project research has been conducted using unclassified sources. To ensure the factual accuracy of the available data, we have endeavored to supplement this material with consultations with knowledgeable present or former government officials or nongovernmental specialists as appropriate. While we are not able to publicly thank them for their not-for-attribution comments, we nonetheless remain grateful for their assistance.

At the same time, others can and should be singled out for their support. As successive directors of the National Defense University's Center for Counterproliferation Research, Bob Joseph and John Reichart actively encouraged this project. Members of the center's staff provided numerous comments, critiques, and helpful suggestions at various stages of the research process, and—proving once again that no good deed goes unpunished—suffered through more whiteboard exercises than any of us would probably care to remember. Seth Carus, Read Hanmer, Rebecca Hersman, Todd Koca, and Richard Love helped shape this manuscript in subtle (and sometimes not so subtle) ways, while Jeff Bennett, Jacky Hardy, Derek Smith, and Steve Smith provided expert research assistance at pivotal junctures. Similarly, a number of students enrolled at the National War College, the Industrial College of the Armed Forces, and other National Defense University elements over the past few years have provided sound, in some cases direct, insights into particular cases.

Duncan Clarke, Marianne Cusimano, Burcu Akan Ellis, Iris Gonzalez, Pete Hayes, and Robert Litwak each read the manuscript and made numerous comments. Early in the project we benefited considerably from interactions with Tony Beilenson, Steve Cambone, M. D. B. Carlisle, Hank Cooper, John Deutch, J. James Exon, Bob Gallucci, Neil Joeck, Dick Johnson, Marcel Lettre, John Macartney, Doug MacEachin, Dave McCurdy, Dan Poneman, Bill Schneider, Henry Sokolski, Suzanne Spaulding, and Bill Wise. As the project progressed, we also profited from insights provided by Bruce Bennett, Paul Bernstein, Steve Black, Elaine Bunn, Ash Carter, Zack Davis, Lew Dunn, Steve Flanagan, Greg Giles, Ron Henderson, Bob Kadlec, David Kay, Jim Miller, and Forrest Waller, among others.

Collectively, these outstanding individuals provided a great service to the authors, whether in the form of particularly insightful discussion, useful technical review, or well-elaborated (and much-appreciated) interpretive commentary. Technical corrections and analytic suggestions have been incorporated where appropriate. Nevertheless, whatever misjudgments exist remain those of the authors alone.

Combating Proliferation

CHAPTER 1

Proliferation 101

A Dynamic Threat, An Evolving Response

> The gravest danger to our Nation lies at the crossroads of radicalism and technology. Our enemies have openly declared that they are seeking weapons of mass destruction and evidence indicates that they are doing so with determination. . . . History will judge harshly those who saw this coming danger but failed to act.
>
> —PRESIDENT GEORGE W. BUSH, 2002

The Nature of the Threat

On November 14, 1994, President William Clinton issued Executive Order 12938, declaring a "national emergency" resulting from the proliferation of nuclear, biological, and chemical weapons—weapons of mass destruction (WMD)—together with their means of delivery.[1] The continuing spread of these weapons constituted, he argued, an "unusual and extraordinary threat to the national security, foreign policy, and economy of the United States." This order built on concerns articulated by both the administration of his predecessor, George H. W. Bush, and Congress and was reaffirmed and extended annually through the end of the decade. Similarly, the incoming administration of George W. Bush underscored both the severity of the problem and its evolutionary nature. Central to the new administration's security strategy were measures designed to actively counter the effects of WMD proliferation.[2] Indeed, underscoring the gravity of this security challenge, the administration subsequently issued a first-ever national strategy to combat WMD.[3]

Throughout the early to mid-1990s, US and international efforts designed to halt or counter WMD proliferation appeared to pay considerable dividends. Indeed, this period witnessed some stellar advances: nuclear dismantlement in the Soviet successor states of Ukraine, Belarus, and Kazakhstan; apparent success in stopping or rolling back elements of the WMD programs of Iraq, Libya, and the Democratic People's Republic of Korea (DPRK); the indefinite and unconditional extension of the Treaty on the Nonproliferation of Nuclear Weapons (NPT); the completion and signing of the Chemical Weapons Convention (CWC); and a strengthening of and expanding membership in a number of regimes designed to enhance supplier restraint. Although evident problem areas remained, some analysts expressed optimism about the long-term prospects for nonproliferation, while others took solace in the new Defense Counterproliferation Initiative, which would complement traditional "nonproliferation" resources.[4] Even if preventive efforts failed in some cases, the United States, its forward-deployed troops, and its allies and friends abroad presumably would be adequately protected against WMD threats as a result of these expanded US efforts to counter their spread and their commensurate strategic and operational impact.

Yet, on balance, the proliferation problem appeared to worsen as the 1990s wore on. A series of high-profile violations of international agreements or significant challenges to them, an evident determination on the part of important regional actors to acquire WMD, and a number of proliferation surprises called this optimistic appraisal of early 1990s nonproliferation into question. At the beginning of the decade Director of Central Intelligence (DCI) William Webster offered the vague, unclassified assessment that "ballistic missiles are being developed or acquired by a growing number of countries." In his view, this was "a particularly alarming prospect because many of them are also in the advanced stages of developing nuclear, chemical, and biological warheads that could turn ballistic missiles into weapons of mass destruction."[5] By 1994 the Department of Defense (DOD) had reported that "at least twenty countries—many of them hostile to the United States and its friends and allies—have now or are seeking to develop nuclear, biological and/or chemical weapons and the means to deliver them," and "more than twelve countries have operational ballistic missiles and the means to deliver them."[6]

By 1999 John Lauder, head of the Director of Central Intelligence Nonproliferation Center, had testified that the intelligence community had identified more than fifty states as suppliers, conduits, or potential proliferant states. The continued relevance of nuclear proliferation was underscored by the unforeseen 1998 Indian and Pakistani nuclear tests, as well as by lingering suspicions over the status of the illicit North Korean and Iranian nuclear weapons development programs. Moreover, according to the intelligence community, "at least" sixteen states maintained active chemical weapons programs, "perhaps" a dozen continued their pursuit of offensive biological weapons programs, and a growing number of states endeavored to acquire the relevant technologies to produce increasingly capable ballistic and cruise missile delivery vehicles or to develop the indigenous capabilities to do so.[7]

Together with evident continuing demand, the arguably accelerating diffusion of weapons-related technologies implies a trend line in which, all things being equal, the problem will continue to worsen in the years ahead. According to then former (and future) Secretary of Defense Donald Rumsfeld, chairman of the 1998 Commission to Assess the Ballistic Missile Threat to the United States, "There is the advent and acceleration of trade among second-tier powers, to the point that the development of these capabilities is almost self-sustaining; that is to say that they now each have various things they know that the others don't know. And to the extent they trade them—whether it's knowledge or physical pieces of equipment or elements or components or technicians—the result is that they are able to move forward in a development path that is vastly different from ours, vastly different from the Soviet Union and certainly, considerably more rapid."[8]

Indeed, the DOD now views the use of chemical and biological weapons as a "likely condition" of future warfare.[9] But this judgment is not necessarily confined to possible armed conflict between state actors. The 1990s also saw increased interest on the part of various subnational actors—from Aum Shinrikyo to Hamas to al-Qaeda—with respect to the acquisition of WMD.[10] Intelligence discoveries in Afghanistan in the context of Operation Enduring Freedom (2001–2) that al-Qaeda, according to DCI George Tenet, was "working to acquire some of the most dangerous chemical agents and toxins," "pursuing a sophisticated biological weapons research program," and "seeking to develop a nuclear device" and "may be pursuing a radioactive dispersal device" only underscored the changing nature of the proliferation problem.[11] If Aum Shinrikyo's use of the chemical agent sarin failed to sound the clarion call, then al-Qaeda certainly has.

The proliferation enterprise is neither static nor necessarily straightforward but rather dynamic and often ambiguous. Predicated on disparate facts that require key analytic judgments relating to the intentions and capabilities of reputed proliferant states (both supply- and demand-side), it is a complex and difficult intelligence challenge. Accurately interpreting the range of political, technological, and other developments that affect the evolving WMD threat requires both a range of collection techniques and multiple analytic methodologies. These, in turn, presuppose sufficient resources allocated for the task, an appropriately trained workforce, and an attentive consumer community.

Similarly, the policy challenges inherent in effectively combating WMD proliferation are acute; designing and implementing coherent, sustainable, and effective country-specific and global responses has proven a difficult challenge. In turn, effectively countering WMD proliferation involves meeting difficult operational challenges, the prospects for which are often constrained by intelligence limitations or technology shortfalls. Indeed, the US experience in combating proliferation in the 1990s and beyond highlights the challenges inherent in efforts to accurately assess the issue area, illustrates a series of difficult policy trade-offs, and underscores the complex dynamics and evolving nature of relations between the intelligence and policy communities. This book explores each of these issues in the context of diverse case studies related to WMD and missile proliferation.

Proliferation Intelligence and Producer-Consumer Relations

Conventional wisdom articulates a relatively straightforward role for intelligence in the making of US foreign policy. Intelligence is designed to support national-level decision making by policymakers and tactical-level operations by the military and other consumers. While an ideal type, the so-called intelligence cycle is at the core of this relationship.[12] In this construct, policymakers first specify the range, relative importance, and issues of concern to the intelligence community.[13] The intelligence community then collects the relevant data through appropriate means.[14] These data are subsequently processed, exploited, and analyzed, and then assessments are produced and disseminated to appropriate policy or operational consumers. Finally, analyses are reviewed by consumers, who then provide feedback to the intelligence producers, input that retasks, modifies previous tasking, or requires limited or no follow-up. There are times when this "normal" process develops as described above; however, often it does not, although performance likely varies across the subject matter in question or the country covered, through different means of exploitation, and over time.

In practice, the available empirical data suggest that requirements often are ill-specified or poorly defined; collection proves infeasible or is unduly delayed; analyses are overtaken by events or perceived by consumers as unhelpful, inaccurate, or irrelevant; data disseminated compete for limited consumer attention; and feedback is infrequent or nonexistent.[15] Consumers view intelligence community products as one of a number of sources of information to consider. They are often dissatisfied with what they perceive as inadequate, erroneous, or counterproductive analyses; sometimes confused or disturbed by the many different views presented by different intelligence community actors on specific issues; and disappointed by the net performance of an intelligence apparatus with a budget of approximately $27 billion to $35 billion per year.[16]

Producers themselves are often dissatisfied with what they perceive as sparse or unclear guidance and feedback, unrealistic "crystal ball" expectations and unwarranted criticism, the politicization or perceived misuse of intelligence, and the inattentiveness or cold-shoulder treatment of policymakers, which in effect marginalizes or excludes intelligence output from policy judgments. Over time, intelligence producers have variously attempted to maintain an arms-length relationship with consumers in order to help prevent the corruption of intelligence or pursued a close or proximate relationship in order to maximize the utility of intelligence.[17] Striking an appropriate balance that both enhances the utility of intelligence products and maintains their integrity has proven a difficult challenge, particularly with the rise of Congress as a key policy consumer.[18] This is particularly true in the WMD arena, as the rapid evolution in 1990s-era threat assessments relating to the proliferation of ballistic missiles strongly suggests.

Ballistic Missile Proliferation: Evolving Assessments

The interplay throughout the 1990s between intelligence producers and policy consumers in the area of WMD proliferation suggests that the rules governing their relationship have evolved in subtle yet important ways. With respect to ballistic missile proliferation, for instance, one senior intelligence official argued in the summer of 1998 that the same briefing could be taken to the Democratic White House and the Republican-led Congress, to considerably different effect. This official recalled one particular instance in which those briefed in the White House interpreted the threats ballistic missiles posed to the United States as "modest but manageable threats" that would "certainly not call for the creation of an expensive national missile defense." That same week, those briefed on Capitol Hill saw "a significant and growing" national-security threat that "clearly warranted the development of an effective ballistic missile defense system."[19]

This discrepancy in interpretation reflects the political climate surrounding the proliferation of ballistic missiles and the design of appropriate and effective policy responses. Moreover, the limited availability of "facts" or their roundly disputed nature imposes a key constraint on "objective" intelligence analysis. This interpretive gap results from a number of concerns, including ambiguous or evolving data, differing evaluative metrics, disagreements over the scale, scope, and timing of perceived threats to the United States, and disputes over policy aimed at combating these security challenges. Moreover, states' increasingly sophisticated capabilities and techniques in deception and denial, the continuing diffusion of weapons-related technologies, and hardening perceptions in key states and regions of the advisability to acquire, develop, or produce WMD further complicate sound assessment.[20]

The ballistic missile dimension of the WMD problem has, of course, been at the center of a political firestorm for some time. Indeed, ever since President Ronald Reagan's 1983 speech proposing a strategic defense initiative, debates over the cost, implications, feasibility, and desirability of deploying advanced defensive systems have taken center stage. Particularly since the 1991 Gulf War, in which the Iraqi government of Saddam Hussein employed a number of conventionally armed ballistic missiles against coalition and Israeli targets, questions over both the specific nature of the threat and the appropriate policy and military or technical responses have been acute. Not surprisingly, divisions have been rampant over each question. A 1995 National Intelligence Estimate, NIE 95-19, for example, assessed that "in the next 15 years no country other than the major declared nuclear powers will develop a ballistic missile that could threaten the contiguous 48 states or Canada."[21] The conclusions of the National Intelligence Council (NIC) were roundly disputed by missile defense advocates, and key limitations—such as the document's lack of specificity on critical assumptions, its overstated certainty of analytic judgment, and its apparent failure to consider "alternative futures"—were deemed methodologically flawed by the General Accounting Office.[22]

Subsequently, Congress authorized a bipartisan Commission to Assess the Ballistic Missile Threat to the United States to help "red team" the intelligence community's assessment. The commission, chaired by former Secretary of Defense Donald Rumsfeld, concluded in June 1998 that

- Concerted efforts by a number of overtly or potentially hostile nations to acquire ballistic missiles with biological or nuclear payloads pose a growing threat to the United States;

- The threat to the U.S. posed by these emerging capabilities is broader, more mature and evolving more rapidly than has been reported in estimates and reports by the Intelligence Community;

- The Intelligence Community's ability to provide timely and accurate estimates of ballistic missile threats to the U.S. is eroding; and

- The warning times the U.S. can expect of new, threatening ballistic missile deployments are being reduced.[23]

The commission highlighted three "crucial factors" shaping the contemporary proliferation threat: (1) new ballistic missile and WMD programs no longer followed the patterns previously set by the superpowers; (2) extensive foreign and technical assistance was readily available, not a "wildcard" (as NIE 95-19 had declared) but rather a "fact"; and (3) states were highly motivated to conceal important elements of their programs. The cumulative effect of these factors was an emergent threat landscape that appeared to be quite different from the past. In this context, the commission called for an "expanded approach to intelligence that assesses both inputs and outputs in other countries' ballistic missile programs" in order to "capture both sooner and more accurately the speed and magnitude of ballistic missile proliferation in the post–Cold War world and to assess, in time, the various threats this proliferation poses to the United States."[24]

The Rumsfeld Commission's findings were soon bolstered by North Korea's launch of an unanticipated three-stage Taepodong-1 (TD-1) medium-range ballistic missile (MRBM), a test flight of the Pakistani Ghauri MRBM (itself a close copy of the North Korean Nodong), and an attempted test of the Iranian Shahab-3 MRBM later that summer. Not surprisingly, in light of these alarming events, the political fallout from NIE 95-19, and the high-profile report of the Rumsfeld Commission, the NIC issued a revised NIE in September 1999 that was in stark contrast to its assessment just four years earlier. The revised NIE projected both possible and likely missile developments through 2015. The new assessment found that the intelligence community's conclusions were constrained by limited information, engineering and other technical assessments, and deception and denial efforts.[25] A 2001 revision concluded that the United States "most likely will face ICBM threats from North Korea, Iran, and possibly from Iraq," while "one to two dozen countries will probably possess a land-attack cruise missile capability by 2015."[26] Such differing assessments stem from an evolution of the threat environment, including both an increasing number of suppliers and an emergent network of states that provide assistance to and share technical developments with one another, and from a change in assessment methodology.

For policymakers, the value of intelligence judgments that do not appear to conform to emerging empirical evidence is suspect: if the intelligence community is politically unwilling, methodologically unable, or analytically incapable of providing "useful" assessments, can the community inform sound policy? How seriously should policymakers view a fifteen-year estimate rendered obsolete in less than four years? Conversely, absent such assessments, how can policy officials both understand the true nature of the evolving threat and design effective policy responses? For intelligence producers, on the other hand, there are few smoking guns to prove events or rapidly evolving capability, and the argumentative or contestable nature of the comparatively few or less-than-straightforward facts available contributes to an environment in which analysis and interpretations inevitably vary. Moreover, the politically charged arena in which such assessments of ballistic missile proliferation play out presents a formidable challenge to sound analysis: to what extent can analysts carefully, but usefully, proceed through such an evident political minefield? How can the intelligence community improve the accuracy of its estimates, enhance its credibility, and retain policy relevance?

The North Korean ballistic missile development program illustrates the substantial analytic challenges in this area (see chapter 3). From the production of a substantial number of Nodong MRBMs based on a single 1994 test (and the weapon's rapid transfer to both Iran and Pakistan) to an unanticipated third-stage addition to the TD-1 MRBM launched in August 1998, surprises that underscore both the alternative technological pathways pursued by this state and its growing capabilities abound. Debates over the nature, extent, and relative importance of the North Korean ballistic missile program have also been fueled in part by the increasing public availability of satellite images. Once the exclusive purview of intelligence analysts and policy officials with appropriate security clearances, images such as those taken by commercial firms and displayed in public forums may affect both the course and the tenor of discussions relating to the evolving nature of the threat. Graphic displays of the relatively primitive technology currently fielded by Pyongyang have led to disparate analytic conclusions (see fig. 1.1). Where the Federation of American Scientists' John Pike sees "the mouse that roared" in North Korea's "singularly-unimpressive facility," the Center for Security Policy's Frank Gaffney cautions that "if crude will do, then we're fools to ignore capabilities that have the potential to do us grave harm."[27]

Intelligence Challenges and WMD Proliferation

The evolving assessment relating to ballistic missile proliferation under-scores both the difficult nature of analytic judgments in this area and their in-herent contestability in the larger political arena. Perceptions of politicized in-telligence, that is, generally, intelligence produced or withheld in support of a larger political agenda, are harmful to the credibility of the intelligence com-munity and detrimental to sound public policy. Whether such estimates are intentionally skewed by those who produce them or selectively interpreted or ignored by those who consume them, their relative value is undermined by the highly charged political implications of their findings.

While informed public debate on the evolving nature of the threat and, of course, on the possible range of policy responses is clearly warranted in a dem-ocratic setting, it can be taken too far. The damaging and, especially in the 1990s, apparently common practice of leaking sensitive information and using it in public forums for partisan or other political purposes only jeopardizes in-telligence objectivity and curtails its utility. As the congressionally mandated Commission to Assess the Organization of the Federal Government to Combat the Proliferation of Weapons of Mass Destruction, chaired by John Deutch, for-mer DCI, found in 1999, "Good intelligence and the rough-and-tumble of the open political process do not always mix. . . . To be agile and well-informed, policy needs disinterested intelligence. To be relevant, intelligence efforts must address policy concerns."[28]

Moreover, the accuracy of intelligence products is suspect not only in the ballistic missile arena, but also in the rapidly advancing and information-limited issue area of WMD proliferation more generally. For example, the scope and composition of the Iraqi WMD programs uncovered by UNSCOM in the wake of the 1991 Gulf War are revealing (see chapter 5). Charged with not only determining the extent of these programs but also dismantling them, UNSCOM brought to light substantial information that apparently was un-known to the United States and other member states of the international com-munity. At the outset of the conflict, in January 1991, Baghdad was apparently within six months to two years of completing an operational nuclear device; had produced a range, and considerable quantity, of chemical agents; and pos-sessed weaponized stocks of biological agents, including anthrax, botulinum toxin, and aflatoxin.[29] These findings sent shock waves through both the pol-icy and intelligence communities, the former asking pointed questions relat-

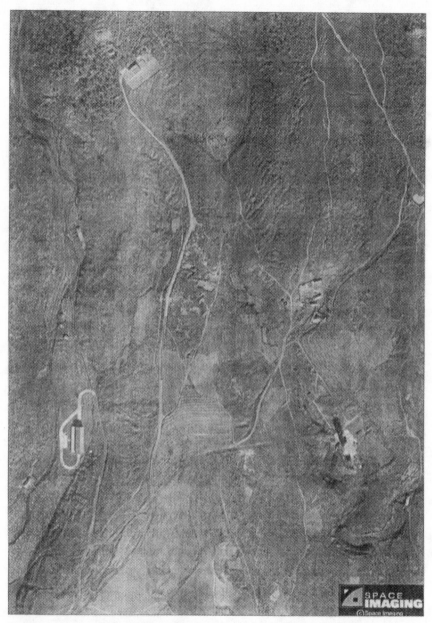

Figure 1.1. Satellite imagery showing the North Korean Nodong launch facility *(above)* and detail of the launchpad *(on facing page)*
(Federation of American Scientists, www.fas.org/nuke/guide/dprk/facility/nodong-2 .htm and www.fas.org/nuke/guide/dprk/facility/nodong-3.htm). Ikonos satellite image by Space Imaging

ing to the nature and extent of evident information gaps and the latter working overtime to answer the mail.

Responding to questions relating to the unexpectedly advanced status of
Iraq's nuclear and other WMD programs, Secretary of Defense Les Aspin declared, "We don't want to face those surprises again." Advancing a principal
rationale for the just-announced Defense Counterproliferation Initiative in
December 1993, he concluded, "If you can't prevent, you have to protect."[30]
Yet, even after a series of "full, final, and complete disclosures" by the government of Iraq and despite more than seven years of intrusive inspections, it is
clear that the full extent of the Iraqi programs remains unknown.[31] Indeed,
many of those who were most involved in this disarmament effort routinely
raised the likelihood of their continued existence, Iraqi government protestations to the contrary notwithstanding, through the 2003 overthrow of Saddam
Hussein's regime.[32]

If the extent and capabilities of the Iraqi programs rang alarm bells in Washington in the wake of the 1991 Gulf War, so too did the depth and scope of the Soviet (and possibly Russian) BW program, revealed in the twilight of the Cold War (see chapter 3). Not only had the Soviets apparently *not* discontinued their offensive BW program when they ratified the Biological and Toxin Weapons Convention (BWC) in 1972 but they had embarked on an ambitious weapons development program that would continue through at least the end of the Cold War.

In 1989, even as the US military stopped vaccinating its troops for smallpox—presumably because there was no intelligence-validated threat—and the relevant Army-run defensive research program was transferred to the civilian Centers for Disease Control and Prevention, credible information relating to the status of Soviet efforts came to light. The defectors Vladimir Pasechnik and, three years later, Ken Alibek revealed a vast, secretive Soviet BW effort that apparently far exceeded prior assessments.[33] Their testimony was a real coup for the British and American intelligence communities, but the severity and long-standing nature of the intelligence gap, together with emerging information relating to Soviet BW technical capabilities, operational plans, and doctrine, dramatically underscored intelligence limitations in this area. More disturbing still, Alibek and others remain concerned that post-Soviet Russia actively continues its offensive BW activities.[34]

Both the Iraqi WMD and Soviet/Russian BW activities highlight important intelligence limitations. The intelligence community's ability to accurately assess the BW capabilities of these or other states is constrained by a number of factors, including rapid technological advances and the diffusion of such technology, the often dual-use attributes of the relevant production equipment, and the "legal" nature of defensive or peaceful BW research and development activities—which are virtually indistinguishable from offensive activities by capability if not intent—permitted under the BWC.[35]

Nor are the prospects for satisfactory intelligence performance necessarily better in other domains. With respect to nuclear weapons, for instance, the US government was reportedly surprised when in 1991 South Africa declared that it had produced six nuclear devices and had decided to dismantle its development program.[36] Similarly, despite the declared intention of Bharatiya Janata Party (BJP) leaders in India to test nuclear weapons once elected to office, the United States was apparently surprised when that state did in fact test five such devices in May 1998 (see chapter 4).[37] In other cases, such as North Korea's nuclear weapons development efforts, the intelligence community has discerned significant activity but has proven unable to agree on the specific parameters or quantity of the material produced or, for a prolonged period, on the program's current status (see chapter 3); or as in the Iraqi case, it has simply been unable to verify the extent of the various WMD programs or to determine their operational status (see chapter 7).[38]

Moreover, there are obvious and continuing collection and analytic difficulties associated with the prospect of fissile material leakage from facilities in Russia and the other New Independent States. The large quantities of fissile material stored under questionable circumstances, coupled with the absence of a reliable inventory and the known desire for such material by select state and subnational organizations, allows for the possibility of undetected smuggling activities.[39] Finally, if state-level actors are difficult to monitor effectively, subnational groups present at least as great a challenge. Prior to the cult group Aum Shinrikyo's 1995 use of the chemical agent sarin in the Tokyo subway, for instance, few US law-enforcement or intelligence officials considered that group to be a threat to national security: "They simply were not on anybody's radar screen."[40]

At other times the intelligence community has performed its collection and analytic tasks well, but the policy responses have been criticized as inappropriate, unwarranted, or ineffective. For instance, although the intelligence community uncovered substantial information relating to China's nuclear and missile assistance to Pakistan throughout the 1990s, the "appropriate" policy responses were widely disputed (see chapter 2). Similarly, the intelligence community's extensive reporting on Russian missile and nuclear assistance to Iran throughout the 1990s prompted the US president and vice president to share sensitive information with their counterparts in Moscow—a one-way street that not only failed to halt such assistance but may have adversely affected US collection capabilities (see chapter 5).[41]

On other high-profile issues, it appears that the policy community acted either on intelligence that may not have been as solid or in a manner not consistent with the relative certainty of the assessments. For example, it will probably never be known conclusively whether the Chinese vessel *Yin He* was in fact engaged in transfers to a third party of technology related to chemical weapons, as US intelligence suggested, or whether it was instead involved in legal trade-related activities, as the People's Republic of China claimed (see chapter 6). The intelligence could have been incorrect, or the illicit cargo might instead have been dumped prior to boarding; either way, the policy community acted and was criticized internationally for this unsuccessful early post–Cold War interdiction.[42]

Similarly, the extensive international condemnation of the 1998 US cruise missile strike against an alleged chemical weapons–related facility in Sudan prompted considerable open discussion of sensitive information and public challenges both to the veracity of the intelligence judgment and to the policy community's justifications for the attack (see chapter 6).[43] Finally, US targeting in the 1998 Desert Fox campaign suggests that information on specific capabilities of adversaries is likely to remain limited and that there is acute constraint on military operations designed to counter WMD acquisition, development, or use. And even when capabilities are known the policy community may not opt to destroy them for fear of collateral damage or other adverse results (see chapter 7).[44]

Together, these and other high-profile WMD-related events in the 1990s suggest a number of important insights into the evolving nature of the WMD problem, the substantial challenges relating to intelligence collection and analysis in this issue area, and the difficulties inherent in designing appropriate policy responses to these challenges. Among the more salient lessons and implications are the following:

- Regimes, treaties, and diplomatic and other arrangements notwithstanding, WMD will continue to spread both horizontally (i.e., to other actors) and vertically (i.e., improved capabilities on the part of individual proliferant states) to individual states and particular regions of proliferation concern, and in some cases to subnational organizations as well. Thus, the future proliferation landscape may differ considerably from that of the past.
- The diffusion of weapons-related technologies appears to be occurring along an accelerated trajectory, enabling would-be proliferators to acquire or improve WMD-related capabilities on a relatively compressed timeline.
- Surprise is likely, both technologically and politically, particularly with respect to the hardest collection targets (which are also the most likely proliferators). Appropriate policy and operational responses should seek to mitigate the likelihood and consequences of intelligence surprise.

- US and allied intelligence gaps may be severe; contemporary threat assessment must therefore incorporate alternative assessment methodologies and, in some cases, move beyond "validated" requirements.
- These gaps are compounded by robust deception and denial activities, alternative weapons development pathways, and the introduction of increasingly sophisticated technologies that challenge collection techniques.
- In an effort to help alleviate these growing gaps, US intelligence will likely be called upon to increase its information-sharing arrangements both on a bilateral basis and with international organizations. Such arrangements require the striking of a proper balance between the risks to intelligence sources and methods and the positive benefits that may accrue from such relationships.
- When problems are identified, it will of course be difficult to achieve policy consensus domestically, let alone to act in concert internationally, and to engage effectively on an operational level as appropriate.
- Indeed, some potential response options—e.g., interdiction, preemption, and counterforce—are likely to be controversial even when there is perfect information (attainment of which is highly unlikely).

Combating Proliferation: An Emergent National Strategy

Central to the national-security strategy articulated by President George W. Bush is the proposition that "America is now threatened less by conquering states than we are by failing ones . . . less by fleets and armies than by catastrophic technologies in the hands of the embittered few."[45] In this post–September 11, 2001 logic structure, "the enemy is terrorism," but we will make "no distinction between terrorists and those who knowingly harbor or provide aid to them."[46] At the same time, the continuing proliferation of nuclear, biological, and chemical weapons, together with their associated ballistic and cruise missile delivery vehicles, enables "even weak states and small groups" to obtain "a catastrophic power to strike great nations."[47] Neither terrorism nor WMD and missile proliferation is a new phenomenon; for many years states in regions of security concern to the United States and its friends and allies have aggressively pursued WMD and missile capabilities or have engaged in or sponsored terrorism. What is new is the national prominence given to the prospective conjuncture of these twin scourges in the form of a security strategy that has both elevated the prominence of each issue on the national agenda and posited a nexus between them that constitutes a combined threat greater than the sum of its parts.

Perhaps most striking is the administration's avowed determination that "we cannot let our enemies strike first," underscoring that the risk of inaction may in particular cases outweigh the risk of action. Faced with a "looming" threat, a set of "new deadly challenges [that] have emerged from rogue states and terrorists," the United States "will, if necessary, act preemptively" to "forestall or prevent hostile acts by our adversaries."[48] Indeed, the United States seeks to advance its security along two parallel and mutually reinforcing lines, pursuing a proactive, full-court press against emergent security challenges emanating from the proliferation-terrorism nexus and strengthening homeland and transforming military capabilities to deter, protect against, and mitigate the effects of an attack. Thus, even as "our best defense is a good offense," the administration seeks both to devalue the attractiveness of WMD and missiles and to diminish the adverse consequences to US interests should adversaries execute such attacks.[49] In underscoring the grave and gathering dangers posed at the intersection of continued WMD proliferation, rogue or failing states, and the prospect of catastrophic terrorism, the Bush administration has replaced America's traditional *nonproliferation*-centered approach with what is, in essence, a national *counterproliferation* strategy.

Key Analytic Judgments

The urgency accorded the threat by the Bush administration stems from four fundamental judgments: (1) that the spread of WMD and missile capabilities poses substantial challenges to US national security and to that of US friends and allies; (2) that WMD and missile capabilities have and will continue to proliferate; (3) that the use of these weapons against US forward-deployed forces, US friends and allies, or even US or allied homelands is increasingly likely; and (4) that while the intelligence community has given credible strategic warning of an intent to acquire, develop, or improve WMD capabilities by key adversaries of the United States, specific tactical warning is, and is likely to remain, problematic.

WMD proliferation and terrorism pose a clear and present danger to US national security. A principal lesson of the 1991 Gulf War was the need to be prepared to fight WMD-armed regional adversaries. US forces were inadequately prepared to confront Iraqi chemical and biological weapons, and most US coalition partners were even less well prepared. Moreover, postwar revelation of the scope of Iraqi WMD activities shocked the national-security community, surprising even "informed" observers and highlighting serious potential vulnerabilities in US regional-security strategies and warfighting plans. While Iraq did not, ultimately, use chemical or biological weapons in the Gulf War, its manifest ability to do so, coupled with its evident (and largely undetected) technical progress, underscored the emergence of a major post–Cold War defense planning challenge.[50]

More recently, President Bush reportedly concluded that "the Pearl Harbor of the twenty-first century took place" on September 11, 2001, when al-Qaeda terrorists attacked the World Trade Center and the Pentagon. Declaring that "the primary mission of this administration is to find [the perpetrators] and catch them," he argued that the United States "cannot allow a terrorist thug to hold us hostage."[51] Later in September, Bush declared that Afghanistan would be merely the first stop in the unfolding "global war on terrorism": "It does not end there. It will not end until every terrorist group of global reach has been found, stopped and defeated."[52]

As counterterrorism operations unfolded, it became clear that the Bush administration viewed the problems of terrorism and rogue states armed with WMD as inherently linked, if not inseparable. Whereas the United States initially focused exclusively on the threat of "global terrorism," the president declared in his January 2002 State of the Union Address that the United States could "not permit the world's most dangerous regimes to threaten us with the world's most destructive weapons," a charge that brought WMD proliferation within the scope of the counterterrorism campaign, centered around what he called an "axis of evil"—Iraq, Iran, and North Korea.[53] Just two days later, Secretary of Defense Donald Rumsfeld further elaborated the administration's evolving position that US counterterrorism and counterproliferation goals converged in key areas: "The real concern at the present time is the nexus between terrorist networks and terrorist states that have weapons of mass destruction . . . something that is totally different than existed in previous periods, and [that] poses risks not of thousands of lives, but hundreds of thousands of lives."[54] In the rubric of the Bush administration's national-security strategy, "we must adapt the concept of imminent threat to the capabilities and objectives of today's adversaries," which rely on "acts of terror and, potentially, the use of weapons of mass destruction."[55]

WMD-related capabilities have and will continue to spread. The starting point for the Bush administration's national-security strategy is the reality of a post-proliferated international-security landscape. Were established multilateral mechanisms more effective in their nonproliferation function, capabilities would not, presumably, continue to spread. The intricate network of nonproliferation treaties and regimes built over the past several decades share one fundamental feature: they have not prevented *determined* states from developing nuclear, chemical, or biological weapons or increasingly capable missile and related delivery systems. South Africa, for instance, successfully developed and produced six nuclear devices despite its purported adherence to the NPT; North Korea acknowledged in October 2002 that it had variously reprocessed plutonium and enriched uranium in order to develop nuclear weapons both prior and subsequent to its withdrawal from the NPT; Iran is recognized as the most recent state to have cheated on the NPT, and there are other self-declared, opaque, and virtual nuclear proliferants potentially waiting in the wings.[56]

Similarly, despite the voluntary, and unenforceable, gentlemen's agreement among supplier states to restrain from exporting technologies that would enhance the prospects for development of ballistic missiles in key aspirant states, key countries of concern—for example, Iran, North Korea, Pakistan, and India—have made steady, incremental progress along this front, a trend that will likely continue. All told, treaties and regimes in the nuclear and missile arenas have not prevented acquisition or development of weapons capabilities, although in general they have likely served to slow the pace of development. Yet, the multilateral constraining mechanisms that were only partly successful in the past are unlikely to be as successful in the years ahead in a context of continuing "foreign assistance" by key suppliers, a growing network of "secondary" suppliers, the continuing insecurity (and large quantity) of fissile materials resident in the post-Soviet states and elsewhere, evident advancements in indigenous weapons-related technological capabilities among lesser-developed states, and the potential availability of germane expertise together threaten to erode traditional supply-side constraints.[57]

This challenge is even more acute in the chemical and biological weapons arenas. With respect to the former, the US government assesses that "many CW [chemical warfare] agents . . . are simple to produce. They are often based on technology that is at least 80 years old and sometimes older, putting them well within reach of virtually any Third World country that wants them." While newer agents, such as the reputed *novichok* class of next-generation nerve agents developed by Russia, may be "more difficult" to produce, the "technology for these agents is widely available in the public domain."[58] While a majority of nations are signatories to the CWC, which prohibits the development, production, acquisition, retention, stockpiling, transfer, and use of chemical weapons, it is unlikely that this treaty has ended potential CW threats to US or allied equities. The twin realities of technology diffusion over time and growing interest by particular states and subnational actors in capabilities that are viewed as force multipliers or mass-casualty implements together suggest that chemical weapons, along with the infrastructure needed to develop and produce them, will remain permanent features of the international-security landscape.

With respect to biological weapons, supply-side controls face even more daunting prospects. According to the Office of the Secretary of Defense, "Virtually all the equipment, technology, and materials needed for biological warfare agent research and development and production are dual-use." As a result, offensive programs "are relatively easy to disguise within the larger body of legitimate commercial activity, as no specialized facilities are required," and "any country with the political will and a competent scientific base can produce toxins or infectious agents, which include viruses, bacteria, and rickettsiae."[59] While only three or four nations were thought to have offensive BW programs at the time the BWC entered into force, almost three decades later the situation continues to evolve. Government analysts warn that in addition to a larger number of states with offensive programs, "credible biological warfare capabilities are becoming more advanced," a "trend [that] leads us to believe that the likelihood of biological weapons use will increase in the coming years."[60]

The continuing demand for biological weapons and the relative ease with which any offensive effort can be concealed, together with the growing availability of weapons-related technologies and expertise and a continuing revolution in biotechnology that could significantly alter the threat environment in the years ahead, suggest that determined states—and possibly certain subnational actors, whose chances would likely improve with state support—face few real constraints in establishing, developing, or improving offensive programs once there has been a national decision to do so. Indeed, even after the post–Gulf War disclosures by the government of Iraq and despite more than seven years of intrusive inspections, UNSCOM was unable to account for critical elements of the Iraqi BW program. Among the gaps in the "select and incomplete" history of the program were "considerable uncertainty" regarding weaponization; "consistently understated" agent production; an "incomplete" declaration of imports of equipment and raw materials; "omitted" planning references; "thoroughly planned" research and development despite Iraqi claims that they were "unplanned"; and, finally, an absence of Iraqi evidence "concerning the termination of its offensive program."[61]

And if UNSCOM was unsuccessful on this front, it is not surprising that its successor—UNMOVIC—had no greater success along a truncated timeline on the road to war in 2002 and fewer personnel and other supporting resources dedicated to its operation. Indeed, UNMOVIC was unable to resolve any of the outstanding BW-related issues raised by its predecessor. Until the scientists, engineers, and administrative personnel and program leadership tell the story of Iraq's accomplishments (and failures) on the BW front, it is unlikely that that state's program will be fully and appropriately characterized. There may also be some missteps along the way, as when two mobile Iraqi trailers were publicly declared BW-related—a judgment later reconsidered.[62]

Use is likely. Coupled with the judgment that capabilities will continue to proliferate is the concern that adversary WMD use against US forces, US friends and allies, and the US homeland is perhaps increasingly likely. While the DOD concluded as early as 1997 that the use of chemical and biological weapons would be a "likely condition" of future warfare, the new wrinkle here is the perceived scope of vulnerability and the plausibility of direct threats to "rear-area," especially civilian, targets, potentially far removed from an overseas theater of operations.

This approach is integral to the administration's national-security strategy, which starts from the premise that the security landscape has undergone a profound transformation. In this new era, according to the White House's *National Security Strategy of the United States of America,* key regional states and terrorist organizations "are determined to acquire weapons of mass destruction, along with other advanced military technology, to be used as threats or offensively to achieve the aggressive designs of these regimes." As a result, there is a "greater likelihood" that rogue states and terrorists "will use weapons of mass destruction against us."[63] The companion *National Strategy for Homeland Security* is even more pointed: "Our enemies are working to obtain chemical, biological, radiological, and nuclear weapons for the purpose of wreaking unprecedented damage on America." Should these actors successfully acquire or develop such weapons—the technology, expertise, and material for which is spreading "inexorably"—they are "likely to try to use them."[64]

In the early-twenty-first-century security environment the intersection of "radicalism and technology" arguably links the security of the US homeland to events overseas more directly than at virtually any other time in the nation's history. It also serves to extend the modern battlefield beyond force-on-force considerations to the full range of civilian noncombatants, an expansive target set for which "losses would be exponentially more severe" than those of September 11, 2001, "if terrorists acquired and used weapons of mass destruction."[65]

Warning is problematic. Clearly, the prevention of specific attacks will result from successful and timely collection, analysis, and dissemination of intelligence and counterintelligence data. Yet, with respect both to WMD proliferation and to terrorism, strategic and tactical warning are prone to failure. Indeed, there are evident reasons to believe that the United States and, by extension, allied nations and the international community as a whole will find it increasingly difficult to track the development of WMD and missile capabilities by key states in a timely and accurate manner. Following on high-profile proliferation "surprises," DCI Tenet testified in March 2000 that a contemporary international-security environment characterized by "rapid change makes us even more vulnerable to sudden surprise."[66]

The propensity for surprise has four principal causes: (1) improved deception and denial efforts on the part of would-be proliferants, which, when successful, pose acute collection and analytic challenges; (2) increasing access to dual-use technologies that effectively mask the intentions of proliferant states; (3) the availability of expertise that proliferants can draw on to advance WMD and missile programs; and (4) accelerating technological progress as information and advanced technologies become increasingly available worldwide. Tenet concluded that the risk of surprise was not only a core feature of the intelligence landscape but also increasingly difficult to counter effectively: "The hill is getting steeper every year."[67] In addition to an evidently narrowing intelligence-collection window, the research, development, and acquisition community has warned that defenses will lag offenses with respect to chemical and especially biological arms.[68]

At the same time, getting a handle on proliferant *capabilities* is likely to be considerably easier than collecting, analyzing, and disseminating accurate and timely information on their *plans* and *intentions*.[69] It is virtually axiomatic that the proliferators of greatest concern also represent some of the hardest intelligence targets; and while some key indicators can be revealed through technical means, uncovering planning documents, informed and current perspectives on WMD-related issues, or the intentions of key program or senior leaders is a daunting task that ultimately will be only as credible as the human intelligence upon which such judgments are predicated.

These are acute intelligence challenges in both the terrorism and proliferation contexts and a central reason why the DOD has started to move away from "threat-based" planning approaches and toward "capabilities-based" ones in an effort to "anticipate the capabilities that an adversary might employ to coerce its neighbors, deter the United States from acting in defense of its allies and friends, or directly attack the United States or its deployed forces."[70] As Secretary of Defense Donald Rumsfeld argued in September 2002, on the road to a possible war with Iraq, "the last thing we want is a smoking gun. A gun smokes after it has been fired. The goal must be to stop Saddam Hussein before he fires a weapon of mass destruction against our people. . . . In the age of WMD, the objective is not to protect the 'rights' of dictators . . . it is to protect the lives of our citizens. . . . after such weapons have been used it is too late."[71]

CHAPTER 2

Standards of Evidence

Intelligence Judgments and Policy Determinations

> If India builds the bomb, we will eat grass or leaves, even go hungry, but
> we will get one of our own. We have no alternative.
> —PRIME MINISTER ZULFIQAR ALI BHUTTO, 1965

> I confirm Pakistan possesses the atomic bomb.
> —PRIME MINISTER NAWAZ SHARIF, 1994

Since the late 1960s Pakistan has secretly endeavored to develop nuclear
weapons. The "opaque" status of its program effectively ended, however, with
a series of six nuclear tests conducted in May 1998—a response to India's five
tests carried out earlier that month—providing an indisputable public confirmation that Islamabad had achieved its objective. Through the years, the longstanding Pakistani quest was aided both by weak Western export controls and
by direct assistance from the People's Republic of China (PRC) and was motivated both by Indian nuclear activities and by manifest security challenges on
the subcontinent. Moreover, coupled with each state's nuclear aspirations have
been ballistic missile development programs. This offense-driven arms spiral has
yielded increasingly capable, mass-destructive arsenals deployed by these neigh-
boring states. In any future conflict between them, these weapons, whether they
are used or their use is threatened, are likely to play a significant role.

For the United States, Pakistan's successful development of nuclear weapons
and its continuing improvements in ballistic missile capabilities constitute a
clear failure of US national policy.[1] The intelligence community warned US policy officials as early as the early 1980s that, Pakistani and Chinese protests to
the contrary notwithstanding, Pakistan's nuclear and missile efforts continued
unabated and China remained a key supplier for Islamabad's programs in both
areas. Yet the historical record shows that US nonproliferation objectives often

were superseded by higher, more pressing policy concerns. Indeed, despite the assertions of Richard Kennedy, ambassador-at-large in the Reagan administration, that "we are not faced in South Asia with the choice between our nonproliferation goals and our strategic interests" and that "we have never once deviated from our commitment" to nonproliferation, Pakistan's ultimate success suggests otherwise.[2]

Similarly, the Clinton administration consistently gave commercial objectives priority over nonproliferation objectives and, in the process, raised the evidentiary bar for intelligence relating to Chinese nuclear and missile assistance to Pakistan to virtually unachievable levels. Over time, it became commonplace to "review" or ignore, often for extended periods, information that would otherwise mandate sanctions against China for its proliferation supply activities. In practice, the administration adopted the posture that, as State Department spokesman James Foley argued, "an intelligence judgment is not in and of itself necessarily a sufficient basis for a sanctionability determination under U.S. law." But administration officials never offered any guidance on how such "determinations" would be made. Rather, sanctions were periodically imposed on specific "entities" presumably beyond government control; more frequently, they were simply waived after discussions with officials in Beijing.

Pakistan's progress in the nuclear and missile arenas and China's role as an important supplier in both raise two central questions. First, what is the relationship between, and the relative importance of, nonproliferation and other principal objectives in US policy? Second, what is the role of intelligence in the making of national policy? Lessons learned from the case studies provide important insights into the nature of the relationship between information inputs and policy outcomes.

Pakistan and the Bomb

An Evolving Nuclear Program

Pakistan's defeat in the 1971 Indo-Pakistani war, together with India's successful 1974 nuclear test, galvanized domestic support in Islamabad for an ambitious but clandestine program of nuclear weapons development. Led by Abdul Qadeer Khan and supported over the years by key military and civilian leaders, the Pakistani program proceeded along both the plutonium and enriched uranium routes. A nonsignatory to the NPT, Pakistan was not obligated to place its nuclear-related facilities under International Atomic Energy Agency (IAEA) safeguards; nor was it entitled to benefit from international nuclear assistance (intended for civilian applications) that might be offered in this context. Thus, Pakistan's program relied heavily on smuggling and black-market transactions to secure the relevant hardware and material necessary for the successful design, assembly, testing, and production of nuclear weapons. These products came from a variety of sources in a number of Western states and greatly aided Islamabad's quest.[3]

The most significant assistance, however, came from the PRC. In response to India's 1974 nuclear test, the Chinese leadership offered its "firm and resolute support" to Pakistan in its "just struggle in defense of its national independence and sovereignty against foreign aggression and interference, including that against nuclear threat and nuclear blackmail."[4] Beijing, leery of New Delhi's regional ambitions, became a key supplier of nuclear- and missile-related goods and services to Pakistan. Among the many transactions, both overt and clandestine, China reportedly provided nuclear material, design, and production assistance.[5] As early as 1983 the State Department argued that there was "unambiguous evidence that Pakistan is actively pursuing a nuclear weapons development program."[6] Within three years many observers concluded that Pakistan had procured sufficient fissile material for at least one nuclear device, a conclusion reinforced in a Special National Intelligence Estimate (SNIE) produced that year.[7] By 1990 the intelligence community reportedly had estimated that Pakistan had assembled sufficient material and weapons components for at least six and as many as ten such devices.[8]

Assessments of Pakistan's nuclear capabilities became alarmingly relevant in the early months of 1990. In a series of events reminiscent of the 1987 Brasstacks crisis, insurgent activities by militant Kashmiri separatists and alleged Pakistani support led to increased tension between India and Pakistan, again raising the specter of war between the two antagonists. Both nations had significant military forces in the area, and the rhetoric in each country reached vitriolic proportions. When the crisis reached its apex, it appeared that neither India nor Pakistan—both ruled by weak minority governments—was willing or able to back down from the burgeoning crisis.

At that point US intelligence agencies allegedly intercepted a message ordering the Pakistani Atomic Energy Commission to assemble a nuclear weapon.[9] The possible nuclear aspect of the crisis was played up in the media, and some accounts, particularly a disconcerting article written by Seymour

Hersh, suggested that the two nations were on the brink of a nuclear exchange. In his accounts Hersh cited "official" sources claiming that a convoy of trucks had been sighted leaving a suspected nuclear storage site and that the Pakistanis had F-16 aircraft on full alert.[10] US officials also apparently perceived that the nuclear status of the two antagonists complicated the already difficult issue of Kashmir. Deputy Director of the CIA Richard Kerr called the episode "the most dangerous nuclear situation" since the Cuban Missile Crisis, "as close as we've come to a nuclear exchange." Deputy National Security Adviser Robert Gates, called upon by President Bush to negotiate a stand-down on the subcontinent, feared that although "both sides were blundering toward a war we were afraid . . . would go nuclear," the two governments would be "too weak to stop a war."[11]

The 1990 Indo-Pakistani crisis ultimately concluded without warfare, but the 1998 round of nuclear testing, the 1999 Kargil crisis (and Kashmir's still unresolved status), and ongoing ballistic missile development programs in both countries underscore both the continuing nature of the offensive arms competition and the vivid possibilities for future crises.

Pakistan and US Foreign Policy

Policy trade-offs. In 1977 and again in 1979 the United States curtailed economic and military aid to Pakistan pursuant to amendments to the 1961 Foreign Assistance Act (FAA) sponsored by Senator John Glenn (D-OH) and Representative James Symington (D-MO), respectively. The former provision mandates cutting off military and economic assistance to countries that deliver or receive from another country nuclear enrichment equipment, material, or technology. The latter offers a waiver provision should the president *(a)* determine that an aid cutoff is contrary to the national interest and *(b)* receive "reliable assurances" that the country in question will neither acquire nor develop nuclear weapons or assist other nations in doing so. A subsequent amendment sponsored by Senator Glenn in 1981 gave Congress the authority to call for a renewed suspension of aid within thirty days should it "disapprove" of assistance sent pursuant to the certification. With the Soviet invasion of Afghanistan and the Islamic revolution in Iran that year, however, many US officials viewed Islamabad as a key ally in a troubled region. Yet, as Deputy Assistant Secretary of State Jack Miklos observed at the time, that country's nuclear activities presented the United States with a "very real policy dilemma." Although Pakistan was "important to us and to the region," he argued, its "current nuclear activities . . . restrict our ability to assist it in meeting its considerable security and economic requirements."[12]

Yet the historical record reveals that geopolitics would trump nonproliferation concerns in US policy toward Pakistan for at least the next decade. Indeed, Warren Christopher, then deputy secretary of state, instigated a pattern in early 1980 in "ask[ing] the Congress . . . to permit resumption of assistance" notwithstanding "our deep concerns about Pakistan's nuclear activities."[13] In 1981 the Reagan administration requested a six-year, $3.2 billion aid package for Pakistan, arguing that the US provision of security assistance (including loans to facilitate the purchase of F-16 aircraft) would both help Islamabad meet its evident conventional military needs and at the same time inspire Pakistani nuclear restraint.[14] Congress approved this request, in the process providing a six-year waiver to Glenn-Symington, making Islamabad the third largest recipient of US assistance, after Israel and Egypt.

Congressional sentiment. In appropriating the requested funds, Congress arguably acted in support of the administration's position and, in the process, agreed to a tacit, if not explicit, prioritization of US foreign-policy objectives for Pakistan in which nuclear issues were of secondary importance. By the mid-1980s, however, key congressional nonproliferation advocates became more outspoken about their concerns. Senator Alan Cranston (D-CA) declared in a June 1984 floor statement that he was "today releasing substantial new evidence that Pakistan has acquired all the capability necessary to produce their own nuclear weapons." For that reason, "U.S. security policies must be premised on the fact that Pakistan now has the designs, the hardware, the plants and the personnel capable of producing several nuclear weapons per year."[15]

In October of that year Cranston argued that promises of an "exclusively peaceful dimension" to the "ongoing nuclear program" by Pakistan's President Mohammed Zia ul-Haq to the contrary, "it appears that the Government of Pakistan is not keeping its word." Equally important, Cranston's "new evidence" publicly raised the question whether there had been a "serious intelligence failure" or a "deliberate misrepresentation of the facts by the Reagan administration" perpetuated in order to avoid punishing Pakistan for its nuclear activities as required by law. He charged the administration with an "unwise and unacceptable politicization of intelligence" and noted with respect to Chinese nuclear assistance that "certain Reagan administration State Department officials have a vested interest in obscuring, withholding or downright misrepresenting the facts about Pakistan's program."[16] Cranston's bottom line was that three years of "lavish U.S. military and economic assistance have not stopped the Pakistani nuclear weapons drive," and it was time to draw "a nonproliferation line in the sand."[17]

Critics of Cranston's efforts, such as Senator James McClure (R-ID), argued that "our security relationship has, in fact, slowed the movement toward a [Pakistani nuclear] weapons program." McClure worried that a curtailment of military assistance—as proposed by Cranston, should Pakistan cross the "nuclear threshold"—could "easily lead to the worst of all possible outcomes: that is, a nuclear-armed Pakistan, hostile to the West and unwilling or unable to continue confronting the Soviets."[18] Other proponents of Pakistani aid, such as Senator John Johnston Jr. (D-LA), suggested that while "there is some question" that Pakistan may be moving toward a nuclear program, he queried whether "there is any clear evidence" to that effect. His prescription: "If we want to get the Pakistanis not to build a nuclear device . . . then let us urge them as friends, and let us apply leverage as friends, as members of an alliance . . . and not as what would then become fickle former friends who have no further influence. That is the way to achieve nuclear nonproliferation."[19]

Months before this spirited policy debate, Dr. Abdul Qadeer Khan announced that Pakistan had succeeded in producing enriched uranium at the Kahuta plant. Moreover, concurrent with the June debates, three Pakistani nationals were indicted for attempting to smuggle fifty krytons (electronic switches used in nuclear weapons), a controlled item, out of the United States. Finally, persistent media reports that the PRC had assisted Pakistan's nuclear weapons program, together with the absence of international safeguards at Kahuta, contributed to growing proliferation concerns.[20] The Reagan administration responded to these allegations in a September letter to President Zia threatening "grave consequences" should the Kahuta enrichment facility be used to enrich uranium beyond the discussed 5 percent threshold. The government of Pakistan reportedly responded a few months later promising not to produce weapons-grade uranium.[21] At the same time, despite protestations by the Chinese government that "we do not engage in nuclear proliferation ourselves, nor do we help other nations to develop nuclear weapons," the Reagan administration also deferred consideration of a commercial nuclear cooperation agreement pending satisfactory resolution of US concerns relating to China's aid to Pakistan. Said White House spokesman Larry Speakes, "[We] want to be sure that what we understand and the Chinese understand are the same thing."[22]

Legislative remedies. While the anticommunist alliance of key Reagan administration officials and their supporters on Capitol Hill prevailed in these 1984 debates, their success was short-lived. The following year saw the passage of two important congressional amendments to the FAA of 1961. One of these, sponsored by Representative Steven Solarz (D-NY), prohibited aid to any non-nuclear weapons state that exported (or attempted to export) illegally from the United States "any material, equipment, or technology which would contribute significantly to the ability of such a country to manufacture a nuclear explosive device" if the president determined that such material was intended for that purpose. While this amendment had obvious implications for Pakistan's efforts to acquire nuclear-related technologies, the other provision was of much greater concern not only to officials in Islamabad but also to Reagan administration officials intent on providing assistance to Pakistan. Sponsored by Senator Larry Pressler (R-SD), this amendment declared that no military assistance, equipment, or technology could be sold or transferred "unless the President shall have certified in writing . . . that Pakistan does not possess a nuclear explosive device" and that the proposed aid program "will reduce significantly the risk that Pakistan will possess a nuclear explosive device."

Reportedly, Islamabad crossed the 5 percent enrichment threshold—in contravention to promises made to administration officials—prior to the beginning of fiscal year 1986, the first year that President Reagan had to provide the certification required by the Pressler amendment. With some 120,000 Soviet troops deployed near the Pakistani border in Afghanistan, however, and the continuing imperative of US military assistance to a key regional ally, the Reagan White House provided the necessary certification.

In Leonard Spector's view, the administration's lack of confrontation translated into a de facto acceptance of Islamabad's move toward the production of highly enriched uranium. It underscored that the Pakistani government had "correctly read American priorities," that the administration "was aware of its advances at Kahuta and was prepared to look the other way."[23] Despite the conclusion of a SNIE the following year that Pakistan had produced weapons-grade fissile material, President Reagan issued the necessary nonpossession certification, reportedly on the premise that Pakistan had not yet fabricated particular weapon components and therefore did not "possess" a nuclear device.[24]

NUCLEAR NONPROLIFERATION AND PAKISTAN:
Key Provisions of US Law (Excerpts)

Glenn Amendment to section 669 of the Foreign Assistance Act (FAA) of 1961 (1977): "No funds made available to carry out the Foreign Assistance Act of 1961 . . . may be used for the purpose of providing economic assistance. . . , providing military assistance or grant military education and training, providing assistance under chapter 6 of . . . that Act. . . , or extending military credits or making guarantees, to any country which the President determines delivers nuclear enrichment equipment, materials, or technology to any other country on or after August 4, 1977, or receives such equipment, materials, or technology from any other country on or after August 4, 1977" (22 US Code 2799aa).

Nuclear Non-Proliferation Act of 1978: "No source or special nuclear material hereafter exported from the United States may be enriched after export without the prior approval of the United States for such enrichment. . . ," and "no major critical component of any uranium enrichment, nuclear fuel reprocessing, or heavy water production facility shall be exported under any agreement for cooperation . . . unless such agreement for cooperation specifically designates such components as items to be exported pursuant to the agreement for cooperation" (42 US Code 2153a).

Symington Amendment to section 669 of the FAA and the Foreign Military Sales Act (1979): "The President may furnish assistance which would otherwise be prohibited under such subsection if he determines and certifies in writing to the Speaker of the House of Representatives and the Committee on Foreign Relations of the Senate that: (A) the termination of such assistance would have a serious adverse effect on vital United States interests; and (B) he has received reliable assurances that the country in question will not acquire or develop nuclear weapons or assist other nations in doing so. Such certification shall set forth the reasons supporting such determination in each particular case" (22 US Code 2799aa).

Symington Amendment to section 620E of the FAA (1981): "The President may waive the prohibitions of section 2799aa of this title with respect to any grounds for the prohibition of assistance . . . to provide assistance to Pakistan if he determines that to do so is in the national interest of the United States" (22 US Code 2375[d]).

Glenn Amendment to section 669 of the FAA (1981): "(a) A certification under paragraph (1) of this subsection shall take effect on the date on which the certification is received by the Congress. However, if, within thirty calendar days after receiving this certification, the Congress enacts a joint resolution stating in substance that the Congress disapproves the furnishing of assistance pursuant to the certification, then upon the enactment of that resolution the certification shall cease to be effective and all deliveries of assistance furnished under th[at] authority . . . shall be suspended immediately" (22 US Code 2799aa).

Pressler Amendment to section 620E of the FAA (1985): "No military assistance shall be furnished to Pakistan and no military equipment or technology shall be sold or transferred to Pakistan . . . unless the President shall have certified . . . that Pakistan does not possess a nuclear explosive device and that the proposed United States military assistance program will reduce significantly the risk that Pakistan will possess a nuclear explosive device" (22 US Code 2375[e]).

Solarz Amendment to section 670 of the FAA (1985) curtails foreign assistance to any country that the president determines "(B) is a non-nuclear-weapon state which, on or after August 8, 1985, exports illegally (or attempts to export illegally) from the United States any material, equipment, or technology which would contribute significantly to the ability of such country to manufacture a nuclear explosive device, if the President determines that the material, equipment, or technology was to be used by such country in the manufacture of a nuclear explosive device" (22 US Code 2799aa-1).

Glenn Amendment to section 670 of the FAA (1994), referring to sanctions to be imposed should the president determine a violation of the Nuclear Proliferation Prevention Act of 1994: "The United States Government shall terminate assistance to that country under the Foreign Assistance Act of 1961 . . . sales to that country under this Act of any defense articles, defense services, or design and construction services, . . . licenses for the export to that country of any item on the United States Munitions List" and "all foreign military financing." The United States will also deny "any credit, credit guarantees, or other financial assistance by . . . the United States Government . . . any international financial institution" or "any United States bank" except those "for the purpose of purchasing food or other agricultural commodities" (22 US Code 2799aa-1).

Nuclear Proliferation Prevention Act of 1994: "The President shall impose the sanction . . . if the President determines in writing that, on or after the effective date of this part, a foreign person or a United States person has materially and with requisite knowledge contributed, through the export from the United States or any other country of any goods or technology . . . to the efforts by any individual, group, or non-nuclear-weapon state to acquire unsafeguarded special nuclear material or to use, develop, produce, stockpile, or otherwise acquire any nuclear explosive device" (PL 103-236, 103rd Cong., 2nd sess. [30 April 1994]).

Brown Amendment to section 620E of the FAA (1995) seeks to clarify the restrictions of the Pressler Amendment: "The prohibitions in this section do not apply to any assistance or transfer provided for the purposes of . . . (A) International narcotics control. . . , (B) military-to-military contact. . . , (C) peacekeeping. . . , (D) antiterrorism assistance. . . ," but "restrictions shall continue to apply to . . . F-16 aircraft" (22 US Code 2375-ae2-4).

(*continued*)

> **Agriculture Export Relief Act** (1998) amends the Glenn Amendment to section 670 of the FAA (1994) to permit "any credit, credit guarantee, or financial assistance provided by the Department of Agriculture to support the purchase of food or other agricultural commodity" (PL 105-194, 105th Cong., 2nd sess. [14 July 1998]).
>
> **India-Pakistan Relief Act of 1998:** "The President may waive for a period not to exceed one year upon enactment of this Act with respect to India or Pakistan the application of any sanction or prohibition (or portion thereof) contained in section 101 or 102 of the Arms Export Control Act, section 620E(e) of the Foreign Assistance Act of 1961, or section 2(b)(4) of the Export Import Bank Act of 1945" (vetoed).

In early 1986, when "pressures . . . which warranted the initiation of a major U.S. assistance program [in 1981 had] not abated," the Reagan administration declared its intention to provide Pakistan with a second six-year, $4.02 billion assistance package beginning in October 1987. According to Assistant Secretary of State for Near Eastern and South Asian Affairs Richard Murphy, US security assistance "serves to encourage Pakistani nuclear restraint and to undercut any perceived security need for acquisition of a national nuclear deterrent."[25] The US foreign-policy dilemma was acute: how to ensure that, simultaneously, US laws were upheld, US nonproliferation interests were promoted, a nuclear arms race in South Asia was averted, and US support for Pakistan in the context of a Soviet-invaded Afghanistan continued.

Key officials in Islamabad argued both that US law unfairly discriminated against Pakistan and ignored similar Indian transgressions and that cutting off aid would only remove any inhibitions in the Pakistani nuclear program.[26] The White House agreed, arguing in January 1988 that disrupting the flow of assistance to Pakistan—a "pillar" of the US relationship with that state—would be "counterproductive for the strategic interests of the United States, destabilizing for South Asia, and unlikely to achieve the nonproliferation objectives" sought by Congress.[27] Congress, for its part, both appropriated most of the requested assistance funds for fiscal year 1988 and, while neither repealing the Symington or the Solarz amendment nor issuing a six-year waiver of the former (as in 1981), provided a thirty-month waiver of the Symington provision. In doing so, the legislative branch again acquiesced to the administration's implicit prioritization of policy goals in South Asia.

The Pressler amendment and its discontents. The underlying logic of President Reagan's fiscal year 1986 "nonpossession" certification required by the Pressler amendment continued, in modified form, through the end of the decade. Although Islamabad was clearly flirting with the development of nuclear weapons and had evidently achieved notable successes in this area, it appeared that Pakistan would continue to be certified as long as it did not actually possess an assembled nuclear weapon, conduct a nuclear test, or otherwise publicly flaunt its programmatic advances.[28] President Reagan's 1988 certification is revealing: "The statutory standard as legislated by Congress is whether Pakistan possesses a nuclear explosive device, not whether Pakistan is attempting to develop or has developed various relevant capacities." Nevertheless, Reagan also warned that "Congress should be aware that as Pakistan's nuclear capabilities grow, and if evidence about its activities continues to accumulate, this process of annual certification will require the president to reach judgments about the status of Pakistani nuclear activities that may be difficult or impossible to make with any degree of certainty."[29] Supporters of a tacit, if not explicit, policy choice that prioritized anticommunist concerns over those relating to nonproliferation and thus of continued aid to Pakistan despite evident progress in the nuclear arena faced an increasingly difficult task.

In May 1989 DCI William Webster testified that "clearly, Pakistan is engaged in developing a nuclear capability."[30] In line with Reagan's 1988 warning, the 1989 certification issued by President George Bush was reportedly made only after the new Pakistani prime minister, Benazir Bhutto, agreed to suspend the further production of weapons-grade uranium.[31] Bhutto, addressing a joint session of the US Congress in June that year, stated, "Speaking for Pakistan, I can declare that we do not possess nor do we intend to make a nuclear device. That is our policy."[32] In his certification Bush declared that the government of Pakistan "is fully aware of the requirements of US law governing security assistance and of the serious consequences that would ensue . . . should it prove impossible to make the certification required by law." He also warned that "our ability to certify depends on evidence that the assurances given by the Prime Minister are being implemented."[33] Yet, within the next year, and in the context of the 1990 crisis with India, Pakistan apparently proceeded to manufacture and assemble the cores for a number of nuclear weapons from previously produced weapons-grade uranium.[34] In October 1990, after Soviet troops had withdrawn from Afghanistan, Bush refused to make the certification required by Pressler. Accordingly, the United States suspended its military assistance to Pakistan.

One element of US security assistance was low-cost financing for Pakistan's purchase of a variety of US-manufactured military equipment, including a pending order for twenty-eight remaining (of sixty initially purchased) high-performance F-16 fighter aircraft approved by Congress the previous year. Although the financing was subject to the terms of the Pressler amendment, Islamabad nonetheless continued to make payments on these purchases after the aid cutoff—$608 million in fiscal years 1991–93—presumably in order to be able to receive the remainder of the order should assistance recommence. Senator Glenn queried why Pakistan continued to send money "when they knew that U.S. law would not enable them to receive the planes," comparing the behavior to that of an investor "buying a stock of a company whose assets are under lien in the hope that the lien will somehow be removed."[35] Threats of Pakistani legal action against the United States for alleged breach of contract, US efforts to transfer the aircraft in question to a third country (and repay Pakistan with the proceeds), and other proposed remedies would keep this issue front and center for much of President Clinton's term of office. And Pakistan, for its part, would attempt to address what Foreign Secretary Shahryar Khan called a "credibility gap" on the issue both by acknowledging its nuclear weapons progress and by attempting to convince Bush administration officials that Islamabad had subsequently frozen the program rather than proceed "in an unwise direction."[36]

In addition to the controversy surrounding the suspended Pakistani purchase of fighter aircraft, other issues also quickly arose in the absence of a "non-possession" certification. Despite the Pressler amendment's requirement that all military-related assistance be terminated, the Bush administration continued its efforts to facilitate the improvement and maintenance of Pakistani conventional arms. Under questioning by Senator Pressler in 1992, Secretary of State James Baker explained that while "we have indeed cut off all foreign assistance" as a result of noncertification, "we have carefully reviewed the [Pressler] amendment, we have reviewed the legislative history, and as a legal matter we do not believe it applies to commercial sales or exports controlled by the Department of Commerce." Under this interpretation, munitions and spare parts necessary to the maintenance of the Pakistani military's existing capabilities would be treated on a case-by-case basis. "Commercial sales are limited," Baker argued to Senator Pressler, and "none are being approved that would contravene either the letter or the spirit of your amendment."[37]

Further elaborating Secretary Baker's position, the State Department's principal deputy legal adviser, Michael Matheson, subsequently testified, "In the absence of express language to the contrary, statutory references to assistance do not include the licensing of commercial arms exports conducted by private parties."[38] Senators Glenn, Cranston, Pressler, and others questioned the administration's interpretation of the Pressler amendment, arguing that the premise of the amendment was to force a Pakistani trade-off between nuclear and conventional arms. Glenn charged that the administration, seeking maximum flexibility in its policy toward Pakistan, had willfully misinterpreted the Pressler provision. While administration officials could seek to change the law, he said, "they do not, however, have the right to ignore the law or to break it, which is what we are seeing happen under present circumstances."[39] Pressler, for his part, recalled deliberately using the "broadest possible" language to present Pakistan with the "starkest possible choice: either adhere to your promise not to develop nuclear weapons or lose your conventional weapons supply, including the spare parts and other equipment that makes your existing arsenal operational."[40]

Echoing Glenn, Pressler concluded that the State Department "was looking for a way to help Pakistan despite a very clear statutory prohibition" and that in the process "the will of Congress was thwarted."[41] While the State Department rejected this interpretation, subsequent independent legal opinions offered by the nonpartisan Congressional Research Service and the nongovernmental Lawyers Alliance for World Security largely supported Pressler's interpretation of the mandatory arms (both government-to-government *and* commercial sales) and aid cutoff required by law.

Seeking to dispel charges of a politicized interpretation of the Pressler amendment, Matheson testified that the State Department's legal advisers "were not pressed by policy officials to reach any particular result" in their statutory review of the legal provision. The review conducted by the legal adviser's office, he argued, had determined that commercial sales were beyond the scope of the Pressler amendment. Rather than insidious machinations at Foggy Bottom, he argued, the administration's licensing policy "was developed only after we had advised that there was legal flexibility."[42] At the same time, Deputy Assistant Secretary of State for Near Eastern and South Asian Affairs John Malott confirmed that the administration's intent was to "preserve some degree of flexibility." Arguing in the spirit of his predecessors, Malott stated that "to totally cut them off . . . would work against our common interest in trying to prevent the proliferation of nuclear weapons."[43] That is, despite the manifest failure of this approach, as represented by the president's evident inability to certify, the State Department intended to continue its policy approach toward Pakistan regardless of the likely proliferation-related results.

Chinese Missile Assistance

Concurrent with nuclear weapons development, Pakistan attempted to deploy increasingly capable ballistic missiles. Indeed, the 1990s witnessed considerable improvements in Islamabad's missile capabilities resulting largely from technology transfers and other assistance from both China and North Korea. As with the evident political difficulties in acknowledging steady advances in Pakistani nuclear capabilities, US policy officials in effect turned a blind eye toward the substantial Chinese assistance in this area. While successive administrations, together with the tacit acquiescence of successive Congresses, prioritized geopolitical concerns more highly than nonproliferation equities in 1980s policy toward Pakistan, geoeconomics reigned supreme in 1990s policy toward China. In each case the intelligence community provided substantial information on the nature of proliferation-related activities in question, and a minority of the policy community argued for more stringent measures to counter the weapons development processes. The cumulative effect of policy inaction was a nonproliferation death by a thousand cuts.

Supply and Demand

In conjunction with its nuclear program, Islamabad actively sought increasingly capable delivery vehicles for its developing nuclear weapons. Even as Pakistan purchased advanced fighter aircraft (which likely could be modified to deliver a nuclear payload) from the United States in the mid-1980s, it also sought and received China's assistance with the Hatf-1, a short-range ballistic missile (SRBM) of Pakistani manufacture with an effective range of approximately eighty kilometers.[44] In a continuing effort to increase the range and accuracy of its delivery systems, Pakistan worked closely with China, as well as North Korea, to develop and field improved ballistic missiles.

The PRC's longstanding assistance to Pakistan is part of a larger pattern of active support for proliferation to a number of lesser-developed states in the Middle East and Asia. The Chinese government traditionally has argued that the "prevention of proliferation is not in itself the ultimate goal" and often has rejected arguments that might "restrict or harm economic, scientific and technological development in developing countries" or "impair the independence and sovereignty of any nation." It has considered the volume of its exports "limited" and proclaimed that its arms transfers were regulated by three principal concerns: (1) the export of such weapons "should help the recipient nation increase its appropriate defence capacity"; (2) the transfers "must not impair peace, safety or stability regionally or globally"; and (3) the weapons trade should not "interfere in sovereign states' internal affairs."[45]

Interpreting this official Chinese stance, former US ambassador to China James Lilley suggests that PRC export behavior has been justified "for decades, even centuries" first by "high sanctimonious rhetoric," second by Realpolitik, and finally by "victimization."[46] In Lilley's view, arms transfers generate revenue for China's defense establishment, encourage political support from significant regional states such as Iran or Pakistan, and remind the United States and others that the PRC is an important player on the world scene. In parallel, former Deputy Assistant Secretary of Defense Mitchell Wallerstein concludes that the PRC emphasizes the "foreign-policy and commercial gains of sharing sensitive technology with proliferant states" and upholds an "ambivalent" nonproliferation policy pending a conclusive national decision regarding China's interests in meeting global nonproliferation norms. Until then, the Chinese leadership appears to find it necessary to "balance its obligations" under the international arms control and nonproliferation regimes to which it adheres and its "perceived need to use exports—including many that are weapons of mass destruction–related—to sustain its domestic defence industries."[47]

While these analysts emphasize the commercial aspect of China's arms sales, others offer geostrategic interpretations of China's proliferant behavior. According to Bates Gill, by the 1980s Iran's "revolutionary policies and strong stand against outside influence meshed well" with the PRC's efforts to both maintain independence from the superpowers and build Chinese regional influence.[48] Similarly, former head of the Director of Central Intelligence Nonproliferation Center Gordon Oehler argues that China has regarded Pakistan as a "counterbalance" to India, a state that declares China to be the underlying rationale for its development of nuclear weapons. For this reason, the PRC "has held back few weapons and technologies in support of this relationship."[49] Daniel Byman and Roger Cliff echo these views, arguing that strategic concerns "include a desire to strengthen foes of China's rivals and to expand China's political influence in regions such as the Middle East and Southeast Asia."[50]

Within this context, it appears that following India's February 1988 test of the Prithvi SRBM, China agreed to provide Pakistan with increased missile-related technology and other assistance, including the direct transfer of China's M-9 and M-11 missiles, with ranges of approximately six hundred and three hundred kilometers, respectively.[51] One year later Pakistan claimed to have successfully tested two surface-to-surface missiles with ranges of approximately eighty and three hundred kilometers and a payload capacity of roughly five hundred kilograms.[52] Almost a decade later, in February 1998, Pakistan successfully test-launched the Ghauri MRBM. While officials in Islamabad declared that this was an "indigenously developed missile," the work for which "was entirely done by our scientists," close observers note that the Ghauri appears to closely resemble the North Korean Nodong MRBM and probably incorporates Chinese technology.[53] This accomplishment underscores a notable feature of missile proliferation: the increasing availability of "secondary" suppliers, whose activities occur largely outside the purview of Western-oriented supply-side regimes but whose transfers and assistance are steadily transforming the security landscape in key regions.[54]

While newly elected Prime Minister Benazir Bhutto publicly denied that she sought Chinese or North Korean ballistic missile assistance during her official visits to each state in late 1993, it is plausible that the Ghauri MRBM originated in that time period. According to Joseph Bermudez, while Chinese leaders "had no desire to further damage" relations with the United States, they "perceived as legitimate Pakistani defense concerns" and developed a plan intended to assist Islamabad without unduly antagonizing Washington. Rather than transferring intact missile systems (as before), China would instead "continue to finance the establishment and expansion of a ballistic missile infrastructure" in Pakistan and "provide the soft technology and engineering" for what would become the Ghauri. North Korea would "serve as a conduit for a portion of the PRC assistance" and "provide hardware and components" from its Nodong and Taepodong MRBM programs, while China would provide components in those areas in which North Korea "was still struggling."[55] While the publicly available literature is vague concerning the components transferred, as well as the timing and extent of Chinese and North Korean assistance, it appears that China *(a)* had transferred complete M-11s by 1992, *(b)* clandestinely exported a substantial number of components related to the M-11 throughout the 1990s, and *(c)* helped Pakistan build a production facility for the M-11, providing blueprints, expertise, and relevant materials. Moreover, the implication of China and North Korea's collective efforts is clear: Pakistani success in developing and, reportedly, fielding both SRBMs and an MRBM capable of delivering unconventional payloads.

Promises Made, Promises Broken

In 1988, China sold to Saudi Arabia a number of Dong-Feng 3A (CSS-2) intermediate-range ballistic missiles (IRBMs) and to Syria and Pakistan shorter-range M-9 and M-11 missiles, respectively. While these transfers both diminished China's "credibility as a country committed to the cause of nonproliferation" and underscored its clear intent to transfer missile systems to interested parties, they also called into question the viability of the newly established Missile Technology Control Regime (MTCR).[56]

The MTCR was an informal export control agreement aimed at preventing the spread of ballistic and cruise missiles capable of delivering a 500 kg warhead to ranges greater than three hundred kilometers. The MTCR was initially designed to counter nuclear warheads, but control guidelines were expanded in 1993 to include biological and chemical warheads as well.[57] MTCR members voluntarily agree to abide by the guidelines of the regime, which seek to prohibit or restrain the export of two categories of technologies: Category I in general covers all finished missile systems and unmanned aerial vehicle systems that exceed th MTCR range and payload limitations. Category II addresses "materials, components, and technologies that could aid in the development of proscribed systems.

While most Group of Seven, or G-7, countries became founding members of the regime, neither the Soviet Union nor China participated. Instead, US diplomatic pressure resulted in a pledge by Chinese premier Deng Xiaoping to visiting US Secretary of Defense Frank Carlucci, an ambiguous assurance that "China would exercise restraint on missile sales, because restraint may be warranted under certain conditions."[58] US concerns were evidently well placed. Over the next several years the PRC would export intact missile systems, their constituent components, and/or their underlying production equipment or infrastructure to a number of states that were of concern with respect to proliferation, including Pakistan, Iran, and North Korea.[59]

The George H. W. Bush administration. The 1991 Gulf War, which saw extensive use of Iraq's Scud-based ballistic missile force and the threat of chemical and biological warfare, was a watershed event for the Bush administration with respect to nonproliferation policy.[60] As a result of the Gulf War experience and the perceived growing threat of proliferation in the Middle East and other regions, on July 13, 1992, President Bush announced "a set of principles to guide our nonproliferation efforts in the years ahead." The president argued that the demand for WMD, delivery systems, and key technologies was expanding and that export controls alone could not reliably halt the flow of sensitive materials. In order to combat the spread of such weapons, the United States needed "to employ the full range of political, security, intelligence and other tools at [U.S.] disposal."[61]

In the area of ballistic missile proliferation one of the key tools was the MTCR, of which the United States was a founding member. The United States sought to tie penalties to violations of the MTCR, which, as a "gentlemen's agreement," lacked a real enforcement mechanism. Under the terms of the Arms Export Control Act, the Export Administration Act (as amended by the 1990 Missile Control Act), and the National Defense Authorization Act of 1991, violations of the MTCR required the automatic imposition of sanctions.[62]

The administration's renewed emphasis on nonproliferation was put to the test in 1991, when intelligence reports reportedly surfaced suggesting the presence of launch vehicles for the Chinese-made M-11 ballistic missile in Pakistan.[63] If the policy community judged that a missile transfer occurred, it would trigger US sanctions under a provision of the 1990 defense authorization bill against any state that violated the MTCR. The Bush administration therefore took action in late April 1991, blocking the export of US-manufactured satellite components to the PRC. The decision was based on what White House Press Secretary Marlin Fitzwater called "serious proliferation concerns," which included not only the alleged missile transfer to Pakistan but also purported Chinese nuclear assistance to Algeria and missile aid to several Middle Eastern countries.[64] The decision to block the export was significant for two reasons, according to the White House: first, it "highlights our concern about nuclear proliferation," where China was suspect, and second, it "shows that where there are legitimate concerns, even when it involves China, we are willing to act."[65]

Several weeks later the White House took additional steps, blocking the sale of high-speed supercomputers to China in May and prohibiting the approval of any new satellite licenses to China pending satisfaction of US concerns over the transfer of missile technologies. The administration also made specific determinations that the Chinese Precision Machinery Import and Export Corporation and the China Great Wall Corporation both had transferred missile technology to Pakistan and accordingly sanctioned the entities as required by public law. However, much to the dismay of congressional Democrats and other observers, President Bush did not halt the renewal of China's most-favored-nation trade status. In June 1991 the United States also engaged China in talks aimed at convincing it not to sell missiles to Pakistan and Syria. Although the talks failed to produce any agreement halting the potential sales, Chinese Foreign Ministry spokesman Wu Jianmin confirmed that "a very small number" of SRBMs had been sold to Pakistan.[66]

The missile issue occupied center stage until October 18, 1991, when the PRC, along with the other permanent members of the UN Security Council, pledged to refrain from selling weapons that would exacerbate conflicts or regional tensions.[67] In mid-November a visit by Secretary of State James Baker resulted in a verbal statement to Baker by Chinese officials reaffirming their commitment to "observe the guidelines and parameters" of the MTCR if the United States would remove the sanctions imposed on the two Chinese corporations in May.[68] Although Secretary Baker considered this commitment to be the most significant accomplishment of his visit, the *New York Times* editorialized, "The Chinese have made and broken promises to the United States about missile exports several times, so the value of their commitment to Mr. Baker can only be tested over time."[69]

Indeed, less than three months after Baker's visit to Beijing the intelligence community reported that China had possibly transferred guidance units for the M-11 missile to Pakistan.[70] These reports emerged as the White House was preparing to lift the sanctions imposed in May 1991. Chinese Premier Li Peng met with President Bush at the United Nations at the end of January 1992 and reportedly stated that China would provide a written version of the verbal commitment offered in November. Although the February 1992 letter sent by Chinese Foreign Minister Qian Qichen was "not as explicit as we would have liked," one White House official suggested that "we got enough in the letter to make us believe these [sales] are covered."[71]

Despite this reputed progress, concern over Chinese sales remained in the intelligence community and especially in Congress, where many Democrats believed that the steps taken by the administration were insufficient. Senator Joseph Biden (D-DE), in particular, was wary of this latest PRC commitment, calling for a closed session of the Senate to debate the issue in support of legislation to make proliferation a condition for renewal of the PRC's most-favored-nation trade status.[72] Biden's bill and its House counterpart both

CHINESE MISSILE TECHNOLOGY TRANSFERS AND US POLICY ISSUES, 1991–1999

1991

March US intelligence discovers the sale of Chinese-made M-11s to Pakistan. Launchers for the missiles are spotted in Pakistan as well.

June The US press reports that China confirms the sale of M-11s to Pakistan.

1993

July A memo from Treasury Secretary Robert Rubin and National Security Adviser Anthony Lake tells President Clinton the United States should "balance US competitiveness against a strong but not yet conclusive case for sanctioning China."

August State Department spokesman Mike McCurry announces that the Clinton administration will impose Category II sanctions against China for the M-11 transfers.

November The White House reportedly considers lifting the ban on communications satellites imposed two months earlier.

1994

January The Commerce Department is allowed to approve the sale of a satellite to China, effectively lifting a portion of the Category II sanctions.

July Amid claims from the US intelligence community that the Clinton administration has ignored evidence of proliferation, the White House states that until the M-11 trade is admitted to by one of the parties, no sanctions will be imposed (see June 1991 above).

September Pakistan reportedly pays $15 million to the China Precision Machinery Import and Export Company for M-11 transfer.

October Secretary of State Warren Christopher and Chinese Foreign Minister Qian Qichen announce "Joint Declarations" between the United States and China, lifting the remaining sanctions in place from August 1993. China agrees not to export any ground-to-ground missiles. The administration says that this "represents a global and verifiable ban on Chinese exports of missiles under 300 km."

1996

April The Clinton administration resumes US government subsidized loan guarantees for exports to China.

June On the thirteenth, the intelligence community reports with "high confidence" that Pakistan has obtained M-11 missiles from China and that Pakistan had developed nuclear warheads for them. The following day, the State Department reports that the policy community has not yet made a sanctionability determination.

August The US intelligence community concludes that Pakistan is secretly building a missile factory outside Islamabad, with blueprints and equipment provided by China.

1997
June The press reports that China is helping Pakistan develop an indigenous missile production program.

The Commerce Department announces that sanctions will be imposed on Chinese "entities," including the Chinese Academy of Engineering Physics, the Institute of Applied Physics and Computational Mathematics, and others.

1998
March The United States announces that it intends to sell missile technology to China, despite its being barred under current human-rights sanctions. The plan offers inducements to prevent technology transfers to Pakistan and Iran.

May The State Department announces that it is concerned about continued Chinese proliferation of WMD.

June The Clinton administration drops plans to pressure China to agree in writing to broad export controls of missile technology.

Gordon Oehler, former DCI Nonproliferation Center director, tells a Senate committee that the administration's determination to avoid imposing sanctions on China led to pressure on his office to downplay evidence that Beijing had sold thirty-four nuclear-capable M-11 missiles to Pakistan in 1992.

November The United States and China meet to bilaterally work toward China's joining the MTCR. The United States voices concern that China had again transferred missile technology to Pakistan and Iran.

1999
April A Commerce Department report states that $15 billion worth of sensitive, high-technology equipment has been sold to China over the past decade.

September A National Intelligence Estimate states that China has transferred complete M-11 missiles to Pakistan. State Department spokesman James Foley responds that "an Intelligence Estimate is not in and of itself necessarily a sufficient basis for a sanctionability determination under U.S. law."

passed in their respective chambers, with Biden confidently proclaiming that "today will mark the point beyond which there can be no excuse on the part of any senator for ignorance of the sobering facts of Chinese proliferation practices" and that the legislation would "lock in" China's commitment to its pledges.[73] Senator Lloyd Bentsen (D-TX) echoed this sentiment, stating that Congress needed to "tell the Chinese that there's a price to pay for its policy of repression and indiscriminate arms sales."[74] These concerns notwithstanding, the president soon moved to lift the sanctions imposed nine months earlier; as with US policy on Pakistan's nuclear weapons development, the gap between official US policy and its rhetorical underpinnings remained.[75]

Remarkably, just one year after these sanctions were lifted China again was caught in the act. Reports emerging in December 1992 indicated that China had transferred additional M-11 missiles to Pakistan, apparently in violation of the commitment made to senior Bush officials.[76] According to media accounts, approximately two dozen missiles or related components had been photographed as they were being unloaded at the Pakistani port of Karachi.[77] Administration officials expressed concern over the reports, but rather than make a specific determination that China had broken its commitment from the previous year, they argued that there was only "very strong circumstantial evidence" of Chinese impropriety.[78] Within days the administration acted further, blocking the transfer of a supercomputer that had been approved by the State Department and the Commerce Department and threatening further sanctions if the intelligence reports were confirmed. However, in the context of the US presidential election, by the end of President Bush's tenure in office this issue had largely fallen off the radar screen. The PRC, for its part, pressed for a resumption of trade and a series of high-level bilateral meetings with the incoming Clinton administration.[79]

The pattern of behavior established in the Bush era would continue to characterize Sino-American relations with regard to proliferation issues in general and to missile technology transfers to Pakistan in particular through the end of the decade and beyond. When evidence surfaced that China had transferred sensitive materials in violation of international requirements or promises, US officials confronted their Chinese counterparts and requested an explanation or clarification. The PRC would deny that any such transfers had taken place but would make commitments to abide by the relevant international regimes. Sanctions, if they were imposed, would be lifted soon after China had appropriately renewed prior commitments. China would then resume technology transfers. This pattern continued and arguably intensified during the Clinton administration.

The Clinton administration. Ironically, during the 1992 election campaign Governor William Clinton frequently attacked President Bush for being soft on China. The Bush decision to decouple human rights and other conditions from the renewal of China's most-favored-nation status was often a target for Clinton's campaign-trail criticism. However, as the new Clinton administration faced the same proliferation problems that had confronted the Bush administration, officials quickly fell into a pattern similar to that established during the previous administration. While nonproliferation was a declared priority for the incoming team, other issues were of evidently greater importance to the new administration. As the administration's new national-security strategy of "engagement and enlargement" suggested, economic ties with other nations would play a major role in ensuring American prosperity and spreading American and democratic values around the world. Indeed, geoeconomics would become a dominant force behind US foreign policy during the Clinton era, and as the record on China and Pakistan showed, other policy goals—including nonproliferation—would often take a back seat.[80]

M-11 redux. While eclipsed initially, the issue of missile transfers to Pakistan did not fade away but arose again in May 1993 as the administration was concluding a review of its China policy and preparing to revisit China's most-favored-nation status. Reports resurfaced of the alleged 1992 transfer of additional M-11 missiles or components thereof from the PRC to Pakistan, again citing evidence from satellite photography and other sources.[81] Intelligence officials briefed key congressional committees on the issue, indicating that such reports had grown "more numerous and more persuasive" since initially circulated. At the same time, some administration officials concluded that while "we keep getting information about the possibility of such transfers" and "the weight of evidence was heavy," the evidence was "strongly suggestive but not conclusive."[82] State Department spokesman Joseph Snyder echoed this sentiment, saying that the United States had "not determined that China transferred M-11 missiles to Pakistan."[83] Pending consultations with the PRC, further action would not be taken.

That the available intelligence was insufficient to support a sanctions determination remained the official position of the administration until August 1993, when in the face of mounting evidence that missile technologies had been transferred Undersecretary of State for International Security Affairs Lynn Davis made the determination "that certain Chinese and Pakistani entities had engaged in missile-related transfers that required the imposition of sanctions under U.S. law."[84] The so-called Category II sanctions to be imposed by the United States blocked new export licenses for materials on the MTCR Annex lists.[85] According to State Department spokesman Michael McCurry, while there was "unambiguous evidence that a Category II transfer has occurred," there was still "ambiguity on the question of whether or not a Category I transfer has occurred."[86] The sanctions were intended to remain in place for two years. The State Department estimated an annual loss of $400–500 million in sales to US businesses as a result of the sanctions.

China and Pakistan strongly objected to the sanctions. Chinese Foreign Ministry spokesman Wu Jianmin stated that the sanctions were "entirely unjustifiable," while the Chinese embassy in Washington declared that the sanctions were "a wrong judgment based on inaccurate intelligence."[87] The Pakistani government did not deny that China had recently transferred missiles but instead argued that the sanctions were unjustified because no treaty violation had occurred: "These missiles did not violate the MTCR. Both Pakistan and China have assured the United States on this point."[88]

Not surprisingly, US businesses were equally vocal in criticizing the decision to impose sanctions. Michael Sun, vice president of Hughes Network Systems (a Hughes Aircraft subsidiary heavily involved in satellite communications–related projects with the PRC) lamented the likely effects of the sanctions, stating, "This is not going to help our business. . . . Every time I meet with Chinese officials they give me a 15-minute lecture complaining about American policy." In his view, "sometimes you have to ask the question why you as an American company get hit more than anyone else."[89]

Whether or not lobbying by Hughes Chief Executive Officer C. Michael Armstrong or other US entities with business connections in China had any effect, by mid-November 1993, just three months after the determination, there was already talk of relaxing some of the sanctions on satellite exports.[90] In January 1994 the Commerce Department, over the objections of the State Department, authorized the export of three commercial satellites for launch on Chinese rockets.[91] (The Commerce Department had previously taken the position that since these were commercial rather than military satellites, the sanctions should not apply.)[92] At the same time, US officials engaged their Chinese counterparts in negotiations aimed both at "clarifying" the precise nature of

China's previous commitment to abide by the guidelines of the MTCR and at obtaining new assurances.

These negotiations apparently resulted in an October 1994 agreement by the PRC not to ship missile parts that were in violation of the MTCR standards and to work with the United States to promote missile nonproliferation in return for the cancellation of the sanctions imposed in August 1993.[93] As before, China insisted that no treaty violations had occurred. As Chinese Foreign Minister Qian Qichen stated, "China does not engage in proliferation of weapons of mass destruction, including missiles outside the MTCR regime."[94] Chinese officials repeatedly asserted that the performance of the M-11 missile was below the MTCR threshold, which prohibited the export of missiles capable of launching a 500 kg or larger warhead to a range of three hundred kilometers or greater. By contrast, US officials argued that the M-11 was "inherently capable" of crossing this threshold, a judgment reflected in this agreement. US Secretary of State Warren Christopher spoke highly of the joint communiqué, stating that it went "beyond the MTCR requirements" and that "China has now accepted the MTCR definition of [the M-11] missile's inherent capability."[95] Furthermore, Christopher declared that the new agreement represented "a global and verifiable ban on Chinese exports of missiles" meeting the MTCR requirements.[96]

Yet within a year of this new Chinese commitment the issue arose again: new intelligence suggested that China had transferred missile technology to Pakistan. In June 1995 the intelligence community, reportedly based on satellite reconnaissance photographs, intercepted communications, and human intelligence reports, alleged that within the past three months the PRC had transferred additional parts for the M-11 missile to Pakistan.[97] Intelligence officials observed that "virtually the entire U.S. intelligence community" agreed that the storage crates sighted at Sargodha Air Force Base in Pakistan contained M-11 missiles.[98]

Although White House, DOD, and State Department spokesmen reiterated the administration's concern over the transfer, Pentagon spokesman Ken Bacon stated that the "firm, conclusionary evidence" needed to make a sanctions determination was not present.[99] Echoing Bacon's assessment, a State Department colleague stated, "What we need is to know the missiles are there. The intelligence community believes they are there, but they don't know." Given the potential economic impact of sanctions, the official stated, "this is something that we take seriously and that we have a high standard of evidence for."[100]

While this official understood that the State Department's standard of evidence had made the intelligence community "unhappy in the extreme," others were more pointed: "The evidence . . . is incontrovertible that M-11s have been delivered and are there," but the administration is evidently "reluctant to push this forward for political reasons."[101]

Nor was Congress silent as the sanctionability drama unfolded. Representative Howard Berman (D-CA), a cosponsor of the 1990 legislation that mandated sanctions for technology transfers of this sort, questioned the administration's handling of the intelligence reports, stating that "sometimes proof . . . depends on where you want [it] to come from," and criticized China's record of "proliferate, promise not to, proliferate, promise not to, and proliferate."[102] Similarly, Senator John McCain (R-AZ), another cosponsor, acknowledged, "This is a delicate time in U.S.-China relations," but if "we have reliable intelligence that M-11 missiles have been provided to Pakistan by China, then the president must act under law."[103]

Illustrating the gulf between the positions of administration and congressional officials, Arms Control and Disarmament Agency Director John Holum summed up the administration's position as follows: "We are approaching the point where we have to make a sanctions decision related to China based on substantial indications of missile-related trade. . . . We need to keep collecting information. We need to get the Chinese to clarify the information we have."[104] Ultimately the administration chose not to act but rather to deliberately pursue a policy course antithetical to US law through the simple but effective procedural device of raising the evidentiary bar for intelligence to unachievable levels.

Members of Congress nonetheless continued to press the White House for action on the M-11 issue. Senator Jesse Helms (R-NC), chairman of the Senate Foreign Relations Committee, challenged the administration's position, declaring, "I am informed unofficially that there was virtually unanimous agreement" that China had made transfers in violation of the MTCR. Waiting for "further evidence against China," he argued, "is both unnecessary and dangerous"; the administration stood to make a "mockery of U.S. commitments" to nonproliferation by refusing to impose sanctions.[105] Senate Intelligence Committee Chairman Senator Arlen Spector (R-PA) echoed this view: "The intelligence community has done an excellent job in identifying this violation," and President Clinton should impose "the maximum sanctions available under U.S. law." Spector argued that if the president failed to do so or waived the sanctions, the administration "would make our national policy an international laughingstock."[106] This latest missile debate occurred as a Chinese transfer of ring magnets to Pakistan's nuclear program became public, underscoring the hollow claims of intelligence insufficiency. Members of Congress soon threatened to block a $368 million transfer of US military equipment to Pakistan.[107]

A "Virtually Certain" Judgment

The summer of 1996 also saw a critical development on the intelligence front as evidence of continuing missile technology–related transfers mounted, reaching a point where, according to Gordon Oehler, the intelligence community was "virtually certain" that the transfer of M-11 missiles had taken place.[108] Oehler testified that the intelligence community had accurately predicted that the transfer would occur based on the 1990 presence of the M-11 training missile and launcher in Pakistan. When the transfer finally materialized, "the evidence was quite strong at the time, and most agencies in the intelligence community agreed right away that the actual transfer of missiles had taken place."[109] Further intelligence reports traced the missile crates to Sarghoda Air Force Base, where they had been stored since their arrival in Pakistan. Compounding the evidence of missile transfers were reports suggesting that the PRC had also transferred the blueprints for a complete M-11 production facility. Satellite photos indicated that the Pakistanis had begun construction of the facility near Rawalpindi in 1995; the photos reportedly were bolstered by human sources and electronic intercepts.[110]

By the summer of 1996, according to Oehler, "the unanimous view of the intelligence community, including the State Department's Bureau of Intelligence and Research" was that "there was a high likelihood that the missiles themselves were transferred."[111] Prior to this the intelligence community had been divided on a central issue: not whether the missiles were actually there but whether they were "operational." Indeed, the unanimous view of the intelligence community, based on satellite photographs indicating the presence of maintenance facilities and launchers at Sarghoda, was that the missiles were in fact at the base.[112] A dispute reportedly arose between the CIA and the DIA on the one hand and the State Department's Bureau of Intelligence and Research (INR) on the other over the operational efficacy of the M-11s, with INR taking the position that they were not operational.[113] INR reportedly based its position on the proposition that the missiles had not been removed from their crates, let alone used for training purposes.

That the State Department's intelligence arm had finally acknowledged the presence of the missiles in Pakistan, regardless of their operational state or parallel questions concerning whether the M-11s were capable of delivering a nuclear payload, was significant. Yet even after INR made this judgment, some reports suggested that State Department intelligence officials had attempted to persuade NIC Chair Richard Cooper and CIA Director John Deutch to tone down the report's verbiage in order to prevent "undue policy alarms."[114]

Indeed, apparent unanimity among members of the intelligence community was still insufficient for policy officials in the State Department and the White House to make a sanctionability determination. The response was to raise the evidentiary standard for intelligence that would otherwise warrant policy action. National Security Council Senior Director for Nonproliferation and Export Controls Daniel Poneman reportedly quipped to intelligence officials, "You're bringing me pennies; bring me some quarters."[115] Meanwhile, Pakistan and China maintained that there had been no illegal transfers at all. Zamir Akram, the deputy chief of mission at the Pakistani embassy in Washington, blasted reports from "dubious people in so-called intelligence agencies" and with regard to the alleged missile factory stated, "We have no knowledge of such a factory."[116] A PRC embassy official continued to deny the transfers, bluntly stating, "We consider this matter completely closed. There never was any such cooperation. This was discussed when we signed the 1994 agreement."[117] Again, no action was taken against China, and amazingly, two months later, Arms Control and Disarmament Agency Director Holum praised China for its cooperation in nonproliferation, stating, "We find increasingly that China is a constructive partner in a number of our global arms control priorities."[118]

Fudging the facts. Despite the case for sanctioning China from a nonproliferation standpoint, broader foreign-policy considerations mitigated against such a course of action. *Engagement* was the buzzword of Clinton administration policy, and the White House argued that national-security interests would best be served by the United States' remaining engaged with the PRC. China relied heavily on its economic and technological ties with the United States, and US corporations benefited from trade relations as well.

Presumably, these economic connections would provide a source of leverage over the Chinese government, a policy tool to effect behavioral changes in Chinese government policy. However, administration officials saw the automatic nature and sweeping requirements for sanctions mandated under US nonproliferation laws as detrimental to the use of economic leverage. Flexibility was seen as key to the Clinton team's foreign policy, and the imposition of sanctions threatened that flexibility. President Clinton forthrightly explained: "What always happens if you have automatic sanctions legislation is it puts enormous pressure on whoever is in the executive branch to fudge an evaluation of the facts of what is going on. And that's not what you want. What you want is to leave the President some flexibility, including the ability to impose sanctions, some flexibility with a range of appropriate reactions."[119] President Clinton's view was echoed several months later by Secretary of State Madeleine Albright, who railed against what she termed the "proliferation of sanctions" by Congress.[120] Said Secretary Albright, "Sanctions that have no flexibility, no waiver authority, are just blunt instruments. And diplomacy requires us to have some finesse. I can't do business, or the president can't do business, with our hands tied behind our backs."[121]

This desire for flexibility led to conflict with the intelligence community and with key members of Congress over the standards of evidence for missile technology transfers to Pakistan. Presumably, intelligence would be critical input in making sanctionability determinations. Therefore, a successful strategy for avoiding inconvenient information was to simply not complete the required administrative process for reaching such a determination. As Gary Milhollin, director of the Wisconsin Project on Nuclear Arms Control, argued, "The State Department has chosen not to complete the administrative process because if it did it would have to apply sanctions and give up its engagement policy."[122] While State Department spokesman James Foley eventually argued that "an intelligence judgment is not in and of itself necessarily a sufficient basis for a sanctionability determination under U.S. law," neither he nor other US officials ever publicly articulated what would in fact be required to make such a judgment.[123]

Rather, as Gordon Oehler testified, "Because of their interest in wanting to preserve their negotiating flexibility . . . there was going to be little likelihood that evidence would ever be high enough" for the imposition of sanctions, the evidentiary bar for which was "already up there very high."[124] According to Oehler, raising the standards for actionability of intelligence was an acute source of frustration and concern for intelligence analysts, who were "very discouraged to see that fairly regularly, their work was . . . summarily dismissed by the policy community, with a statement that 'it isn't good enough, it isn't good enough.'"[125] Nor was this limited to the missile arena. There was similar frustration over policy inaction following nuclear-related ring magnet transfers from China to Pakistan, prompting CIA Director John Deutch to declare at a 1996 White House cabinet meeting, "If you're not satisfied with the intelligence on this, you will never be satisfied with any intelligence on anything else."[126]

On Capitol Hill, the Clinton administration's handling of Chinese missile transfers provoked outrage. Over time the failure to implement required sanctions led to several important hearings in which members of Congress sharply criticized the administration's apparent disregard of US nonproliferation laws. Senator Ted Stevens (R-AK), for instance, concluded that "maybe the administration is so narrowly interpreting our laws that we'd have the situation that if a country moved a missile or a poison gas or a bacterial warfare system piece by piece, grain by grain, you couldn't do anything about it until all the grains were there, and then it would be a fait accompli. . . . You're very narrowly interpreting what we thought was very specific legislation."[127] Nor was this a partisan cry, as Senator Carl Levin (D-MI) suggested: "I think we have not lived up fully to our domestic requirements in terms of the imposition of sanctions where evidence is plenty clear, or clear enough for me at least."[128] In one 1998 hearing, Senate Foreign Relations Committee Chairman Jesse Helms flatly declared: "I regret the appalling . . . legal hijinks of the administration in trying to avoid sanctioning Communist China for its missile proliferation," as well as the administration efforts to "dumb down U.S. intelligence."[129]

The price of engagement. The Clinton administration's belief in liberal democratic precepts arguably led it to overlook China's broken promises, to ignore or avoid congressionally mandated sanctions, and to fail to take action supportive of its oft-heralded commitment to nonproliferation. Indeed, such was the commitment to "engagement" that the White House arguably sought to advance commercial gains above all other policy considerations.

For example, according to a secret 1998 National Security Council memorandum leaked to the *Washington Times,* the United States "would offer . . . expanded commercial and scientific space cooperation with China (in limited areas) if China meets our conditions for joining the MTCR and controlling its missile-related exports to Iran, Pakistan, etcetera."[130] The proposal, which was disavowed following post-leak criticism, also would offer a blanket presidential waiver of the sanctions imposed on satellite launches that followed the 1989 Tiananmen Square massacre. Senator Jon Kyl (R-AZ) opined that he was "absolutely" opposed to any such deal, stating, "It raises the question: How many times do we have to be fooled?"[131] Representative Curt Weldon (R-PA) expressed similar sentiment over the proposal, which in essence offered advanced US missile technology in return for more dubious Chinese promises to end missile proliferation: "We shouldn't have to entice them with offers of next-generation missile technology to get them to comply [with the MTCR]."[132] Nevertheless, during visits to China in March and May by senior-level US officials, including the secretary of state, the United States proposed MTCR membership to China with the hope that an agreement could be signed when President Clinton visited in June 1998. Chinese officials were unpersuaded.

At the same time, the White House vigorously sought waivers in the case of Chinese applications for lucrative satellite launches, prohibited by the Tiananmen sanctions. Just as President Bush had done before him, Clinton signed every "national interest" waiver that crossed his desk in this area. Domestic political concerns and economic arguments, such as the number of jobs affected, evidently played an important role in the waivers' approval.[133] Gary Milhollin testified that "a satellite launch is one of the most lucrative things a Chinese aerospace company can get from the U.S." and that by shifting the licensing authority to the Commerce Department in 1996, "the administration has surrendered one of the most important levers America has to stop Chinese missile proliferation."[134]

Revitalizing the M-11 drama, in September 1999 the NIC released an unclassified summary of the NIE "Foreign Missile Developments and the Ballistic Missile Threat to the United States through 2015." The report declared that the security situation in South Asia "provides one of the most telling examples of regional ballistic missile and nuclear proliferation," stating conclusively—and for the first time publicly—that "Pakistan has Chinese-supplied M-11 short-range ballistic missiles" and "Pakistan has M-11 SRBMs from China."[135] This NIE followed the April 1998 test launch of the Ghauri MRBM built with Chinese assistance, the May 1998 nuclear tests, and the June 1998 hearings outlining the M-11 saga.

Once the NIE summary had been publicly circulated, State Department spokesman Foley acknowledged that "the transfer of complete M-11 missiles to Pakistan could meet the requirements for triggering sanctions under the U.S.

missile sanctions law."[136] However, Foley continued, "it is important, though, to make a distinction between a judgment by the intelligence community, in other words an intelligence judgment, which obviously is important to informing policy and making policy determinations and judgments and the matter of a legal determination as required under the law." While intelligence was necessary to inform policy, it was insufficient for making an appropriate "determination"—in the end, a policy judgment. Foley assured reporters that "we're going to be continuing to look at this very closely."[137] In July 2000, in the context of new reports of Chinese transfers to Pakistan, State Department spokesman Philip Reeker argued the now-familiar mantra that although the administration was "concerned that China doesn't exercise sufficient control of missile exports to Pakistan . . . we have no reason to conclude that they have acted in a manner inconsistent with their 1994 commitment."[138]

During a visit to China, John Holum took this line of reasoning one step further, echoing the hollow policy judgment of the early Clinton administration: "It is important for Americans to recognize that China has in a very short time covered an extremely long distance in terms of nonproliferation and arms control."[139] But Holum's bottom line is revealing: "We raised our concern that China has provided aid to Pakistan and other countries" in direct contravention of the 1994 commitment; "the issue remains unresolved."[140]

Conclusion

It has been more than a decade since the intelligence community first detected the presence of training equipment that suggested the impending transfer of M-11 ballistic missiles to Pakistan. Intelligence suspicions about Pakistan's nuclear efforts date back even further, to the early 1980s and late 1970s. Since that time, Pakistan has tested the Ghauri MRBM, a delivery system developed with extensive Chinese and North Korea assistance, and revealed its nuclear status, in May 1998. During the twenty-year period from the late 1970s to the late 1990s, consecutive US administrations stated that nonproliferation was an important US policy goal, and the congressional sentiment on the issue was expressed in the legislation enacted by Congress. Yet when evidence suggested that the relevant US legislation had been violated and that US nonproliferation policy should warrant particular courses of action, other policy considerations were consistently weighed more heavily. In the case of Chinese-Pakistani nuclear cooperation in the 1980s, nonproliferation clashed with the need to maintain Pakistan as an ally against Soviet expansionism in South Asia. During the 1990s, nonproliferation considerations emerged subordinate to the presumptive economic benefits of continued "engagement" with China. One-time policy trade-offs or exceptions to national policy were repeatedly made in the context of broader geopolitical or geoeconomic policy goals, and nonproliferation faded to a distant second priority.

These cases underscore the clear differences in relations between an incumbent administration and Congress and between policy and intelligence officials. They also foreshadow an evolving nonproliferation environment and a requirement for both traditional and innovative approaches to countering WMD proliferation.

Epilogue: after the tests. Almost immediately after India and Pakistan conducted their series of nuclear tests in May 1998, the United States imposed wide-ranging sanctions on both countries. However, within two months both the executive and the legislative branch began to seek ways to lessen or waive the sanctions imposed by US law. Assistant Secretary of State for Near East and South Asian Affairs Karl Inderfurth declared that it was necessary to reengage both India and Pakistan in negotiations and that the stringent sanctions were interfering with those efforts: "It is clear that we will need greater flexibility than the law currently allows to tailor our approach, influence events and respond to developments. In this regard . . . we seek waiver authority for all the sanctions currently in place against India and Pakistan."[141] There was considerable support for this approach in Congress, as evidenced by legislation introduced by Senators Mitch McConnell (R-KY) and Sam Brownback (R-KS) to ease sanctions on agricultural products. McConnell's proposed bill passed in the Senate with a vote of 98 to 0, prompting supporter Senator Gordon Smith (R-OR) to declare, "With the action of the U.S. Senate today . . . America has been spared the spectacle of watching its government wrestle its farmers to the ground merely because our laws on nuclear nonproliferation were unable to control the spread of nuclear weaponry on the subcontinent."[142]

The McConnell bill became the Agriculture Export Relief Act of 1998 (PL 105-194), which exempted food and agricultural purchases from nuclear nonproliferation sanctions for a period of one year.[143] President Clinton remarked after signing the bill, "We need to make sure that our sanctions policy furthers our foreign policy goals without imposing undue burdens on our farmers. . . . This action allows us to send a strong message abroad, without ignoring the real needs of those here at home."[144] The day after this legislation was signed, Pakistan held a wheat auction; if the law had not been signed, US wheat producers would have been prohibited from participating. That same day, July 15, 1998, the Senate approved the Brownback amendment, which gave the president authority, after consulting with certain congressional committees, to waive most of the sanctions imposed by the Arms Export Control Act, except for those applying to military assistance, arms sales, and sensitive technology exports.[145] Senator Brownback used the hearings on this amendment to question the continuing utility of sanctions in general: "It's clear, from the bind we find ourselves in, that our sanctions law is due for an overhaul, not just as it applies to India and Pakistan, but as an instrument of foreign policy."[146]

Echoing the familiar pattern first enshrined in the Reagan administration, when faced with competing interests—in this case economic goals—nonproliferation policy was again placed on the back burner. Just three years later, in the context of a global war on terrorism and offensive military action in Afghanistan, sanctions on both India and Pakistan would be lifted entirely. And China, of course, would again be caught transferring ballistic missile technology to Pakistan—despite a renewed November 2000 commitment otherwise.[147]

CHAPTER 3

Through a Glass Darkly

Estimative Uncertainties and Policy Trade-offs

The spread of nuclear, biological, and chemical weapons and their attendant delivery systems is better viewed as a dynamic process than as discrete events or particular outcomes. Forecasting trends, divining intentions, and estimating capabilities are central to understanding the proliferation enterprise. The intelligence community is charged with assessing this changing landscape, collecting information on and analyzing events in particular countries, the transactions between them, and their interactions with subnational actors of concern.

Yet as former NIC Chairman Joseph Nye cautions, "In a world where rapid change has become the norm, uncertainties abound."[1] Fragmentary or inaccurate data, key information gaps, active deception and denial measures, and evolving intentions by actors of concern present substantial challenges to intelligence analysts in the WMD arena. As former Deputy Director of the CIA John Gannon suggests, "In a perfect world, intelligence always heads off the bad guys at the pass before they can do any damage. In an *almost* perfect world, we catch them red-handed with the smoking gun. But, in our *far less than perfect* world, no matter how hard we work or how many assets we bring to bear, we still may be able only to find pieces of an ominous puzzle."[2]

When faced with an absence of significant information or when facing acute time constraints, the analytic community often tries to determine the larger picture as if all the facts were available. Analyzing the known facts and structuring the remaining uncertainties, estimative intelligence deals in the realm of possibility, presenting a plausible range of alternative scenarios, often with probabilities assigned, in an effort to "help policymakers interpret the available facts, to suggest alternative patterns that available facts might fit, [and] to provide informed assessments of the range and likelihood of possible outcomes."[3] This is a time-tested process; Sherman Kent, the father of modern US intelligence, argued in the earliest days of the CIA that such estimates may have great value when they are "soundly based in reliable descriptive data, reliable reporting, and proceed from careful analysis."[4]

At the same time, close observers such as Mark Lowenthal have criticized important gaps as "annoying" at best and "both crucial and frightening" at worst.[5] While there is no guarantee that better intelligence necessarily leads to better decisions, policy debates often hinge on input provided by the intelligence community. Notable factual or interpretive uncertainties, critical information gaps, and discrepancies in intelligence judgment between intelligence producers frequently bump up against the "rough and tumble" of the policy process.[6] The often acrimonious debates in the 1990s over the evolving scope and nature of the ballistic missile threat to the United States, US friends and allies, and forward-deployed US forces are a clear case in point (see chapter 1). Important estimative uncertainties and difficult policy judgments interacted significantly in two other relatively recent high-profile proliferation-related cases: the extent, capability, and status of the North Korean nuclear weapons program and the Soviet (and perhaps Russian) offensive biological weapons program, discussed in turn below.

North Korea and Nuclear Weapons

In addition to its aspirations for advanced ballistic missile technology (see chapter 4), North Korea maintains a longstanding interest in nuclear weapons.[7] As with Pyongyang's pursuit of ballistic missiles, there is considerable uncertainty about nuclear weapons development efforts. Although technical and other means provide important details, key gaps evidently exist in US information regarding the status and scope of North Korea's efforts, particularly over how much plutonium the DPRK has produced and whether it has produced a nuclear weapon. These uncertainties had become a source of disagreement within the intelligence community and between the intelligence and policy communities by the early 1990s, when it appeared that North Korea was preparing to undertake a major expansion of its efforts. By default, when the DPRK threatened to withdraw from the NPT in 1993, that state had become, in essence, the world's smallest de facto nuclear power.

Over time, imagery, inspection data, and human reporting have provided important information on North Korea's evolving capabilities. As Robert Carlin suggests, "The process of discovery has not been easy; in fact, it is more complex than is often realized."[8] The North Korean nuclear program originated in the 1950s, and although uncertainties abound, some aspects of this program are evident.[9] Over the years, considerable attention has focused on the Yongbyon nuclear research complex as the epicenter of North Korean nuclear efforts. Home to the major facilities of North Korea's program, Yongbyon was the site of its three known nuclear reactors: a 2–4 megawatt thermal (MWt) reactor built by the Soviet Union in 1965–67, an indigenous 5 megawatt electric (MWe) reactor built during the 1980s, and a 50 MWe reactor that began construction in 1984.[10]

In addition to the three reactors, Yongbyon also houses a massive, six-story, 600 foot long reprocessing facility, ostensibly referred to by North Korea as a "Radiochemistry Laboratory," that began construction in 1987.[11] In addition to the facilities at Yongbyon, North Korea also inaugurated construction of a fourth, even larger, 200 MWe reactor in 1989 at T'aech'on, thirty kilometers west of Yongbyon.[12] The reactors housed at Yongbyon were presumably a source of concern to US officials since their designs were optimized for plutonium production and, North Korean claims to the contrary, lacked the signatures of civilian power reactors.[13] In addition, the new reprocessing facility represented a puzzling development for a country rich in natural uranium unless nuclear weapons development was the state's ultimate objective.[14]

Taken together, the known features of the North Korean nuclear infrastructure seemed to indicate that the DPRK was pursuing the plutonium path to nuclear weapons development. If this was correct, the new facilities constituted a major expansion of the country's ability to produce the requisite fissile material. When completed, the two new reactors would produce a combined total of approximately 200–300 kilograms of plutonium annually, in addition to the 7 kilograms produced by the existing 5 MWe reactor. The reprocessing facility would have the capability to process 100–300 tons of spent reactor fuel and to separate 200 kilograms of plutonium annually, or sufficient fissile material for perhaps twenty to thirty nuclear weapons per year.[15]

Key Information Gaps

While Pyongyang's longstanding inclination to develop nuclear weapons is clear, the specific details of North Korea's nuclear program remain elusive. Indeed, considerable uncertainty continues over how successful the DPRK's program has been, and even the full scope of its nuclear infrastructure is not publicly known. For policymakers, these uncertainties present an evident quandary: how to halt or at least contain North Korea's nuclear aspirations. The possibility that North Korea has produced enough plutonium for at least one nuclear weapon would have to figure prominently in any policy deliberations. Two major points of contention emerged early on between analysts in the various US intelligence agencies, between policy officials, and between the intelligence and policy communities: (1) how much plutonium, if any, the North Koreans had been able to produce; and (2) whether Pyongyang had successfully constructed any nuclear weapons.

How much plutonium? How much plutonium North Korea may have produced is partly revealed by that state's declarations, defectors' testimony, and additional efforts by the intelligence community and other parties. According to formal declarations during the May 1992 IAEA inspections, approximately 90 grams of plutonium were reprocessed from "damaged" fuel rods from the 5 MWe reactor at Yongbyon in March 1990.[16] In 1989 this 5 MWe reactor was shut down and the fuel rods were removed, possibly for reprocessing. Yet in spite of these two data points, open-source estimates of plutonium production vary widely, from a low of 5 kilograms to a high of 24 kilograms.[17] Estimates produced by the intelligence community are apparently more tightly grouped, in the range of 6–12 kilograms.[18]

How many weapons? When North Korea threatened to withdraw from the NPT in 1993, two questions arose: Had North Korea produced any nuclear weapons with this plutonium? If so, how many? Answers to these important questions would depend on assessments of how much plutonium was required for a viable weapon and how much progress the DPRK had made in overcoming technical issues related to weapons design and production.[19] Not surprisingly, as with the amount of plutonium produced, estimates of the country's weapons status varied considerably. But an NIE issued in late 1993 apparently concluded that there was a "better than even" chance that the state had already developed one or two nuclear weapons, a view supported by every member of the intelligence community except the INR.[20]

In the context of these information gaps, suppositions, and a prospective or fledgling North Korean nuclear stockpile, US policy officials attempted to develop coherent and effective policy responses to the growing nuclear crisis.

The 1994 Crisis and US Responses

Through the first quarter of 1994 the international community weathered a North Korean standoff with the IAEA that nearly resulted in that state's withdrawal from the NPT. However, less than one year after the apparently successful resolution of that crisis another urgent matter arose. On April 1, 1994,

North Korea shut down the 5 MWe reactor at Yongbyon in preparation for the removal of the fuel rods.[21] Five weeks later, the North began removing the fuel rods from the reactor in defiance of US threats that such actions would result in an end to diplomatic discussions and the likely imposition of sanctions.[22] The international community expressed concern over the potential amount of plutonium that the DPRK could obtain from the rods if it decided to proceed with reprocessing. This situation presented a grave challenge to US nonproliferation policy and put policymakers to work trying to craft an acceptable and verifiable solution.

US nonproliferation policy and response options. It was evident that North Korea, a potentially hostile nation apparently intent on developing nuclear weapons and in noncompliance with its international obligations, posed a substantial challenge to US nonproliferation policy. How the United States and the international community dealt with this issue could affect future nonproliferation efforts with other states, such as Iran. Early statements by US officials conveyed the impression that the United States would take a firm stand on the issue, resolute in its efforts to halt the DPRK's illicit activities. In one November 1993 media appearance, for instance, President Clinton stated that "North Korea cannot be allowed to develop a nuclear bomb. We have to be very firm about it."[23] The president's statement was echoed a month later by Secretary of Defense Les Aspin: "We will not let the North Koreans become a nuclear power. . . . We have a policy that has been consistent from the very beginning . . . nuclear weapons in the hands of North Korea is not acceptable."[24]

Just five months later, however, this seemingly unambiguous stance was softened as Defense Secretary William Perry stated, "Our policy right along has been oriented to try to keep North Korea from getting a *significant* nuclear-weapon capability."[25] Perry's statement, delivered as the 1994 crisis reached its zenith, indicated a possible shift in the Clinton administration's position: in order to halt future North Korean nuclear weapons–related activities, the administration might be willing to live with that state's possessing one or two weapons. If the administration had in fact come around to such a position, it represented a dramatic swing from its earlier statements, as well as a critical policy trade-off.

Whether the principal policy goal was to completely roll back North Korea's nuclear program or to accept its existence instead and focus on attempting to halt future weapons development activities, it appeared to senior officials that there were three possible "generic options" that could be pursued in order to achieve the desired end: (1) the use of military force; (2) the imposition of sanctions; and (3) "to try to force compliance through an agreement of some sort."[26] Each of these proposed approaches posed potentially severe hazards, shortfalls, and trade-offs, discussed in turn below.

Military force: destruction—how viable an option? One of the possible solutions to the North Korean nuclear issue considered by US officials and supported by some nongovernmental specialists was the use of military force against DPRK nuclear facilities. Those advocating this view drew parallels between the 1981 Israeli strike against the Osirak nuclear reactor and the current situation. This sentiment was not limited to the media or nongovernmental organizations; indeed, several members of Congress were vocal in their support for such action. For their part, senior administration officials seriously considered military operations against the North's nuclear facilities. To that end, they met repeatedly with senior military officials to discuss how best to bolster US forces in Korea and how to prosecute effective military operations on the Korean Peninsula in the context of a potentially nuclear North.[27]

Several key difficulties served to undermine, constrain, or make less politically palatable particular military options, including targeting difficulties resulting from a lack of firm intelligence on the location and extent of the DPRK's nuclear infrastructure,[28] the apparent lack of adequate munitions to ensure destruction of hardened or deeply buried targets, the need to minimize collateral damage,[29] and the fear that any military action by the United States could trigger an all-out North Korean response and possibly result in a larger conflict costing hundreds of thousands of lives.[30] Air Force Chief of Staff General Merrill McPeak stated candidly that air strikes were "not a very attractive option, quite frankly," because "we don't know if the North Koreans have nuclear material off-site about to be weaponized. We don't know where that is so we don't know how to attack it."[31] General Gary Luck, commander in chief of US forces in Korea, concluded that a general war on the Korean Peninsula could cost trillions of dollars—based on the cost of waging the war and the resulting economic impact on the United States and other nations in the region—and a "low sided" estimate of a million lives lost.[32] In the end, the Clinton policy team held the use of military force as a last resort, hoping to achieve successful resolution of the crisis through diplomacy or international sanctions.

Imposition of sanctions: an equally dangerous solution? Clinton's advisers focused instead on financial solutions to the nuclear issue, with the pursuit of sanctions seemingly an attractive policy tool. Although diplomacy would eventually become a preferred policy position, there was reportedly an initial lack of confidence in the ability of diplomacy to achieve a satisfactory resolution of the crisis. One assessment, broadly reflective of the conventional wisdom, forecast that "the North initially will resist or delay the decision to dismantle facilities and transfer spent fuel [to a third nation]."[33] As it became increasingly clear that the DPRK would not comply with IAEA demands, senior policy officials began to push for sanctions.

Yet, like military actions, economic sanctions also raised the specter of war, as North Korea repeatedly stated that it considered the imposition of sanctions to be a hostile act. Moreover, it was unclear that sanctions would ultimately be effective. This presented a clear dilemma, as Secretary Perry recounts: "We were prepared to go to sanctions . . . [but] had no confidence that going to sanctions would have stopped that nuclear program."[34] In the end, Secretary Perry and others concluded that sanctions were "not a satisfactory solution, but it was the best we thought we could do," even if "we will have to take seriously the risk of war."[35] By early June 1994 the United States had started to actively lobby UN Security Council members to impose sanctions and at the same time to bolster US military forces in Korea.

A diplomatic approach: the Agreed Framework. As the United States and the Security Council began to move toward sanctions, former President Jimmy Carter intervened, acting on a standing invitation to travel to North Korea, with the hope of achieving a peaceful resolution to a crisis that appeared headed for war. During Carter's visit there were indications from North Korean leader Kim Il Sung that he might be willing to halt his nation's nuclear program in return for US concessions, opening a possible door to the peaceful resolution of the crisis.

Carter was able to obtain two concessions from North Korea: (1) an agreement on rules that would allow international inspectors to visit the two disputed sites; and (2) a proposal that the fuel rods removed in April 1994 be stored in another country.[36] Carter's efforts and the DPRK response offered a potential diplomatic solution. Shortly thereafter the United States accepted the offer, and high-level talks in Geneva between the United States and North Korea were scheduled. These negotiations led to the so-called Agreed Framework, signed in October 1994. It sought to advance four principal objectives: (1) "replace the DPRK's graphite-moderated reactors and facilities with light-water (LWR) power plants"; (2) move toward "full normalization of political and economic relations" between the United States and North Korea; (3) encourage the United States and the DPRK to "work together for peace and security on a nuclear free Korean Peninsula"; and (4) "work together to strengthen the international nuclear nonproliferation regime."[37]

Under this agreement, the eight thousand fuel rods in dispute would be placed under IAEA supervision, preventing North Korea from reprocessing them. The so-called proliferation-resistant reactors to be provided would, presumably, replace North Korea's purportedly more proliferation-prone production reactors. By granting the IAEA the right to make intensive inspections of North Korean facilities and by supplying the DPRK reactors with the required fuel and components that they could not manufacture indigenously, the Agreed Framework also attempted to increase the amount of international control over the North Korean program. What is perhaps most important, while it did not eliminate the DRPK nuclear problem, the Agreed Framework delayed North Korea's efforts to produce nuclear weapons. In doing so, the agreement sought to buy time in which the United States and its allies could develop and pursue other potential solutions to the nuclear issue. In this sense the Agreed Framework was a qualified, if perhaps stopgap and temporary, success for US nonproliferation policy.

Contending interpretations of a "frozen" program. Clinton administration officials heralded the Agreed Framework as a major step toward ending North Korea's weapons program and redirecting its nuclear efforts to more benign ends. Ambassador Robert Gallucci, who negotiated the agreement for the United States, stated in a press conference, "The program will no longer exist. That's extremely important from our perspective."[38] When asked about the monitoring and verification aspects of the agreement, Secretary Perry stated that "in terms of monitoring this agreement, I think we have high confidence in being able to do that."[39] Verification and monitoring were to be provided by IAEA inspectors and US national technical means.[40] As required by law, President Clinton certified to Congress that the DRPK was in compliance with the Agreed Framework.[41] In 1998 Deputy Assistant Secretary for East Asian and Pacific Affairs Rust Deming stated that "the North's indigenous nuclear program at Yongbyon remains frozen, the canning of the D.P.R.K.'s spent fuel is now virtually complete and under IAEA seal, as are the reprocessing plant and reactors."[42] For Special Envoy Charles Kartman, the Agreed Framework was and must remain "the centerpiece of U.S. policy toward the D.P.R.K. for some time to come."[43]

Staunch advocates notwithstanding, the Agreed Framework also had its detractors. Critics in Congress, in the nongovernmental sector, and in the media questioned whether the agreement served the best interests of the United States, whether it unduly rewarded a proliferant state, and whether it truly halted DPRK nuclear weapons development activities. Ironically, while some critics argued that the agreement was too far-reaching in its provision of light water reactor technology and fuel oil, others observed that the agreement might have been too narrowly constructed: even if it successfully halted work at Yongbyon indefinitely, the agreement would not necessarily spell an end to North Korean nuclear ambitions or developmental efforts.

Senator Sam Nunn (D-GA) feared that the agreement would have negative consequences for US nonproliferation policy, speculating that other nations "may get the signal that if they get their program to a certain point . . . then at that stage they have huge leverage."[44] In testimony before the Senate Armed Services Committee several months after the Agreed Framework was signed, Gary Milhollin, of the Wisconsin Project on Nuclear Arms Control, argued that the DPRK's main purpose in signing the agreement and obtaining the light water reactors was delay.[45] Milhollin argued that by demanding the new reactors, which would take years to complete, the DPRK had successfully delayed US and IAEA inspections for at least five years. This delay was critical because "if North Korea has not made a bomb yet, it has five years to produce one secretly, because surprise inspections are effectively barred until then."[46] The North Korea Advisory Group, chaired by Representative Benjamin Gilman (R-NY), concluded in November 1999 that "although the 1994 Agreed Framework was essentially aimed at eliminating North Korea's ability to make nuclear weapons, there is significant evidence that nuclear weapons development is continuing, including its efforts to acquire uranium enrichment technologies and its nuclear-related high explosives tests."[47]

Yet such criticism missed a key achievement of the Agreed Framework, according to Assistant Secretary of Defense Ashton Carter: "What is being traded here is ten years of [the DPRK's] operating [graphite moderated] reactors, and thereafter, continuing to build and operate these reactors, against what happens under the framework agreement, which is ten years of no reactors, followed by a period where they operate [light water] reactors, which are not pro-liferation proof by any means, but proliferation resistant. So, if you compare the world without the agreement to the world with the agreement—in both the near term and the far term—the comparison is favorable to the agreement."[48] The 1999 review of US policy toward North Korea conducted by former Defense Secretary William Perry found that "within the Agreed Framework, the DPRK's ability to produce plutonium at Yongbyon is verifiably frozen."[49] However, Perry's report also concluded that the Agreed Framework did "not verifiably freeze all nuclear weapons-related activities," and thus the United States still needed to maintain its vigilance and seek to supplement the Agreed Framework with additional agreements.[50]

Compliance concerns and Kumchangni. North Korean compliance with the agreement soon became a contentious topic. Representative Dan Burton (R-IN), for instance, remarked in 1995, "I want you all to know that communists are not always trustworthy. . . . They've lied to us numerous times in the past."[51] The possibility that North Korea would use covert, underground or other facilities to continue its nuclear efforts in violation of the Agreed Framework remained a matter of concern to some observers. As Andrew Mack suggests, "It is very difficult to believe that the paranoid North has not taken the obvious precaution of keeping a significant part of its nuclear program in hiding."[52]

Lending credence to such fears, various intelligence assessments apparently concluded that North Korea was possibly continuing its nuclear program covertly. By the late 1990s DIA analysts reportedly had compiled a list of ten facilities that the agency believed could be related to an ongoing covert program.[53] Of particular concern was the underground facility being constructed near Kumchangni that US intelligence discovered in late 1998. Also, reportedly based on satellite imagery and other intelligence sources, DIA analysts assessed that it could be a clandestine nuclear site and estimated that it was large enough to hold a reactor and a reprocessing facility.[54] A brief standoff arose when US officials demanded access to the facility for inspections and North Korean leaders agreed to provide access—for $300 million. An agreement for continued food aid was ultimately reached in May 1999, and inspections were conducted that month and again in May 2000. In each case inspectors found no evidence to reveal the facility's true purpose or to confirm that the DPRK was continuing its nuclear weapons development activities.[55]

Yet despite the lack of conclusive evidence one way or the other, persistent reports of hidden and underground facilities nonetheless strained relations between policy officials and the intelligence community. Intelligence analysts found increasing evidence of continued North Korean nuclear activities; while some policymakers were alarmed by such allegations and sought sterner measures, others proved eager to protect the agreement.[56] Sometimes this led to heated exchanges between administration officials. During congressional testimony in July 1998, for instance, Secretary of State Madeleine Albright and DIA Director Lieutenant General Patrick Hughes clashed on this issue in an unusual public display. When asked for her assessment of a recent DIA intelligence report concerning a suspected North Korean storage installation that potentially housed components for nuclear weapons, Secretary Albright replied that she had only learned of the report two weeks earlier.[57] At that point General Hughes entered the fray: "Madame Secretary, I have to correct the record. You were briefed on that intelligence a year ago."[58]

Day of Reckoning

The Agreed Framework did not eliminate the North Korean nuclear program. Given that neither the United States nor the IAEA knew the full extent of North Korea's nuclear activities or infrastructure, the goal of completely eliminating the nuclear program proved unrealistic. Although the agreement remained in force through December 2002, it became evident over time that the DPRK had in fact continued its efforts to develop nuclear weapons. While plutonium reprocessing did not begin again until early 2003, North Korean officials acknowledged that they had pursued the uranium option as well.[59] Reportedly, these efforts were actively facilitated by a US ally: Pakistan.[60]

At least one important issue remains unresolved, namely, the uncertainties surrounding the scope and accomplishments of the North Korean program. Because of estimative uncertainties, the policy ultimately chosen to deal with the North Korean nuclear problem necessarily focused on known elements of the program. Yet several years after the framework was negotiated, many of the gaps that had plagued intelligence analysts and policymakers in the early 1990s remained. It is still reportedly unknown, for instance, how much plutonium that state recovered during the late 1980s and early 1990s, and is it not known with great confidence whether the DPRK successfully produced any nuclear weapons during the same time period.

New reports indicating that North Korea may have moved or added to nuclear-related sites underground, beyond the reach of IAEA inspectors, are clearly troubling. Certainly, 2002 revelations that Pyongyang had secretly pursued the uranium route in parallel bode ill. The uncertainty is thus compounded, setting the stage for political or technical surprise (see chapter 4). In this context, policymakers are likely to find themselves faced by situations not very different from those of 1993–94, presented with a similar range of unpleasant options for resolving a developing crisis. And as before, how US officials and appropriate international organizations handle North Korean treaty and other violations will foreshadow the constraints—or, more likely, limitations—of the exact nonproliferation response. And without a doubt, states such as Iran will be watching.

The Soviet/Russian BW Program

As in the North Korean nuclear case, estimates of the Soviet offensive BW program varied considerably. Unlike in the North Korean case, however, a robust deception and denial effort appears to have effectively masked the sheer magnitude of the Soviet effort, including many of its advanced technical achievements. While some innovative policy efforts endeavor to cope with the Soviet BW legacy, acute concerns remain over the current status of the program, policy trade-offs inherent in the responses pursued, and future prospects for effective verification.

During the Cold War the Soviet Union pursued a massive BW program involving dozens of institutions, tens of thousands of workers, and the equivalent of billions of dollars in funding. However, for much of that period US intelligence analysts apparently substantially underestimated the full scope of Soviet efforts. While US officials understood that the Soviet Union maintained an offensive BW program in defiance of international accords, key details, including its scope and resources, its specific technical capabilities, and its operational employment doctrine, were evidently lacking. Reports from key defectors in the late 1980s and early 1990s filled at least some of these gaps but in the process also underscored just how advanced the Soviet program was. This new information also raised important considerations regarding the post-Soviet status of offensive activities. Have the programs been halted, as President Boris Yeltsin claimed in 1992, or do they in fact continue, as many analysts and policymakers suspect?

Past Soviet and possible ongoing Russian biological weapons efforts have substantial policy and military implications for the United States. With respect to policy, there are clear implications for arms control regimes, particularly the 1972 BWC, as well as ongoing nonproliferation and threat reduction activities. On the military side, implications include the manner in which the Soviets thought about biological weapons use—which differed greatly from US doctrine and use concepts—and the technical accomplishments of the program as a whole, including its successful development of novel threat agents or those with enhanced performance characteristics.

US Estimates of Soviet BW Efforts

Early Cold War estimates. By the end of World War II, US intelligence agencies were aware that the Soviet Union was pursuing an offensive BW program. It was a matter of concern to Western military leaders at the time because they feared that a Soviet Union lacking the atomic bomb would turn to biological weapons as a substitute.[61] The specific details of the Soviet program, or how it compared with the US or British programs, were apparently unknown to US analysts, as collection limitations precluded a sound assessment of the Soviet effort. As a result, many early reports were based on human intelligence gleaned from defectors and other individuals who had fled the Soviet Union, as well as information found in defeated Nazi Germany's intelligence files. This intelligence included reports from individuals who were peripherally or directly involved with the BW program at lower levels (e.g., animal handlers, janitors), which evidently provided some information on the locations and sizes of Soviet BW facilities.[62]

Intelligence from the German Wehrmacht indicated a Soviet BW effort dating back to the 1930s and identified several sites involved in the program, including Vozrozhdeniya Island in the Aral Sea.[63] Human reporting also suggested that the Soviets had conducted several tests of various delivery systems in Mongolia using plague, anthrax, cholera, and glanders, the first three of which were referred to by the code name Golden Triangle.[64]

Although they were unable to verify much of the information contained in the Wehrmacht's intelligence files, Western intelligence agencies considered the information to be adequate evidence that the Soviets were pursuing particular biological weapons–related research and development activities. US intelligence agencies were also aware that the Soviet Union, like the United States, had captured personnel from Unit 731 and other elements of the Japanese BW program that had been active in Manchuria during World War II, appropriating their knowledge for use in Soviet activities.[65] An NIE from 1957 reportedly found that "relatively little is known about the nature and magnitude of the Soviet BW program, particularly its offensive aspects."[66]

Bolstered by increasingly capable imagery intelligence (IMINT), US agencies developed information suggesting that the Soviets maintained at least six sites dedicated to BW research, many of which were located west of the Ural Mountains.[67] Ironically, however, increased reliance on IMINT may have actually compounded the uncertainties regarding the offensive Soviet BW efforts due to mirror imaging.[68] Early intelligence reports indicated that the Soviets were working with the same set of pathogens, or a close derivation thereof, as the one on which US offensive activities centered. Consequently, analysts surmised that the structure of the Soviet program would resemble that of the US effort. Thus, when analysts sought to identify and characterize Soviet BW facilities using IMINT, they looked for facilities that resembled their US counterparts. According to Gary Crocker, senior adviser for politico-military affairs in the State Department's INR, "In the old days . . . we were looking at mainly a military program. So we sort of sized it and based what we could see in terms of the military program and somewhat mirror imaging back even to our own past programs that were military."[69]

In some ways the assumptions of US intelligence analysts were proved correct. The Fifteenth Directorate of the Soviet Ministry of Defense was the lead agency for BW research and development from 1945 to 1973, and it controlled BW stockpiles and primary production facilities even after that date. However, these assumptions contributed to important oversights regarding the critical role of Biopreparat, an ostensibly civilian pharmaceutical concern established in the early 1970s.[70] By the early 1960s, gaps notwithstanding, the prevailing view within the US Army's Chemical Corps was that "the Soviet potential for biological operations is believed to be strong, and could be developed into a major threat."[71]

While specific Soviet BW capabilities remained shrouded in mystery, discerning Soviet intentions proved equally difficult, if not more so. To what extent should the Soviet program be judged as *offensive*, as opposed to *defensive*, in nature? Examination of IMINT and scientific journals provided insufficient data to discern motives or plans, and at best might provide particular insights into specific aspects of a program or the general contours of the overall program. The biological agents identified presented legitimate public health concerns within the Soviet Union, but they were also being investigated in the context of US offensive activities and thus, some argued, provided a rationale for Soviet defensive research. Moreover, in spite of having identified a possible test site near the Aral Sea, US intelligence could not prove that the Soviets were testing actual weapons. Nor could they identify likely delivery systems. Thus, leadership intent, the nature of the program, and the status of Soviet advancements were key gaps in US information about Soviet efforts.

At the same time, there was general agreement that the Soviet Union clearly had the *potential* to pursue an offensive program. To a greater or lesser extent, nongovernmental specialists echoed this general view. At the 1968 London Conference on Chemical and Biological Warfare, for instance, D. E. Viney argued that "the Soviets are clearly in a position to embark on large-scale manufacture of biological agents if ever they decide to," but "there is no reason to assume that they have formulated a military requirement of this kind, or ever will."[72] As the United States terminated its own offensive BW program and pushed for the international ban on biological weapons that culminated in the 1972 BWC, these gaps would soon loom larger as questions arose regarding Soviet compliance with this new treaty.

The BWC, Soviet compliance, and the Sverdlovsk incident. The BWC aimed to eliminate the acquisition, development, production, stockpiling, and use of biological and toxicological weapons. Article 1 of the convention expressly prohibits parties to the treaty from developing, producing, stockpiling, or otherwise acquiring or retaining "microbial or other biological agents, or toxins whatever their origin or method of production," as well as "weapons, equipment or means of delivery designed to use such agents or toxins for hostile purposes or in armed conflict."[73] The treaty makes an exception for "defensive" research, allowing parties to retain quantities of agents that are commensurate with "prophylactic, protective, or other peaceful purposes." However, it fails to define the line between offense and defense, a clear source of diplomatic discord and analytic ambiguity.

The Soviet Union acceded to the BWC in 1975, but concerns arose almost immediately with respect to Soviet compliance. These concerns were only exacerbated by a lack of effective verification protocols in the treaty, which, according to Robert Harris and Jeremy Paxman, "led to a campaign in the Western press the like of which had not been seen since the scare stories of Russian 'disease factories' in the early fifties."[74] Imagery reportedly indicated that "there is evidence that within recent months the Soviet Union has been constructing or expanding facilities which appear to be biological arms production plants, having very high incinerator stacks and large cold storage bunkers that could be used for stockpiling the weapons."[75]

US officials were uneasy about calling the Soviets to task for possible violation of the BWC for fear of revealing too much about US imagery capabilities, the lack of absolute certainty regarding the role of the facilities in spite of photographic evidence, and the reality that "the Russians could insist these are simply new pharmaceutical plants and it would be hard for us to prove otherwise."[76] This "dual-use" dilemma would continue to plague US and international efforts to assess the Soviet program and those of other suspect proliferant states in the years ahead. Because many of the technologies and the equipment used in the research, development, or production of BW agents also have civilian utility, judgments must be based more on perceived intent than on extant capability.

There were at least some concrete indicators of Soviet noncompliance. In April 1979, for instance, reports of an anthrax outbreak in either Novosibirsk or Sverdlovsk (there was initial confusion over where the outbreak took place) began to appear first in a Russian émigré newspaper and subsequently in a British news magazine. In a surprise move, TASS, the Soviet central news agency, was authorized to announce shortly after the incident that an outbreak had in fact occurred and that sixty-four people had died as a result of intestinal anthrax caused by contaminated meat sold on the black market.[77] Others quickly discounted the official Soviet explanation; a large-scale gastrointestinal anthrax outbreak was arguably less plausible than alternative hypotheses, including an aerosol release.

To help resolve these interpretive discrepancies, US diplomats repeatedly requested an explanation of the events from Soviet officials through the mid-1980s, stating that they had received "no satisfactory responses" to US concerns over the incident.[78] As with prior allegations of Soviet offensive work with viral agents, including Ebola, Marburg, and Lassa Fever, in an active disinformation campaign the Soviet government charged its diplomats with blaming Western "misinformation" departments for such false allegations; the Soviet mantra remained, "At present, the Soviet Union does not possess any bacteriological (biological) agents or toxins, weapons, equipment or means of delivery."[79] Indeed, the Soviet version of the events in Sverdlovsk was reinforced in the late 1980s by additional Soviet statements and in an article published in *Science* by US scientists who were allowed to visit Sverdlovsk and conduct research. The team, led by Matthew Meselson, of Harvard, concluded,

"Contrary to the U.S. government version, there is no evidence of inhalatory anthrax. . . . It is clear that the U.S. version of the Sverdlovsk anthrax outbreak is in need of careful and objective review."[80]

Western intelligence eventually concluded that there was evidence enough to believe that an outbreak of pulmonary anthrax had broken out in Sverdlovsk as a result of an inadvertent aerosol dissemination from Compound 19, a military laboratory located in the city. At a September 1986 BWC compliance-review conference, US ambassador Donald Lowitz reiterated US concerns over the incident and stated, "We have determined that the facility at Sverdlovsk . . . has responsibility for research, development, production, and storage of biological warfare agents."[81] In 1992 Boris Yeltsin admitted what intelligence analysts and policy officials had long suspected: that the accident at Sverdlovsk had been related to weapons-related research.[82] Years later Meselson recalled, "What we had thought and said to be plausible . . . was actually entirely wrong."[83]

Assessment Revised

Concurrent with the Cold War's end was an increase in the information Western intelligence agencies acquired with respect to the Soviet BW program, stemming principally from two factors: defections by three key Biopreparat personnel, who brought with them a wealth of information on the organization and scope of the Soviet BW program; and a series of agreements that allowed Western, principally US and UK, inspectors direct access to some of the facilities involved in the civilian side of the Soviet BW program. Finally, immediately following the Soviet Union's 1991 collapse there was a significant increase in official statements from the new Russian government concerning past Soviet BW efforts. Together, these sources helped establish the long-elusive contours of the Soviet effort. But they would prove unable to resolve a central issue, namely, the post-Soviet status of Russian offensive activities in the BW arena.

Intelligence from key defectors. In October 1989 the United Kingdom received a significant defector: Vladimir Pasechnik, formerly director of the Institute for Ultra-Pure Biological Preparations in Leningrad, part of Biopreparat. For the first time, Western intelligence services gained access to someone with firsthand knowledge of the Soviet Union's BW efforts.[84] The information that Pasechnik brought with him was alarming. Pasechnik revealed that the Soviet Union had developed or was in the process of developing lethal, vaccine-

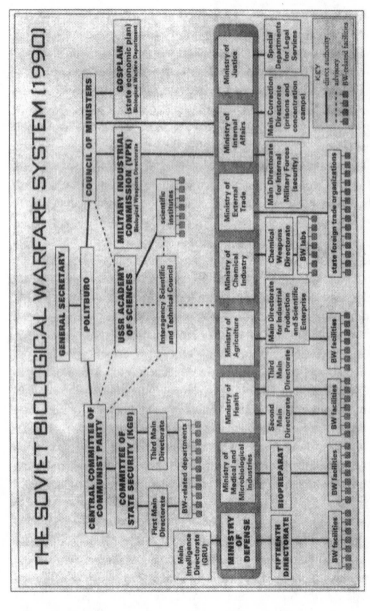

Figure 3.1. Organizational chart outlining the structure of the Soviet biological warfare program, 1990 (Ken Alibek with Stephen Handelman, *Biohazard: The Chilling True Story of the Largest Covert Biological Weapons Program in the World—Told from the Inside by the Man Who Man Ran It* [New York: Random House, 1999], 293)

resistant strains of biological agents, including plague and tularemia; that the Soviet Union had engaged in weapons testing at a site in the Aral Sea; and that biological weapons had been integrated into Soviet war plans at all levels.[85] He also drew attention to the role of Biopreparat in the Soviet BW program, which at that time boasted scores of locations throughout the Soviet Union, more than thirty thousand employees, and an annual budget in the hundreds of millions of dollars (see fig. 3.1).[86] Finally, Pasechnik asserted that the program to develop a more lethal variant of the plague bacterium, a so-called superplague, had been a top priority for Biopreparat in the second half of the 1980s.[87]

Western intelligence agencies were aware of Biopreparat but apparently did not know of the organization's role in the BW program or the vast scope of its clandestine efforts. Pasechnik's information greatly enhanced the ability of Western agencies to track what was going on inside Biopreparat, and his reports about one affiliate, the Leningrad Institute, featured prominently in US-UK inspections that took place in 1991. Frank Malinoski, who represented the US Army Medical Research Institute of Infectious Diseases, or USAMRIID, during these inspections, observed that Pasechnik "detailed sufficiently the extent of [the biological weapons program], that it was clear they had been doing a number of things in violation of the treaty." In Malinoski's view, Pasechnik's information was "confirmed by what our intelligence community had gathered from a number of different areas over time."[88]

In October 1992, approximately three years after Pasechnik's defection, the United States received another key figure from the Soviet BW program: Kanatjan Alibekov (later, Ken Alibek), first deputy director of Biopreparat. According to Alibek, Biopreparat had been created in 1973, after the Soviet Union signed the BWC, "to establish an entity that wouldn't have any 'footprints' of previous BW activity in the Soviet Union."[89] "Ostensibly operating as a civilian pharmaceutical enterprise," Biopreparat "could engage in genetic research without arousing suspicion." According to Alibek, "It could participate in international conferences, interact with the world scientific community, and obtain disease strains from foreign microbe banks—all activities which would have been impossible for a military laboratory."[90] The relationship between Biopreparat and the military was in theory that of producer and customer; the military issued tasks to Biopreparat, which then produced the required product for final delivery to the military. The Soviet military also continued its own autonomous development of biological weapons.[91]

With respect to the overall Soviet BW program, US analysts learned from (or

confirmed through) Alibek that the Soviet program included not only the ef-
·forts of the Ministry of Defense and Biopreparat but also those of the Ministries
of Agriculture, Health, and External Trade, the Soviet Academy of Sciences, and
the Soviet Committee for State Security (KGB). In addition to the offensive BW
efforts carried out by the Ministry of Defense and Biopreparat, the Ministry of
Agriculture developed anticrop and antilivestock agents and the Ministry of
Health conducted research into lethal and nonlethal toxins and pathogens in
an effort code-named Program Flute, which aimed to develop "psychotropic
and neurotropic agents for use by the KGB in special operations."[92] The Ministry of Health's Medstatistika, the Soviet Academy of Sciences, the KGB, and
the Ministry of External Trade provided intelligence and resources for the Ministry of Defense and Biopreparat programs.

Alibek also shared information on how the Soviets viewed BW and how
they planned to use biological weapons in time of war. In the Soviet view, biological weapons were not battlefield weapons per se but operational and strategic weapons to be used alone or in conjunction with strategic nuclear
weapons.[93] Cluster bombs and spray tanks would be used to deliver agents deep
into enemy rear areas, while SS-18 intercontinental ballistic missiles would
carry biological warheads to the enemy's homeland.[94] According to Alibek, BW
agents were selected for use at different levels based on their respective characteristics and effects. At the strategic level these included smallpox and plague;
at the operational level, tularemia, brucellosis, glanders, and Venezuelan
equine encephalitis; and at the strategic/operational level, anthrax, Q-fever,
and Marburg hemorrhagic fever.[95]

Overall, Alibek's assessment was that the Soviet Union was far ahead of the
United States in both the technical and scientific areas of biological weapons
development and production, as well as in concepts of employment. When the
United States ended its offensive BW program in 1969, it was arguably at the
forefront of research. Yet, advanced as it was at the time, the US program paled
over time in comparison with the vast Soviet effort. By the end of the Cold War
the Soviet Union appears to have surpassed the United States in some areas, notably weaponization and other areas of technological expertise (e.g., genetic engineering of biological agents). In April 2000 the General Accounting Office concluded that "former Soviet biological weapons scientists have at least a 20-year
lead over the United States in their understanding of biological weapons."[96]

In 2000, US intelligence agencies began to debrief Sergei Popov, a third defector from the Soviet BW program. Popov came to the United States in April

1992 and for several years conducted research at the Texas University Medical Center. It was only when he joined Alibek at Advanced Biosystems Inc. eight years later that he was fully debriefed by intelligence personnel.[97] While at Biopreparat in the 1980s, Popov was involved in cutting-edge research that applied the latest developments of the biotechnology revolution to offensive BW research. Alibek recalls that Popov's work was part of two larger projects known as Bonfire and Metol, which sought to use genetic engineering to develop new toxin weapons as well as antibiotic-resistant strains of existing bioweapons.[98] In November 1989 Popov presented to colleagues some of his work on a strain of the bacteria *Legionella* with myelin-producing genes inserted. This new bacterium first produced mild symptoms of pneumonia but was followed, after the symptoms of *Legionella* infection had disappeared, by a metabolic reaction to the myelin genes that resulted in paralysis, brain damage, and death.[99] The implications of such a bacterium, if it were weaponized, are staggering: "the infectious agent would be gone by the time it began its killing, leaving few or no traces for medical detectives trying to understand the cause of the havoc."[100]

Although Popov stated that this bacterium, which he described as his "most successful research," was, to his time-dated knowledge, never produced or weaponized, this achievement illustrates the potential impact of rapid advances in science and technology on the future of BW.[101] In Popov's view, "if somebody wants to employ genetic engineering in creating weapons, the most exciting discoveries are still ahead."[102] Genetic engineering, recombinant DNA, and other emerging techniques offered the potential not only for new pathogens and agents but also for the revival of what bioweaponeer William Patrick III has referred to as the "oldie moldies," classical BW agents such as anthrax and tularemia, among others.

Indeed, the potential for genetic modification of classical BW agents was dramatically, if inadvertently, demonstrated by a group of scientists working on a pest control project in Australia in 1998. As part of an experiment aimed at causing infertility in field mice, scientists inserted interleukin-4 genes, which play a role in controlling the immune system, into the mousepox virus, a relative of the much deadlier smallpox virus.[103] As a result, the mice not only were rendered infertile but died. Even more alarming was the fact that the new "super-mousepox" had the same effect on mice that had been vaccinated against mousepox.

The scientists' public announcement of their findings in February 2001 caused quite a stir in government and media circles.[104] Popov, working in what was in the late 1980s the world's most advanced BW laboratory, was at the cutting edge of offensive research. Two decades later, scientists working in the private sector had begun to replicate some of the advanced techniques practiced by Popov and his colleagues. Technology diffusion and information flow over time, coupled with continuing advances in biotechnology, foreshadow a gloomy future for BW in which defensive countermeasures will sorely lag developing offensive capabilities.

Intelligence from inspections. In October 1990 the United States, the United Kingdom, and the Soviet Union came to an agreement regarding inspections of suspected BW facilities. In order to address US-UK concerns over Soviet compliance with the BWC, the agreement allowed inspections of select nonmilitary facilities in all three countries. The joint US-UK team arrived in the Soviet Union in January 1991 and inspected four facilities: the Institute of Immunology in Lyubchany, the All-Union Scientific Research Institute for Applied Microbiology in Obolensk, the Vektor laboratory complex near Novosibirsk, and the Institute for Ultra-Pure Biological Preparations in Leningrad. Although the inspections were hampered by extensive denial, delay, and deception efforts on the part of the Soviet hosts, what the inspectors were able to see was startling. Frank Malinoski, a US inspector, observed that "this was a massive program. . . . They had production capacity that was on a scale that no one in the U.S. or the UK would expect to be necessary if you were in a defensive posture."[105] Alibek, who organized the inspections, noted that when the inspectors got their first glimpse of the Soviet research facilities, "they were unbelievably shocked."[106]

Soviet deception efforts were partly successful: inspections of the Institute of Immunology, for example, revealed nothing indicative of offensive BW work but clear evidence of vaccine production. However, at Obolensk the inspectors were more successful. Following a lead given to British intelligence by Pasechnik, the US-UK team discovered a "large six-sided steel chamber" that showed evidence of being used for explosive dissemination tests.[107] At the main research center at Oblensk—Corpus One—British microbiologist David Kelly saw evidence that the Soviets were working with a genetically engineered strain of plague in order to increase its hardiness and survivability, while other inspectors noted the presence of giant fermenters in the labs, including at least four fermenters twenty feet in height, each having a capacity of more than 10,000 liters. The group's Soviet handlers acknowledged that each of the eight floors of Corpus One could produce more than 900 liters of a particular biological agent per week, which in the view of the inspectors far exceeded the needs of any defensive-oriented program.[108]

The final two facilities provided the Western inspectors with still more evidence of alarming developments by Soviet scientists. At the Vektor laboratory, in Siberia, the inspectors observed a sophisticated computer modeling system for plotting the behavior of aerosols under diverse conditions. The inspectors also saw a large aerosol test chamber not unlike that at Oblensk and noted that Vektor scientists were conducting extensive virus research, especially on Marburg hemorrhagic fever. And perhaps of greatest consequence, the inspectors discovered that these scientists were working with the smallpox virus. Not only did this work possibly violate the BWC, it also showed that the Soviets had violated World Health Organization (WHO) strictures by moving the smallpox virus from the Ivanovsky Institute for Viral Preparations, one of two designated repositories for the virus established after the WHO declared smallpox eradicated in 1980.[109] The final site visited by the inspectors was the Leningrad Institute for Ultra-Pure Biological Preparations, Pasechnik's former institution. In light of the inside information that the inspectors had obtained from Pasechnik, the Soviets went to great lengths to cast the institute's activities as peaceful in nature. Nevertheless, the inspectors noted the facility's two-story explosives test chamber, a huge aerosol test chamber, as well as special dryers and milling equipment, none of which had practical applications for defensive research.

After returning from the Soviet Union, the joint inspection team produced a two-hundred-page report on its findings, including supporting photographs, audiotapes, and videotapes. The inspection team reportedly made five major findings. First, they uncovered key indicators—"the type and configuration of the equipment and the huge BW production capacity"—that confirmed that the Soviets were pursuing a massive offensive BW program run by both the Soviet military and Biopreparat, "the largest such programme that the world had ever known." Second, they noted the close and extensive contacts between Biopreparat and the Soviet military. Third, they uncovered evidence of specific violations of the BWC and other agreements, "including smallpox research, genetic engineering of dangerous pathogens, and explosive aerosol testing." Fourth, the inspectors noted the extensive denial and deception efforts undertaken by the Soviets to conceal the work that was under way at the inspected Biopreparat facilities, including sanitization of laboratories to preclude sample taking, removal of equipment, and the rushing of inspection tours to prevent any in-depth investigation. Finally, the inspectors found that their counterparts were less than forthcoming with facts and resorted, when pressed, to a standard rejoinder relating to the "defensive" nature of all research conducted.[110] A Soviet delegation that included then Deputy Director of Biopreparat Kanatjan Alibekov visited former US sites shortly thereafter.[111]

This avenue of data collection would not remain open for long. In September 1992 Russia, the United States, and the United Kingdom negotiated and signed a second, more formal document covering multilateral inspections known as the Trilateral Agreement. Western negotiators considered this to be a key agreement because it established procedures for reciprocal visits to facilities in the three countries, allowing "unrestricted access, sampling, interviews with personnel and audio and video taping" and permitting inspectors to visit any nonmilitary site they asked to see.[112] What was perhaps even more important for Western specialists, the Trilateral Agreement also stated that at some point in the future Western observers would be permitted to inspect Russian military facilities. Although the locations of these military facilities and a clear timetable for the beginning of such inspections were not outlined in the agreement, Western negotiators nevertheless considered it to be a key concession on the part of the Russians.[113]

While US officials hoped that the informal arrangement that led to the 1990–91 inspections would be formalized under the 1992 Trilateral Agreement, the process was drawing to a close. Since a handful of reciprocal inspections in 1993 there have been no further visits. Indeed, Sir Percy Cradock, a former British intelligence official, pronounced something of a postmortem for the agreement:

> The trilateral process is stalled. There is little enthusiasm for meetings with Russian officials who consistently lie, and who demand that the UK and US undergo a programme of visits to any Western facility chosen by the Russians—none of which has anything to do with biological warfare—in exchange for limited access to Russian BW facilities. Until we receive a credible account from the Russian government of the Soviet BW programme which they inherited . . . we will remain concerned about a continuing Russian capacity for biological warfare. We just don't know why they are so determined not to allow access to the BW facilities run by the military.[114]

Russian government statements and actions. In 1992 Russian President Boris Yeltsin publicly confirmed that the Soviet Union had in the past pursued an offensive BW program in violation of the BWC and asserted that it had been terminated in 1991. On April 11, 1992, Yeltsin issued a presidential decree "on ensuring the implementation of international pledges in the sphere of biological weapons," which would ensure Russian compliance with the BWC and cut funding for such programs by 30 percent and personnel by 50 percent.[115] Months later, after the signing of the Trilateral Agreement in September of that year, Russian Deputy Foreign Minister Grigory V. Berdennikov echoed Yeltsin's statement, stating that "the Soviet Union was violating this convention and was running a program in the sphere of offensive biological research and development, which had been declared unlawful by the convention. These activities were in progress from 1946 until March of 1992. They were discontinued by the decree of the Russian President."[116]

Russia also agreed to fully disclose its past efforts to the United Nations. The relevant documentation was submitted after some delay, apparently on the part of military hardliners who resisted efforts at transparency, and failed to meet British and American expectations. It only outlined four BW production and testing centers, even though at that point in time US and UK officials were aware of more than twenty such facilities, and failed to address issues and concerns raised by the Sverdlovsk incident, Pasechnik's defection, and the 1991 inspections.[117] The Russians also repeatedly extended Yeltsin's deadline for dismantling the offensive program, and Yeltsin failed to follow through on a pledge to dismiss General Yuri Kalinin, one of "the old guard of biological cold warriors," from his post as director of Biopreparat.[118] In September 1992, six months after Yeltsin's first pledge to dismantle the BW program, State Department spokesman Richard Boucher stated, "To date, we do not have the kind of concrete actions that would indicate that the Russian government has effectively terminated the illegal Soviet offensive biological weapons program."[119] In 1993 the Arms Control and Disarmament Agency warned that the status of the program . . . remains unclear," a judgment evidently shared by other agencies.[120] Alibek echoed this concern, repeatedly articulating his belief that Russian scientists continued to carry on research into offensive BW. Others, such as Lieutenant Colonel Yevgeni Tulykin, former personnel director at Compound 19, in Yekaterinburg (formerly Sverdlovsk), made similar assertions regarding Russian military BW facilities in Yekaterinburg, suggesting that the plant was continuing its offensive BW work.[121]

Implications

The past Soviet BW program and the possibility of a continuing Russian program carry several important policy implications for the United States, its friends and allies, and the international community as a whole. Absent an effective, enforceable verification mechanism, international activities designed to control the spread of biological weapons remain predicated on state-level declarations, national intelligence capabilities, and bilateral arrangements. While the Soviet program was unprecedented in its scale and perhaps unsurpassed in its technical and operational achievements, other state actors are doubtless able to replicate successful Soviet measures undertaken to conceal the existence of an offensive program. Coupled with the continuing spread of weapons-usable technologies and expertise, biological weapons constitute a growth area within the WMD continuum. Indeed, the Soviet experience highlights at least four challenges inherent in any effort to properly characterize and effectively respond to states pursuing BW.

Timely and accurate threat assessment. The Soviet case underscores the difficulties inherent in trying to accurately assess a state's BW program. While analysts long surmised that the Soviet Union was engaged in suspect research activities, it was not until credible defector testimony unraveled key secrets that judgments on its "offensive" nature could be reliably made. And if analysts missed available indicators in such a large-scale program and against such a well-resourced collection target, there is a great likelihood of critical gaps in coverage of other proliferant states.

Worse still, these gaps are often compounded by inadvertent mirror imaging. Extrapolating from one state's known technical capabilities, organizational structures, or development pathways is fraught with peril. It is sometimes inaccurate, as with the prior US assumption that military programs would be housed in military institutions—as were those of the United States or the United Kingdom—rather than (or in addition to) in civilian facilities, as in the Soviet case. It is frequently misleading, as with the erroneous assumption that since US weaponeers had not been able to master the intricacies of weaponizing pneumonic plague by the time the offensive program ended, other states would be similarly constrained; certainly, Soviet weaponeers solved this problem and proceeded to genetically modify the agent to maximize its lethal potential.[122] Finally, it is often unhelpful, as with the assumption that aflatoxin (as well as other agents) has no discernible militarily-relevant purpose, so Iraqi efforts to research, produce, and weaponize the agent remain a mystery.[123]

While some actors may view BW as weapons of last resort and others may view them as usable solely against finite or discrete target sets, the Soviet case suggests that at least some proliferant states have a considerably more varied employment doctrine. These capabilities may be fully integrated into military operational plans, with BW intended for both military and nonmilitary targets. Nor are proliferant states' BW capabilities static: while classical BW agents will remain a core security challenge to the United States for some time, the research of Sergei Popov and others suggests that the continuing revolution in biotechnology has the potential to substantially alter the traditional BW problem in the years ahead.

The "dual-use" enigma. The trilateral inspections process underscored the critical importance of dual-use equipment to the manufacture of biological weapons. According to the Office of the Secretary of Defense, "Virtually all the equipment, technology, and materials needed for biological warfare agent research and development and production are dual-use." As a result, offensive programs "are relatively easy to disguise within the larger body of legitimate commercial activity, as no specialized facilities are required," and "any country with the political will and a competent scientific base can produce toxins or infectious agents, which include viruses, bacteria, and rickettsiae."[124] The continuing demand for biological weapons and the relative ease with which any offensive effort may be concealed, together with the growing availability of weapons-related technologies and expertise and a continuing revolution in biotechnology that could significantly alter the threat environment, suggest that determined states—and possibly particular subnational actors, whose chances would likely improve with state support—face few real constraints in establishing, developing, or improving offensive programs if there is a national decision to do so.

Yet judgments predicated on the latent capability to develop such a program are inherently uncertain. While research and development facilities and relevant production technologies provide clear mobilization potential, assessments of a state's intentions are far more important and far more difficult to make. As commonly practiced, intelligence is an inherently conservative art form; it generally relies on information collected to make judgments rather than extrapolating to the universe of possibilities. While policymakers often prefer judgments on the *known,* the *possible,* and the *likely,* intelligence analysts are often unable to accurately forecast the evolution of a state's actual capabilities or leadership intentions. Indeed, in the enigmatic biological weapons arena, specific, complete, and current information on such restrictive data are among the hardest types of intelligence to collect.[125]

Duplicity, denial, and deception. The Soviet case illustrates the inherent difficulties in trying to uncover secret and highly compartmentalized information from a state that masks its weapons-related activities. The 1975 Soviet ratification of the BWC was apparently intended more for concealment and deception that for demilitarization. Indeed, the apparent ease with which the Soviet Union violated the treaty and set up its massive program highlighted one of the major shortcomings of the BWC. Article 1 requires that signatories never "develop, produce, stockpile or otherwise acquire or retain" pathogens or toxins except for defensive purposes. States parties to the convention are required to destroy all existing stockpiles within nine months of the treaty's entry into force. The absence of any intrusive verification measures or inspection protocols and the probability that states intent on carrying out an illicit program might not be caught proved to be the treaty's Achilles' heel.

Yet this difficulty relates more to the inherent nature of BW than to the efficacy of specific response measures, including arms control treaties or negotiated bilateral verification processes. With respect to Iraq, for instance, even after a series of post–Gulf War "full, final, and complete disclosures," and despite more than seven years of intrusive inspections, UNSCOM was unable to account for critical elements of the Iraqi BW program. Among the gaps in this "select and incomplete" history of the program were "considerable uncertainty" regarding weaponization; "consistently understated" agent production; an "incomplete" declaration of equipment and raw material imports; "omitted" planning references; "thoroughly planned" research and development, despite Iraqi claims that they were "unplanned"; and finally, an absence of Iraqi evidence "concerning the termination of its offensive program."[126]

The absence of cost-free policy options. If proper characterization of a state's BW capabilities and plans presents an arduous analytic challenge, so too does the design of effective policy responses. The arms control route has run its course, as Undersecretary of State John Bolton suggests: "The time for 'better than nothing' protocols is over. It is time for us to consider serious measures to address the BW threat. It is time to set aside years of diplomatic inertia. We will not be protected by a 'Maginot treaty' approach to the BW threat."[127] With respect to Russian BW capabilities, it appears that the trilateral process has run its course as well. One innovative set of efforts designed to address the BW legacy in Russia and other formerly Soviet states relate to site-specific scientific research and other cooperative endeavors at particular civilian facilities under the auspices of the Cooperative Threat Reduction (CTR) program.[128]

In this context, CTR funds have been used to dismantle the former Biopreparat anthrax production facility in Stepnogorsk, Kazakhstan. Similarly, research projects funded with CTR funds may have helped counter brain drain to Iran or other states of proliferation concern. And they have provided access to select Biopreparat facilities and personnel, allowing US officials some measure of transparency into activities at select installations. Still, since government cooperation is required, efforts to dismantle the Soviet BW program are likely to succeed only to the extent permitted by the Russian government.

For the United States, these threat-reduction efforts also present clear oversight challenges and policy trade-offs, for example, with respect to the difficulties inherent in verifying that funding recipients are not concurrently sharing their expertise with other proliferant states or with respect to the fungibility of program funding, the potential that US funding inadvertently permits the Russian government to divert at least a portion of the resources available for offensive purposes or to commit resources to other, perhaps less than desirable activities. Nor is it clear that the small-scale pattern of cooperation established at a handful of civilian sites will ultimately extend to military sites. BW-related CTR activities to date have not cleared up uncertainties relating to past and possibly continuing offensive BW activities; at best, they have provided both a window into the activities of particular institutes and a vehicle to help reduce the prospect of diversion of material or expertise that remain part and parcel of the Soviet BW legacy.

Conclusion

The North Korean nuclear program and the Soviet/Russian BW program illustrate how information gaps create policy difficulties. In each case, US intelligence analysts understood that programs were under way but could not determine the full extent or status of those programs. While North Korean revelations in 2002 of a continued nuclear weapons development program have erased some uncertainties, considerable gaps shroud Russian BW activities more than a decade after the Cold War's end. And policy efforts to address these thorny proliferation programs have both been less than successful and carried substantial trade-offs. For instance, the Agreed Framework signed with North Korea shut down the overt aspects of that state's nuclear program at Yongbyon, but it proved unable to halt other covert efforts. Similarly, while site-specific cooperation has occurred in the Russian civilian sector, little is known about activities by the purported military BW program or whether offensive BW efforts in some former Biopreparat institutes have in fact been terminated. Because of the uncertainties inherent in each case, US policymakers run the continuing risk of inadvertently contributing to the problem they seek to counter.

In all likelihood, other aspiring proliferants remain astute observers both of Russian and North Korean tactics and techniques designed to conceal their clandestine activities and of US and international responses. As they become more adept at masking their efforts through denial and deception measures—whether Iraq (chapter 5), North Korea (chapter 4), India (chapter 4), or others—or become more aware of specific US intelligence capabilities, the net margin of analytic uncertainty is only more likely to increase in the years ahead. This raises the prospect of intelligence surprise, a key feature of the emerging security landscape.

Intelligence Surprise

Deception, Innovation, Proliferation

On May 11, 1998, India announced to the world that it had initiated a series of five nuclear tests at its Pokhran test range in Rajasthan. These explosions broke the country's twenty-four-year self-imposed moratorium on nuclear testing. Both the US intelligence community and US policymakers were caught by surprise. Just a few months later, in East Asia, North Korea startled the world by launching a three-stage rocket. Not only did the missile's overflight of Japanese territory provoke sharp diplomatic discord but its unexpectedly sophisticated technical parameters again caught policymakers by surprise. The intelligence community was reportedly unaware of the existence of a third stage, which, while not entirely successful, Pyongyang later declared to be an attempted satellite launch. The congressionally mandated blue-ribbon Commission to Assess the Ballistic Missile Threat to the United States concluded in this context that "deception and denial efforts are intense, and often successful, and U.S. collection and analysis assets are limited."[1]

Two years later, DCI George Tenet testified that there was a high risk of continued surprise in a contemporary international-security environment characterized by "rapid change [that] makes us even more vulnerable to sudden surprise."[2] In his March 2000 congressional testimony, Tenet outlined four principal reasons for this risk. First, and in his view most important, is the increasing sophistication of denial and deception efforts on the part of proliferant states. Would-be proliferants now routinely employ measures designed to deny the United States a window on both their evolving intentions and their improving capabilities. Second is the increasing availability of dual-use technologies that effectively mask the intentions of proliferant states. While nonproliferation measures have traditionally been predicated on a technology-denial strategy, existing arms and export control regimes do not sufficiently impede the spread of many weapons-related technologies, particularly those with civilian applications as well as potential military purposes. In the chem-

ical and biological arenas, the continuing spread of dual-use technology re-
duces the visible signatures of a proliferant's weapons-related activities.

Third is the availability of expertise that proliferants can draw on to advance
nuclear, biological, chemical, and missile programs. The supply-side labor sur-
plus brought on by the collapse of the Soviet Union differentiates the contemporary environment from its Cold War corollary; the growing indigenization of production capabilities will further enlarge this specialized labor pool.
Finally, the pace of technological progress is accelerating as information and
advanced technologies become increasingly available worldwide. Even as
1940s-era technology continues to suffice for some weapons-related applications, recent and continuing advances stand to significantly ease research, development, and production difficulties and may also facilitate the concealment
and localization of production activities.

As the Indian and North Korean illustrations suggest, surprise in the proliferation context may be either political or technological in nature. These unexpected high-profile incidents raise several important issues for the intelligence, operational, and policy communities in the proliferation arena. For
intelligence producers the challenge is twofold: both to field technologies or
recruit assets that enhance the prospects for collection in this tough environment and to develop improved capabilities and methodological approaches
that enhance analytic output. For intelligence consumers the task is similarly
daunting. Policymakers must develop strategies to diminish the attractiveness
of adversaries' acquisition, development, and use of WMD, while operators
must seek to mitigate the effects of proliferation surprise by continuing to improve the military's ability to operate more effectively in WMD environments.
These imperatives are even more important if, as Tenet concludes, the risk of
surprise not only is an immediate feature of the intelligence landscape but is
becoming increasingly difficult to counter: "The hill is getting steeper every
year."[3] The Indian and North Korean case studies that follow emphasize the
difficulty of reading a proliferant's evolving intentions and developing capabilities, respectively.

Misreading Intentions: India's Unexpected Nuclear Tests

In 1974 India conducted what it referred to as a "peaceful nuclear explosion," announcing immediately thereafter a moratorium on future tests but

making its nuclear weapons potential clear. Twenty-one years later US satellites detected activity at the Pokhran test site. Analysts believed that this activity was indicative of preparations for another nuclear test. In an effort to prevent a nuclear arms race on the subcontinent the United States sent a letter of demarche to the Indian government presenting evidence of India's test preparations.[4] This use of diplomatic pressure was successful in dissuading India from testing a nuclear explosive device. However, just two and a half years after this apparent success in diplomatic dissuasion, India successfully carried out its clandestine preparations. In Senate Intelligence Committee Chairman Richard Shelby's view, this represented "a colossal failure of our intelligence gathering."[5]

The Jeremiah Report

Not surprisingly, this "colossal failure" led to widespread calls for reviews to determine how the intelligence community had failed to provide strategic warning, and CIA Director Tenet soon commissioned retired Admiral David Jeremiah to lead an inquiry into the matter. Although the report remains classified, many of the group's conclusions were made public. These provide important insights into the nature of the evolving proliferation problem, the modus operandi of the intelligence community, and emergent collection and analytic requirements. The report identifies several major factors that contributed to the failure to predict the Indian tests, including analytic biases on the part of intelligence officials and policymakers; successful denial and deception efforts on the part of India; technical or resource shortfalls characterized by a lack of adequate, reliable human intelligence (HUMINT) sources; and an overreliance on an overwhelming quantity of satellite imagery, while having an inadequate staff to fully exploit it.

Analytic bias. The Jeremiah Commission considered analytic biases on the part of the analytic community to be a principal factor in the warning failure, concluding that an "underlying mindset" in both the intelligence and policy areas had led to mirror imaging on the part of analysts. Mirror imaging, or "assuming that other states or individuals will act just the way we do," can undermine objective analyses.[9] It was widely held among US analysts and officials that the BJP government would behave in a "rational" manner. Rationality, however, was evidently defined differently in Washington and New Delhi.

At the time, the United States was actively seeking to improve its diplomatic and economic relationship with India. If India were to conduct nuclear tests, the United States would be required by law to impose significant, wide-ranging sanctions on India. Thus, officials in the United States calculated that the Indian government would not risk losing the economic benefits of an improved relationship with the US government. As Admiral Jeremiah stated during an unclassified report outbrief, "We had a mindset that said everybody else is going to work like we work. Why would anyone throw away all the economic advantages associated that they would lose with testing, why would they hazard all that stuff when there is no reason to do that?" His bottom line: "We don't think like the other nation thinks."[7]

The evident mirror imaging is particularly significant in light of numerous public statements on nuclear weapons made by both BJP officials and figures in the Indian nuclear program.[8] In February 1998 the BJP released its party manifesto, stating that it planned to "exercise the nuclear option" and "declare India a nuclear weapon state" after coming to power.[9] During the subsequent elections in March, BJP politicians highlighted the nuclear issue and promised to conduct nuclear tests if elected.[10] US analysts apparently believed that Indian politicians, perhaps not unlike some of their US counterparts, would ignore or fail to implement promises made during the campaign.[11] In fact, even though CIA analysts were aware of the BJP manifesto issued in February, an agency report from the same time period reportedly discounted the rhetoric.[12] Following the elections and the formation of the new BJP government, India conducted its first-ever strategic defense policy review, and numerous public officials, including the prime minister, the defense minister, and the army chief of staff, stated that India should consider or proceed with "inducting" nuclear weapons into its arsenal. India's atomic weapons commissioner weighed in on the issue in March, stating that he was ready to conduct tests as soon as political leaders gave the green light.[13]

Both intelligence analysts and policy officials may have misread Indian intentions in part due to the BJP's prior, if brief, tenure of office in May 1996. At the time, the BJP's line of nationalist rhetoric, especially on nuclear weapons, was publicly known throughout India and by the press.[14] Almost immediately after the 1996 elections, Prime Minister Atal Bihari Vajpayee reportedly gave permission to the Defence Research and Development Organization and the Department of Atomic Energy to begin preparations for nuclear tests. The preparations apparently reached the point where at least one weapon was placed in a test shaft, but ultimately the test did not take place.[15] As in 1995, US intelligence detected test preparations, and a letter of demarche was sent to the Indian government. However, it appears that the decision to halt the test was more a result of internal Indian politics than of US policy intervention. The BJP's ruling coalition was weak, and Vajpayee and his advisers judged that a nuclear test would be too controversial to survive an impending confidence vote in the Indian parliament; the prime minister ultimately decided not to pass the consequences of a BJP nuclear decision on to a future government. These concerns were well founded, as on May 28, 1996, the BJP received a no-confidence vote and the successor government promptly canceled the tests.[16]

At the time of the 1998 tests, public statements by the BJP were not the only sources available for US assessment. A considerable volume of news reporting in both India and Pakistan, including even English-language Indian newspapers readily accessible to US analysts, conveyed a substantially similar message.[17] Upon discovering the apparent discounting or omission of such sources, Senator Daniel Patrick Moynihan (D-NY) asked, "Why didn't the CIA find this out? The question is why don't we learn to read? What's the State Department for? The political leadership in India as much as said they were going to begin testing."[18] One example of publicly available speculation on the impending tests was a newsletter published on May 7, 1998, by Sikh separatists claiming that its sources had reported "feverish nighttime activity" at India's Pokhran site, signs of an imminent nuclear test.[19] Other articles soon followed in both Indian and Pakistani newspapers. While sound analysis required judgments as to the quality and volume of information available and needed to discount background "noise," the availability of *potentially* valuable information from these outlets underscores the important need to improve collection and analysis of open-source data. Indeed, the information revolution of the 1990s greatly increased both the volume and the accessibility of open-source information, an area that intelligence analysts should seek to fully exploit.[20]

"An effective denial activity." The Jeremiah report identified Indian denial and deception efforts as a major contributor to the warning failure. Deception and denial measures span a range of often overlapping activities, including, for example, concealment and camouflage of facilities to obscure their true purpose, false or planted information to mislead foreign intelligence agencies, or convoluted procurement methods that shield desired end uses.[21] During the unclassified press conference reporting the findings of his commission, Admiral Jeremiah commented on India's deception efforts, ruefully stating, "I guess I'd rather not say that it was a success on the part of anyone in keeping secrets

from us. But, in fact, that happens and some of that occurred here." He later added, "I would certainly say that they had an effective denial activity."[22] Similarly, Senator Sam Brownback observed during hearings on the Indian tests that "India did all it could to deny the international community forewarning of these tests."[23] Nor was this interpretation limited to US officials. Indian researcher G. Balachandran, for instance, also concluded that India had carried out a well-orchestrated denial and deception plan aimed at US collection and analysis: "It's not a failure of the CIA. It's a matter of their intelligence being good, our deception being better."[24]

Thus, at the same time that key BJP members were publicly campaigning on a pronuclear platform, Indian officials were carrying out a concerted effort to conceal nuclear test preparations. In particular, the deception and denial program attempted to foil US reconnaissance satellites and to mislead US officials regarding the BJP's position on nuclear testing.[25] While these efforts were not conducted on the same massive scale as Iraqi activities, there are significant similarities. They also serve as evidence to support what David Kay, a former (and future) weapons inspector in Iraq, considered to be one of the most important lessons of weapons inspections in Iraq: "Determined proliferators pay close attention to sources and methods with a view to countering them."[26]

It is possible that the 1998 intelligence failure stemmed in part from a 1995 success, both strategic warning and dissuasion of a planned test by India. In the 1995 case, US satellites detected evidence that India was preparing its facilities at the Pokhran test range.[27] US Ambassador to India Frank Wisner Jr. delivered a letter of demarche to the India government, reportedly including satellite photos of the test site as part of a diplomatic strategy to prevent the test. While New Delhi did not carry out its 1995 test, it is possible that the demarche inadvertently revealed extant US monitoring capabilities and therefore contributed to the 1998 surprise. Insofar as proliferant states are able to learn the sources or methods of US collection activities, those capabilities may prove ineffective in future cases.[28] One indicator of the potentially deleterious long-term effect of Wisner's dispatch was that the pattern of events at the test site was altered. Close observers note that since 1995 "India's test site has been kept in a permanently high state of readiness, so as to minimise the need for 'suspicious movements' of vehicles and equipment in the run-up to an explosion."[29] Also, some of the equipment from the 1995 preparations was apparently left in situ, reducing the setup activities that would be required for a subsequent test.[30]

While open presentation of intelligence may serve worthwhile policy goals, Kay observes, "the underlying algorithms and weaknesses of these methods will become much more widely understood."[31] The risks inherent in such activities must therefore be weighed carefully against both short-term and long-term policy requirements, in the immediate situation and for collateral activities. As former CIA Director James Woolsey underscores: "As we go around delivering demarches to [countries] on what they should and should not do, almost always the information comes from intelligence, and it therefore reveals something about intelligence sources and methods."[32]

At the same time, defeating established collection techniques, particularly heavily used imagery and signals intelligence, is sometimes possible. In this case, Indian officials probably used information surmised from the 1995 demarche and apparently supplemented this information with data from indigenous satellites to plot the orbits of US satellites in order to estimate periods conducive to clandestine preparation.[33] R. R. Subramanian, for instance, concludes that Indian scientists determined roughly when American satellites would be in position and endeavored to relocate people and equipment during periods when the satellites were not overhead.[34] More broadly, recent advances in information technology have facilitated the open exchange of previously closely held satellite data; as a result, satellite watchers routinely plot the trajectory of known overhead assets.[35]

Finally, in parallel to the denial activities discussed above, the Indian government undertook a deliberate disinformation campaign. Specifically, some US officials believe that the Indian government deliberately stated that New Delhi would consider retracting prior nuclear policy declarations.[36] After the March 1998 elections and the formation of the BJP government, the Hindu nationalist party noticeably toned down its nationalist rhetoric, including statements on nuclear policy.[37] For instance, the new prime minister, Atal Bihari Vajpayee, stated on March 18, 1998, that while India intended to keep its nuclear options open, "there is no time-frame," a position George Fernandes, the new defense minister, reiterated the next day.[38] Furthermore, Nagendra Nath Jha, a senior BJP foreign-policy adviser, reportedly told officials at the US embassy in New Delhi that India planned to conduct a review of defense policy that would take three to six months and that no tests would be conducted before that review was completed.[39] In April, Bill Richardson, US representative to the United Nations, met with Prime Minister Vajpayee and left with the apparent impression that there would be no tests.[40]

After the tests, National Security Adviser Sandy Berger stated, in reference to Richardson's April visit, "Collectively . . . the government of India was not forthright with Ambassador Richardson."[41] Similarly, State Department spokesman James Rubin stated that the Indian government had "engaged in a campaign of duplicity," acting in a manner "inconsistent with high-level representations made to the United States Government."[42] The Indian government, for its part, issued a press release on May 18 stating that claims by "senior U.S. administration officials that they have been 'seriously misled' by Indian interlocutors" were false: "In the twenty or more meetings referred to by US Spokesman [sic], India never gave any assurances or guarantees. On the contrary, it was clearly pointed out that no assurances can be given."[43] Whether deliberate disinformation or egregious misreading of intentions, concludes George Perkovich, "for every bellicose sign emanating from India, a reassuring diplomatic sign also could be found."[44]

Technical and resource limitations. The failure to detect the Indian nuclear tests also revealed significant limitations in deployed intelligence community capabilities, according to Admiral Jeremiah. The inadequacy of HUMINT assets around the world was one prominent shortcoming singled out by DCI Tenet shortly before the tests.[45] Indeed, the status of HUMINT in India was particularly poor; according to the Jeremiah panel, the CIA had "no spies worthy of the name" in the country.[46] While the CIA evidently had tried to recruit intelligence operatives in India, apparently it had met with little success, and reportedly it had few, if any, HUMINT assets at the top levels of the Indian government, where the decisions regarding testing were ultimately made.[47]

In general, human sources offer several key advantages to intelligence agencies, such as the potential for recruiting well-placed sources in political and military decision-making processes, the ability for operatives to introduce false or misleading information to other governments, and the ability to gather information on activities whose "signatures" are not very noticeable (e.g., terrorism or drug trafficking).[48] These potential benefits, however, are matched by difficulties that include the fact that HUMINT, unlike signals or imagery intelligence, cannot be handled remotely and may have important political consequences if handlers are uncovered by a target state's counterintelligence service; the difficulty in recruiting foreign nationals who have access to desired information, as well as the reliability of such contacts; the susceptibility of

HUMINT to deception; and the security needed to protect these unique sources from deliberate or inadvertent unmasking.[49]

In 1998 the Jeremiah panel concluded that the heavy reliance on satellite imagery engendered its own set of problems. While such technical means regularly yield a substantial volume of *potentially* useful data, analysts appear to have been overwhelmed by the deluge of incoming imagery. Reportedly, only one imagery analyst was regularly assigned to examine satellite photos related to India's nuclear program.[50] The result, according to Admiral Jeremiah, was that "there is an awful lot of stuff on the cutting room floor at the end of the day that we have not seen."[51]

At the same time, the satellites themselves were high-demand assets. The Pokhran test site reportedly was not considered a critical priority warranting continuous coverage.[52] Misconceptions regarding Indian nuclear intentions, together with the small number of trained and dedicated analysts and evidently competing demands for imagery from higher-priority areas, in effect reduced the amount of coverage over India and opened a significant window for concealment activities at the test site. It is perhaps unsurprising that signs of activity at Pokhran were apparently overlooked, lost in collateral activities, or treated as background noise. Thus, the first clearly understood signal came from statements by Indian officials immediately following the tests.

Ironically, just one week before the tests, Tenet observed that the CIA's capabilities "had eroded," that HUMINT assets were spread too thin, and that too much emphasis was being placed on satellite imagery. The volume of imagery was ten times what it had been a decade earlier, a volume generally overwhelming to analysts.[53] Budget constraints in the wake of the Cold War both reduced the assets available to the intelligence community and led to an overreliance on particular capabilities. As a result, although the CIA has identified more than fifty countries of proliferation concern (as suppliers, demand states, or conduits), in Tenet's view, it is unable to effectively and consistently monitor them all. Testifying in open session, Tenet observed that "we focus much of our intelligence collection and analysis on some 10 states," but "even concerning those states there are important gaps in our knowledge. Our analytical and collection coverage against most of these states is stretched, and many of the trends that I just noted make it harder to track some key developments, even in states of the greatest intelligence focus."[54]

Tenet's testimony was tantamount to a judgment that further strategic surprises in the proliferation arena would be likely, an argument that should have made the policy community reel. Collection and analysis priorities are established by policymakers, and resource levels ultimately are determined by the Congress. While the national-security policy community clearly views the proliferation of nuclear, chemical, and biological weapons as a leading challenge to America's security, the intelligence community is unlikely to provide credible strategic warning of important proliferation-related developments if it does not have adequate resources or appropriate tools or if the policy community is inattentive to developments in the field. In this case, while there were clear procedural and interpretive intelligence shortcomings, the relative lack of emphasis on and resources devoted to observing India's test site suggests that the "intelligence failure" was equally attributable to the policy community. Indeed, as former DCI James Woolsey argued shortly after the event, "Insofar as there has been a failure of the U.S. Government . . . to understand what direction the BJP might take," it is also "a failure of academics, of think tanks, of the press . . . of Congress, of the executive branch as a whole." In this view, it was "not just an intelligence failure, per se," but a policy failure as well.[55]

Technical Surprise: North Korea's Taepodong-1

While the Indian nuclear case well illustrates the challenge of political surprise, North Korea's concurrent development of the TD-1 MRBM illustrates what Congressman Curt Weldon (R-PA) called "an extremely troubling technical surprise."[56] On August 31, 1998, North Korea conducted a ballistic missile test from its Musudan-ri launch site. Still reeling from the aftershocks of India's nuclear tests in May, senior national-security officials boldly announced that the United States had not been surprised by this first test of the TD-1 MRBM but rather had been aware and had prepared for the impending launch by deploying appropriate collection assets in the theater.[57] Specifically, in mid-August US intelligence detected preparations at the Hwadaegun missile test facility that, combined with deployments by the North Korean navy into the East Sea, were suggestive of a test launch (similar activities preceded the May 1993 Nodong test).[58] By August 27, US air and sea assets were in place to monitor events should a launch occur. In particular, the United States deployed a broad package of assets to observe the launch.[59]

Immediately following the launch, DOD spokesman Major Bryan Salas underscored that "we weren't surprised by the firing." Other government sources reiterated that "we knew it was coming" and that the missile "acted the way it was supposed to."[60] Yet, this apparent success would be short-lived. Several days after the test the DPRK unexpectedly announced that it had not conducted a ballistic missile test but rather had "succeeded in launching the [DPRK's] first artificial satellite aboard a multi-stage rocket."[61]

Despite initial assessments to the contrary, after reviewing the substantial amount of data collected from the launch, the US government reached concluded that the DPRK had in fact attempted to launch a satellite. Although the DPRK launch was only partly successful, it was an unexpected and alarming development. Indeed, several features of the test caught the intelligence community off guard. US officials were surprised as much by the fact that a nation as impoverished as North Korea would attempt to launch a satellite as by the fact that the rocket both had a third stage and had undergone successful stage separations during its flight. Apparently, the North Korean missile program was not thought to have overcome these technological hurdles. Coming on the heels of the Rumsfeld Commission's July report (see chapter 1), this technology surprise led the intelligence community to reevaluate its assessment of the DPRK missile threat as well as its process for creating such assessments more generally.

TD-1 Assessments

The Taepodong was first revealed in 1994, when North Korea displayed mock-ups of two new ballistic missiles, each with two stages. US intelligence analysts dubbed these the Taepodong-1 and Taepodong-2 (TD-2) missiles.[62] The TD-1 and TD-2 programs were apparently started in 1990–91 and represented a major advance in North Korean missile technology.[63] Prior to this point, North Korean missiles had been single-stage vehicles, but the two new missiles appeared to have multiple stages. Based on analysis of the two mock-ups, some analysts surmised that the TD-1 consisted of a Nodong first stage mated to a Scud-C second stage and that the TD-2 was composed of a new first stage and a Nodong second stage.[64] When the mock-ups were first noticed in 1994, the range of the TD-1 was estimated to be about twelve hundred kilometers and that of the TD-2, thirty-five hundred kilometers.[65] Generally, the new missiles were not assessed to be capable of reaching the continental United States, but they would be able to threaten most of East Asia and might be able to reach US territories in the theater. Various range figures appeared over the next several years, but unclassified estimates generally assessed the TD-1 to have a range

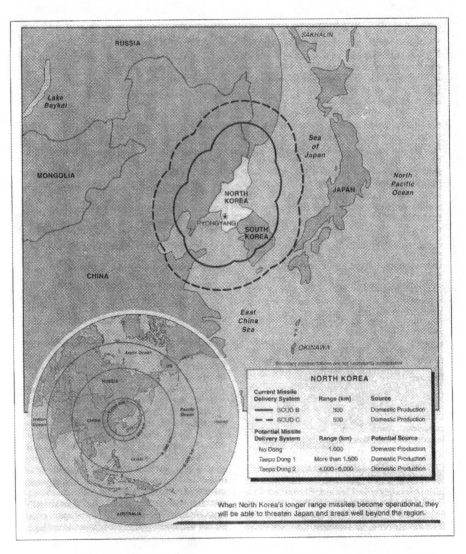

Figure 4.1. Estimated range of current and potential North Korean ballistic missiles (Office of the Secretary of Defense, *Proliferation: Threat and Response* [Washington, DC: GPO, 1997], 7)

of fifteen hundred to twenty-two hundred kilometers and the TD-2, four thousand to six thousand kilometers (see fig. 4.1).[66]

The DOD, for instance, judged in 1997 that "both TaepoDong missiles represent a significant technological departure from the proven SCUD designs." Yet it cautioned that the DPRK's "little experience" in flight-testing its missiles and the fact that it had never tested multistage ballistic missiles and related technology "could complicate North Korea's ability to evaluate, improve or repair flaws in its missile designs."[67] Other observers thought that the Nodong represented the upper limit of what could be achieved using Scud technology and that any longer-range missiles, such as the Taepodong, would require a new engine, new capabilities such as multistaging, and probably a significant amount of external assistance. David Wright, for instance, argued that the structure of the Taepodong series did "not make technical sense" and that the TD-1 had "a poor design that could lead to structural problems during boost phase."[68]

The Taepodong program figured prominently in the July 1998 report of the congressionally mandated Commission to Assess the Ballistic Missile Threat to the United States, chaired by former (and future) Secretary of Defense Donald Rumsfeld. The commission focused on the TD-2, as this missile was believed to pose the greatest threat to the United States. While acknowledging that the "status of the system's development cannot be determined precisely," the commission assessed that a TD-2 test flight could be conducted within six months of a decision to do so. Should the DPRK judge the missile test to be a success, the TD-2 "could be deployed quickly."[69] (Although these statements did not explicitly refer to the TD-1, they were apparently extrapolated from the commission's assessment of the Nodong program and, as such, would apply to both the TD-1 and the TD-2.)

When the Rumsfeld Commission's report was released in July, the intelligence community stood by its earlier assessments, in particular a March 1998 judgment that was substantially similar to NIE 95-19 but somewhat modified in light of the considerable criticism that document had engendered (see chapter 1).[70] Tenet allowed that there were some differences between the commission's timelines and those of the March 1998 assessment but said that he still believed that "the conclusions of our report were supported by the available evidence and were well tested in community debate."[71] Similarly, in September 1998, at the Carnegie Endowment for International Peace, National Intelligence Officer for Strategic and Nuclear Programs Robert Walpole stated, "We are in basic agreement with the Commission on North Korea. While they did not indicate so in their paper, I assume they do not disagree with our judgments that a Taepo Dong I or a Taepo Dong II could be tested this year."[72]

The Threefold Nature of Technological Surprise

Anticipated vs. apparent capabilities. In spite of the intelligence community's initial confidence in its assessment of the August 31, 1998, launch, subsequent investigations proved that assessment inaccurate in important respects. The official DPRK news agency released a statement shortly after the launch claiming that it had not been a ballistic missile test but an attempted space launch and that the DPRK had successfully placed a small satellite into low Earth orbit.[73] Skeptical of North Korea's claim, US analysts nonetheless reexamined the data from the test. On September 15, DOD officials announced, "We believe that North Korea attempted to launch a satellite and failed."[74] Others, such as the Japanese Defense Agency, continued to view the event as a multistage missile test. Shortly after the DOD announcement, US defense and intelligence officials reportedly judged that despite Pyongyang's claims to the contrary, the DPRK's attempt had ultimately faltered because of a third-stage failure.[75] As the story unfolded, three technical aspects of the TD-1 launch came as surprises to the intelligence community: the solid-fuel third stage, the new, single-nozzle first-stage engine, and the satellite itself.

Although it may not have worked exactly as intended, the TD-1's third stage was a major advance for the North Korean program. Prior to the TD-1, all North Korean missiles had been single-stage vehicles. Some analysts, such as Joseph Bermudez, have argued that the third stage was adapted from an HQ-2/SA-2 surface-to-air missile and represented the first solid-fuel motor North Korea had employed.[76] Equally significant was the fact that the TD-1 underwent successful stage separation in flight while maintaining stability, a technical feat of which most US analysts did not believe North Korea capable.[77] David Wright, for instance, argued that "staging is commonly assumed to be a significant technical hurdle" for aspiring proliferators, requiring "a more complicated guidance and control system" than that needed for less complicated missiles, such as the Scud. Wright noted that China, however, when faced with a similar staging problem, had found a relatively simple solution to this presumably complex issue.[78] Whether or not China (or another state) had shared its solution with the North Korean scientists, the launch had "demonstrated the most important elements of long-range missile technology," including "successfully separating three stages."[79] CIA Director Tenet argued similarly in his February 1999 threat assessment to Congress: "North Korea's three-stage Taepo-Dong 1 . . . demonstrated technology that, with the resolution of some important technical issues, would give North Korea the ability to deliver a very small payload to intercontinental ranges including parts of the United States although not very accurately."[80]

A related technical surprise was the post-test revelation that the TD-1 had a single-engine first stage. Prior to the test, analysts reportedly had assessed that a cluster of four Scud engines powered the TD-1. Conventional wisdom held that clustering the engines was the best course of action, if not the only one, open to the DPRK that did not involve designing a completely new engine. About a year after the test launch, North Korea publicly displayed its TD-1, confirming its "single engine exhaust."[81] Echoing the Rumsfeld Commission's findings, Joseph Bermudez concluded that the engine was new, based on a scaling up of the original Scud engine, possibly with the assistance of former Soviet missileers.[82]

A third surprise was the existence and attempted orbiting of the satellite itself. Pyongyang claimed that the satellite, named Kwangmyongsong 1, had successfully been placed in orbit. However, neither US nor other observers have publicly reported evidence that the satellite had achieved this feat. Nevertheless, it would appear that despite the extreme poverty and hardship in North Korea, and in the context of considerable international humanitarian relief efforts, the leadership of that state decided to undertake a satellite program four or five years prior to the attempted launch.[83] One possible motivation is competition with South Korea, which received international acclaim when it launched its second research satellite in 1993. The DPRK satellite was reportedly developed with Chinese assistance, and such assistance allegedly continues with the Kwangmyongsong 2 satellite.[84] The depth of North Korea's commitment to a space program, especially after the death of Kim Il Sung, is uncertain, but the reputed Chinese influence on Kwangmyongsong 1 is indicative of a troubling pattern of foreign assistance and contacts with other proliferant states in North Korean missile and space programs.[85]

Foreign assistance. The connections noted between the DPRK and other countries highlight the importance of technology and information suppliers and how they factored into North Korean technical achievements. Indeed, such foreign connections were a feature of the North Korean missile program from its inception. Throughout the program, North Korea benefited from covert contacts with China, Russia, and other supplier states. At the same time, some assistance was obtained by diverting materials legitimately imported from countries like Japan.[86] According to the CIA, even after the launch "North Korea continued procurement of raw materials and components for its ballistic missile programs from various foreign sources, especially through North Korean firms based in China," and "firms in China have provided dual-use missile-related items, raw materials, and/or assistance to . . . North Korea."[87] Together, these activities significantly expedited the DPRK's ballistic missile development efforts.

Chinese–North Korean cooperation on missile development programs is longstanding. In the mid- to late 1970s China and North Korea began to collaborate on the development of a ballistic missile known as the DF-61.[88] This cooperation soon ended because of a change in the political climate in Beijing, but the episode provided North Korean scientists and technicians with valuable experience. Moreover, although the DF-61 program was canceled, it appears that the links remained intact and that China continued to export technology to that state. In 1994 the DIA reportedly concluded that a significant type and quantity of Chinese missile-related technology was flowing to North Korea. The DIA highlighted similarities between the North Korean TD-2 and the Chinese CSS-2.[89] Others, such as Joseph Bermudez, argue that throughout the 1990s DPRK missile scientists traveled to China for training and possible technology exchange.[90] Not surprisingly, the PRC has denied such allegations.

The composite open-source record suggests that not only have these types of exchanges evidently continued but other weapons-related materials and technologies have been transferred to North Korea. In 1998, for instance, China reportedly supplied North Korea with special steel that could be used to manufacture missile frames.[91] Similarly, a 1999 report suggested that China had shipped "accelerometers, gyroscopes and special high-technology machinery" to North Korea, items that could be used to improve guidance systems and missile-fabrication techniques.[92] Additional shipments of fiber-optic gyroscopes and specialty steel followed later that same year.[93] In the view of the intelligence community, China remains an important supplier of material and expertise for North Korea's missile efforts.[94] These transfers continue despite numerous US protests and repeated Chinese promises to uphold the spirit of control regimes, including the MTCR (see chapter 2).

Other reports allege Russian involvement, both direct and indirect, in North

Korean programs. These allegations focus on attempts by North Korean proxy agents to recruit former Soviet missile designers and builders. The issue of a Russian brain drain became more alarming in October and November 1992, when Russian police intercepted more than sixty Russian missile scientists reportedly departing Moscow for North Korea.[95] A Russian national apparently employed by the DPRK government and posing as a Russian government official had recruited the scientists, many of whom were from the Makayev Design Bureau.[96] Affiliated with the Russian Ministry of Defense, this bureau was responsible for the design of the Scud missiles, as well as for the design of several Soviet submarine-launched ballistic missiles.

More recently, a German missile expert has suggested that rather than being indigenous designs or improvements on the Scud, the DPRK's missiles are actually made from Russian components that are merely assembled in the DPRK.[97] John Pike, of the Federation of American Scientists, similarly concluded that the design of the North Korean missile was "clearly a knockoff of the [Russian] SS-4," but he did not attribute this to the use of components brought directly from Russia. In fact, Pike argues that Russian involvement in the DPRK program ended in the early 1990s, and while the Soviet Union (and, through at least the early 1990s, Russia) may have been involved early in Pyongyang's efforts, "the paper trail ended eight years ago."[98] Others, such as Henry Sokolski, disagree, concluding that Russia continues to indirectly assist the DPRK. Russia is providing significant assistance to Iran's ballistic missile program, and Sokolski suspects that some of that knowledge may reach North Korea, at least indirectly, through its Tehran contacts.[99] As a result of the substantial Russian and Chinese assistance to North Korea over the years, in 2001 the intelligence community judged that "North Korea is nearly self-sufficient in developing and producing ballistic missiles."[100]

Other countries that have provided assistance to the DPRK's ballistic missile programs are part of an emerging rogue network of WMD and missile proliferators who share technology, funding, expertise, and other resources.[101] The Rumsfeld Commission found that these states "have increased incentives to cooperate with one another."[102] While NIE 95-19 called "foreign assistance" a "wildcard," the commission found that "extensive technical assistance" was readily available from foreign sources.[103] The commission also noted that through "trade and their own indigenous efforts, these second-tier powers are on the verge of being able to provide to one another, if they have not already done so, the capabilities needed to develop long-range ballistic missiles."[104]

External financial and material assistance, especially from Middle Eastern states, was a feature of the North Korean missile program from its earliest days. The DPRK's Scud-based program began in the late 1970s, when North Korea imported Scud missiles from Egypt in order to reverse engineer them.[105] In the 1980s, during the Iran-Iraq War, Iran provided financial assistance to North Korea's Scud programs in return for finished products, establishing a financial and supply relationship that continues today.[106] Pakistan also maintains a longstanding relationship with North Korea, one that dates back to the 1970s and involves the transfer of not only missile technology but also, reportedly, nuclear technology.[107] The Nodong program received significant assistance from both Pakistan and Iran, which subsequently produced their own versions of the North Korean missile.[108] In this vein, Iran and Pakistan have conducted launches with missiles that are based on the Nodong, providing data to North Korean scientists and diminishing the need to conduct further tests in North Korea.[109] While Russian and especially Chinese assistance have greatly facilitated the North Korean missile program, the recent collaboration between Iran, Pakistan, and the DPRK in missile development suggests that other states may be contributing to or already benefiting from the Taepodong program.[110] In David Fulghum's view, "The evidence points to Russian-derived technology paid for and supplied via Iran."[111]

Alternative pathways. That North Korea's technological advances have surprised both intelligence and nongovernmental specialists illustrates clearly that aspiring missile proliferators may not follow the Soviet or American development models with respect to either their technological pathways or their deployment timelines. While the US experience in developing ballistic missiles was characterized by high technical standards and extensive flight testing prior to deployment, the North Korean case suggests that other states may pursue different paths or uphold different standards. To assume that there is a single pathway or development process is to mirror image. As the Rumsfeld Commission concluded, "Newer ballistic missile and weapons of mass destruction . . . development programs no longer follow the patterns initially set by the U.S. and the Soviet Union. These programs require neither high standards of missile accuracy, reliability and safety nor large numbers of missiles and therefore can move ahead more rapidly."[112] Echoing this finding, Robert Walpole, the national intelligence officer for strategic and nuclear programs, subsequently testified on a central judgment of the 1999 NIE on this issue: "Emerging long-range missile powers do not appear to rely on robust test programs to ensure a missile's accuracy and reliability."[113]

Moreover, the DPRK programs benefit from legacy technologies rather than requiring innovative research and development. Simple and proven hardware and software are likely to have a higher reliability rate than unproven technologies and are likely to require less extensive testing of components or systems.[114] The baseline technology for the North Korean missile program is the Soviet-designed Scud missile; all North Korean missiles, at least through the Nodong series, appear to represent improvements on and evolutions of the foundational Scud design, in service for almost forty years and based on World War II–era, liquid-fueled rocket technology. In this seamless view, the TD-1 missile represents the latest step in a growing line of DRPK ballistic missiles with increasingly longer ranges, from rudimentary copies of the Soviet Scud missile up through the TD-2, currently under development.

Parallels to North Korea's Nodong program are evident in the development of the TD-1. The Nodong missile, in either its Nodong-1 or Nodong-2 variant, is widely believed to constitute the first stage of the TD-1. Both missiles are based on Scud technology and underwent rapid, truncated development programs. According to the open literature, the Nodong was successfully test-launched only once. That one 1993 test launch reportedly reached five hundred kilometers, which was apparently successful enough for North Korea to deploy the system in the 1995–97 time frame and to export the missile abroad.[115] Official US statements confirm that the Nodong development program is likely completed, but uncertainty remains about the number and location of actual deployments.[116] The Rumsfeld Commission judged that "the No Dong was operationally deployed long before the U.S. Government recognized that fact."[117]

Sales of the missiles and transfer of components and technology to Pakistan and Iran started as early as 1995. While Jung-Hoon Lee and Il Hyun Cho estimate that the DPRK had deployed four brigades of nine launchers each by 1999, Joseph Bermudez believes that it had produced from fifty to one hundred Nodong missiles by then, perhaps twelve to twenty-four of which were sold abroad. Other estimates range from a low of a half-dozen to a high of more than one hundred deployed Nodong missiles fielded since the 1993 test.[118] Given the likely prospect of continued collusion between Pyongyang, Tehran, and Islamabad, it is possible that the TD-1 will proceed along the lines of the Nodong.[119] Indeed, Pyongyang reportedly announced shortly after the August

1998 test that it would be ready to export the TD-1 beginning in 2000 for a price of $6 million each.[120] While the DPRK's voluntary test and export moratorium helped diminish the urgency of this threat, a resumption of exports would profoundly affect the security environment in regions of acute proliferation concern.

Coping with Surprise

Surprise is and will likely remain a key feature of the proliferation landscape, a feature for which the intelligence, policy, and operational communities must prepare. In his 2001 confirmation hearing for the post of secretary of defense, Donald Rumsfeld highlighted the "importance of considerably improving our intelligence capabilities so that we know more about what people think and how they behave and how their behavior can be altered and what the capabilities are in this world."[121] The Indian and North Korean cases illustrate the political and technological dimensions of surprise and the difficulties it creates for both intelligence officials and policymakers alike. In the Indian case, a misreading of the BJP government's intention led the intelligence community to miss preparations for the nuclear test series. In the North Korean case, analysts underestimated the technical capabilities of that state's missile. Both events highlighted shortcomings in the intelligence community's ability to predict and deal with such situations.

Yet several years after these events there are mixed signs of progress with respect to the intelligence community's efforts to deal with surprise. The Jeremiah Commission recommended more rigorous analysis, realigning collection priorities, balancing human skills with technical collection means, better integration of capabilities, and an integrated management structure. The intelligence community has followed some of these recommendations, but it will take time to fully implement change.

At the same time, spurred in part by the recommendations of the Rumsfeld Commission, the intelligence community's assessment of the ballistic missile threat continues to improve in quality. For example, new information gained from the DPRK's 1998 TD-1 launch and the alternative technologies suggested by the Rumsfeld Commission prompted the intelligence community to reexamine its process for generating threat assessments. As a result, the assessed ballistic missile threat to US interests has undergone profound change. While a 1995 NIE assessed that "no country other than the major declared nuclear powers will develop a ballistic missile that could threaten the contiguous 48 states or Canada," in 2002 the NIC estimated that by 2015 the United States "most likely will face ICBM threats from North Korea, Iran, and possibly from Iraq."[122] In the view of William Schneider, a member of the Rumsfeld Commission, "The Intelligence Community has now given credible strategic warning of a ballistic missile threat to the United States."[123]

Proliferation surprise has not been limited to the Indian and North Korean cases discussed in this chapter or to the scope and achievements of the Soviet offensive biological weapons program discussed in chapter 3. And should CIA Director Tenet be proven correct, there are likely to be additional strategic and technical surprises ahead. Indeed, numerous factors underlie proliferators' ability to achieve surprise, including the potential overexposure of US intelligence efforts and capabilities, robust denial and deception efforts on the part of proliferators, and the persistence of mind-sets that may lead to flawed judgments or mirror imaging. As the Indian and DPRK cases demonstrate, these factors create constraints and difficulties for both intelligence analysts and policymakers alike.

In order to mitigate the effects of proliferation surprise, the United States "must prepare for a range of operating conditions and regional circumstances," moving toward a "capabilities-based" approach to defense planning.[124] Appropriately preparing for and mitigating the effects of surprise requires that the United States retool its collection and analytic capabilities. The Indian and North Korean cases show that there are inherent limitations to the ability of the intelligence community to understand the evolving intentions of potentially hostile nations and to ascertain their developing capabilities. The intelligence community should endeavor to implement key recommendations offered by Admiral Jeremiah, former (and future) Defense Secretary Donald Rumsfeld, former DCI John Deutch, and others, whose aggregate suggestions center on a number of core themes, among them the need to

- Retool intelligence capabilities, both human and technical, to meet emerging challenges. National technical means are useful for some aspects of intelligence collecting, but they cannot replace the value of HUMINT in discerning intentions; greater focus on human asset recruitment appears to be warranted.
- Reexamine the methods by which assessments are generated with the goal of generating broader-based threat assessments, supplementing

traditional analysis with red-teaming, better integrating regional and functional analysis, and making better use of all-source analysis.

- Develop and field new capabilities in intelligence collection and analysis technologies and seek to better integrate planning for collection planning against priority proliferation targets.

- Err on the side of overreporting, since the consequences of a missed warning can be much more serious than those of a false alarm. The director of central intelligence should ensure that intelligence is responsive to the needs of policymakers and that regular and frequent conferences between policy agencies and the intelligence community continue. The policy community, in turn, should promulgate and periodically review guidance to ensure clear tasking priorities for collection and analysis, seeking to appropriately balance the requirements of current intelligence with those of longer-term research and analysis.

- Develop sufficient proliferation-related depth and analytic capabilities throughout the intelligence community. Without in-depth, informed, and objective analysis, the targeting of collection assets will be poor and the information collected will not be translated into useful, policy-relevant intelligence. Sound analysis must consider both the technical aspects of WMD and missile development, acquisition, and production processes and the regional and indigenous political and security concerns that lead nations to acquire them.[125]

CHAPTER 5

Intelligence Sharing

Prospective Risks, Potential Rewards

While the United States can, and should, seek to autonomously develop capabilities and plans to effectively counter the proliferation of nuclear, biological, and chemical weapons and the transfer of related technologies, the ultimate success of America's longstanding campaign against strategic weapons proliferation requires the active support of like-minded states. Indeed, information exchanges, combined exercises and military training, the development of shared policy positions, and coordinated economic leverage are key elements of both the non-and counterproliferation strategies pursued by the United States. To this end, both the nineteen-member North Atlantic Treaty Organization's WMD Centre (and related NATO entities) and a set of important bilateral relationships with key partners will factor heavily into the prospects for ultimate success in this complex, dynamic, and critical issue area.[1]

Yet there is an inherent tension between sharing sensitive information with partners in US efforts to counter WMD proliferation and the protection of intelligence sources and methods. Sometimes the risks of "burning" sources may outweigh the net benefits gained by concerted multilateral action. At other times US policy objectives can be met most expediently, and perhaps most soundly, through the judicious sharing or exchange of sensitive information with foreign governments or even, occasionally, particular international organizations. Indeed, the 1990s cases involving the high-profile US efforts to deal with Russian arms transfers to Iran and the saga of US support to UNSCOM are illustrative of the pitfalls and possibilities that result from intelligence sharing. In both cases the United States had clearly articulated policy goals, and senior policy officials determined that the best way to achieve these objectives was to actively engage the other parties involved, including the sharing of sensitive information.

In the Russia-Iran case, the United States wanted to end the potentially dangerous transfers of nuclear and ballistic missile technology and materials to

Iran, a state widely understood to be actively engaged in the development of WMD and ballistic missile delivery systems.[2] With respect to Iraq, the United States pursued a set of interrelated objectives: preventing the reconstitution of its WMD programs, diminishing the Iraqi threat to US friends and allies in the region, and encouraging the removal of Saddam Hussein from power. While the Russia-Iran case featured bilateral intelligence sharing, the UNSCOM case called for information sharing with an international organization. Yet in each case, while some successes are evident, the sharing of information alone proved insufficient to achieve the specified policy goals, and it appears that intelligence assets were compromised in the process. Like the global war on terrorism that commenced in September 2001,[3] the US campaign against strategic weapons proliferation must include the concerted efforts of friendly bilateral, "neutral" or third-party internationals and, perhaps on occasion, less-than-friendly states to improve the likelihood of ultimate success.

Russian Nuclear and Missile Transfers to Iran

With the 1991 collapse of the Soviet Union and the resulting economic dislocation, US officials became deeply concerned about the fate of the vast formerly Soviet arsenal and feared that both weapons-related technologies and expertise were at risk of diversion.[4] Of particular concern were nuclear- and missile-related transfers from Russian companies, institutes, and other "entities" to select regional states. While Iran has nuclear and missile aspirations, Tehran has not, despite considerable investment, achieved the indigenous capability to develop, produce, and maintain either nuclear weapons or medium- or longer-range ballistic missiles.[5] Rather, it remains largely reliant on technologies and expertise supplied by Russia, China, and North Korea to advance its nuclear and missile programs. In the view of Stephen Sestanovich, "Iran is taking advantage of Russia's economic woes and large reservoir of defense technology and scientific talent to accelerate development of an indigenous ballistic missile capability."[6] By the end of the 1990s, Russian and other assistance had significantly enhanced the Iranian programs.

Calibrating the US Response to a Fluid Security Environment

In an effort to prevent further transfers, US officials engaged in high-level consultations both to inform Russian authorities of US concerns and to assist the Russian government in taking steps to halt the flow of technologies and expertise.[7] Beginning in 1995 and continuing through the end of the decade, this issue was on the agenda of virtually every presidential summit (often annual) and meeting of the vice-presidential bilateral commission (often semi-annual). The Clinton administration also appointed two successive special envoys to help resolve the issue favorably. One key facet of the US strategy to stem these transfers involved the sharing of sensitive information with authorities at the highest levels of the Russian government. Another was the deliberate policy to incentivize Russia through a range of economic benefits and other cooperative programs. While many of these programs attempted to redress the hemorrhaging of technologies and expertise to Iran, over time, select recipients of US assistance also came to be suspected of involvement in such transfers.

Indeed, US policymakers were informed by the intelligence community of the unsavory, proliferation-related illicit activities of a number of Russian companies and institutes. These entities were, in Ambassador Robert Gallucci's understanding, "in some cases institutes, in some cases universities, in some cases for-profit organizations that have roots back in the Soviet system and some not."[8] The Russian Space Agency (RSA), for instance, received both significant US assistance for projects relating to the International Space Station and substantial US contracts for commercial satellite launches.[9] Glavkosmos, a commercial RSA subsidiary, became suspect over time because of allegations of assistance to the Iranian missile program (see table 5.1).

Among the nuclear-related concerns was an agreement by Russia's Ministry of Atomic Energy (Minatom) to complete two Iranian nuclear reactors at Bushehr. Construction of these reactors had been started by a German company hired by Shah Reza Pahlavi but halted by the Shah's overthrow and the Iran-Iraq War in the 1980s. In the early 1990s Russia signed a contract with the new Iranian government to complete the two reactors using Russian designs, which led to additional agreements for closer nuclear cooperation between Russia and Iran and the construction of additional reactors (see table 5.2). While civil cooperation in the nuclear arena is not proscribed by international convention, US analysts long suspected that Iran's civilian nuclear cooperation would extend, whether formally or tacitly but clandestinely in either case, to the military sphere.[10]

Some, such as Minatom spokesman Vyacheslav Syachev, insinuate a sinister motive for US allegations of Russian proliferation, declaring that "competition . . . makes [the United States] speak of mythical Iranian nuclear threats,

Table 5.1. Russian transfers of missile-related materials and technology to Iran

Category	Recipient	Equipment	Manufacturer	Exporter	Status
Materials and components	Unknown	21 tons of maraging steel	Unknown, possibly Inor Production Association	MOSO and Yevropalas 2000	Intercepted
	Unknown	Composite material used for ballistic missile warheads	NII Grafit	Unknown	Intercepted
	Unknown	Turbopumps for RD-214 (SS-4) liquid-fuel rocket engine	Samara State Scientific and Production Enterprise	Samara State Scientific and Production Enterprise	Canceled
	Unknown	Components of RD-214 (SS-4) liquid-fuel rocket engine	NPO Trud and NPO Energomash	Unknown	Alleged
	Unknown	Unspecified missile-guidance components	Polyus Scientific Research Institute	Unknown	Alleged
	Unknown	620 kg of special alloys and foils	Inor Production Association	Rosvooruzheniye	Alleged
Manufacturing and testing equipment	Unknown	Wind tunnel and related facilities	Russian Central Aero-hydrodynamic Institute (TsAGI)	Rosvooruzheniye	Alleged
	Unknown	Unspecified missile-manufacturing equipment	Inor Production Association	Rosvooruzheniye	Alleged
	Unknown	Measurement equipment used in rocket engine tests	NPO Trud	Unknown	Alleged

Training and know-how	Sanam Industries Group	Training of Iranian students in missile design	Baltic State Technical University and Moscow Aviation Institute	Suspended
	Unknown	Missile specialists traveled to Iran under false documents	Komintern Plant, Tikhomirov Institute	Suspended
	Unknown	Training of Iranian students in missile design	Bauman Moscow State Technical University	Unknown
	Unknown	Suspected transfer of dual use technology	Glavkosmos	Unknown
	Unknown	Recruitment of Russian experts to work on Iranian missile programs	Federal Security Service (FSB)	Alleged

Source: Adapted from Fred Wehling, "Russian Nuclear and Missile Exports to Iran," *Nonproliferation Review* 6, no. 2 (1999): 135, 139.

Table 5.2. Russian transfers of nuclear-related materials and technology to Iran

Category	Recipient	Equipment	Manufacturer	Exporter	Status
Reactors	Bushehr Nuclear Power Plant	One VVER-1000 light water power reactor	Zarubezhatomenergostroy	Minatom	Ongoing
	Bushehr Nuclear Power Plant, possibly others	Three additional power reactors	Zarubezhatomenergostroy	Minatom	Under negotiation
	Atomic Energy Agency of Iran	One 30–50 MWt research reactor	Zarubezhatomenergostroy	Minatom	Under negotiation
	Unknown	One 40 MWt heavy water research reactor	Probably Zarubezhatom-energostroy	Scientific Research and Design Institute of Energy Technologies (NIKIET)	Under negotiation
	Unknown	One APWS-40 desalinization plant	Experimental Machine Building Design Bureau (OKBM)	Minatom	Unknown
Enrichment, mining, and milling	Unknown	Uranium conversion facility	Unknown	NIKIEET and Mendeleev University of Chemical Technology	Under negotiation
	Atomic Energy Agency of Iran	Gas centrifuge plant	Unknown	Minatom	Canceled
	Alleged facilities in Yazd Province	Assistance to mining and milling operations	Unknown	Unknown	Unknown
Nuclear materials	Bushehr Nuclear Power Plant	LEU fuel rods for VVER-1000 reactor	Novosibirsk Chemical Concentrate Plant	Minatom	Planned
	Unknown	2,000 tons of natural uranium	Unknown	Minatom	Unknown
Training and know-how	Bushehr Nuclear Power Plant	Training for physicists and technicians		Kurchatov Institute and Novovoronezh Nuclear Power Plant	Ongoing

which are not confirmed by the facts."[11] Similarly, in the ballistic missile area, US attention was focused on reports of transfers of the Soviet SS-4 IRBM technology and its RD-214 rocket engine, special materials such as maraging steel for missile components, and educational opportunities for Iranian students at Russian educational and research institutes. Yuri Savelyev, rector of the Baltic State Technical University, warned that if Russia did not provide the technical assistance, "North Korea and China are ready to offer Iran help with new rocket programs."[12]

US officials approached their Russian counterparts with concerns about these and other transfers, offering an array of incentives in return for Russian tightening of export controls. As part of these efforts to persuade Russian officials of the scope and gravity of the problem, senior US officials shared specific intelligence with Russian officials on particular transfers and the entities involved. According to Ambassador Gallucci, "The process was one, quite frankly, of the U.S. offering demarches to Russia about activities that we saw, sharing information and intelligence about what we saw was happening between these entities and the Iranian missile program."[13]

The underlying US presumption was apparently that of a benign but weak Russian state that was either unaware of the activities of these companies and commercial enterprises or simply unable to prevent these transactions.[14] As a senior White House official reportedly stated in 1997, "You cannot overemphasize the extent to which the Russian Government exercises imperfect control over Russian individuals and entities that are looking to make money in order to survive." As such, "the Russian government has limited resources and ability to control this problem."[15]

During the early 1990s, US officials encouraged Russian leaders to move toward the implementation of tighter export controls to strengthen the legal basis for halting these types of transfers. At the same time, US officials asked Russian authorities to take steps to halt some of the more egregious offenders and provided intelligence to bolster US claims. In Henry Sokolski's view: "The assumption was that if we talked with the Russians about proliferation, if we showed them what was going on, they would act. And we did. We gave them very good intelligence. . . . We asked them, look, here's the intelligence on what we call the dirty dozen of activities that we still think are going on, please clean them up. . . . We hoped that if we shared, if we were open, that they would respond. That if we dealt simply with the top, the bottom would follow."[16]

These demarches involved high-level meetings between US and Russian officials. Twice in 1997 Ambassador Frank Wisner was dispatched to Russia as a special envoy to discuss the proliferation problem with the Russian government, followed by additional visits by his successor, Ambassador Gallucci. In parallel, this issue became a regular feature on the agenda of the U.S.-Russian Commission on Economic and Technological Cooperation, established in 1993 to increase US-Russian bilateral cooperation on space, energy, trade and investment, defense conversion, health and medicine, science and technology, the environment, and agriculture.[17] Through this medium, Vice President Al Gore dealt directly with his counterpart on particular US proliferation concerns, as in February 1997, when the United States presented specific evidence that Iran had tested a missile engine based on the Soviet-era SS-4 missile.[18] Similarly, in a May 1995 presidential summit President Clinton reportedly passed "a six-page intelligence report on Iran's nuclear bomb-making ambitions" to his counterpart in an effort to convince the Russian president to cancel the estimated $1 billion nuclear deal with Iran.[19] While the United States evidently has longstanding intelligence-sharing arrangements with its closest allies—for example, Canada, Australia, New Zealand, and the United Kingdom—it was a novel feature of the post–Cold War US-Russia security "partnership" articulated by the Clinton administration.[20]

Intelligence Sharing: Process and Outcomes

With reference to unclassified sources alone, it is difficult to determine the specific intelligence data passed to the Russians or, of course, the quality of the information provided. However, it is possible, through a close examination of official statements and related media accounts, to piece together a rough outline of where particular intelligence reports may have originated and what information was shared. This intelligence was characterized by officials cited in news accounts as "what help is coming from which institute" in order "to show them the reasons for our concerns."[21] Sources and methods used to obtain information on the entities involved and on several of the suspected transfers reportedly included the use of undercover assets and contacts within Russian industry, some of whom were directly involved in suspected transfers.[22]

Moreover, in addition to US sources and methods, media accounts suggest that some of the information passed to the Russians originated with Israeli sources. Israel apparently obtained "significant, credible intelligence" about Iran's WMD and missile intentions and foreign assistance in those programs from its covert agents operating in Iran and shared its findings with US intelligence agencies, which reportedly corroborated it with their own information.[23] These reports named specific Russian companies, institutes, and enterprises that were engaged in suspicious transactions and exchanges with the Iranians. For example, one 1997 *Washington Times* article, based at least in part on Israeli information, discussed explicit cooperation between three Russian entities and the Iranian Shahid Hemmat Industries Group.[24] The contracts between these three Russian entities were part of cooperative efforts between Russian entities and the Iranian Defense Industries Organization in the area of liquid-fueled ballistic missiles.[25]

Later that same year, US officials reportedly learned from Israeli intelligence "the names of senior Russian officials involved" in assisting Iran's missile program and "identified the Russian companies working on the project."[26] The information also reportedly included "a copy of the $7 [million] contract between a Russian company and the Iranian organisation in charge of the missile project."[27] With the Israeli contribution, the list of entities with suspicious ties to Iran had grown to more than twenty by July 1997.[28] At least some of this information was reportedly passed along to Russian officials; at times it dealt with transfers of specific technologies or missile components, including the alleged transfer of technology related to the RD-214 engine of the SS-4 missile.[29]

How successful was this process in halting Russian transfers to Iran? A judgment on this key question is predicated on assessments of two related issues. First, to what extent did intelligence sharing and cooperation with the Russian government lead to a decline or cessation in the transfers of nuclear and missile technology and components to Iran? Presumably, significant steps taken by the Russian government to crack down on the entities of concern could be considered a measure of policy success. Second, to what extent were the goals of intelligence sharing met without undue consequences to US intelligence sources and methods? Arguably, US efforts to halt proliferation to Iran could not be considered entirely successful if they resulted in the elimination or neutralization of specific sources or particular methods that would allow US intelligence agencies to detect any future activities either sanctioned by the Russian government or conducted on an unauthorized basis by semiautonomous Russian entities.

Russian actions. After the United States began sharing intelligence with senior Russian officials, there were some positive signs of Russian cooperation in containing transfers to Iran. The Russian government appeared to be taking US requests to halt transfers to Iran seriously and acting on the intelligence provided by US envoys. For instance, in 1997 the Russian Federal Security Service reportedly canceled a contract between Iran and the Scientific Production Association to develop missile motors; foiled an effort to pass classified materials on aviation engineering, probably from the Central Aerohydrodynamic Institute (TsAGI); and expelled a representative of the Iranian embassy in Moscow for allegedly attempting to obtain documentation on missile designs.[30] In 1998, Azerbaijani customs officials seized twenty-two tons of maraging steel allegedly of Russian origin bound for Iran.[31] Ambassador Wisner concluded in January 1998 that "for their own interests, the Russians are getting serious about closing the gap between what they've repeatedly said and what's actually happening."[32] Ambassador Gallucci similarly concluded later that year that "steady progress" on the part of the Russians was evident from the summer of 1997 through the summer of 1998, resulting in "a smaller and smaller number of problem cases."[33] The policy take, as viewed by White House nonproliferation specialists, was that "the Russians have made commitments to us. . . . And sometimes timely interventions can make a difference. So we're trying to ascertain what they know and help them to stop it."[34]

In this context, Russian authorities also took concrete steps toward improving export controls. US pressure helped Russian officials in this task, especially as it applied to establishing norms and regulations to prevent proliferation.[35] In January 1998 the Russian government enacted a system of comprehensive "catch-all" export controls that allowed the government to "consider any issue that does not formally fall under the restrictions of export control regimes but relates to dual-use technology."[36] In turn, these "catch-all" controls directly influenced new export control legislation that took effect in July 1999 requiring the establishment of internal export control compliance programs at Russian firms that routinely trade in sensitive military and dual-use technologies.[37]

Russian authorities appeared ready to take action against those entities that were in violation of these new export controls and to crack down on suspect shipments destined for Iran. In July 1998 the official Russian news service, TASS, reported that the Russian Government Commission on Export Control was examining accusations of export control violations by numerous Russian entities and announced that the government would press criminal charges against any company found to be in violation.[38] These companies included Glavkosmos, the INOR Scientific Production Center, the Grafit State Scientific

Research Institute, the Polyus Scientific Research Institute, the Tikhomirov Instrument-Building State Research Institute, the Komintern Plant, the MOSO Company, Evropalas 2000, and the Baltic State Technical University.[39] The Komintern Plant, the MOSO Company, and Evropalas 2000 were involved in an intercepted shipment intended for Iran of maraging steel, a special steel alloy that can be used in producing missile frames and fuel tanks.[40] The INOR Scientific Production Center also allegedly shipped the special alloy to Iran using an intermediary that declared the shipment was zinc-plated iron.[41] Glavkosmos, the Grafit State Scientific Research Institute, and the Polyus Scientific Research Institute were suspected of shipping missile-related material and technology, such as laser gyroscopes and basalt fibers.[42] The Baltic State Technical University, which administered an educational exchange program for Iranian students, received significant attention from Russian authorities, being investigated on national-security grounds first in July 1998 and again in December 1999 at the behest of the United States.[43] Following the second investigation, Russian authorities terminated the program after determining "that Baltic State was indeed transferring expertise that could be useful to Iran's missile program" and took similar action against educational exchange programs at the Bauman State Technical University and the Moscow Aviation Institute.[44]

Russian authorities also canceled contracts with Iran for the construction of facilities or the transfers of technologies that were suspected of being destined for Iran's nuclear and missile programs. These included a wind tunnel for Iran's missile program to be built by TsAGI and Rosvooruzheniye, the state arms export agency, and a contract to supply missile manufacturing equipment and components from the INOR Scientific Production Center.[45] Moreover, US authorities also attempted to prompt Russian authorities to act on specific shipments, as in September 2000, when the United States attempted to convince the Russian government not to sell Iran technology and equipment for a laser isotope separation plant.[46] Russian authorities agreed to halt the sale as a "goodwill gesture" to the United States but argued that the laser system would not contribute to Iran's nuclear weapons efforts and insisted that the laser was intended "only for medical, industrial, and scientific purposes."[47]

More recently, in January 2001, US and Israeli officials alerted Russian authorities to a suspicious shipment of high-strength aluminum destined for Iran. Although Russian authorities inspected the ship and declared that its cargo was destined for use in a joint Ukrainian-Iranian civilian aircraft program, US and

Israeli officials suspected that it was destined for the manufacture of gas centrifuge rotor blades.[48]

Russian government complicity? According to Prime Minister Viktor Chernomyrdin, through 1998 "Moscow ha[d] not transferred to Iran or any other country missile or nuclear technologies in violation of the prevailing international regime."[49] One year later Prime Minister Sergei Stepashin echoed this view, arguing, despite an abundance of both open-source and covertly collected information shared by the United States, that "nobody has proved that it is Russia who supplies missile technologies to Iran."[50] While the underlying US presumption seemed to be that the Russian government was not involved in the illicit transfers to Iran, the specter of a quasi-privatized, obviously weak or incapable state raised the possibility that sensitive Russian technologies or technical know-how could leak either without the knowledge of the relevant Russian authorities or with their tacit complicity.

Former CIA Director James Woolsey takes the argument one step further, suggesting that a Russian individual could at the same time be an executive in a major Russian firm, a Russian intelligence officer operating under cover, and a senior member of a Russian organized crime group.[51] As Russian transfers continue, the CIA warns that the Russian "government's commitment, willingness, and ability to curb proliferation-related transfers" are suspect.[52] Others have argued that Russia retains a deliberate policy of "selective proliferation."[53] Many simply do not believe then Prime Minister Yevgeny Primakov's 1999 statement that Russia is "doing everything to prevent leakage of weapons of mass destruction" and is "abiding by absolutely every international standard concerning export."[54]

Others, such as the Foreign Ministry's Victor Mizin, argued that "there is no such thing as a private or independent defense manufacturing facility. . . . They are tightly controlled by the Ministry of Defense."[55] Thus, if groups were "constantly undermining" the regimes that should regulate Russian-Iranian contacts in the missile area, at least a degree of state complicity was suspect.[56] Indeed, some of the entities affected by US sanctions or Russian government investigations claimed that they had carried out their activities with the full knowledge of Russian authorities. For example, Baltic State Technical University's Yuri Savelyev argued that his "educational" program to teach Iranian engineering students advanced missile building techniques had been created with the full knowledge of the Ministry of Defense and the Federal Security Service.[57]

To date, the senior-most Russian official to argue in this vein was Deputy Foreign Minister Yuri Maslyukov, who observed that US fears over Russian technology transfers to Iran were "entirely justified." In his view, "some of the cases that they [the Americans] have presented have turned out to be true," and there were possibly many ongoing Russo-Iranian exchanges that Russia had uncovered that the American government did not know about.[58] Not surprisingly, Maslyukov's comments were later "clarified" by the Russian government, and he was censured for them.

The Russian government's official response to such allegations is outright denial. Russian authorities have consistently requested additional intelligence from the United States concerning alleged transfers to Iran by Russian entities. When that intelligence has been provided by US officials, its accuracy has been questioned by government authorities, and the judgment that Iran has been pursuing weapons of mass destruction has equally been seen as suspect.[59] For instance, Vladimir Moskvin, a senior staff member of the Russian Ministry of Foreign Affairs, argued that the "periodically revealed sporadic contacts" between Russians entities and Iran were not part of a Russian government strategy and that in the future the United States "should provide as much factual backup as realistically possible."[60]

Similar arguments were also put forth by Russian nongovernmental organizations and meshed with the official government position that no such transfers had occurred. Vladimir Orlov, director of the Moscow-based PIR-Center for Policy Studies, for example, argued that "there is not a single confirmed fact of a leakage of critical materials and technologies from Russia to Iran." Instead, in his unsubstantiated opinion, there was "a pile of unsupported accusations of Russia in this regard, with references mostly to the US and Israeli intelligence sources."[61] One statement issued by the Federal Security Service went so far as to suggest that US spies who had provided information on illicit transfers might be "defective."[62]

Impact on sources and methods. In sharing sensitive information, senior policy officials calculated that the risks to intelligence sources and methods were outweighed by the prospective policy gains. Arguably, however, presenting such detailed intelligence data to the Russians led more to a diminished effectiveness of US assets than to an ultimately successful nonproliferation policy. As Russian officials learned of specific Israeli and US intelligence capabilities, they evidently began to take steps to counter these intelligence sources. According to Kenneth Timmerman, "The state security apparatus in Russia is . . . using information that [the United States] provided them in what used to be called the Gore-Chernomyrdin forum to better conceal the proliferation activities." In his view, the Russian security services had achieved a tremendous counterintelligence coups: "The more intelligence the United States shares with Russia on its missile transfers to Iran . . . the more skillful the Russians have become in disguising that activity."[63]

Both US and Israeli officials also expressed concern about the security implications of sharing critical intelligence with Russian authorities. As Representative Douglas Bereuter (R-NE), a member of the House Intelligence Committee, noted, "There is some evidence we did share information in the past which caused us to lose resources."[64] General David Ivry, a senior Israeli Ministry of Defense official, similarly lamented the sharing of intelligence in the Gore-Chernomyrdin Commission context, concluding that "whenever Gore provides more information to Chernomyrdin about the missile programs, we see the Russians seeking to identify the sources of that information and close them off."[65] One clear result was that suspect entities, while often suspending particular transactions, would be reincarnated elsewhere: "They shut down one company, and transfer its contracts to someone else."[66] Perhaps lending credence to this, one Russian news article published shortly after the United States imposed sanctions in 1998 noted that of the companies sanctioned, the MOSO Company "disappeared in 1998," the Moscow Aviation Institute "dissolved in 1995," and the location of another, Evropalas 2000, "has not been discovered."[67]

In addition to complicating future intelligence-collection efforts, the intelligence-sharing process likely resulted in the outright elimination of particular sources. Notwithstanding evident information gaps in the public domain, covert contacts apparently were an important source of information on Russo-Iranian transfers for both US and Israeli intelligence agencies. The open-source literature suggests at least one instance in which a clandestine source was eliminated as a result of intelligence passed to Russian authorities. Israeli intelligence provided to US officials and passed on to the Russians in late 1997 was reportedly so detailed that it inadvertently revealed the sources of the information contained in the report.[68] According to a senior Israeli military intelligence official, "From the intelligence point of view, it hurt. American efforts were compromised as well." In this assessment, "previous sources [were] no longer available," Israeli intelligence operations in both Iran and Russia had been "severely damaged," and both Russian and Iranian authorities had increased their vigilance as a result of the information provided.[69]

Transfers Continue

It became increasingly apparent over time that Russian transfers to Iran would continue indefinitely. In January 2000, for instance, the Russian government reaffirmed its nuclear agreements with Iran and its intention to expand nuclear cooperation between the two countries.[70] In November of that year Russia officially renounced a secret aide-mémoire signed by Gore and Chernomyrdin in 1995 committing Russia to halt conventional arms transfers to Iran by 1999.[71] Four months later Russia announced that it had negotiated a new multi-billion-dollar arms trade agreement with Iran.[72] The CIA warned in 2001 that Iran's success in gaining technology and materials from Russian entities had "helped accelerate Iranian development of the Shahab-3 MRBM, and continuing assistance likely supports Iranian efforts to develop new missiles and increase Tehran's self-sufficiency in missile production." Moreover, Russian assistance "enhances Iran's ability to support a nuclear weapons development effort even though the ostensible purpose of most of the assistance is for civilian applications."[73]

The Russian government's unwillingness to investigate problematic contacts between Russian entities and Iran also suggests a lack of resolve. While the Russian government reportedly began an investigation of nine entities identified by the United States in 1998, six months later Ambassador Gallucci lamented that the investigation "which was launched with such optimism, at least on our part . . . has not produced any real results in which there was a conclusion that anyone acted really inappropriately. There's been no prosecution."[74] Nor did the Russian investigations include what the United States considered to be key institutions in the transfer of technology to Iran, such as the RSA, Rosvooruzheniye, or the Federal Security Service.[75]

During 1998, in response to pressure from key members of Congress, the Clinton administration imposed sanctions on many of the entities in question, including those allegedly being investigated by the Russian government; by January 1999 twelve Russian entities had been sanctioned.[76] Russian officials countered by stating that the Russian Federal Security Service had thoroughly investigated three of the sanctioned companies and found no evidence of violations.[77] According to a statement issued by the Federal Security Service in

January 1999, "As a result of a very scrupulous investigation we can state that the . . . organizations [under investigation] have never violated the international requirements for export control and non-proliferation of weapons of mass destruction and means of rocket delivery."[78] Yet in Deputy Secretary of State Strobe Talbott's judgment, the problem of arms transfers to Iran was "getting worse, not better."[79]

Nor was this conclusion limited to government officials. Kenneth Timmerman, for instance, surmised that the Russian government and security services were well aware of the transfers of technology and expertise to Iran since they were responsible for approving academic exchanges, visa applications, and other special permits for access to classified materials.[80] "This is across the board; it's a Russian government effort," he concluded. "We're not talking about rogue efforts, we're not talking about isolated engineers. We're talking about efforts which have been sanctioned at the very highest levels of the Russian government."[81] Similarly, Fred Wehling judged that "credible reports continue to suggest that the Russian government has either turned a blind eye to the activities of Russian defense firms in this area or has actually assisted their efforts."[82] In Ambassador Gallucci's candid appraisal, by January 1999 "progress [had] come to a halt."[83]

An Intelligence-Sharing Postmortem

Despite intelligence sharing and high-level diplomatic pressure from the United States, Russia's transfers of technology, expertise, and materials to Iran's nuclear and ballistic missile programs continue. Though there were some apparent successes when the United States was able to prod Russian authorities to halt certain specific shipments, such as the shipment of maraging steel intercepted by Kazakhstan or the TsAGI wind-tunnel contract canceled by the Russian government in 1997, the aggregate pattern of Russian assistance continues. From an intelligence standpoint, it is likely that these few, small-scale successes were outweighed by the clear risks to collection methods and particular sources. From a policy standpoint, these interdictions, while laudable, were insufficient to declare positive resolution of the large-scale (and continuing) problem.

This raises an important consideration: the need to balance the actionability of intelligence products with the risks to those sources and methods. As with India's nuclear tests (see chapter 4), intelligence communicated to Russian authorities likely revealed US and Israeli capabilities and, in the process, contributed to improved Russian deception and denial efforts.

The fact that transfers did not end, serious and continuing allegations regarding the Russian government's complicity, and the potentially deleterious impact of intelligence sharing on sources and methods together suggest that the trade-offs made by the United States in pursuing its policy options did not achieve the desired outcome. In fact, with the refutation of the 1995 Gore-Chernomyrdin *aide-mémoire*, the strengthening of nuclear cooperation and renewed arms sales between Russia and Iran announced in 2000 and after, and the continued impact of Russian assistance on Iranian WMD and missile programs, it would appear that the opposite was achieved.

US-UNSCOM Relations and the Iraqi Arms Inspection Saga

Intelligence collaboration between the United States and UNSCOM was a timely and innovative approach to a tough proliferation problem. While bilateral information exchanges occur with some frequency, direct intelligence support to an international organization or multilateral intelligence sharing in general is less frequent. In this case, the goals of UNSCOM and the United States were generally in accord, as both sought to verifiably destroy Iraq's nuclear, biological, chemical, and longer-range missile programs. US officials decided that assisting UNSCOM in fulfilling its mandate furthered US policy goals vis-à-vis Iraq, and they determined that the potential payoff from supplying significant intelligence platforms and products to the inspectors outweighed the potential risks to sources and methods.

UNSCOM was unprecedented, and its mandate was ambitious. Whereas other international arms control treaties and inspection regimes relied on the consent of member states to carry out their activities, UNSCOM operated in a recalcitrant state, with a mandate for forcible, ultimately noncooperative, arms elimination. As the inspection process became increasingly confrontational in the 1990s, and as the intricate web of denial and deception that Iraq spun around its closely guarded WMD and missile programs grew more dense, UNSCOM and the United States began to cooperate more closely in intelligence collection and analysis. Ultimately, however, by the close of the decade, when UNSCOM ceased operations, neither entity had prevailed in the central objective of a verifiably WMD-free Iraq.

Iraq's WMD and Missile Programs and UNSCOM's Post–Gulf War Creation

The Iraqi WMD problem. The Iraqi invasion of Kuwait in August 1990 and the subsequent formation of a US-led coalition brought the issue of Iraq's WMD and ballistic missile programs to the forefront of the US agenda. During the force deployment of Operation Desert Shield and planning for Operation Desert Storm, coalition military planners became increasingly concerned about the potential threat posed by Iraq's WMD and ballistic missile capabilities (see table 5.3). Iraq's chemical weapons capabilities were generally understood by 1990 because of Iraq's extensive use of such weapons during its 1980–88 war with Iran. The war also demonstrated Iraqi interest in ballistic missiles both as means of delivering chemical weapons and as instruments of terror.[84] Iraq was also thought to be pursuing both biological and nuclear weapons, although there was little evidence available in 1990 to suggest the scope, status, or developmental timelines for such programs (see chapter 7).[85]

In this context, coalition planners anticipated that Iraq might use its special weapons in an effort to counter coalition forces. However, except for Scud missiles armed with conventional explosive and concrete warheads launched against Israel and Saudi Arabia, Iraq refrained from using these weapons during the air and ground campaigns.[86] With the coalition victory over Iraq, the Security Council sought to eliminate Iraqi WMD capabilities.

The ceasefire and UNSCOM's mandate. Measures to reduce Iraq's ability to threaten its neighbors were central to the postwar security agenda. UN Security Council Resolution 687, the ceasefire agreement that ended the conflict, required Iraq to "unconditionally accept the destruction, removal, or rendering harmless, under international supervision," of all its nuclear, chemical, and biological weapons and components, as well as all ballistic missiles with a range greater than 150 kilometers. UNSCOM was expressly created to ensure compliance. Inspections focused on Iraqi biological, chemical, and missile capabilities and were carried out in coordination with the IAEA, which was charged with uncovering and destroying Iraq's nuclear weapons program.

To aid UNSCOM and IAEA efforts to carry out this mandate, Iraq was required to provide UNSCOM with a declaration outlining the locations and details of the facilities, equipment, products, and other key attributes of its unconventional activities. This comprehensive documentation was intended to

Table 5.3. Principal Iraqi WMD targets during Operation Desert Storm

Samarra Chemical Weapons Production and Storage (10)	Qabatiyah Ammunition Storage
Habbaniyah Chemical Weapons Precursor Production I	Ash Shuyabah Ammunition Storage Northeast
Habbaniyah Chemical Weapons Precursor Production II	Ad Diwaniyah Ammunition and Storage (4)
Habbaniyah Chemical Weapons Precursor Production III	An Nasiriyah SW Ammunition Storage Point (4)
Salman Pak Biological Weapons Research and Production (4+)	Mosul Airfield
Abu Ghurayb Suspect Biological Weapons Production	Taji Ammunition Depot
Abu Ghurayb Biological Weapons Production/Vaccine Plant	H-3 Airfield
Taji Suspect Biological Weapons Storage	K-2 Airfield
Taji Suspect Biological Weapons Production	Kirkuk Airfield
Latifiyah Suspect Biological Weapons Production	Al Taqqadum Airfield
Al Qaim Superphosphorus Production Plant	Baghdad Nuclear Research Institute/ Al Tuwaitha
Kirkuk Ammunition Depot West	Al Jarrah Airfield
Habsaniyah Ammunition Depot	Qayyarah West Ammunition Depot
Tikrit Ammunition Depot	Tallil Airfield Chemical Weapons Storage Bunker
Karbalah Ammunition Storage Depot (1)	Kirkuk Storage & Ammunition Depot
Fallujah Ammunition Depot South (2)	Qayyarah West Airfield

Sources: DIA, "CBW Targets during Desert Storm," www.gulflink.osd.mil/declassdocs/dia/19950825/950825_049pgv_94d.html, accessed April 2001; CIA, Office of Weapons, Technology and Proliferation, "CIA Report on Intelligence Related to Gulf War Illnesses," 2 August 1996; Iraq Interagency Biological Warfare Working Group, "Targeting Priority against Iraq BW Facilities," 14 January 1991, www.gulflink.osd.mil/declassdocs/dia/19961031/961031_950811_0173pgv_91d.html, accessed April 2001; *Gulf War Air Power Survey*, vol. 2, *Operations and Effects and Effectiveness* (Washington, DC: GPO, 1993), pt. 2, p. 316.
Note: More than fifty-one targets are identified here; other targets are not referenced in open literature. Numbers in parentheses indicate multiple targets struck at one site.

serve as the baseline for destruction and dismantlement activities. As for chemical weapons, Iraq declared the Al Muthanna State Establishment Complex, a sprawling facility covering twenty-five square kilometers, as its sole CW research, development, production, and weapons-filling facility; identified CW storage facilities at the Al Bakr Air Base, the Al Matasim aerodrome, and the Al Fallujah Proving Ground; and detailed the agents and munitions that the country produced.[87] In the missile area, Iraq declared that it possessed fifty-two

Scud missiles with thirty chemical and twenty-three high-explosive warheads and ten mobile launchers.[88] With regard to biological weapons, the Iraqi declaration amounted to a single sentence: "Iraq does not possess any biological weapons or related items as mentioned [in UN Resolution 687]."[89] Finally, in the nuclear area, Iraq claimed that it did not possess any of the nuclear materials proscribed by the ceasefire resolution.[90]

Inspection complications. As UNSCOM began its inspections in mid-1991 to verify the Iraqi declarations, several key points regarding Iraq's WMD and missile programs became apparent. First, the infrastructure and facilities that Iraq had developed to research, develop, and produce WMD and ballistic missile delivery systems were far more extensive and advanced than previously estimated. Over time, UNSCOM inspections revealed that the coalition planners and other observers had significantly underestimated the true scope of Iraq's programs prior to the Gulf War.[91] Second, the inspections eventually exposed the incomplete nature of Iraq's first WMD and missile declarations. By October 1991, six months after the declaration, inspectors had discovered almost ten times the number of CW shells and bombs originally declared by Iraq.[92] Between 1992 and 1996 Iraq prepared at least four "full, final, and complete disclosures," each of which was rejected by UNSCOM experts as being not very full, far from final, and nowhere near complete.[93] Significant quantities of undeclared material increasingly challenged the notion that the entire UNSCOM disarmament exercise would be completed in a relatively brief period of time. The continuing requirement for inspections and the understanding that they might continue for some time contributed to the erosion of political will and support for the numerous rounds of confrontation between Iraq and UNSCOM.

Finally, and perhaps most importantly, Iraq made considerable efforts to interfere with the investigations and to conceal documentation and other evidence from UNSCOM inspectors. Iraqi personnel repeatedly attempted, often successfully, to deny UNSCOM inspectors access to facilities; documents and equipment were removed from suspect sites; and other facilities were thoroughly sanitized to preclude thorough investigations.[94] Further complicating the accounting process, Iraq also claimed to have unilaterally destroyed WMD munitions and materials prior to the commencement of UNSCOM inspections. Collectively, Iraqi actions constitute one of the most extensive denial and deception efforts ever mounted by a proliferant state.

Former IAEA inspector David Kay describes a system of concealment with four overlapping layers: a political layer; a procurement and acquisition layer, aimed at obtaining materials for Iraq's WMD programs while circumventing international export control regimes and concealing the true purpose of the purchases; a facilities and activities layer, designed to conceal the true nature of facilities involved in WMD and missile programs; and an inspections layer, charged with deceiving international inspectors.[95] Scott Ritter, formerly a senior UNSCOM official, recalled that the Iraqi leadership "opted to pay lip service to compliance" and in fact held a "high-level meeting in which Iraq made strategic plans for concealing the existence of their entire biological weapons program, their entire nuclear weapons program, the bulk of their modern chemical weapons production program, and their entire indigenous missile production capability."[96] As UNSCOM inspections progressed, increasing resources were required to counter the Iraqi concealment mechanism, prompting the development of new investigative tactics, more intrusive methods, and innovative information-collection capabilities and analytic processes.

The Information Assessment Unit. To this end, UNSCOM created the Information Assessment Unit (IAU). The IAU played an important role in planning and executing inspections, in directing aerial reconnaissance efforts, and in obtaining information from inspection reports, aerial surveillance, supporting states, the public media, and Iraqi declarations. In addition to data collection, the IAU was responsible for identifying gaps in UNSCOM's available information and for developing strategies to fill them. The IAU also had two major roles that related directly to intelligence sharing between UNSCOM and outside intelligence agencies. The IAU was responsible for maintaining contacts with the "relevant agencies" of supporting governments and for requesting and obtaining information from those agencies.[97] Supporting governments and their respective intelligence and commercial agencies possessed significant information, such as data from enterprises that had supplied materials and components to Iraqi programs, technical analysis capabilities, and other relevant intelligence data.[98]

The decision to rely on support from many different nations was a conscious one on the part of Rolf Ekeus, UNSCOM's first chairman. Tim Trevan, political adviser to the chairman through 1995, concluded that "one of Rolf's great strengths and one of his brilliant insights was that from the very first American intelligence brief he realized that UNSCOM could not afford to be totally dependent on one source—or in those days two sources, the United

States and the United Kingdom—because it could be vulnerable to being manipulated on the basis of intelligence handed to it."[99] According to UNSCOM officials, more than forty nations provided support to UNSCOM, offering "intelligence materials and equipment for gathering information relevant to [UNSCOM's] work," such as "experts, information, equipment, finance and in-kind help like laboratory analysis or helicopters."[100] In Ekeus's view the IAU "changed the character" of states' sharing of intelligence with UNSCOM "from a mere trickle to a broad stream of data, supported by professional and multi-layered cooperative efforts." It ultimately made UNSCOM "much better informed about most aspects of Iraq's activities related to its weapons of mass destruction programs than . . . any individual government."[101]

US intelligence support to UNSCOM. In addition to its role as liaison with supporting governments and outside intelligence agencies, the second major responsibility of the IAU was directing aerial surveillance operations on behalf of the executive chairman. This task required a strong link between UNSCOM and US intelligence agencies, a high-profile illustration of national-level intelligence support to the multinational organization. As David Kay suggests, this "marked a watershed in the willingness of the U.S. intelligence community to share with an international inspectorate its high-quality intelligence product, including a broad range of NTM [National Technical Means], HUMINT, and measurement and signature intelligence (MASINT), and equally the willingness of the UN system openly to receive and act upon such information."[102]

From the beginning, the UNSCOM leadership realized that aerial surveillance capabilities were a vital prerequisite for accurately verifying Iraq's WMD and missile declarations and for ongoing monitoring of key sites. The organization sought to acquire an aerial surveillance component that eventually included helicopters provided by Germany and Chile and high-altitude surveillance aircraft provided by the United States. The US contribution included an Air Force U-2 reconnaissance plane and pilot made available to UNSCOM beginning in August 1991.[103] The U-2 flights were an important addition to UNSCOM's efforts, and the information gathered during the flights was used to support on-site inspection planning, infrastructure monitoring and verification efforts, and the search for undisclosed facilities.[104] The executive chairman of UNSCOM was responsible for developing and approving the flight plans with the assistance of the IAU, once that unit came into being.[105]

Originally such missions were assigned on a priority basis, but the establishment and expansion of the IAU allowed UNSCOM to develop tasks focused on particular sites.[106] Based on identified UNSCOM monitoring requirements, the IAU typically generated plans for approximately two or three U-2 flights per week focusing on targets of specific interest. The executive chairman would then approve the plans and inform the Iraqis of the dates and plans of the flights.[107] After the flights were completed, the United States assisted the IAU in processing, assessing, and interpreting the resulting imagery.[108] The actual imagery became the property of UNSCOM, was independently assessed by UNSCOM analysts, and was retained at the IAU and UNSCOM offices in New York.[109] Because of the extensive use of the U-2 aircraft and "other independent monitoring assets," concludes former UNSCOM inspector Jonathan Tucker, "the locus of information and expertise on Iraq's WMD programs has shifted . . . from national intelligence agencies to the United Nations itself."[110]

UNSCOM Findings

UNSCOM performance through 1995. Despite Iraq's incomplete and misleading declarations and considerable deception and denial activities, UNSCOM made measured progress throughout the first four years of inspections, especially in the chemical weapons and ballistic missile areas. By early 1995 there was a sense of optimism among many UNSCOM staff members, and the UNSCOM leadership generally appeared satisfied with the progress that had been made.[111] A June 1995 UNSCOM report to the Security Council reiterated earlier findings that UNSCOM "has essentially completed the accounting of proscribed ballistic missile capabilities" and "has completed the destruction of Iraq's identified chemical weapon facilities, stockpiles and production equipment."[112] In the chemical arena, UNSCOM succeeded in uncovering and destroying 480,000 liters of chemical agents (including mustard, tabun, and sarin), more than 28,000 chemical munitions (shells, rockets, bombs, and missile warheads), and some 1.8 million liters and 1.04 million kilograms of 45 different CW precursor chemicals.[113] While some issues remained unresolved, particularly with respect to Iraq's efforts to develop the nerve agent VX and advanced binary chemical weapons, UNSCOM officials apparently considered them to be "no longer significant."[114] In the chemical and missile arenas, enough was accomplished to allow for the beginning of ongoing monitoring and verification efforts, which were designed largely to provide unmanned, long-term monitoring of Iraqi facilities to ensure that illegal programs were not reconstituted.

Substantial concerns remained, however, with respect to Iraq's nuclear weapons program and especially its biological weapons program. With respect to the former, the IAEA eventually concluded that Iraq had been within two years of successfully completing work on a nuclear explosive device when the Gulf War derailed these activities.[115] Since its initial declaration, Iraq had consistently and adamantly maintained that it had not pursued an offensive BW program. Initially, UNSCOM inspections failed to uncover any evidence that directly contradicted the Iraqi claims, but they did produce important information concerning the scope of Iraq's biological research activities and supporting infrastructure.[116]

Indeed, a number of indicators suggested that Iraq had in fact pursued an offensive BW program. For example, while Iraq claimed that the Al Hakam factory was engaged in legitimate commercial ventures (including pesticide production), the technical characteristics of some equipment at the factory did not appear to be useful for this purpose.[117] Moreover, UNSCOM inspectors, with the assistance of supporting governments, had gathered information regarding Iraq's procurement and consumption of growth media used to produce biological organisms and believed that the acquired amounts were inconsistent with Iraq's alleged peaceful applications.[118] Finally, UNSCOM obtained evidence that Iraq had acquired pathogenic organisms, operated a large aerosol-inhalation chamber, and maintained other specialized BW-related equipment, such as spray dryers and filling machines.

Faced with this evidence, Iraq admitted on July 1, 1995, that there had been large-scale military production of BW agents at the Al Hakam plant, including significant quantities of botulinum toxin and anthrax. In spite of this important revelation, Iraq maintained that it had never weaponized the agents and that production had only taken place in 1989 and 1990, after which all stocks of BW agents had been unilaterally destroyed.[119]

General Kamal's chicken farm. In August 1995, however, a series of events exposed the incompleteness of Iraq's recent BW-related admissions and the inadequacy of UNSCOM's findings regarding the extent of chemical and missile destruction and dismantlement. On August 7, 1995, General Hussein Kamal Hassan arrived in Jordan with his brother, their wives (Saddam Hussein's daughters), and their families. Kamal's defection was a singularly important event since he was not only a senior figure in the Iraqi leadership but also the former head of Iraq's WMD and missile programs. As minister of industry and minerals and former director of the Military Industrialization Corporation,

Kamal was a potential gold mine of information regarding Iraq's WMD and missile efforts. According to Stephen Black, the official UNSCOM historian from 1993 to 1998, Kamal himself provided "few details and little specific evidence to the Commission," but in response to Kamal's defection the government of Iraq provided an information windfall in an effort to limit the damage.[120] Within a week of the defection, the Iraqi government asserted that Kamal had been responsible for the illicit concealment of the true scope of Iraq's WMD and missile efforts and requested that the UNSCOM chairman travel to Baghdad to discuss the matter further.

During the course of these discussions, Iraq made new disclosures regarding its missile development and BW efforts to date, revealing not only the prior production of significant quantities of particular biological agents but also their weaponization status. The Iraqi government also revealed that the indigenous Scud missile program had advanced further than previously admitted. During the visit, Chairman Ekeus and his team were asked to visit the Haider Farm, a chicken farm allegedly owned by Kamal located approximately thirty-five kilometers southeast of Baghdad. At the farm inspectors found several hundred thousand pages of original documentation regarding Iraqi WMD and missile programs.[121]

The information contained in the recovered documents and new Iraqi disclosures was startling, calling into question UNSCOM's earlier assessments regarding the scope and accomplishments of the Iraqi WMD and missile programs and revealing that the programs were much more advanced than previously assessed. With regard to missile programs, the documents indicated that Iraq had been carrying out clandestine missile research until at least 1993. In addition, the inspectors found plans for a missile with a range of three thousand kilometers, and Iraq admitted that a project aimed at achieving indigenous production capability for Scud engines—Project 1728—had been successful.[122]

In the chemical arena, the new information undermined Iraq's previous declaration concerning its limited success in developing and weaponizing chemical weapons and also revealed that Iraq was pursuing an active research, development, and trial program for the nerve agent VX. This latter discovery was of great concern to the inspectors, as Iraq had previously admitted to experimenting with VX only in a laboratory setting during the period from April 1987 to September 1988.[123] Based on the new information, UNSCOM concluded not only that Iraq had produced VX on an industrial scale but that it had done so in quantities possibly as high as several hundred metric tons.[124]

Information on Iraq's BW efforts remained scarce, but the information recovered indicated that contrary to its initial assertions, Iraq had developed "a mature, offensive biological warfare programme" comprising at least five BW production sites and had produced significant amounts of several BW agents: 4,000 gallons of botulinum toxin, 1,800 gallons of anthrax, 530 gallons of aflatoxin, 90 gallons of *Clostridium perfringens,* and a limited quantity of ricin.[125] In addition to the documentation found at the chicken farm, UNSCOM inspectors also recovered an album of photographic documents relating to Iraqi BW equipment, munitions, and test results, as well as scores of boxes and other containers filled with computer disks, videotapes, and microfiche. Iraqi officials revealed that BW agents had been not only produced but also weaponized and admitted to having filled 166 aerial bombs and 25 Al Husayn missile warheads with anthrax, botulinum toxin, and aflatoxin.[126] Video footage also suggested that Iraq had experimented with using aircraft, including the French-made Mirage F-1, as delivery systems—ideal platforms for aerosol dissemination of biological pathogens.

In the aftermath of Kamal's defection and the subsequent series of Iraqi disclosures, the unavoidable question arose: how had Iraq been able to hide such an amount of documentation and related materials from the UNSCOM inspectors for four years? In the early phases of UNSCOM's inspections there had been skepticism about Iraq's intention to comply with disarmament requirements. One early UNSCOM report concluded that "the elements of misinformation, concealment, lack of cooperation and violation of the privileges and immunities of the Special Commission and IAEA have not created any trust in Iraq's intentions."[127] Over the following four years numerous inspections were conducted in an effort to alleviate concerns about hidden documents, weapons, or related materials but "did not yield material evidence of hidden Iraqi WMD assets."[128]

The chicken-farm incident revealed the lengths to which Iraqi authorities would go to conceal the true scope of Iraqi programs from UNSCOM inspectors. Statements from Kamal and information gleaned from the chicken-farm documents confirmed Iraq's ongoing efforts to conceal its remaining WMD and missile stocks and raised questions about the portion of Iraq's capabilities that might remain hidden.[129] The stark recognition that they had been misled by Iraq for years led UNSCOM officials to conclude that previous methods of operating would not be sufficient to pierce the robust veil of Iraqi denial and deception. According to Scott Ritter, UNSCOM inspector and head of the commission's Concealment Unit, "The revelations led to a decisive shift away from the hopelessly flawed material balance approach to verification and active pursuit of the concealment mechanism."[130] The new investigative methods developed by UNSCOM following the chicken farm disclosures would prove to be a source of acute confrontation between UNSCOM and Iraq.

"Shaking the tree" and efforts to counter the concealment mechanism. In addition to overhead reconnaissance support, US intelligence agencies, together with their British and Israeli counterparts, became principal supporters of UNSCOM's effort to evade Iraqi concealment activities, an effort that became known popularly as "shaking the tree."[131] Open-source accounts suggest that the major US contribution to this strategy took the form of electronic eavesdropping equipment to monitor Iraqi conversations.[132] According to Barton Gellman, the "shake the tree" process followed a general procedure: "There will be an open effort by UNSCOM inspectors to come upon a sensitive site. Simultaneous with that, there will be covert efforts to look and listen to what the Iraqis are doing in response to the UNSCOM approach."[133] One important feature of these efforts was the use of ground-based radio scanners to listen in on Iraqi communications, which allowed UNSCOM to develop an understanding of "how they were being gamed by the Iraqis and [devise] a plan for beating the Iraqis at their own game."[134]

Over time, however, some personnel with direct knowledge of the operation alleged that UNSCOM eventually became co-opted by the United States for its own purposes. As Scott Ritter charged, "The US decided this system is too sensitive to be run by UNSCOM. They bullied their way in and took it over. Now any data collected by this activity is not being assessed by UNSCOM. Now, the US gained 100 percent access and is not feeding any of it back."[135] Such accusations made their way into the media, reinforcing the idea that UNSCOM was increasingly becoming a tool of US interests and that US and UNSCOM interests diverged. In UNSCOM Chairman Richard Butler's view, the organization "was particularly hurt by Scott Ritter's carrying on." While Butler "did approve some kinds of technical assistance from intelligence bodies to penetrate the wall of deceit that was put up to prevent us from doing our work," Ritter's claim "that I somehow sold the store to the CIA is dramatically untrue."[136]

For the United States, according to Undersecretary of State Thomas Pickering, since the invasion of Kuwait in August 1990 "our fundamental goal is to counter the threat the Iraqi regime poses to U.S. national interests and to the peace and security of the Gulf. This goal remains unchanged from the time of Desert Storm."[137] Cooperation with UNSCOM offered US intelligence agencies the clear opportunity to penetrate "what is arguably the best insulated security and counterintelligence operation in the world."[138] The interests of UNSCOM in defeating the Iraqi concealment mechanism and of the United States in monitoring Iraqi WMD programs would appear convergent.[139] The reputed eavesdropping effort involved a system to intercept Iraqi microwave communications colocated with UNSCOM monitoring equipment, a set of cameras installed at approximately three hundred sites around Iraq to monitor activities at suspect facilities. The alleged purpose of monitoring such communications was to "eavesdrop on sensitive conversations as part of an effort to overthrow" Saddam Hussein.[140]

By surreptitiously tapping into UNSCOM's monitoring system, US intelligence agencies reportedly sought to obtain information to further US policy goals. Against this opportunity US officials had to weigh the costs to UNSCOM's credibility if the covert piggybacking operation was uncovered, but "the stakes were so high in the conflict with Iraq, and the probability of discovery so low, that they deemed the risks worth running." Apparently, a decision was made not to inform the UNSCOM leadership of the covert US operation because of concern over continued US access to this new source of intelligence and the possibility that UNSCOM's operations might change in the future.[141]

Publicly, both the US government and the UNSCOM leadership denied that any illegal or covert eavesdropping took place. State Department spokesman James Rubin stated, "It is my understanding that at no time did the U.S. work with anyone at UNSCOM to collect information for the purpose of undermining the Iraqi regime."[142] UNSCOM Chairman Richard Butler refuted the allegations, arguing that such claims by Iraq were propaganda, "without foundation, and not a shred of credible evidence has ever come to light suggesting otherwise."[143] Butler maintained that he knew of no instance in which UNSCOM information was directed toward military planners. In his view, the charge that he had been "co-opted" by the United States was "quintessentially ludicrous," a "belly laugh," a "joke"; this "intelligence issue has been played with such dramatic success by Iraq, and its friends, including in the Secretary General's office, that it's a travesty." Illustrating the complexities and sensitivities of information sharing in a multilateral context, however, Butler acknowledged the politicized nature of the UN body. "I am aware," he declared shortly before his resignation, "that members of UNSCOM's staff were leaking assessments and reports and information to their sending governments. And I'm not talking about Americans. I'm talking about other nations. I'm trying to get away from this single focus that somehow we were done over by the United States."[144]

Clinton administration officials often evinced a "no compromise, no surrender" stance in public rhetoric, trumpeting an "unparalleled, second-to-none record in supporting UNSCOM."[145] This support included the deployment of military forces to the region and the threat of military force to compel Iraq to comply with the UN Security Council resolutions. However, by the end of 1998 there were some indications that the administration was tiring of resorting to the threat of military force in response to Iraqi intransigence.[146] A top-level review of US policy toward Iraq reportedly came to two major conclusions. First was that Saddam was setting the agenda; the United States needed to take the initiative from the Iraqis and maintain it. Second was the propensity of UNSCOM inspections for triggering confrontations, increasingly viewed as a hindrance to US policy goals.[147]

In order to address these two issues, senior Clinton administration officials apparently sought to restrain the scale of UNSCOM's inspections in order to prevent acute confrontations. In late 1998 media reports suggested that the administration had taken steps to halt at least half a dozen inspections and succeeded in doing so in five cases. The administration's stated goal was "to control the pace of confrontation with Iraq to create the best conditions in which to prevail," although critics maintained that an additional purpose was "to prevent the inspectors from exceeding the administration's diminishing capacity to protect them."[148] Reports also alleged that the United States withdrew some of its intelligence support to the commission at about the same time.[149]

The end of UNSCOM. By the end of 1996 UNSCOM had developed and implemented these new, increasingly effective investigative methods to deal with Iraq's concealment mechanism. UNSCOM inspectors attempted to address some of the more significant outstanding issues, notably the production of VX, Iraq's BW history, and the processes and organizations that concealed information and evidence from the inspectors. In light of these increasingly intrusive UNSCOM activities, Iraqi officials grew even more uncooperative and recalcitrant. Iraq began to demand changes in the composition of UNSCOM inspection teams, refusing to allow US inspectors to deplane once they arrived

Table 5.4. Sites associated with Iraq's WMD and missile programs

Sites Associated with Iraq's Nuclear Program

Tuwaitha Nuclear Research Center	Akashat Mine
Tarmiya	Al Qaim
Al Atheer	Rashidiya
Al Furat	Al Sharqat
Al Jesira	Petrochemical-3 Center
Abou Obeydi Airbase	Al-Numan Factory, Baghdad

Sites Associated with Iraq's Biological Warfare Program

Agricultural & Water Research Station, Al-Fudhaliyah	Al-Qa'a Qa'a, Latifiyah
Agricultural Aviation Division, Khan Bani Sa'ad	Al-Rasheed Air Base, Baghdad
Airfield 37, near Ramadi	Al-Taji
House at Al-Amiriyah, Baghdad	Asma School, Al-Hindaya
Al-Adile Stores (Kimadia)	HQ Air Force Technical Depot, Taji
Al-Azzizziyah	Jarf Al-Sakr
Al-Dabash Stores	Jurf Al-Nadaf
Al-Fao	Nasr State Establishment, Taji
Al-Faris Factory, Al-Amiriyah	Project 144, Taji
Al-Hakam Factory	Serum & Vaccine Institute, Amiriyah
Al-Hazen Ibn Al-Haithem, Salman	Site 85, near Latifiyah
Al-Kindi Company, Abu Ghraib	State Enterprise for Heavy Engineering, Daura, Baghdad
Al-Manal, Daura, Baghdad	State Establishment for Mechanical Engineering, Iskanderiah
Al-Mansuriyah	Store No. 6, Misbah, Baghdad
Al-Mohammediyat	Technical Research Center, Salman
Al-Meshada, Taji	Tigris Canal, near Fallujah
Al-Muthanna, Samara	University of Baghdad
Al-Nahrawan, near Baghdad	University of Technology, Baghdad
Al-Nibai	Military Industrial Commission

Sites Associated with Iraq's Chemical Warfare Program

Muthanna State Establishment (MSE)	H1, H2, H3 Multipurpose Pilot Plants (MSE)
P8 Plant (MSE)	Inhalation Chamber (MSE)
P7 Plant (MSE)	Aerial Bomb Workshop (MSE)
Multipurpose Plant, Dhia (MSE)	Filling Station (MSE)
Multipurpose Plant, Malek (MSE)	Fallujah 1,2,3
Multipurpose Plant, Mohammed (MSE)	Mamun Precursor Plant (Fallujah 2)
A1 Multipurpose Plant (MSE)	TMP Precursor Plant (Fallujah 2)
A2 Multipurpose Plant (MSE)	Equipment Stores (Fallujah 2 and 3)
A3 Multipurpose Plant (MSE)	Muhammadiyat

Table 5.4. continued

Sites Associated with Iraq's Ballistic Missile Program

Taji	Badr State Establishment
Rafah	Qadisiya State Establishment
Khadimiya	Saddam State Establishment
Shahiyat	Qa'Qa State Establishment
Wazeriya	State Establishment for Automobile Industries
Qa'Qa	State Establishment for Mechanical Industries
Dora	Salahaldeen State Establishment
Yawm Al Azim	Kindi State Establishment
Thu Al Fiqar	Nida Factory
Taj Al Marik	Harith Factory
Nasser State Establishment	Numan Factory

Sources: UNSCOM, "Major Sites Associated with Iraq's Past WMD Programs," 3 December 1997; idem, *Report to the Security Council on the Status of Disarmament and Monitoring,* S/1999/94, 29 January 1999.

in Baghdad and denying other inspection teams entry into suspect facilities on the grounds that American "spies" were on the teams.[150]

Iraq's behavior resulted in several intense confrontations between the inspectors and their Iraqi interlocutors. When UNSCOM was actually able to conduct inspections, it did so in the face of intense Iraqi efforts to interfere with and impede the inspectors' activities. Inspectors were routinely denied access to facilities, forbidden to use audiotaping or videotaping equipment, denied interviews with Iraqi personnel, and shown facilities that clearly had been sanitized in preparation for UNSCOM visits.[151] Faced with Iraqi recalcitrance, UNSCOM inspectors pulled out of Iraq for what would be the final time in December 1998, shortly before Operation Desert Fox (see chapter 7).

UNSCOM's final accounting. After Desert Fox, Iraq refused to allow the inspectors to return. Lingering allegations that the United States had used UNSCOM as a cover for its own espionage activities created (or reflected) a split in the Security Council and curtailed the prospect of continued inspections for four years. In January 1999 Butler issued UNSCOM's final report. The report contained an extensive listing of the facilities related to Iraqi WMD and missile programs, much larger than any of Iraq's "full, final, and complete" disclosures (see table 5.4).

That UNSCOM inspectors were able to compile such an accounting of Iraq's WMD and missile programs in the face of such an intense and effective denial and deception program speaks highly of the commission's personnel and the efforts of states to provide relevant information. Yet, in spite of this evident success, the UNSCOM final report also outlined areas in which inspections had not been able to obtain a complete report of Iraqi activities. With respect to ballistic missiles, UNSCOM could not account for the supposed but unverified unilateral destruction of VX-filled, BW-filled, and conventional missile warheads; the fate of some five hundred metric tons of missile propellants; and the location of approximately seven complete ballistic missiles and numerous major missile components. The prime chemical weapons issues remaining included the status and details of Iraq's VX development and production efforts; discrepancies in the material balance of chemical weapons declared by Iraq (the fate of thousands of munitions Iraq claimed to have expended in the Iran-Iraq War, lost shortly after that war, or unilaterally destroyed); and the location of CW production equipment removed from Iraq's main CW facility. The report lamented continuing ambiguity surrounding Iraqi BW efforts, whose existence had only been definitively confirmed in 1995.

The numerous "full, final, and complete disclosures" submitted by Iraq after that time were rejected after being "assessed by the Commission and by international experts as incomplete, inadequate and containing substantial deficiencies."[152] The lack of full disclosure about the scope and scale of Iraq's BW development, production, and weaponization programs prevented any real UNSCOM accounting in this area. Ominously, the commission underscored the importance of recognizing "that Iraq possesses an industrial capability and knowledge base, through which biological warfare agents could be produced quickly and in volume, if the Government of Iraq decided to do so."[153]

Epilogue: The Iraq Saga Continues

With the departure of UNSCOM inspectors in December 1998, the United States lost a significant source of information regarding the status of Iraqi WMD and missile programs. Although UNSCOM was an international organization and, despite Iraqi propaganda to the contrary, the United States did not direct the commission's actions, there is little doubt that the United States benefited from its intelligence-sharing relationship with UNSCOM. The highly intrusive inspections provided a valuable, if unofficial, source of HUMINT, observing the actual facilities, viewing documentation, and interviewing Iraqi personnel. According to the CIA, "having lost this on-the-ground access, it is more difficult for the UN or the US to accurately assess the current state of Iraq's WMD programs."[154]

In this context, the Office of the Secretary of Defense warned in 2001 that "this abeyance and our previous judgments about Iraq's intentions raise concern that Iraq may have begun . . . reconstitution efforts and that it will again be able to threaten its neighbors."[155] This view was echoed by former UNSCOM chief Richard Butler, who stated that "elementally" Iraq was as dangerous at the close of the millennium as it had been at the beginning of the decade. Although UNSCOM did successfully eliminate substantial portions of Iraq's existing WMD and missile capabilities, Butler opined that Saddam Hussein "clearly continues to have the motive and means to threaten great danger, and now the opportunity for renewed weapons development, given the extended absence of international arms control in Iraq."[156]

Absent intrusive, on-the-ground inspections, the only individuals likely to know the status of particular programs are the Iraqi scientists, engineers, administrators, and civilian and military officials involved in the programs. In December 1999 the Security Council voted to create a new inspection agency to take over UNSCOM's mission. Known as the United Nations Monitoring, Verification, and Inspection Commission, or UNMOVIC, this new agency hoped to build on UNSCOM's successes and at the same time to distance itself from UNSCOM's politically charged legacy. Yet this difficult task would prove elusive. Illustrating the tremendous divide among Security Council members, Russia, China, and France—Iraq's main supporters on the Security Council—abstained from the vote to create the new agency.[157]

At the same time, however, even before the Security Council passed the resolution creating UNMOVIC, staunch supporters of rigorous inspections began to refer to the organization derisively as "UNSCOM Lite."[158] These critics pointed to the numerous restrictions on UNMOVIC's operations, such as the perceived requirements to be culturally sensitive and less confrontational than UNSCOM, which would almost certainly limit the agency's effectiveness.[159] And though UNMOVIC would presumably be allowed to inspect any location in Iraq, the organization would likely be under pressure from Iraq and those nations that wanted the sanctions lifted to complete their inspections as quickly as possible. Under such conditions, critics worried, inspections would be a sham, unable to uncover Iraq's likely reconstituted and deeply hidden programs and potentially falsely concluding that Iraq had complied with the relevant Security Council resolutions. France and Russia even blocked UN Secretary General Kofi Annan's first choice as director, former UNSCOM Chairman Rolf Ekeus. As a result, the leadership fell to Hans Blix, former head of the IAEA, himself a controversial choice given his agency's previous failure to uncover Iraq's nuclear program.

The government of Iraq steadfastly refused to allow inspectors back into the country through December 2002. Anticipating eventual inspections, Blix opined that "intelligence is valuable. Defectors do not come knocking at UNMOVIC headquarters. They go to governments, and it is valuable to have much of that. . . . I don't think where the intelligence comes from really matters—it is the critical examination to which it is subjected that counts." Hoping to avoid the espionage allegations that plagued UNSCOM, Blix cautioned would-be providers that UNMOVIC was "not in the intelligence-trading business. We are not an intelligence organization. We are not giving anything to suppliers in return. We are not an espionage organization, whatever Iraq has said." Yet some exchange of information was virtually certain: "In order for us to get information that is relevant, it may well be that we will have to describe to intelligence providers what we are interested in."[160]

When UNMOVIC finally commenced field operations in late 2002, Blix's stance apparently was initially met with less-than-helpful support from nations, including the United States.[161] Shortly before inspections began, Blix softened his view, expressing a desire for more than "very supporting words" from the United States and other nations: "Of course we would like to have as much information from any member state as to evidence they may have on weapons of mass destruction and, in particular, sites."[162]

In the view of some US officials, the stated absence of a quid pro quo and concerns over appropriate safeguards of sensitive information would preclude substantial support. According to one unnamed senior official, "Based on our historical experience with UNSCOM, they had a very difficult time keeping information from falling into Iraqi hands."[163] Nevertheless, as inspections mounted, Secretary of State Colin Powell acknowledged that the United States was sharing some "significant" intelligence with UNMOVIC. At the same time, Washington was evidently holding back some of its most sensitive data until it was determined that inspectors "are able to handle it and exploit it. . . . It is not a matter of opening up every door that we have. . . . The means by which we get this information is so sensitive, and if it is not handled properly or exploited in the right way, we will lose that channel."[164] Yet, the US stance also evidently softened over the next few months. Addressing the UN Security

Council in February 2003, Secretary Powell indicated that while he could not "tell you everything that we know," the United States was providing "all relevant information we can to the inspection teams for them to do their work."[165]

Conclusion

One important lesson from the Russia-Iran and UNSCOM cases is the need to strike an appropriate balance between the actionability of intelligence and the potential risks to sources and methods. Like other tools available to policymakers that make use of intelligence products, such as demarches or military action, bilateral or multilateral intelligence sharing can have a negative impact on intelligence-collection capabilities. There is a clear danger that policymakers may become so focused on achieving short-term objectives that they lose sight of the potential long-term consequences of such actions.

To the extent that media reports are accurate, in the Russia-Iran case short-term successes against a few entities engaged in transfers were achieved at the cost of a potential increase in the difficulty of obtaining future information; Israeli human sources in Russia were reportedly curtailed, if not eliminated, as a result of releasing too much information to Russian authorities. Similarly, intelligence assistance from the United States and other nations helped UNSCOM to counter Iraqi denial and deception efforts and no doubt provided US intelligence agencies with valuable information on Iraq. However, the alleged eavesdropping program contributed to the decline of UNSCOM's credibility as an independent entity and ultimately to the end of the inspection regime. The departure of UNSCOM inspectors from Iraq evidently had an adverse effect on US intelligence collection in Iraq.

In short, intelligence sharing is a potentially risky, if sometimes necessary, enterprise. When undertaken, intelligence-sharing or data exchanges must be conducted with a full appreciation of the potential risks involved. Yet despite the obvious downside potential, intelligence sharing need not be dismissed as a pointless exercise or one that is so fraught with danger that it should never be attempted. As in other policy areas, decisionmakers will be required to prioritize objectives and resources, making difficult trade-offs when necessary. Although US policy goals were not completely achieved in either the Russia-Iran or the UNSCOM case, the United States arguably benefited from the intelligence-sharing relationship that it established with UNSCOM. Although Iraq was not completely and verifiably disarmed and UNSCOM inspections subsequently halted, the United States and the international community learned more about the scale and scope of Iraq's WMD and missile programs and infrastructures than they had known before.

While at least one Clinton administration official considered intelligence sharing with UNSCOM to be "unique," it is clear that this was not in fact a one-time phenomenon.[166] Indeed, there are a range of plausible scenarios in which, in order to achieve its policy goals, the United States would likely undertake the sharing and exchanging of information with close allies, international organizations, and perhaps other nations as well.

CHAPTER 6

Military Support

Intelligence in an Operational Context

Post–Gulf War revelations regarding the scope and achievements of Iraqi nuclear, biological, and chemical programs underscored an emergent reality of the international-security environment: that over time, determined proliferants would likely succeed in surreptitiously acquiring or developing WMD-related capabilities. Traditional supply-side measures, including national export controls and international regimes or other agreements designed to mitigate the spread of weapons-related technologies, continue to play an important role in US policy. However, the classic technology-denial approach holds generally unfavorable long-term prospects with respect to preventing new WMD states from arising or capping extant capabilities in existing WMD states.

While Iraq was central to this developing calculus, it was hardly unique: the Soviet collapse carried the latent prospect of a supply-side supermarket for aspiring proliferants even as recent developments in demand-side states such as Pakistan, South Africa, Iran, and North Korea suggested that each had achieved considerable successes in the nuclear, biological, and/or chemical arenas. In this context the administration of President George H. W. Bush elevated the relative importance of WMD and ballistic missile proliferation, declaring that "the proliferation of weapons of mass destruction may profoundly challenge our national security in the 1990s."[1]

In conjunction with the outgoing Bush administration's heightened focus on proliferation issues, the incoming administration of President William Clinton sought both to improve intelligence support to military operations and to develop a military that would be more capable of fighting in WMD environments. While the Cold War demanded that the intelligence community focus principally at the national strategic level, both the Bush and Clinton teams attempted to retool this capability, arguing that national imperatives required improved tactical and operational intelligence support in general, but with special attention to programs, policies, and plans to counter WMD proliferation.

In December 1993 Secretary of Defense Les Aspin launched the Defense Counterproliferation Initiative. "We're looking for intelligence that is militarily useful, not only diplomatically," he explained.[2] While diplomacy would continue to play a central role, "the priority would be on intelligence that could be used to support military operations in the field."[3] This priority was subsequently reiterated in Presidential Decision Directive 35, which outlined intelligence-collection and analysis priorities for the intelligence community. In an address to the staff of the CIA more than two years after the directive was signed, President Clinton reiterated that his administration's first priority was "supporting our troops and operations."[4]

This shift in balance between the strategic and operational levels carries with it important implications for the policy, intelligence, and operational communities. It raises key questions regarding standards of evidence or levels of confidence in intelligence assessments and the attendant diplomatic risks of inaccurate, incomplete, or outdated information; the actionability of sensitive information versus potential risks to sources and methods; and the ability to undertake effective counterproliferation operations.

This chapter discusses the perils and prospects for interdiction operations and military strikes against proliferant targets, with emphasis on the 1993 *Yin He* interdiction and the 1998 al-Shifa strike, respectively. In each case, US policymakers, acting on what they considered to be accurate and reliable intelligence reports on matters of declared national interest, authorized military actions in an effort to counter suspected chemical weapons–related activities. Underscoring the potentially acute difficulties in forcibly countering proliferation on the international stage through activities short of war, the operations were severely challenged: the suspect proliferants criticized the action, the international community balked, and US policy officials were left to defend in open forums the disputed actions of a post–Cold War superpower against select states in the developing world. The nature and interpretation of the information obtained, the behavior of the proliferants in question, and the character of the US response together underscore the imperative of a multidimensional counterproliferation strategy and the difficulties inherent in its effective implementation.

Interdiction Operations and the *Yin He*

The 1993 Defense Counterproliferation Initiative was designed to "strengthen prevention" while "adding protection as a major policy goal."[5] In Secretary Aspin's view, nonproliferation "combined global diplomacy and regional security efforts with the denial of material and know-how to would-be proliferators."[6] Yet, the emergent post–Cold War security environment would require more than the traditional approach, with its emphasis on diplomacy, undertaken by the United States in conjunction with its presumably like-minded partners in the international community. Beyond demarches, or as an adjunct to them, interdiction operations became an oft-employed tool in the early 1990s. Interdiction "entails disruption of sources of procurement and supply for proliferant WMD and missile programs, whether by law enforcement agencies tracking down illicit acquisitions or by military forces operating covertly and, typically, on the high seas."[7] Such operations require accurate and timely intelligence, a commodity often difficult to obtain and use effectively; and since the burden of proof rests with the enforcing entity rather than with the proliferant state, interdiction carries an inherent potential for failure. Yet to the extent that such operations can be effectively implemented, their potential successes may yield significant political or operational victories in an expanded post–Cold War campaign to constrain WMD proliferation.

Interdiction Efforts under George H. W. Bush

From mid- to late 1991 the United States actively tracked the *Mupo*, a North Korean freighter that had left its home port in July of that year. US analysts assessed that the ship was carrying a load of Scud-C ballistic missiles destined for Syria. In addition to the concern of missiles being shipped to the volatile Middle East, US officials also suspected that Israel might take unilateral military action to prevent the ship from reaching its presumed destination.[8] In this context US officials made no secret of the fact that they were tracking the *Mupo* and stated that the ship could be subject to inspections as it passed through the Red Sea and the Suez Canal.[9] However, before entering the Red Sea in October, the ship abandoned its original itinerary and sailed down the coast of Africa before eventually returning to North Korea in January 1992. According to the *Washington Times*, US officials believed that this decision was brought about by the publicity the case attracted, as well as the threats of Israeli military action.[10]

Approximately one month after the apparent resolution of the *Mupo* incident, other freighters originating in North Korea generated considerable interest among US officials. Acting on a tip reportedly from Israeli intelligence, US analysts began tracking another North Korean freighter, the *Dae Hung Ho*, which left port in February with a course toward the Middle East. Administration officials believed that the *Dae Hung Ho* was attempting to redeliver the *Mupo*'s cargo—Scud missiles and possibly equipment for missile manufacturing—to Syria possibly via Iran or another third country.[11] As with the *Mupo*, US officials underscored publicly that they were tracking the ship's every move: on the record, State Department spokeswoman Margaret Tutwiler stated that "we would like to see these transfers stop."[12] In the US Congress, Senator John McCain (R-AZ) submitted a resolution calling on states party to the MTCR to condemn North Korea's actions and requesting that the DPRK halt the *Dae Hung Ho*'s delivery.[13] Bush administration officials apparently deliberated about intervention options prior to the ship's reaching its destination, asserting a right to board and search the vessel.[14] When asked about possible US courses of action, President Bush answered, "We're always contemplating options."[15]

The intended goal of this saber rattling was to persuade the North Koreans to turn the ship around without delivering its cargo, as the *Mupo* had done months before. Yet despite intense aerial and surface surveillance, the *Dae Hung Ho* managed to slip by US warships in the Persian Gulf region, possibly by hugging the coastline and blending in with coastal boat traffic, and arrived at the Iranian port of Bandar Abbas on March 9.[16] Several days after the ship arrived in Bandar Abbas, large containers were unloaded from its cargo hold, but US intelligence reportedly could not determine their contents.[17] At about the same time, two other suspect vessels were successfully intercepted by US warships; after their cargoes and destinations were checked, they were allowed to continue on their respective courses. The Iran-flagged freighter *Iran Salaam* claimed to be carrying "steel and drilling material" destined for Chah Bahar in Iran, while the North Korean–flagged *Dae Hung Dan* claimed to be carrying commercial cargo to southern Africa.[18]

With the US Navy's evident lack of success, some news reports suggested that it had failed to conduct a thorough investigation of the ship. Pentagon spokesman Pete Williams argued that the North Korean ship was not the "highest priority" for Navy ships in the region: "There are a lot of arms sales going on in the world that we don't like, but that doesn't mean we have the legal authority to stop them."[19] This apparent attempt to downplay the incident was in stark contrast to the position of General Joseph Hoar, commander of the US Central Command (CENTCOM), who assumed full responsibility for the incident: "If you're looking for the guy who let the [freighter] go through, you're looking at him."[20]

The Navy's apparent failure to track the ship despite the significant resources it had devoted to the task triggered an investigation by the House Intelligence Committee, whose chairman, Representative Dave McCurdy (D-OK), considered the incident an embarrassment to the country.[21] At the same time, Syrian President Hafez al-Assad accused the United States of playing "international pirate," the Iranian government claimed that the United States "was waging psychological warfare against the Islamic state," and North Korean Vice President Li Jong Ok refuted US allegations that the ships were carrying missiles.[22] Israeli officials, who had provided the initial information to the United States, made no public statements on the failure to intercept the suspect ships and their alleged missile cargoes. Privately, however, some Israeli officials reportedly expressed dismay over the US failure and attributed it to apparent unwillingness to prevent the missiles from being delivered: "The U.S. doesn't have the ability to stop a North Korean ship?" asked one official. "Either it wants to or it doesn't."[23]

Interdiction under William Clinton

The Clinton administration appeared to share its predecessor's views on the proliferation of WMD and ballistic missiles. "One of the key national security challenges of the post Cold War era," President Clinton stated early in his tenure in office, "is containing the spread of nuclear arms and other weapons of mass destruction."[24] To this end, the Clinton administration successfully persuaded Egypt to intercept and search a French freighter that was headed through the Suez Canal. That ship, the *Ville de Vega*, was bound for Iraq carrying a large quantity of Indian-produced hydrofluoric acid, which can be used in enriching uranium for nuclear weapons.[25] At the request of the United States, the Egyptian navy stopped and searched the vessel and then impounded it when the cargo was discovered. The ship and its cargo were eventually returned to India, which promised to improve its export controls.[26] The *Ville de Vega* incident suggested that interdiction activities would continue on Clinton's watch.

Intercepting the Yin He. In July 1993 the Chinese containership *Yin He* left the port of Tianjin along a regular route that would eventually take it to ports in the Persian Gulf.[27] On July 23, US officials approached the Chinese government claiming that the United States had reliable information suggesting that the ship was carrying two chemicals, thiodiglycol and thionyl chloride, to Iran for use in that country's chemical weapons program.[28] Both thiodiglycol and thionyl chloride are referred to as "dual-use" chemicals, compounds that can be used as precursors for particular chemical weapons but also have legitimate uses in the industrial and commercial sectors.[29] Because these types of chemicals are not limited solely to weapons-related applications, the mere fact that a country possesses a particular dual-use chemical is not *necessarily* indicative of that nation's desire to produce chemical weapons.

The difficulty lies in determining whether a country is using the chemicals for legitimate commercial purposes or for other, weapons-related applications. The US intelligence reports, according to publicized statements, placed the chemicals in two containers with the serial numbers CSAQ 3101 and CSAQ 3102, slated for delivery to the Iranian port of Bandar Abbas.[30] Initially, the United States exercised the diplomatic option, requesting that Beijing order the freighter to return to China in order to prevent the suspected chemicals from reaching Iran.[31] The Chinese government refused this request but agreed to investigate the issue. Eventually Chinese officials concluded that while there were twenty-four cargo containers destined for Iran, the bills of lading and contents yielded no evidence that the chemical were on board the ship.[32] The Chinese investigation reportedly revealed that the containers in question held stationery, hardware, machine parts, and dyestuff that were to be offloaded in Dubai for transshipment to Iran, whose ports lacked the proper facilities for handling cargo containers.[33] Assistant Foreign Minister Qin Huasun stated that "serious and earnest checks" made by Chinese officials had confirmed that "there is neither thiodiglycol and thionyl chloride on the ship, nor is there a bill of lading for them as the U.S. side claimed."[34] The Chinese government also claimed that although the treaty had not yet entered into force, it was adhering to the terms of the Chemical Weapons Convention and was "very serious about the international obligations it shoulders."[35] Moreover, Qin argued that since 1990, Chinese laws had placed export controls on the chemicals in question and prohibited their export to the Middle East.

Despite these protestations, the United States continued its diplomatic pressure and maintained its surveillance of the *Yin He*. By early August US naval and air units were monitoring the *Yin He* as it entered the Indian Ocean on its way to the Persian Gulf region.[36] At the same time, Secretary of State Warren

Christopher publicly reiterated that the information concerning the *Yin He*'s cargo was reliable and that the United States was "trying to find circumstances in which we can inspect the ship. . . . We'll find a way to make sure those chemicals are not delivered into the wrong hands."[37] The United States again requested that the freighter be turned around and that China allow US personnel to inspect its cargo.

The Chinese responded by taking the issue to the international media, publicly criticizing the United States for harassing the ship and accusing Washington of behaving in "an unreasonable and arrogant manner."[38] The state-run media discussed the supposed inconsistencies or inaccuracies in the American allegations, including the ship's point of origin and presumptive destination. Chinese media outlets pointed out that the *Yin He* had departed from Xingang, not Dalian, and that Bandar Abbas was not on the ship's itinerary because the Iranian port lacked the proper facilities for handling cargo containers.[39] Assistant Foreign Minister Qin Huasun stated, "The ship is a regular cargo liner, whose route did not include a stop at any Iranian port. The U.S. side is in fact aware of this. We don't understand what the U.S. motives are in spreading rumors that the ship is bound for Iran."[40] By implication, if US intelligence could not correctly identify the ship's itinerary, could it not also be wrong about the ship's cargo?

Nevertheless, the United States continued to demand that its personnel be allowed to inspect the ship's containers for evidence of the chemicals, although according to international law the United States had no legal authority to search the vessel without China's consent.[41] The PRC refused these requests but suggested that it would be amenable to a search conducted by a third party. While the United States initially declined the offer, it eventually agreed. By the end of August an agreement had been reached whereby the *Yin He* would dock in the Saudi port of Ad Dammam, at which time a joint Sino-Saudi team would search the ship, with US representatives providing technical assistance to the Saudis.[42] The search was originally limited to the 24 containers destined for Iran, but when the search of those containers yielded no chemicals, the United States requested that all cargo containers on board the ship be inspected. When the inspection ended ten days later, the inspectors had found no evidence of the chemicals in any of the ship's 782 cargo containers.

Fact or fiction: a Yin He *postmortem.* The balance of this interdiction saga played out in the international media. China condemned the United States for attempting to assume the role of "self styled 'world cop'" and asserted that the whole incident had been a "show of hegemony and power politics."[43] The reputed US evidence leading to the incident was criticized as inaccurate and unfounded, "no more than hearsay or self-invented stories."[44] The PRC demanded that the United States apologize for its actions and pay compensation to the China Ocean Shipping Company, which owned the *Yin He,* and to the businesses that had cargo on the ship.[45] Iran echoed the Chinese demands that the United States apologize and offer compensation for the incident, denouncing US actions as a "blatant violation of international law and shipping rights regulations."[46] Iranian officials also announced that they would back any of the businesses with cargo on the *Yin He* that wished to pursue legal action against the United States.[47]

US officials maintained that the request for inspections had been justified despite the apparent absence of the chemicals and a weak legal basis for inspections (absent the CWC, not yet in force) in international law. According to State Department spokesman Michael McCurry, "We had information from a number of credible sources that . . . thiodiglycol and thionyl chloride were contained within the cargo on that ship."[48] McCurry and other US officials stated that they "had acted in good faith on intelligence from a number of sources" and that "the dangers of proliferation require us to pursue effective means of resolving concerns when credible evidence of destabilizing transfers occurs."[49] For former CIA Director Robert Gates, the lesson was clear: "If you want an aggressive non-proliferation strategy, you need to act when you have credible information. You're not always going to be 100% successful when the policy moves from rhetoric to action. . . . But I think the message . . . is that the United States is going to be very tough on non-proliferation issues."[50]

Ultimately, the absence of chemicals on the ship led to obvious questions about the fidelity of the relevant intelligence reporting. Yet it also raised the prospect that the cargo might have been dumped overboard en route.[51] Certainly in public, US officials stood by their assessment that the *Yin He* had carried the suspect cargo. State Department spokesman Michael McCurry observed, "I haven't seen any information that suggests that we may have been wrong."[52] US officials gave no official explanations as to why the chemicals had not been found, but they asserted that the United States "had sufficient credible evidence that those items were in the cargo" and that "this case is closed."[53] Privately, analysts suspected that that the crew, upon learning of US suspicions, had dumped the containers overboard: "We very strongly believe it was on the *Yin He*. We inspected it in Dammam, ergo something happened to it in between."[54] Others posited that the containers might have been off-loaded at one of the ship's other ports of call, most likely in Singapore or Jakarta, or instead that the chemicals had never been on board in the first place and US information regarding them had simply been wrong.[55]

The *Mupo, Yin He*, and related cases demonstrate the intrinsic difficulty of implementing an effective interdiction operation and the adverse implications for policy when there is an inability to interdict when and where it is required. These cases also highlight the need to carefully balance the potentially useful information at the strategic level with the potentially actionable at the tactical or operational level. The potential credibility gap between the imperatives for action and the uncertain prospects for successful execution suggests that peacetime interdiction of suspected technology or material transfers may be employed cautiously by a policy community whose public accusations became high drama on the international stage.

The mismatch between specific allegations and inspection findings in this case prompted one reporter to ask State Department spokesman Michael McCurry whether the fact that the suspect chemicals had not been found would "cast doubt on the U.S. Government's credibility when it makes an accusation with regard to China or with regard to anyone else."[56] McCurry responded that he did not believe that the *Yin He* incident would have any future repercussions for actions designed to counter WMD proliferation. Rather, he postulated that "the type of cooperation in this instance" might prove useful in resolving future proliferation issues.[57] Moreover, it is clear that proliferants do not often advertise their intentions, plans, or transfers of WMD-related technologies or material. Indeed, the Chinese government made similar statements regarding the presumably faulty intelligence that the United States had obtained on the *Yin He* and on the purported Chinese transfers of M-11 missiles to Pakistan (for which the United States applied sanctions).[58] As chapter 2 suggests, such concerns were hardly far-fetched.[59] Pakistani success in this area with active Chinese assistance only underscored that the intelligence community might have judged correctly in this case as well. In 2002 the director of the CIA reported that "Iran continues to seek such assistance from Chinese entities."[60]

Retribution: Operation Infinite Reach

While interdiction operations have been a component of US efforts to disrupt, delay, or deny the transfer of WMD- and missile-related materials, the military's role in countering proliferation is broader. The armed forces are also tasked with, among other things, deterring their use, defending against their effects, and destroying targets in wartime (see chapter 7) or other settings as directed.[61] While intelligence is central to these tasks, the political determination to employ military force to counter WMD proliferation has evident risks, including the likelihood of information uncertainty, inaccuracy, or insufficiency; the potential for harmful collateral effects; the prospect of diplomatic fallout or adverse international opinion; and the potential conflict between the actionability of intelligence and the risks to sensitive sources and methods. Operation Infinite Reach, in which the United States launched a cruise missile strike against Sudanese and Afghan targets, cuts across these complex issues. In this operation Clinton administration officials obtained what they argued was accurate and irrefutable evidence linking a Sudanese pharmaceutical plant to chemical weapons precursors, suggesting potential links to Osama bin Laden's terrorist network and possible links to Iraq and demonstrating a clear connection between bin Laden and the destruction of two American embassies in 1998.

The attack rapidly evolved, however, into a broad controversy in which the US government found itself in the uncomfortable position of defending its actions to a wide range of domestic and international critics. In the debate that followed, senior policy officials chose to publicly reveal sensitive information relating to the suspected chemical weapons–related facility. Claims and counterclaims were exchanged as severe doubts were raised concerning the credibility of US intelligence. One illustrative review stated that while "it remains *possible* that at some point in time, a small quantity of a VX precursor chemical was stored or produced in Shifa or transported through or near it," the "evidence available in open sources offers only limited support for the U.S. allegation," and it is "more probable that the Shifa plant had no role whatsoever in CW production."[62] The nature of the evidence in question, together with the extensive public debate, has important implications for the use of military force. Even if it was accurate, the information in this case led to a successfully executed military operation that ultimately culminated in an acute failure of policy and jeopardized intelligence sources and methods in the process.

Setting the Stage: The 1998 Embassy Bombings

On August 7, 1998, US embassies in Nairobi, Kenya, and Dar es Salaam, Tanzania, were rocked by nearly simultaneous car bomb explosions that resulted in more than two hundred fatalities (including twelve Americans) and nearly five thousand casualties.[63] No organization or group claimed responsibility for the bombings, but the inspection led by the Federal Bureau of Investigation, or FBI, concluded that Osama bin Laden, the exiled Saudi millionaire who was the head of the al-Qaeda terrorist network, was ultimately culpable. Indeed, US officials stated early in the process—as four suspects, one of them formerly a personal secretary to bin Laden, were arrested and linked to al-Qaeda—that the investigation was "starting to unravel a wide-ranging conspiracy orchestrated by bin Laden."[64] President Clinton, speaking on the day of the missile strikes, publicly reiterated that "there is convincing information from our intelligence community that the bin Laden terrorist network was responsible for these bombings. . . . We have high confidence that these bombings were planned, financed, and carried out by the organization bin Laden leads."[65] In a December 1998 interview, bin Laden disputed the allegation but expressed clear sympathy for the attacks: he stated that while he "was not involved in the bomb blasts. . . . I don't regret what happened there."[66]

Not only did US government officials conclude that Bin Laden was linked to the embassy bombing attacks but they believed that further attacks would follow. According to National Security Adviser Samuel Berger, "a substantial volume of credible and reliable information" indicated that there were "other attacks planned against U.S. targets around the world." Intelligence apparently had revealed "very specific information about very specific threats with respect to very specific targets."[67] Secretary of State Madeleine Albright promptly directed a variety of measures to protect American citizens and possible targets, including the shutdown of several embassies. Chairman of the Joint Chiefs of Staff General Henry Shelton reiterated that the bombed embassies "might be only the first of two, three or even possibly four attacks."[68]

Indeed, just over a month after the attacks in Tanzania and Kenya a suspected bomb plot was foiled in Uganda. The CIA and the FBI, which had been investigating "a flood of threats worldwide" since the embassy bombings, alerted Ugandan authorities to an apparent plot to bomb the US embassy in the capital, Kampala.[69] In this case the US government did not publicly accuse bin Laden; rather, US authorities concluded that the plotters were at least sympathetic to bin Laden's cause, if not directly linked to it.[70]

Cruise Missile Strike

On August 20, 1998, less than two weeks after the embassy bombings, President Clinton announced that the military had struck "terrorist-related facilities in Afghanistan and Sudan because of the imminent threat they presented to our national security."[71] Eighty cruise missiles were launched from units in the Red Sea and the Indian Ocean at targets in Afghanistan and Sudan. According to Undersecretary of State Thomas Pickering, "The main purpose of the strikes was not retaliation; it was to prevent further terrorist attacks against American targets which we had reason to believe would take place."[72] The targets in Afghanistan comprised a group of terrorist training camps located near Khost, referred to by Secretary of Defense William Cohen as "Terrorist University."[73] The single target in Sudan was a pharmaceutical factory known as al-Shifa, located in an industrial suburb north of the Sudanese capital of Khartoum. This facility was reportedly involved in the production of precursor elements for the nerve agent VX. Allegedly, bin Laden was a major financial supporter of the factory whose intent to acquire WMD was known to US intelligence.[74]

Questions regarding Sudan and chemical weapons first emerged in the 1980s, although few official US sources publicly discussed the allegations that Sudan intended to acquire, develop, and possibly use chemical weapons.[75] In the mid- to late 1980s Sudanese People's Liberation Army rebels operating in the south of the country alleged that the Sudanese government had used chemical weapons against them.[76] In addition to reports from these rebels and from Ethiopian sources, the Monterey Institute of International Studies found numerous allegations of Sudanese chemical weapons use in open-source reporting.[77] The United States investigated such accusations but could not confirm the reports of use against rebels and concluded that evidence of such use was sketchy.[78]

Sudan allegedly also received assistance from Iraq and possibly other nations in the production or procurement of chemical weapons. Reports from Sudanese opposition forces and from media accounts have alleged Sudanese-Iraqi collusion beginning in the 1970s and continuing to at least 2001, but without offering much supporting evidence.[79] According to the State Department, "Sudan and Iraq established very close relations following the Persian Gulf

War," and both were featured on that institution's list of state sponsors of international terrorism.[80] In return for providing facilities for Iraqi use far from the prying eyes of UNSCOM inspectors (see chapter 5), Sudan allegedly received financial assistance from Iraqi military and civilian experts in chemical weapons.[81] According to Undersecretary Pickering, "We see evidence that we think is quite clear on contacts between Sudan and Iraq. In fact, el Shifa [sic] officials, early in the company's history, we believe, were in touch with Iraqi individuals associated with Iraq's VX program."[82] Similarly, State Department spokesman James Foley observed that "there is evidence that Sudan sought help in the pursuit of a CW capability from other countries, particularly Iraq," and that such information "was of utmost concern to us."[83]

US intelligence also reportedly assessed that bin Laden was connected to the plant either directly or indirectly and that the "so-called pharmaceutical plant" was part of a Sudanese military-backed enterprise known as the "Military-Industrial Complex."[84] According to Sudanese and Arab sources, this organization comprised five factories in Khartoum established in late 1992 by the ruling military regime to produce conventional and chemical weapons.[85] Technical and other assistance appears to have been acquired from a number of countries, including Iraq, Russia, Kazakhstan, and Bulgaria, as well as at least one Canadian firm.[86] Senior intelligence officials concluded, "We know that Bin Ladin has made financial contributions to the Sudanese military industrial complex. That's a distinct entity of which we believe the Shifa pharmaceutical facility is part."[87] Reportedly, bin Laden had been working with the Sudanese military on the production of chemical weapons since the mid-1990s.[88] The reputed intelligence take was that "we know that Bin Ladin has worked with Sudan to test poisonous gases and to finance simpler methods of manufacturing and dispensing gas."[89] In sum, bin Laden's apparent links to the Sudanese Military-Industrial Complex and the knowledge that he was intent on acquiring CW capabilities fueled US suspicions that he was tied to operations at the al-Shifa plant. Such a connection posed a hazardous state of affairs; US officials widely agreed that bin Laden had been *seeking* to acquire chemical weapons, but had he succeeded in doing so?

Not surprisingly, as a suspected part of Sudan's broader CW program, the al-Shifa plant came under scrutiny by the US government. US intelligence suspected that the facility had produced several types of precursors for chemical weapons, but one chemical in particular received much of the attention. This chemical was O-ethyl methylphosphonothioc acid, more commonly known as EMPTA, a precursor chemical used in the manufacture of the nerve agent VX. According to the State Department, EMPTA "is not used in commercial applications, does not occur naturally in the environment and is not a byproduct of another chemical process."[90] Because the chemical has no apparent use outside of its role in the production of VX, US intelligence came to the "unambiguous conclusion" that al-Shifa was producing the precursor for use in chemical weapons.[91] The belief that Sudan was producing this chemical strengthened claims of a suspected link with the Iraqi CW program. According to US officials, there are several ways to produce VX, but the method that uses EMPTA is the one that Iraq pursued when it developed its VX stockpiles.[92]

At least two years prior to the missile strikes, US intelligence reportedly had concluded that the al-Shifa pharmaceutical plant was a front operation for less benign purposes than its outward appearance suggested.[93] In spite of its alleged purposes, intelligence officials observed that they "have no evidence, have seen no commercial products that are sold out of this facility."[94] Senior US officials confidently proclaimed that instead of producing life-saving drugs for the people of Sudan, the plant was intended to produce CW precursors. According to National Security Adviser Berger, "We know with great certainty [that al-Shifa] produces essentially the penultimate chemical to manufacture VX nerve gas."[95] Other characteristics of the plant, such as its secure perimeter patrolled by Sudanese army troops, contributed to the intelligence judgment that it was "an unusual pharmaceutical plant" and more likely a site connected to chemical weapons–related activities.[96] The day after the attack, Berger stated with even more certainty that "there is no question in my mind that the Sudanese factory was producing chemicals that are used, can be used, in VX gas. This was a plant that was producing chemical warfare related weapons and we have physical evidence of that fact."[97]

Strike planning: senior-level, closely held. Planning for the strikes against Afghanistan and Sudan began shortly after the investigation of the embassy bombings linked bin Laden to the blasts.[98] According to press reports, only a small group was involved in the planning in order to reduce the possibility of leaks.[99] Outside commentators observed that "few national security issues in Mr. Clinton's presidency were handled with greater secrecy or by a smaller group of people."[100] The core group apparently was made up of only six members: President Clinton, National Security Adviser Berger, DCI Tenet, Secretary Albright, Secretary Cohen, and Joint Chiefs Chairman General Shelton.[101] General Anthony Zinni, the regional commander in chief, was also involved in operational planning.[102] Finally, because the plan involved launching cruise missiles from Navy ships, "the top leadership of the Navy was brought into the planning sooner than other service chiefs—perhaps several days before the strike."[103] The other members of the Joint Chiefs, the attorney general, and the directors of the DIA and the FBI were apparently excluded from the planning stages and were briefed only shortly before the strikes took place.

These evident exclusions caused a stir in the media, which seemed surprised that the service chiefs and the top representatives from the Department of Justice—the agency that was actively investigating the embassy bombings and the bin Laden link—would be absent from such important planning sessions. Attorney General Janet Reno reportedly was not convinced that the evidence in question was sufficient for a military strike, apparently not believing that there was enough information on the links between bin Laden and the embassy bombings and between bin Laden and the targets of the raids.[104] She suggested that the raids be delayed in order to give the FBI more time to gather evidence, arguing that the evidence that had been gathered was not sufficient to meet the standards of international law.[105] The service chiefs, on the other hand, appeared unconcerned that they were not included in the planning sessions since according to current law, the president is not required to involve them in military planning since they are not officially in the chain of command.[106] As Pentagon spokesman Kenneth Bacon suggested, "As is appropriate for any sensitive military operation, planning was limited to those who needed to be involved."[107] Yet although they were not briefed on the operation until the day before the event, they apparently influenced the target set. While the initial target list called for strikes on a reported chemical weapons storage facility also in Khartoum, the Sudanese capital, the absence of a soil sample from that site and concerns over the potential for adverse collateral effects prompted the service chiefs to press for the removal of the second target in Sudan.[108]

The "smoking gun" revealed. In the days following the strike public and international confidence in the administration's assessment of the al-Shifa plant began to wane. Contrary to US statements made on the day of the attacks, the remains of medicine bottles scattered about the ruins of the factory seemed to indicate that commercial medicines had in fact been produced at al-Shifa.[109] Combined with these observations were public statements made by the Sudanese government regarding the role of the al-Shifa plant.[110] Public reports such as these led to further questions about the specific nature of the evidence that had prompted the United States to strike the plant.

Initially, US officials refused to discuss the intelligence in question. The day after the attack, National Security Adviser Berger stated that the US had physical evidence that chemicals were being produced at the plant but was reluctant to discuss it further in public for fear of compromising sources and methods: "The evidence is highly classified. It involves intelligence methods and intelligence sources, and we are not going to release it."[111] Within a few days, DOD, State Department, and other government officials all publicly stated that the United States had irrefutable physical evidence that the chemicals were being produced at the plant. Five days after the attack, US officials indicated that a covert operative had obtained a soil sample from the site that conclusively showed that the chemicals in question were associated with the facility.[112]

Thus, the main impetus for targeting the al-Shifa plant over other possible CW-related targets in Sudan was the fact that the United States had what it claimed was physical proof of CW-related activities at the "pharmaceutical plant." Media organizations reported that several months prior to the strikes US intelligence agencies had infiltrated an operative into Sudan to visit the site and obtain samples of the soil near the plant.[113] Once the samples had been processed, the operative was apparently interviewed and polygraphed to ensure that he had followed procedures. "This is not somebody who we do not have a high degree of confidence in," an unnamed official was cited as saying.[114] Intelligence officials also revealed that laboratory tests conducted on the soil samples had shown that the concentration of EMPTA was approximately three times the amount needed to establish the chemical's presence in the soil.[115] US intelligence officials believed that the chemical had been deposited in the soil "either through airborne emissions or spillage from the manufacturing process."[116]

The soil samples seemed to offer irrefutable proof of the plant's chemical weapons activities. The use of such samples to detect the possible presence of material associated with weapons-related activities falls within a subdiscipline of the growing field of measurement and signature intelligence.[117] MASINT offers means for detecting WMD-related research, development, storage, or production of weapons or materials beyond traditional imagery or signals intelligence. It includes, for example, material sampling, radar, geophysical, infrared, and optical sensors, nuclear radiation, radio-frequency sensors, and multi- and hyperspectral imagery.[118]

In the al-Shifa case one administration official argued, "We have confidence in the soil sample. It categorically demonstrates the presence of a compound good for just one thing—making VX by the Iraqi method."[119] US officials bolstered this claim by stating that the sample had been tested three times and compared with five samples taken from other sites in Sudan, none of which showed any evidence of EMPTA.[120] "We had previously collected samples from other suspected sites in Sudan," stated one State Department official, "but only the sample from the Shifa facility tested positively for chemical weapons precursors. We know of no other factors in the environment that could result in a positive EMPTA signature."[121] Another US official stated that the samples singled out al-Shifa above all other candidate targets: "There were other facilities where there was really hard evidence, but there was not a smoking gun; there was not a soil sample."[122] In the view of Amy Smithson, a senior associate at the Stimson Center, "If they've got a soil sample, they've got 'em. Soil samples don't lie."[123] Former DCI James Woolsey, on the other hand, opined that the decision to strike the plant "should not be the kind of decision made only by three or four people around you of Cabinet level who don't know an EMPTA sample from their left foot."[124]

Postattack disputes. Almost immediately after the attacks the Sudanese government denounced the United States for destroying the plant. Mahdi Ibrahim Mohamed, Sudanese ambassador to the United States, condemned the US attack and argued that "this plant was not manufacturing chemical weapons for terrorists. . . . It was engaged in manufacturing human and veterinary medicine, and was an approved supplier of export medicine under the UN's food for oil program."[125] Sudanese officials maintained that the plant was exactly what it claimed to be: a pharmaceutical factory that produced some 50–60 percent of Sudan's pharmaceuticals.[126] Walter Daum, the German ambassador to Sudan, echoed this view in a report to his superiors, noting that in contrast to US allegations, "the plant had produced antibiotics, antimalarial and antidiarrheal drugs, intravenous fluids, and a few veterinary medicines."[127] These counterclaims cast considerable doubt on the high-profile assertions made by senior US officials, and in the days after the attack US officials reexamined the public record and acknowledged that the plant could have produced medicines, adding, "But that in no way alters the fact that the factory was also producing precursor elements."[128]

According to the plant's designer, engineers involved in the construction, and employees, there was no way that the plant could have produced chemical weapons. Henry Jobe, a US chemical engineer who had designed al-Shifa for the original owner, stated that the plant had been built solely for producing pharmaceuticals and that no dual-use capability had been built into the plan.[129] Thomas Carnaffin, a consulting engineer who worked at al-Shifa from the beginning of construction until 1996, claimed that he had seen no evidence of chemical weapons production and opined that the plant was not properly configured for such activities: its design "just didn't lend itself to making chemical weapons."[130] Jordanian engineer Ahmad Salem, who supervised construction of the plant from 1993 to 1997, concluded that "there is no chance that this factory could be used to produce chemical weapons. It was designed to produce medicine for people and animals."[131] The plant's owner, Salah Idriss, stated through his attorney, Ghazi Suliman, that when he had purchased the factory in early 1998, "we had no idea, and it didn't come across our mind, and we didn't hear any rumors previously, that this factory was involved in chemical weapons."[132]

Others disputed US claims that EMPTA had no commercial utility. In the parlance of the Organization for the Prohibition of Chemical Weapons (OPCW), the agency charged with monitoring and inspections under the CWC, EMPTA is a "schedule 2" chemical. According to Donato Kinigier-Passigli, spokesman for the OPCW, this means that EMPTA has uses "in limited quantities for legitimate commercial purposes." But OPCW officials conceded that there were no extant commercial products that used EMPTA.[133] Still, they noted that some companies, including the Mobil Corporation and International Chemical Industries of America, had previously conducted research into possible commercial applications using EMPTA. While US officials declined to make any public statements regarding the OPCW's findings, off-the-record comments suggest that they did not attach too much importance to those findings: "Just because you identify a chemical agent for commercial uses, that does not mean anyone makes it."[134] While "we're aware of placeholder patents that posit theoretical uses," argued one government source, "we could find no evidence that anyone . . . has attempted to use it commercially."[135]

These questions led to additional scrutiny of the all-important soil sample. Questions arose over how the United States had obtained the sample, the sample's chain of custody, and the process used to test the sample. Chemical experts and others soon offered alternate explanations for the presence of EMPTA in the soil sample. The Sudanese interior minister questioned where the US operative had actually obtained the soil sample, asserting that the majority of the ground around the plant was paved and the remainder was planted with rose bushes: "If you look around, you will not see any soil in the immediate vicinity of our factory premises." Alamaddin al-Shibli, export manager at al-Shifa, agreed with the interior minister: "There's no way to take a sample of soil from this factory, according to the construction of this factory. It's either concrete or cement or carpet."[136]

Some observers proposed an alternative hypothesis, that al-Shifa did not produce EMPTA but the chemical was only stored at the plant or nearby.[137] Other observers suggested that US examiners could have confused EMPTA with related chemicals or disputed that the United States had found the chemical in the concentrations that it claimed. One OPCW inspector who had worked with EMPTA noted that the chemical was highly reactive and would have begun to break down soon after coming into contact with the ground. For this reason, he concluded: "No way it came out of a smokestack or in the effluent. The only way this material could be in the ground is if somebody had emptied a flask . . . and then taken a sample."[138]

Hank Ellison, a former US Army chemical officer, believed that the length of time between sample collection and analysis could have led to EMPTA's being confused with similar chemicals: "I imagine this soil sample wasn't taken under the best of circumstances, by somebody placing it in a cooler and immediately sending it to a lab. And quality control for the storage and manufacture of pesticides and insecticides is not the highest in the world, so that could increase the possibility of seeing similarities in the chemical structure."[139] Specifically, Ellison suspected that analysts might have confused EMPTA with an agricultural insecticide called Fonofos, which has molecular similarities to EMPTA and is common in Africa.[140] If the soil sample obtained by the CIA had not been properly handled in transit, he maintained, such a degraded sample could have been confused with a very similar chemical. In light of these accusations, US intelligence officials defended both their analysis and the procedures employed to test the sample, arguing that their results were correct and that no mistakes had been made. Apparently, the sample had been divided into three parts, and each part had been tested by a laboratory "with a long history of doing quality analysis."[141]

Finally, critics of the US strike on al-Shifa also challenged the links that US officials declared existed between the plant and the Sudanese military; the United States had alleged that al-Shifa was both part of the organization known

as the Military-Industrial Complex and also heavily guarded and routinely patrolled by Sudanese soldiers.[142] Yet in the aftermath of the attack no evidence
of a secured perimeter, such as fences or gates, materialized, and no information was presented to counter Sudanese claims that the plant was not patrolled
by Sudanese soldiers, except for the single night watchman killed in the attack.[143] Bobby May, an American citizen who happened to be in Khartoum at
the time of the attack and claimed to have visited the al-Shifa plant several days
before it was destroyed, observed that there had been no restrictions on visits
to the plant: "One of the places where the Sudanese liked to take you is the
pharmaceutical plant. It was a showplace for them."[144] Thomas Carnaffin, the
British technical manager at al-Shifa, made a similar observation: "It was never
a plant of high security. You could walk around anywhere you liked, and no
one tried to stop you."[145]

Moreover, while the United States alleged that bin Laden had funneled
money to al-Shifa because it was part of the broader Sudanese Military-Industrial
Complex, the plant was evidently privately held. The owner at the time of the
attack, Saudi businessman Salah Idriss, argued that the fact that it was in such
financial hardship undermined allegations of ties to the Sudanese military: "If
it was producing chemical weapons—with the support of the government, for
the sake of argument—how was it left to go through hard times? How could
it be sold to me, with my Saudi backing and connections? And my contacts
with the opposition? It doesn't make sense."[146]

This protestation by Idriss leads to questions concerning the larger issue of
his involvement in the al-Shifa affair. US officials alleged that Idriss was evidently the front man for bin Laden. Yet such claims were undermined by public insinuations that the United States did not know Idriss was the owner of al-
Shifa until after the attack.[147] It appears that rather than being funneled
straight into the Sudanese Military-Industrial Complex, bin Laden's money was
instead laundered by Idriss. Said one administration official, "What we're learning about [Idriss] leads us to suspect that he's involved in money laundering,
that he's involved in representing a lot of bin Laden's interests in Sudan."[148]
One of the key pieces of evidence linking Idriss to bin Laden was the revelation that Idriss had had financial dealings with the terrorist group Islamic
Jihad.[149] Also troubling to US officials were Idriss's links to the National Islamic
Front (NIF), the ruling cabal in Sudan, and to the president of Sudan, Omar
Hassan Bashir.

Indeed, muddling Idriss's claims that he had no strong connections to the

Sudanese government—but rather to prominent opposition politicians—was the fact that he was a self-described "close friend of the president."[150] As for his connections to the NIF, Idriss denied paying off the government, although a report by a private investigator hired by Idriss's American lawyers did acknowledge some connections between Idriss and the NIF's Military-Industrial Complex.[151] The report concluded that because the Military-Industrial Complex reached into so many sectors of the Sudanese economy, there were many links between Idriss and that organization but none evident through the al-Shifa connection.[152] Nevertheless, the US government froze more than $24 million of Idriss's assets four days after the attack "pending investigation of interests of Specially Designated Terrorists" without declaring that Idriss was a terrorist or that he was linked to a designated terrorist.[153] A lawsuit eventually freed Idriss's assets over US government protests: "Our concerns regarding Mr. Idriss are based on sensitive intelligence sources and methods," said a White House spokesman. "We're not prepared to expose these sources for the purpose of blocking Idriss' money."[154]

Conclusion

The *Yin He* and al-Shifa cases illustrate the imperative of achieving effective operational intelligence and the potential difficulties involved, as well as the policy implications of doing so. They exemplify the clear requirement for an appropriate balance between the protection of intelligence sources and methods and the actionability of intelligence. While US policymakers were sufficiently confident in the available intelligence assessments to take action, in each case action ultimately proved counterproductive to the advancement of US counterproliferation interests.

While no credible assessment of the sensitive information in question can be made through a review of the available open-source literature, some comparative generalizations can be drawn. First, despite the evident public failure of the operations, post-event statements from senior US officials reiterate the justifiability of the actions in question and suggest that there may be future requirements for interdiction, preemption, or other military operations. Second, public discussions over sensitive sources or methods will sometimes be counterproductive. With respect to the Chinese freighter, US officials stated that they had credible evidence but did not provide supporting details despite protests by the Chinese government. Following the missile strike in Sudan almost the opposite occurred. After US officials maintained an initial period of silence about evidence supporting the decision to attack, a significant volume of intelligence was revealed in poststrike justifications of the event. Yet it is nearly impossible to disprove a negative—that in effect the absence of evidence aboard the *Yin He* was not, in fact, evidence of absence—or, in some cases, to prove a positive—that even if al-Shifa produced garden-variety pharmaceuticals, it may also have been connected with chemical weapons–related activities. Finally, limited disclosure of intelligence is not new: intelligence was used to support retaliatory bombings against Libya in 1986, in revealing the Soviet role in the downing of Korean Air Lines flight 007 in 1983, and other activities.[155]

However, such revelations can have an adverse impact both on future intelligence-collection efforts an on the credibility of US policy. As former CIA analyst Bruce Berkowitz observed: "The problem is that, after the strike on El Shifa [*sic*], U.S. officials tried to use intelligence as evidence in a court case, and intelligence is usually poorly suited for that task. . . . What's more, it is particularly hard to use intelligence as evidence supporting a policy decision after the fact without compromising intelligence sources. . . . With each round of disclosure in the Sudan incident, more U.S. intelligence sources have been exposed."[156] To the extent states are aware of active US collection activities or even latent capabilities, they can take steps to cover their tracks and deny potentially vital information to the United States. This is a lesson not only of these cases but also of the unanticipated 1998 Indian nuclear tests (see chapter 4), the intelligence-sharing relationship with Russia on proliferation to Iran (see chapter 5), and related activities of would-be proliferants.

In spite of the evident difficulties associated with its successful implementation, military force against WMD- and missile-related targets in states of proliferation concern will remain an important option in the president's policy tool kit. Nonproliferation regimes and treaties have not halted the spread of such weapons; rather, it appears that the US military will be required to confront WMD-armed adversaries in regions of acute interest to the United States.[157] Timely, reliable, and accurate intelligence is a critical element of such operations, as the following discussion of Operations Desert Storm and Desert Fox suggests.

CHAPTER 7

Warfighting in a WMD Context

Intelligence Gaps, Operational Capabilities, and
Policy Implications

In the 1991 Gulf War, US and coalition efforts to destroy Iraq's WMD-related
assets and infrastructure met with only minimal success, underscoring the intrinsic difficulties of intelligence support to counterproliferation operations.
The conflict revealed considerable difficulties in locating, identifying, appropriately characterizing, and destroying nuclear, chemical, biological, and missile-related targets.

Yet the war demonstrated that even when WMD targets were successfully
located, their physical destruction would carry the acute risk of collateral damage. In theory, the release of even one kilogram of a biological agent such as
anthrax in a densely populated urban area might place tens of thousands or
even hundreds of thousands of civilians at risk. As the al-Shifa case examined
in chapter 6 suggests, or as Iraq's charge (discussed below) that the United
States destroyed a "baby milk plant" rather than a legitimate BW-related military target during the Gulf War indicates, such concerns are of critical importance to policymakers. In recent years this has often translated into a caution-
ary note in targeting, with the policy and operational communities being
unable or unwilling to carry out operations in which collateral WMD releases
were likely.

Whether in peacetime or in wartime, counterforce considerations remain
central to policy discussions relating to the use of force against a proliferant
state. This chapter emphasizes the role of intelligence in counterforce operations as it unfolded in Operation Desert Storm and, seven years later, Operation Desert Fox. While over the past several years the acquisition community
has made measured progress in developing military capabilities that diminished concerns over collateral release, it remains unlikely that extant technologies or those on the immediate horizon will eliminate such considerations.
Rather, policymakers and operators will have to contend both with continu-

ing difficulties in target detection and identification and with considerations relating to collateral damage and the prospect of unintended agent release resulting from counterforce operations. These difficulties can have serious diplomatic and operational impacts, potentially constraining the options available for securing US national interests or escalating the cost to the United States or its allies of achieving defined security objectives.

The Operation Desert Storm Air Campaign

The Gulf War air campaign highlighted the difficulty of conducting operations in a CW and BW environment. Of central importance was the planning and execution of military operations in the context of critical information gaps. Intelligence analysts and coalition air-campaign planners had great difficulty identifying the full extent of Iraq's WMD and missile capabilities; as a result, the air campaign was largely unsuccessful in destroying them. While planners entered the conflict aware that Iraq had developed both chemical and (probably) biological weapons, the WMD target set grew by half between Iraq's August 1990 invasion of Kuwait and the January 1991 beginning of the air campaign. When Iraq's Scud missile capability became a high-priority target set, coalition air forces were hard pressed to deal with the problems created by the need to detect, track, and destroy mobile missile launchers. Finally, even "successful" strikes on chemical weapons storage sites raised postwar concerns that US troops might have been exposed to low levels of chemical agent, one possible cause of the oft-referenced "Gulf War Illness."

Target Identification

In the month-long air campaign that preceded the hundred-hour ground campaign of Operation Desert Storm, Iraqi WMD-related targets were given a high priority. Iraq had used chemical weapons in its 1980–88 war with Iran and had developed an infrastructure that permitted self-sufficiency in chemical weapons production. The sophistication of Iraq's doctrine and Iraqi leaders' willingness to use chemical weapons led coalition planners to the prospect that Iraq might use its chemical weapons capabilities to counter actions by coalition ground forces when ground actions commenced. In addition to preventing chemical attacks on coalition troops, a second objective was to reduce Iraq's offensive capabilities and, by extension, its ability to threaten other regional states.[1] US and allied planners sought to achieve these objectives through a combination of deterrence and air strikes on Iraq's WMD infrastructure, a key center of gravity for Hussein's government, whose destruction was "on par with smashing Saddam's regime and dominating enemy airspace as main objectives" of the air campaign.[2] Thus a key issue for military planners was to accurately identify Iraq's WMD-related sites and target them for destruction (see table 5.3).

Generating the target list for Iraq's WMD-related facilities proved to be planners' and decisionmakers' "biggest challenge," according to the DOD's after-action report on the air campaign.[3] Although it was well known that Iraq was pursuing self-sufficiency in the manufacture of chemical weapons and widely held that Iraq was developing biological and nuclear weapons, there was much that coalition air planners did not know about the extent of Iraq's WMD programs and associated infrastructure.[4] Nevertheless, according to Barry Schneider and former Gulf War air commander General Charles Horner, at the time "U.S. officials believed that their knowledge was extensive enough to deal Iraq's NBC/M programs a fatal blow at the onset of hostilities."[5]

Targeting studies conducted in early 1990 by CENTCOM and its subordinate air component, US Central Command Air Forces (CENTAF), reportedly provided the foundation for the Desert Storm plan. These studies covered a wide variety of potential targets in Iraq, but "both target lists clearly lacked adequate information on nuclear, biological, and chemical target sets." The CENTAF target study identified only three WMD-related targets, while the CENTCOM study identified two.[6] Combining these studies with available intelligence, coalition planners were able to identify what they considered to be key installations in Iraq's WMD programs, totaling forty discrete targets as of August 2, 1990, the date on which Iraq's force invaded Kuwait.

The target list expanded as new intelligence surfaced after expanded collection and analysis, growing to some 60 targets by January 16, 1991, the day before the air campaign was launched, along with a total of 121 Scud-related targets. While only 2 biological weapons–related sites had been identified as of early August, by the beginning of the air campaign this number had grown to 19 known or suspected production sites and storage bunkers.[7] Only 2 nuclear targets were identified prior to the start of the air campaign: the Baghdad Nuclear Research Institute at Al Tuwaitha and the Al Qaim superphosphate plant and uranium mine. Other targets included key chemical weapons–related production and storage centers, some of which CENTCOM considered to be "the largest and possibly most sophisticated . . . in the third world."[8]

Results of the Air Campaign

During the course of the air campaign 970 strikes were launched against Iraqi WMD-related targets, roughly 15 percent of the total target set for the air campaign and approximately 5 percent of the total air strikes launched during the war.[9] Initially these strikes were assessed as having achieved considerable success in degrading or destroying Iraq's WMD production and delivery capabilities. According to the DOD's after-action report, *known* Iraqi WMD programs and facilities were severely damaged by air strikes in the coalition's campaign: "At least 75 percent of Iraq's CW production capability was destroyed," "the BW program was damaged and its known key research and development facilities were destroyed," and "damage to the known nuclear weapons program was substantial."[10] There was one interesting twist: when one suspected BW-related facility was destroyed, the Iraqi government permitted Western media sources to tour the ruins of what it called a "baby milk" factory. The Iraqi disinformation campaign led CNN's Peter Arnett to report, "It looked innocent enough, from what we could see." White House spokesman Marlin Fitzwater responded, but without offering supporting evidence, that "that factory is in fact a production facility for biological weapons. The Iraqis have hidden this facility behind a façade of baby milk production as a form of disinformation."[11]

In spite of these apparent successes, postwar inspections by UNSCOM teams revealed that the Iraqi WMD infrastructure was in fact much larger than the air-campaign planners had thought (see chapter 5).[12] In retrospect, the shortfalls in US intelligence were substantial, and the faith placed in prewar assessments of Iraqi WMD programs was, according to General Horner and Barry Schneider, "naïve."[13] As a result, key installations were not attacked, and the setbacks to Iraqi WMD programs were not as substantial as the original estimates suggested. This was especially true of the nuclear program: air-campaign planners had identified only two nuclear-related targets out of the more than twenty later discovered by UNSCOM.[14] Similarly, only nineteen biological weapons–related facilities were targeted, but UNSCOM later discovered forty.

The postwar *Gulf War Airpower Survey* found that due to the "extraordinary measures" the Iraqis had taken to obscure their nuclear program, "the air campaign no more than 'inconvenienced' Iraqi plans to field atomic weapons."[15] The after-action report attributes the "failure" of coalition analysts and planners to uncover the extent of the Iraqi program to a failure to ask "first order questions about the extent to which active deception and concealment measures by the Iraqis might be able to complicate Coalition targeting, or to reduce substantially the effectiveness of even precision bombing," and to "a conceptual failure to think through the range of feasible countermeasures and responses that the Iraqis could take to minimize the effectiveness of bombing against the military programs and capabilities that their leaders value most."[16] With regard to the Iraqi chemical weapons program, the report concluded that "even though air attacks against Iraq's chemical-warfare capabilities fell well short of destroying them completely, it by no means follows that these attacks were militarily futile or served no purpose." Rather, they served the "long-term goal of reducing Iraq's postwar threat to its neighbors."[17]

While in August 1990 there were forty known WMD-related targets, by January 1991 there were sixty, and by July 1992 more than eighty such targets had been identified.[18] This increase more than doubled the August 1990 target list and included not only facilities discovered during the course of the war but also those discovered by UNSCOM inspectors afterward.[19] This information and especially information gleaned from UNSCOM inspections would no doubt assist in future target planning against Iraq. But even after seven years of intensive UNSCOM inspections, "it has not been possible to verify, fully, Iraq's statements with respect to the nature and magnitude of its proscribed weapons programmes and their current disposition."[20]

Detecting Mobile Targets: The Great Scud Hunt

In addition to the threat posed by Iraq's chemical and biological weapons, its extensive Scud inventory also presented coalition air planners with a significant problem. The Scuds gave Iraq the ability to strike targets in coalition rear areas and throughout the Middle East. Though too inaccurate to be of substantial military value when armed with conventional warheads, Iraq's ballistic missiles nonetheless carried significant political and psychological impact and could be mated with unconventional warheads.[21] Thus, eliminating Iraq's Scud missile capability as early in the conflict as possible became a clear political priority for planners to address.[22] As a result, the coalition devoted substantial intelligence and military resources to tracking down and destroying Iraq's Scud launchers in what became popularly known as the "Great Scud Hunt."

Iraq used a combination of fixed and mobile launchers for its ballistic missile forces. Identifying the fixed sites and the number of mobile launchers proved troublesome. In October 1990 planners believed that Iraq had twenty-eight fixed-launch sites and approximately twenty Soviet- and Iraqi-built mobile and transporter erector launchers (MELs and TELs, respectively).[23] As the beginning of the air campaign grew closer, the assessed number of launchers grew. The official postwar after-action reports concluded that "intelligence estimates at the time of the total numbers of mobile launchers and Scuds were sketchy" and that by the time the air campaign began, "key portions of the target set—notably the pre-surveyed launch sites and hiding places used by the mobile launchers—were not identified."[24]

The initial master attack plan developed by CENTCOM did not target mobile Scud launchers but instead focused on the fixed launchers identified in western Iraq, which were among the first targets attacked when the air campaign began on January 17, 1991.[25] Reportedly, CENTCOM viewed attacking mobile missiles as too difficult and strategically insignificant compared with the goal of destroying Iraq's long-term ability to produce ballistic missiles.[26] Moreover, by December 1990 US intelligence reportedly had concluded that Iraq had already deployed and dispersed its mobile launchers to unknown sites throughout the country.[27]

The lack of attention to mobile launchers became a liability on January 18, 1991, when Iraq launched the first of more than forty missile strikes against Israel and coalition leaders found themselves faced with the possibility that Israel would retaliate against Iraq and potentially split the assembled coalition.[28] As missile strikes continued against Israel and targets in Saudi Arabia, coalition planners diverted a substantial number of sorties to tracking and destroying mobile Scud launchers. This was not an easy task, as the DOD later concluded: "The Scud crews had several initial advantages. They fired from pre-surveyed launch positions. Mobile erector launchers are only about as large as a medium-sized truck and moved constantly. This enabled crews to set up relatively quickly, fire, and move before coalition forces could respond. Western Iraq, launch area for targets in Israel, is rugged, a good setting in which to conceal mobile launchers in ravines, beneath highway underpasses, or in culverts."[29]

To counter this threat, campaign planners further tasked intelligence-collection assets, including photoreconnaissance and Joint Surveillance, Target Attack Radar System, or J-STARS, aircraft, US Defense Support Program satellites that detected the heat plumes of missiles as they rose into the atmosphere, and US and British special operations forces (SOF) detached to hunt down the mobile launchers and notify orbiting aircraft of their locations.[30] In spite of these activities, getting information to strike aircraft in a timely fashion remained a key challenge. Indeed, by the time intelligence reached strike assets, it was often obsolete.[31] In spite of improved communication procedures developed over the course of the war, at best it still took an estimated eighty minutes for targeting data to pass from reconnaissance assets to the strike aircraft.[32]

Over the course of the campaign, approximately 1,460 sorties were directed against Scud-related targets, 215 of which specifically focused on destroying mobile launchers; this was roughly one-third more than the number of sorties against WMD-related capabilities.[33] Strikes against Iraq's fixed-launch sites were among the first of the air campaign, but while CENTCOM claimed to have destroyed all twenty-eight identified sites by the end of January, postwar DIA assessments reportedly concluded that as many as half may have survived the war intact.[34] Locating mobile launchers also proved "remarkably difficult even in a desert environment."[35] Even when the mobile launchers were found, pilots tracking them soon discovered another difficulty: sorting out the launchers from decoys and vehicles similar in appearance. In some ways the pervasive inability to discriminate between decoys and actual targets did not fundamentally alter the task of the pilots flying Scud-hunting sorties, as their mission was to destroy "every vehicle that moved in the areas of western Iraq where the mobile scud units were operating."[36] It did, however, complicate battle damage assessment and left a decidedly unclear picture of how many mobile launchers were actually destroyed by coalition forces.

Difficulties in target discrimination resulted in grossly inflated reports of launcher kills from pilots and SOF, who reported destroying between eighty and ninety mobile launchers during combat operations.[37] Yet most, if not all, of these were later judged to be decoys. Indeed, the DOD after-action report observed that "there is no indisputable proof of any TELs or MELs—as opposed to high-fidelity decoys, trucks, or other objects with Scud-like signatures—having been destroyed by aircraft."[38] The reported successes of aircraft and SOF must also be weighed against the prewar estimate of twenty to thirty mobile launchers available to Iraq. These discrepancies suggest that either coalition pilots and SOF substantially overestimated the number of launchers they destroyed or intelligence analysts significantly underestimated the number of launchers Iraq possessed. A more realistic measurement of the effectiveness of the counter-Scud effort was based on the rate of launches rather than the number of launchers destroyed. By the end of January coalition air strikes and SOF had at least one evident effect: a noticeable decline in the number of launches, from an average of five per day early on to one per day toward the end of the war.[39]

Ten years after the war, General Horner recalled that "intelligence was a real problem." He attributed this partially to the "Cold War–centric view" that still existed at the time but also to agency rivalries. "I know there are many good people in the intelligence community," Horner stated, "and I know they do good work. But you should have had to work with the CIA during the Gulf War; then you would understand my anger. The CIA might have been doing wonderful work in Washington, but the intelligence they gathered filtered down to us as little more than gossip."[40] Other Desert Storm commanders also expressed dismay over intelligence performance, including CENTCOM Commander in Chief General H. Norman Schwarzkopf. Like Horner, Schwarzkopf criticized interagency rivalries and conflicts in the intelligence community during the war, stating that such conflicts produced "major areas of confusion."[41] Both for the soldier on the front line and for the policymaker in Washington, the considerable uncertainty surrounding the status and disposition of Iraq's WMD and missile capabilities ill served their respective purposes. After the conflict, consistent with enhanced policy focus, the relative attention paid by the intelligence community to WMD and missile proliferation increased significantly.

Facility Destruction and Collateral Effects

Even when WMD-related targets were "successfully" destroyed, collateral effects often persisted. During the air campaign and the ground war, several chemical units attached to coalition forces detected low-level concentrations of various chemical agents. While neither US nor coalition officials believe that Iraq deliberately employed chemical munitions during the Gulf War, the small quantities of chemical agents detected raised suspicions of collateral agent release, possibly triggered by coalition air strikes on Iraqi CW-related facilities.[42]

In the wake of the conflict, veterans suffering from a variety of medical symptoms collectively known as Gulf War Illness became concerned that the possible release of these chemical agents was connected to the appearance of the symptoms. Although no link between Gulf War Illness and these chemical agents has been established with certainty, the hypothesis that particular symptoms might be related to exposure to Iraqi chemical agents retains support.[43] This issue highlights a number of considerations, including key gaps in US and coalition intelligence data, the potential for collateral agent releases from the physical destruction of CW-related targets, and evident shortcomings in modeling and simulation capabilities to estimate possible exposures effectively and accurately. Indeed, effects modeling of potential poststrike releases

from facilities, including Ukhaydir and Khamisiyah, present often contradictory assessments over time.⁴⁴

Ukhaydir

Coalition aircraft bombed the Ukhaydir ammunition storage depot, believed to be a chemical weapons storage facility, twice during the air campaign,
on January 20 and again on the night of February 13–14, 1991.⁴⁵ Although
planners evidently had their suspicions, the true extent of the site's chemical
weapons inventory was not known until well after the war.

In 1996 another in a series of Iraqi "full, final, and complete disclosures"
to UN weapons inspectors revealed that 6,394 155-millimeter artillery shells
filled with mustard agent had been stored at Ukhaydir at the time of the strikes.
Iraq had originally led UNSCOM inspectors to believe that the rounds had been
stored at the Fallujah Proving Ground during the war. UNSCOM inspections
of Fallujah turned up evidence of 6,380 shells, about 200 of them damaged
enough to allow leakage. Based on the new Iraqi disclosure, UNSCOM inspected the Ukhaydir facility and found evidence, including 3 intact mustard-
filled shells, indicating that chemical rounds had been stored at the site. Furthermore, UNSCOM assessed that the damage to the munitions discovered at
Fallujah actually had occurred while the rounds were stored at Ukhaydir. The
intelligence community agreed with this assessment and concluded, based on
a review of data, that the damage could have occurred during the January or
February air strikes.

Initial models of the Ukhaydir release. Intelligence analysts reviewed available
data to determine whether any agent might have been inadvertently released
by the strikes and, if so, whether coalition forces might have been affected by
any such release (see fig. 7.1). They concluded that the January 20 strike had
ignited an extensive fire in the Ukhaydir complex that might have burned 104
rounds and caused 94 to leak and that the February air strike "may have destroyed as many as 11 mustard-filled rounds and possibly caused the 107 green
rounds to leak after they fell into the resulting bomb crater."⁴⁶ With regard to
the fire-damaged rounds resulting from the first strike, CIA analysts assessed
that most of the chemical agent would have been destroyed in the fire and that
it was unlikely that any surviving agent would have reached coalition troops
in any significant concentration.⁴⁷

Since this analysis was developed before the 1997 UNSCOM inspections of

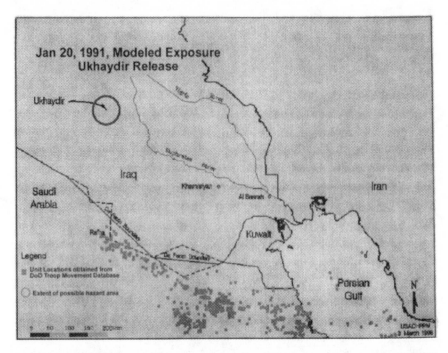

Figure 7.1. Map showing 40-kilometer radius around Ukhaydir and the locations of US forces on January 20, 1991
(DOD, Special Assistant for Gulf War Illnesses, *Possible Mustard Release at Ukhaydir Ammunition Storage Depot* [Washington, DC: GPO, 16 June 2000])

Ukhaydir revealed additional evidence, later that year CIA created a new hazard-transport analysis for the second strike. CIA modelers assumed that the contents of the 11 destroyed rounds, approximately seven gallons of mustard agent, had been aerosolized and that all 107 of the additional damaged shells had leaked their entire contents, approximately ninety gallons of mustard agent. Utilizing these source characteristics and available weather data for the time of release, the CIA model generated a plume of agents 10 to 20 kilometers wide extending 125 kilometers southwest of the Ukhaydir site and covering an area of approximately 1,250–2,500 square kilometers (see fig. 7.2). The CIA model suggested that any plausible agent plume "would have fallen below the general population limit by the time it had gone 40 kilometers in any direction from Ukhaydir." Thus, any release from Ukhaydir from either the January 20 or the February 13–14 strike would not have come within several hundred kilometers of any US or coalition forces.[48]

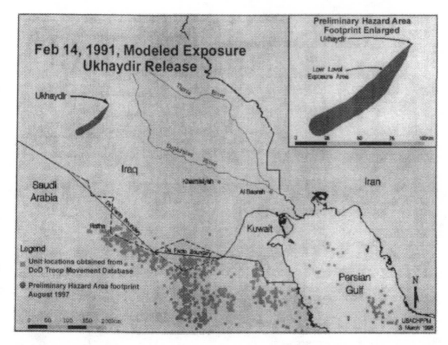

Figure 7.2. CIA preliminary modeling of results of the February 13–14 air strike on Ukhaydir
(DOD, Special Assistant for Gulf War Illnesses, *Possible Mustard Release at Ukhaydir Ammunition Depot* [Washington, DC: GPO, 16 June 2000])

A second look. The DOD also was assigned the task of modeling the potential release plume from the February strikes. The DOD used additional computer models and more detailed weather information than did the CIA, gathering all available weather data, including data from Air Force Special Forces, evidently not previously made available to the CIA. This additional information, together with sophisticated weather prediction software, allowed DOD modelers to recreate local weather patterns at the time of the strike and more accurately estimate agent dispersion under those specific conditions (see fig. 7.3).[49]

The resulting model assumed that the bulk of the agent would have been released within twenty-four hours of the facility's destruction and that the resultant plume would have come closest to coalition troops during this period. The DOD model suggested that the plume actually traveled in a different direction—southerly to southeasterly—from that suggested by the CIA model and posited a considerably smaller net potential hazard area. The illustrative plume was approximately 20 kilometers wide and extended approximately

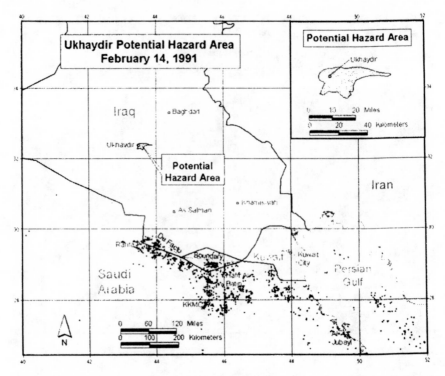

Figure 7.3. DOD modeling of results of the February 13–14 air strike on Ukhaydir, Day 1 (DOD, Special Assistant for Gulf War Illnesses, *Possible Mustard Release at Ukhaydir Ammunition Storage Depot* [Washington, DC: GPO, 16 June 2000])

20–40 kilometers in a south-southeasterly direction from Ukhaydir, covering an area of approximately 800 square kilometers. The DOD also modeled the anticipated behavior of the plume for three days following the attack, after which analysts believed the plume would have fallen below a level for concern, thus posing no real threat to coalition forces.[50] Like the CIA modelers, the DOD modelers concluded that during the three-day period after the strikes the release plume was always several hundred kilometers from coalition forces.

CIA reevaluation. In 1999 the CIA reassessed the potential release at Ukhaydir. Based on UNSCOM inspection data and a reevaluation of previous information, the CIA concluded that neither of the air strikes on Ukhaydir was responsible for the release of the agent. Instead, CIA analysts judged that the rounds had probably been damaged at a third location, where the damaged munitions might have released their contents. The CIA also reassessed the February air strike, concluding, based on the "lack of evidence of damage seen during [the] 1998 UNSCOM inspection," that it was unlikely that chemicals had been released during that attack.[51] The official DOD report on the Ukhaydir incident notes that there is contradictory information about the exact locations of the damaged rounds for both the January 20 strike and the resulting bunker fire and the February 13–14 strike. The lack of conclusive evidence and the differing assessments of CIA and DOD investigators prompted additional investigation. Nevertheless, based on the available data, the DOD report stated that it was unlikely that US troops had been affected by a release of chemical agents from Ukhaydir.

Khamisiyah

For those who argue that Gulf War Illness resulted from exposure to low levels of Iraqi chemical weapons during the war the Khamisiyah case is of prime importance. Whereas the potential releases at Ukhaydir, Al Muthanna, and other sites resulted from combat action, the Khamisiyah release stemmed directly from postwar demolition by US forces. Although the intelligence community identified Khamisiyah as a chemical weapons storage depot and relayed this information to the forces that initially captured the site, the information was not passed along to the troops carrying out demolition operations.[52] As a result, unlike the Ukhaydir incident, which did not affect US troops, the Khamisiyah incident potentially affected a large number of US soldiers.

The Khamisiyah ammunition storage depot contained a hundred storage bunkers in an area of roughly 50 square kilometers located approximately 100 kilometers from the Kuwaiti border. During the ground war US forces initially overran Khamisiyah on February 27, 1991, and follow-on forces arrived several days later to undertake an inventory and conduct destruction of munitions at the site. The troops that initially passed through the site, the 24th Infantry Division (Mechanized), had been warned of possible chemical weapons at the facility, but it appears that this information was not passed along to the follow-on forces, the 82nd Infantry Division (Airborne).[53] A search of several bunkers during the course of the inventory turned up no evidence of chemical weapons, and preparations were made for the demolitions, which were conducted on March 4 and 10. On March 4 a chemical alarm went off, causing troops to don protective gear. However, subsequent tests showed weak or slightly positive indications, while others showed no indications at all and led to commensurate reductions in the mission-oriented protective posture, or MOPP. Apparently, the demolition operations destroyed all one hundred bunkers at the site, as well as several crates of artillery rockets stored in a pit near the depot.

New information and initial CIA-DOD models. Questions arose in the years following the destruction of the Khamisiyah bunkers and the surrounding area. Postwar investigations revealed that chemical weapons had been stored at the site during the war and might have been present when US forces destroyed the munitions. In May 1991 Iraq admitted that more than two thousand 122-millimeter artillery rockets containing the nerve agent sarin had been stored at the Khamisiyah site along with more than six thousand 155-millimeter mustard gas shells.[54] It appears that leaks in some of the rockets prompted Iraq in February 1991 to transfer roughly one thousand of the 122-millimeter artillery rockets to a pit near the facility, which is where they were found and destroyed by US troops. It would seem that those particular US troops may have been exposed to low levels of sarin nerve agent as a result of the demolition operations at Khamisiyah.

However, analysts could not be sure how much of the agent had been released and therefore exactly how many troops may have been exposed. DOD personnel estimated that as many as twenty thousand could have been affected (see fig. 7.4).[55] To determine the possible extent of exposure, the CIA and the DOD were tasked in 1997 with producing several models of the possible release caused by the March 10 demolition. The best information available to modelers indicated that the site destruction might have released a potential 715 kilograms of agent.[56] The models produced two separate plumes, one for the area of first noticeable effects and one for the area of potential low-level exposure. The CIA models were tempered by uncertainties regarding several characteristics of the release, including a lack of concrete information on local weather conditions at the time of the pit demolition, how much agent was contained in the rockets, how much agent was released and what its purity was, and how many rockets were involved in the demolition. The resulting plumes suggest that a significant number of US troops may have been exposed to low-level concentrations of nerve agent.

2000: CIA-DOD reevaluation. In 2000, prompted by the recommendations of an independent review panel of modeling experts to improve aspects of their initial modeling methodology, the DOD and the CIA jointly developed another computer model of the release. For this reevaluation, the modelers had access to improved computer models and additional information on the munitions from UNSCOM inspections.[57] Using the new data and software, the DOD reevaluated its modeling and its projections for the number of US troops potentially exposed (see fig. 7.5).

While initial estimates in June 1996 posited that only four hundred troops might have been affected, within months this number had grown to twenty thousand troops (see table 7.1).[58] Yet the number rose again in 2000, with revised projections of more than a hundred thousand troops possibly exposed to low levels of nerve agent over the four days following the demolition.[59] While the Khamisiyah release was of greatest immediate concern to those investigating Gulf War Illness due to the large number of US troops potentially exposed to low levels of nerve agent, events such as this highlight the important of accurate intelligence, effective communication, reliable hazard prediction, and improved capabilities for defeating agents—all of which would come into play vis-à-vis Iraq seven years later.

Counterforce in Operation Desert Fox

By the end of 1998, UNSCOM inspections of Iraq had been under way for more than seven years. Iraq had made several "full, final, and complete" disclosures of its WMD programs that were, according to UNSCOM, "incomplete, inadequate, and containing substantial difficulties."[60] In December 1998, as a result of continued Iraqi recalcitrance regarding UNSCOM weapons inspections, the United States and Great Britain carried out a series of air and cruise missile strikes directed at air defense and WMD-related targets throughout Iraq. The target planners in Desert Fox benefited from seven years of UNSCOM inspections, which, as discussed in chapter 5, revealed that Iraq's WMD infrastructure and programs were much larger than previously understood. Desert Fox included seven discrete types of targets: (1) the Iraqi air defense network (32 targets); (2) the Iraqi military command and control system (20 targets); (3) security forces responsible for protecting and concealing WMD programs (18 targets); (4) the WMD and missile industrial base (11 targets); (5) Saddam's special security forces, including the Republican Guard (9 targets); (6) airfields (6 targets); and (7) a refinery producing oil products for smuggling in violation of UN economic sanctions (see table 7.2).[61]

While this WMD target list was based in part on data obtained by UNSCOM, the list reflects US and UK selections rather than UNSCOM priorities. When asked about the issue during a press briefing, CENTCOM Commander in Chief

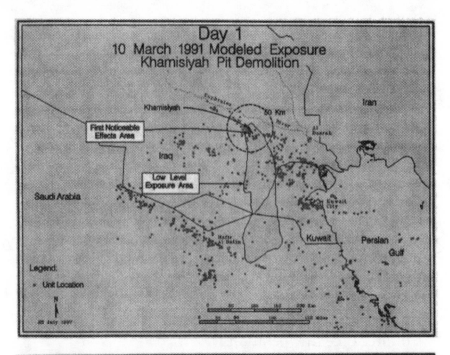

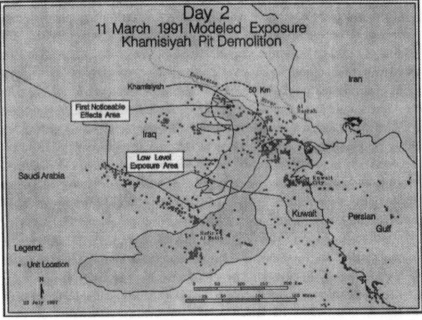

Figure 7.4. CIA 1997 modeling of the Khamisiyah pit demolition on March 10, 1991, and the spread of the agent cloud over the following days
(CIA and DIA, "Modeling the Chemical Warfare Agent Release at the Khamisiyah Pit," 4 September 1997, www.gulflink.osd.mil/cia_092297/, accessed 16 March 2001)

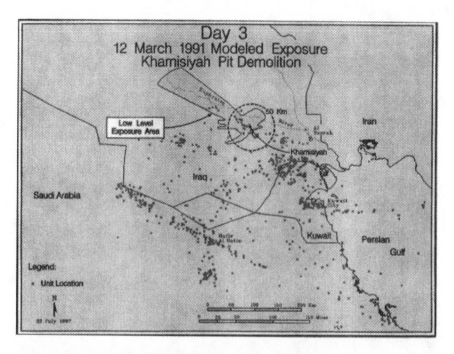

Day 3
12 March 1991 Modeled Exposure
Khamisiyah Pit Demolition

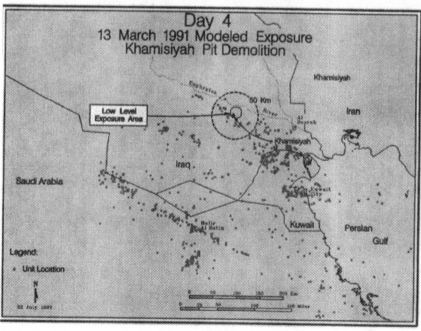

Day 4
13 March 1991 Modeled Exposure
Khamisiyah Pit Demolition

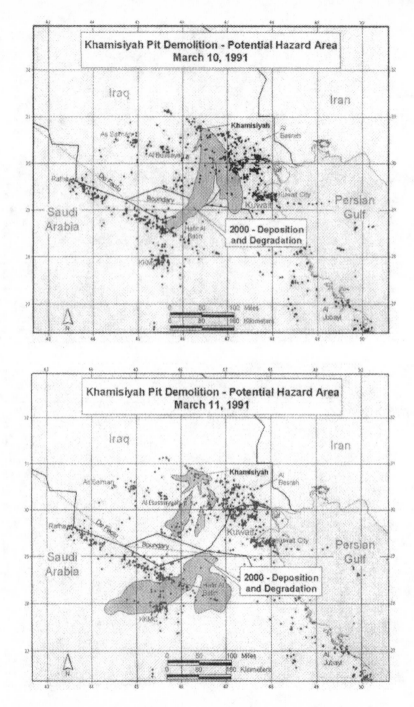

Figure 7.5. DOD 2000 modeling of the potential hazard area resulting from the Khamisiyah pit demolition on March 10, 1991, and the spread of the agent cloud over the following days
(DOD, "U.S. Demolition Operations at Khamisiyah," 7 December 2000, www.gulflink .osd.mil/khamisiyah_ii/, accessed 12 April 2001)

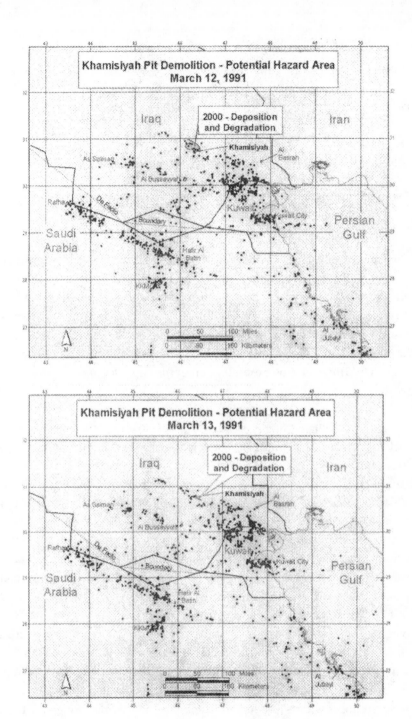

Table 7.1. DOD estimates of US service members possibly exposed to agents as a result of the Khamisiyah pit demolition, 1997 and 2000

Day	1997 Possible Exposures	2000 Possible Exposures
March 10	18,814	45,226
March 11	79,058	61,480
March 12	3,287	4,192
March 13	1,638	0

Source: DOD, *U.S. Demolition Operations at Khamisiyah,* 7 December 2000.
Note: Figures for 1997 represent joint CIA and DOD estimates.

General Anthony Zinni stated, "We see what UNSCOM does and where it goes and what the reports are, but nothing [in] the reports that I have [indicates] any knowledge of any deliberate spying or effort worked through UNSCOM."[62] To outside observers, Desert Fox constituted the world's "first nonproliferation war," demonstrating that "egregious violations of international norms would be punished" and that states such as Iraq "must be held accountable for their actions."[63] However, closer examination of the target set suggests otherwise.[64]

Desert Fox: Bypassed Targets

President William Clinton declared that the mission of US forces was "to attack Iraq's nuclear, chemical, and biological programs, and its military capacity to threaten its neighbors."[65] Yet, out of the hundred targets that were attacked during the campaign only eleven were related to WMD or missiles. Virtually all of the eleven were facilities related to Iraq's ballistic missile programs and other delivery systems.[66] Even these did not constitute all of the possible missile targets, as UNSCOM had identified twenty-two missile-related sites by December 1998 (see table 5.4). The majority of the remaining targets were related to Iraq's air defense network or were key to sustaining Saddam's regime, such as the secret police, presidential palaces, or the Republican Guard.[67]

US officials stated that military planners did not target Iraqi chemical or biological facilities for fear that air or missile strikes might inadvertently trigger the release of an agent, potentially generating massive civilian casualties.[68] The strikes also avoided targeting any dual-use facilities that might have been part of the Iraqi WMD infrastructure, as CENTCOM officials acknowledged: "We targeted nodes within [production] capability. But we did not go for the actual facilities. Our aim all along was to minimize collateral damage or civilian casualties. Any time you go after chemical or biological weapons, you create a

Table 7.2. Iraqi WMD and missile targets struck during Operation Desert Fox

Abu Ghurayb WMD Facility	Taji Missile Repair Facility
Ibn Al Haytham Missile R&D Center	Baghdad University Bio Research Center
Al Kindi Missile R&D Facility	Zaafaraniyah Fabrication Facility (Missile)
Tikirt Presidential Palace	Jabul Makhul Presidential Palace[a]
Radwaniyah Presidential Palace	Al Sava (Sahra) Airfield
Al Karamah Electronics Plant	Talil Airfield

Sources: William S. Cohen, General Hugh Shelton, and Rear Admiral Thomas Wilson, DOD news briefing on Operation Desert Fox, 18 December 1998; idem, DOD news briefing on Operation Desert Fox, 19 December 1998; Tim Youngs and Mark Oates, "'Desert Fox' and Policy Developments," House of Commons Library, International Affairs and Defence Section, 10 February 1999, 49, www.parliament.uk/commons/lib/research/rp99/rp99-013.pdf, accessed February 2001.

Note: In addition to the targets listed, the Iraqi Broadcasting Corporation (IBC) states, "All weapons of mass destruction factories south, southwest and southeast (especially Mahmoudia and Al Yousefia) were hit in the second raid on Thursday night." The IBC also mentions Rashidiya as a target, stating, "Weapons of mass destruction facilities in this area were also hit." The IBC does not specify what exactly these targets were. Presidential palaces were targeted because many were believed to be locations were Iraq concealed materials related to its WMD programs (see IBC, "Military Facilities Heavily Damaged in Baghdad and Other Areas from US/UK Bombing," 18 December 1998, Federation of American Scientists, www.fas.org/news/iraq/1998/12/18/981218-ibc.htm).

[a] The Iraqi Broadcasting Corporation reported that Jabul Makhul was being used as a storage site for materials related to Iraq's nuclear weapons program (see IBC, "Military Facilities Heavily Damaged in Baghdad and Other Areas from US/UK Bombing," 18 December 1998).

risk of dispersing those weapons and hurting civilian populations. You create a plume."[69] This sentiment extended to the highest levels of government. As Secretary of Defense William Cohen remarked, "We're not going to take a chance and try to target any facility that would release any kind of horrific damage to innocent people."[70] For this reason, the bulk of the strikes targeted command and control facilities and ballistic missile–related facilities rather than extant WMD capabilities or infrastructure, allegedly a central justification for military action. Clearly, the targeting of WMD facilities and how to strike them would continue to be a vexing problem for both the operational and policy communities in subsequent engagements.

Conclusion

The Gulf War underscored the importance and intrinsic challenges of countering WMD proliferation. Counterforce difficulties that US military, intelligence, and policy officials have had to deal with include identifying mobile targets, defeating hard targets, mitigating collateral effects, and countering adversary deception and denial techniques. The years since Desert Fox have seen considerable efforts devoted to these areas, resulting in measured progress.

Countering mobile targets. As a result of the Great Scud Hunt, US and allied military forces conducted extensive examinations of new methods for identifying and targeting mobile missile launchers. Although the Desert Storm experience played an important role in spurring the development of new tactics and munitions, Iraq's possession of such missiles was not the only impetus. Other potential military competitors, including China and North Korea, make use of both deep underground facilities and mobile missiles.

While technological advances have diminished the time between target identification and notification of operators, these efforts by potential adversaries make it considerably more difficult to identify, locate, and detect WMD- and missile-related capabilities. Improved electronic data links were developed to allow near-instantaneous communication between reconnaissance and strike assets involved in Scud hunting. In NATO exercises these links have reduced the time needed to pass targeting information to strike aircraft to less than ten minutes.[71]

Efforts have also been made to develop techniques to improve target discrimination and reduce the effectiveness of decoys. As with agent defeat, the Counterproliferation Program Review Committee continues to highlight detecting and defeating mobile targets as priority areas for capability enhancement. In fiscal year 1999, for instance, the Defense Advanced Research Projects Agency spent approximately $47 million on programs to develop advanced sensors and information exploitation systems to defeat enemy deception and camouflage activities and to provide near real-time information and imagery for tracking mobile targets.[72]

Target identification and dual-use considerations. In Desert Fox, US officials thought it would be too difficult to target chemical and biological manufacturing plants since they were often ambiguous.[73] Secretary Cohen argued that "we'd consistently indicated in the past that it's very difficult to try to target biological facilities, manufacturing facilities, since it could take place in a room [of any size]."[74] In planning Desert Fox, reducing collateral damage was a key concern; General Zinni directed planners to "only bomb Iraqi sites that had been identified with a high degree of certainty."[75] The dual-use nature of particular Iraqi chemical and biological facilities was also a key consideration.[76] General Zinni underscored that it was difficult to target chemical or biological facilities "because many of the plants that could produce [CBW] are pharmaceutical plants or agricultural chemical production plants. It's easy, in dual-use facilities like that to produce it."[77] The guidance proffered at the highest levels was "to strike those facilities we could identify that possibly solely produced" chemical or biological agents.[78]

The Desert Fox strikes occurred only months after the Clinton administration destroyed the al-Shifa pharmaceutical plant in Sudan, a suspected chemical weapons storage facility that also reportedly produced pharmaceuticals (see chapter 6). One possible explanation for the administration's caution was the international backlash likely to follow a similar incident.[79] Thus, such potential adversary disinformation strategies as the "baby milk" factory loomed as large in 1998 as they had seven years earlier.

The "agent defeat" problem. One of the key lessons of the Gulf War was a clear requirement to invest in "agent defeat" technology and precision-guided munitions. The deputy secretary of defense's 1994 *Report on Nonproliferation and Counterproliferation Activities and Programs* identified chemical and biological agent defeat as a high-priority area in light of both evident shortfalls in operational capability and the inherent political imperative to minimize collateral damage and reduce the potential for US and allied casualties.[80] Several years later the interagency Counterproliferation Program Review Committee still had not made significant progress in this area. The Air Force Agent Defeat Weapon Program, a program aimed at developing "capabilities and munitions to defeat or neutralize BW/CW agents and their delivery systems with little or no collateral damage," was one of several DOD counterforce programs reviewed by the committee. While some progress was evident, the program had a budget of only $298,000 out of a total DOD counterproliferation budget of approximately $6 billion for fiscal year 1999.[81]

The Air Force Research Laboratory (AFRL) and the Defense Threat Reduction Agency (DTRA) continue to explore potential improvements to counterforce capabilities. AFRL's Munitions Directorate began a weapons development program in the early 1990s but remained largely in the concept-definition phase at the end of the decade. Several designs have been tested over the years, but they have not resulted in a proven nonnuclear capability to adequately defeat chemical and biological agents. A variety of methods for neutralizing or destroying agents have been considered, including incendiary methods and various types of foams and other chemical technologies.[82] In 1999 the AFRL announced a forty-two-month program to develop and demonstrate a warhead that would meet requirements to "disrupt the functioning of fixed ground targets associated with the development, production and storage of chemical and/or biological (CB) weapons; neutralize the maximum possible amount of CB agents residing within the target; and limit the potential for collateral damage."[83] Unfortunately, no potential contractor proved able to develop an adequate technical solution, the demonstration was canceled, and "the acquisition strategy for this weapon [was placed] under reevaluation."[84]

DTRA also sought to develop improved munitions through two Advanced Concept Technology Demonstrations. DTRA's programs have focused on improved responses to the challenges of hardened and deeply buried targets and agent defeat. Some of these programs have attempted to use existing munitions in the US arsenal or to harness viable off-the-shelf technologies, such as the Consecutive Miracles program, designed to attack hardened or underground targets.[85]

Operation Enduring Freedom, the 2001–2 campaign in Afghanistan, suggested that weaponeers would continue to develop munitions to deal with these issues, widening the options available to policy and military officials. In that conflict US forces faced an elusive enemy hiding in a warren of caves. In addition to the use of precision-guided munitions and massive conventional munitions such as the BLU-82 "Daisy Cutter," US forces turned to new munitions to cope with Afghanistan's mountainous terrain.[86] Chief among these were fuel-air and "thermobaric" explosives, which use heat and pressure to destroy targets in caves and tunnels. The latter munitions may also help address the problems of hardened and deeply buried targets and agent defeat, manifest counterforce requirements.

While some promising technologies are being developed, the difficulties associated with destroying WMD-related facilities, weapons, or stocks with minimal collateral damage are likely to remain substantial obstacles both to military planners and to political leaders. Desert Storm highlighted that agent defeat capabilities were lacking, and US combatant commanders identify agent defeat as a priority capability for their warfighting needs. Yet by the end of the millennium the United States still lacked an operational nonnuclear weapon capable of attacking and destroying chemical or biological targets without the substantial and potentially politically unacceptable risk of collateral agent release.[87] More recently, such capability shortfalls have raised the prospect of a future requirement for tailored, low-yield nuclear weapons to resolve the agent defeat problem.

Deception and denial. With respect to adversary deception and denial techniques and the tracking of mobile targets, during Operation Allied Force in 1999 the United States and its NATO allies were able to test new technologies to determine the extent to which they had improved their capability for discriminating between targets and decoys. Operation Allied Force was directed at Yugoslav forces; a primary objective was to force their withdrawal from the Serbia province of Kosovo in order to protect ethnic Albanians in that region. For seventy-eight days NATO aircraft flew continuous sorties against a range of Serbian targets. As in the Iraqi air campaign, US and allied pilots were faced with an extensive denial and deception program aimed at reducing the effectiveness of air strikes and ensuring the survival of Yugoslav forces.[88]

While NATO forces had great success against fixed targets and facilities, the results against mobile targets, particularly tanks, armored personnel carriers, and artillery, were more ambiguous. Initial reports gave the impression that a significant impact had been made on Yugoslav forces: 181 strikes on tanks, 317 on armored personnel carriers, and 857 on artillery pieces.[89] However, subsequent reports indicated that the strikes had been much less effective and that many of the "successful" strikes had actually been strikes on Yugoslav decoys. One report claimed that out of 3,000 guided munitions employed by NATO warplanes, 500 hit decoys and only 50 hit tanks, while another asserted that "only 13 of 300 battle tanks were hit by NATO air bombs" and that "NATO pilots may have been duped by Serb decoys."[90]

The postcampaign review conducted by the DOD found that the initial reports had estimated results about 60 percent greater than the eventual confirmed results.[91] The review also suggested that unlike the deception and decoy efforts in the Gulf War, the Yugoslav deception and decoy efforts became less effective over the course of the campaign as NATO pilots recognized the scale of the deception efforts and "increasingly learned how to deal with Serbian deception tactics."[92] While progress in countering mobile targets is evident, denial and deception efforts are permanent features of today's security landscape. To be effective, US forces must develop an improved operational capability to hold an adversary's assets at risk. Indeed, a continued inability to credibly target and destroy a state's WMD capabilities may have profound and adverse implications for deterrence of adversary WMD use.

CHAPTER 8

Combating Proliferation

Toward a National Strategy

On May 6, 2002, Undersecretary of State for Arms Control and International Security John R. Bolton delivered an address to the Heritage Foundation outlining the threat posed by nuclear, biological, and chemical weapons from key states. In what came as a surprise to many observers, Bolton singled out Cuba, indicating that "the United States believes that Cuba has at least a limited offensive biological warfare research and development effort."[1] He called on the Cuban government to meet its obligations under the BWC and to halt its support to the biological weapons–related programs of other proliferant states.

Bolton's remarks played out against an open-source backdrop of rife speculation and little hard information relating to the suspected Cuban BW program or to WMD-related activities more broadly. To be sure, some analysts had speculated on this issue. Joseph Douglass Jr. and Neil Livingstone, for instance, had charged in 1987 that facilities at Kimonor and Jardin de Orquilles were associated with Cuban activities related to chemical and biological weapons.[2] A 1989 congressional hearing identified Cuba as a potential but doubtful possessor of chemical weapons, but it was not mentioned by name as a state of BW concern.[3] In 1991 Seth Carus observed that "allegations of offensive biological warfare activities have been made concerning fourteen countries in all," including Cuba.[4] The 1993 report of a House Armed Services Committee inquiry into the spread of chemical and biological weapons listed Cuba as a "possible" biological weapons state.[5] Apart from these scattered instances, little mention was made of Cuba and biological weapons until 1998, when Secretary of Defense William Cohen released a DIA report entitled "The Cuban Threat to U.S. National Security." According to that report, Cuba's advanced biotechnology industry "could support an offensive BW program in at least the research and development stage."[6]

Coming as they did on the eve of former President Jimmy Carter's visit to

Cuba, Bolton's remarks touched off a political firestorm. President Carter, for his part, discussed the issue with his Cuban interlocutors, who denied the allegations and took him on a tour of one particular laboratory, and claimed to have seen no evidence to support US charges.[7] National Security Adviser Condoleezza Rice dismissed Carter's decidedly critical take: "You can't show someone a biotech lab and be assured they're not creating weapons of mass destruction. That's not how biotech weapons work. And they're actually very easy to conceal and you need multiple measures to make certain biotech weapons aren't being developed and transferred."[8] Similarly, Assistant Secretary of State for Intelligence and Research Carl Ford opined, "We feel very confident about saying that they're working on an effort that would give them limited BW offensive capability. And that's serious enough to tell you. If we didn't think that it was important . . . we would have looked at the evidence and said: 'This is all bogus and there's nothing here worth reporting.'"[9] Conservatives on Capitol Hill, such as Robert Menendez (D-NJ), expressed gratitude that the administration "has finally come forth with an acknowledgement of Cuba's capabilities. Cuba's biotechnology industry is not just for medical reasons. . . . I think they could be making a variety of things, from anthrax to smallpox to other agents."[10] Similarly, Congressman Lincoln Diaz-Balart (R-FL) observed that Bolton's remarks "begin to put into perspective the debate about Cuba, a terrorist state with biological weapons 90 miles from the shores of the United States."[11]

At the same time, others were less sanguine about the text and the tenor of Bolton's blunt statement. For instance, Major General Gary Speer, of the US Southern Command, indicated that he thought Bolton's statement "got reported as an accusation that the Cubans were . . . that we had evidence that they were actually producing bioweapons. And I'm not sure that is the case."[12] Secretary of Defense Donald Rumsfeld suggested that he had "not seen the intelligence that apparently led Undersecretary Bolton to make those remarks."[13] Secretary of State Colin Powell, in turn, argued that Bolton's speech "was not breaking new ground" and that while "we do believe Cuba has a biological offensive research capability . . . we didn't say it actually had some weapons."[14]

While Cuba resides at the heart of a politically and ideologically charged debate in US foreign policy, the difficulty in assessing the BW threat stems largely from varying interpretations of fragmentary data. Within the BW arena the question where to draw the lines in a dual-use context—at what point BW-related activities become a "program" and when they would be properly characterized as "offensive" rather than "defensive"—presents a vexing analytic challenge. With respect to BW, a weapons capability arguably comprises mobilization potential (e.g., infrastructure, knowledge base, dual-use equipment) as much as it does intact weapon stocks. Thus, virtually any state with an advanced biotechnology or pharmaceutical industry could carry out offensive BW activities following a national decision to do so. Indeed, the Soviet precedent (see chapter 3) underscores that particular states have actively sought to conceal their program-related efforts in the guise of civilian activities. Thus, an assessment of Cuba's BW capability is predicated as much, if not more so, on perceived leadership intentions as on the existence of relevant research and development or production capabilities. Fundamentally, absent the "smoking gun," this is more a policy judgment than an intelligence assessment.

Assessments of Cuba's possible BW program underscore the intrinsic difficulties in WMD threat assessment writ large. Clearly, this is not the only such case of analytic discord; fragmentary indicators and inherent uncertainty are permanent features of the proliferation landscape. This final chapter reviews the nature and scope of the contemporary WMD threat and assesses core challenges to the development and implementation of the emergent US national strategy to counter WMD.

An Enduring Strategic Challenge

The number of actors pursuing nuclear, biological, or chemical weapons or their attendant delivery vehicles has increased significantly over the past couple of decades. The increasing ease of technology and information flow across national borders only compounds this phenomenon. At the same time, a comparatively small number of determined states actively pursue one or another weapon type; these states often seek to deepen existing capabilities. Some, on the other hand, have relinquished already developed capabilities. All told, the proliferation enterprise is dynamic rather than static; as it evolves, so too should policy responses.

For US national-security policy, the challenge posed by key regional actors armed with WMD is acute. In the hands of irresponsible or hostile states or subnational actors, WMD constitute a clear and present danger to US interests in key regions. How the United States and the international community as a whole meet this strategic challenge will bear heavily on the prospects for international peace and security in the twenty-first century. With revelations in

2002–3 of continued North Korean and Iranian nuclear weapons development programs, substantial uncertainties relating to the status of Iraqi special weapons activities, continuing supply-related activities by Russia, China, and other weapons-capable states, and the manifest development of a network of secondary suppliers, the specter of security competition looms large. Traditional diplomatic and economic efforts to restrain WMD development are unlikely to prevent nascent security dilemmas. If this hypothesis proves correct, states in Asia and the Middle East, if not elsewhere, are likely to build capabilities or seek alliances in an effort to safeguard their national interests in evolving regional security environments.

Disaggregating the Problem Set

An unambiguous agenda. Reviewing the record, one sees that the WMD- and missile-related activities of particular states are straightforward. Either states accept and appear completely compliant with their international obligations under the various international treaties and regimes regarding WMD or they reject membership in such conventions outright or do not comply with them. The former represent clear nonproliferation successes, whether because of unilateral decisions or because of US or international pressure, for example, the rollback of South African, Brazilian, and Argentine nuclear and/or missile programs; the suspension of nuclear weapons development activities by Taiwan, South Korea, and other states; and the post-Soviet safe return of special weapons to Russia from Ukraine, Belarus, and Kazakhstan and the attendant dismantlement of program infrastructure in those states.[15] Arguably, these states include the vast majority of the international community, states that seek to uphold traditional nonproliferation norms.

The latter group comprises the "holdouts" or "cheaters," which collectively and individually present substantial policy challenges. This group includes the members of what President George W. Bush in January 2002 dubbed the "axis of evil"—Iran, Iraq (at least through the fall of Saddam Hussein's regime in 2003), and North Korea.[16] These states have vigorously pursued WMD and their delivery means and pose clear challenges to US policy in Northeast Asia and the Middle East. Other states, including India and Pakistan are also clear proliferants, while Israel, Libya, Cuba, and Syria traditionally have been more opaque in their respective quests.[17] Should Libya successfully implement its late 2003 decision to unilaterally renounce its existing WMD capability, it will be the most recent state to follow South Africa's disarmament lead.

Together, this smaller group of recalcitrant or intractable proliferant states pose acute difficulties for the established nonproliferation regime. While, for instance, the status and accomplishments of the Iraqi programs may not be definitively known for some time, Iran has used chemical weapons in combat, is assessed to be actively pursuing biological and nuclear weapons, and continues to improve its ballistic missile capabilities.[18] North Korea continues unabashedly to pursue nuclear and other WMD in contravention of international norms and despite the poor state of that nation's economy.[19] India and Pakistan continue to build and improve their nuclear and missile capabilities, raising the prospect of deliberate or inadvertent nuclear use in any significant future conflict.[20]

Some of these states, such as Iraq, were allegedly members in good standing of international accords such as the NPT when they pursued a clandestine program to develop nuclear weapons (see chapter 6); inspectors from the IAEA gave Iraq a clean bill of health in 1990, while post–Gulf War inspections suggested that Baghdad had come within six months to two years of successfully developing a nuclear explosive device.[21] Other states simply sought to extort concessions from the international community. For example, North Korea supposedly suspended its nuclear activities in exchange for fuel assistance, light water reactors, and other items, including, a move toward the normalization of relations with the United States. Rather than complying with the terms of the Agreed Framework, however (see chapter 3), Pyongyang never declared how much fissile material it had illicitly produced and instead withdrew from the NPT and evicted IAEA inspectors from the Yongbyon facility, blaming "hostile" US policy for its actions in the process. Still other states, such as Israel, have simply refused to join the relevant international regimes.[22]

Since the nature of specific proliferation challenges presented by these states, as well as their underlying motives, varies considerably, it is unlikely that a one-size-fits-all policy will achieve the desired nonproliferation objectives in every case. Rather, the United States, in concert with like-minded partners and relevant international organizations, will need to develop actor-specific strategies in order to roll back existing capabilities and prevent the development of additional ones. Failing this, the United States and its allies will need to develop appropriate hedging strategies against the potential use of WMD by adversaries.

An ambiguous commitment. Other cases are decidedly less straightforward. Of central importance are those states that publicly declare support for established international conventions or select nonproliferation treaties, regimes, or organizations therein but are either unwilling or unable to effectively fulfill their responsibilities or actively pursue a duplicitous export policy. China's activities, particularly in the nuclear and missile areas, are a prime example of such behavior (see chapter 2). Chinese officials have variously championed the free flow of technology across borders and declared an intention to prevent further proliferation, with the trend being toward the latter. In practice, while China has pledged to uphold the spirit of the MTCR and has repeatedly promised US officials to refrain from supplying WMD- and missile-related capabilities, PRC weapons-related technologies have continued to flow to other states, including Pakistan and Iran. Similarly, the Russian government's continued unwillingness, inability, or lack of interest in stemming the flow of weapons-related assistance to Iran presents a clear challenge to US policy and to ultimate prospects for successful nonproliferation (see chapter 5).

The Chinese and Russian cases raise the vexing issue of relative state strength. The nature and number of military, energy, industry, and other state actors in the Chinese decision-making process challenge the unified nature of the state apparatus. Yet while the leadership may be unaware of some individual transactions, the aggregate pattern of PRC export behavior suggests at least some complicity on the part of key officials.

Despite progress in China's declared nonproliferation policy over the last several years, implementation continues to lag. One possibility is that the Chinese leadership has not truly made a commitment to upholding global nonproliferation norms and is torn between three competing principles: adopting responsible and restrained policies that appropriately reflect (in the eyes of the international community) China's increasing status as a regional and global power; using selective proliferation to advance perceived Chinese security interests with respect to a limited number of states; and relying on exports to raise much-needed revenue. It appears reasonable to suggest that while Chinese officials believe that proliferation may in some cases adversely affect long-term PRC security interests, selective proliferation is likely to continue with their tacit approval, if not active support.[23]

Similarly, the contemporary Russian case poses the difficult post-Soviet challenge of a weak state that is either incapable of regulating the outward flow of WMD-related technologies or unwilling to do so. Russian officials often question the accuracy of charges that weapons-related information, technologies, or material have emanated from Russia. At other times they routinely argue that conventional weapon sales do not violate international agreements and that other commercial transactions, such as Russian space-launch and nuclear assistance to India or commercial reactor sales and technical support to Iran, are valid under international law. Indeed, in aggregate it would appear that weapon sales are intended to advance larger Russian foreign-policy considerations and may yield some influence over the foreign and defense policies of friendly states.[24]

Despite the possible negative strategic implications of some exports, short-term profit is a powerful lure; Stephen Blank argues that such "strategic myopia" is widespread.[25] But even if Russian officials are, as then Prime Minister Primakov suggested, "doing everything" to prevent technology leakage, such efforts are clearly inadequate.[26] Despite official Russian assurances, it would be prudent to expect further transfers of technology and continued cooperation—whether direct and state-sanctioned or indirect and without the knowledge of the state—with states of proliferation concern, as well as a modest to minimal official Russian response to such activities ahead.[27] There is little reason to suggest that the pattern identified by Aaron Karp—transfer, then deny, then pledge restraint (but instead continue)—will abate in the near term.[28]

The nonproliferation regime is incapable of preventing deliberate state-level transfers and is unsuited to preventing unsanctioned ones. Thus, if Russian and Chinese transfers are, in fact, authorized by government officials, there is little basis for believing that established international conventions will be able to effectively implement their assigned nonproliferation tasks. But even if such transfers are illicitly made by rogue "entities," there is little international recourse. Nor have bilateral approaches proven much more effective: neither diplomacy, intelligence sharing, sanctions, nor trade incentives have solved this problem. Rather, the cumulative effect of Russian, Chinese, North Korean, and other WMD- and missile-related exports has fundamentally transformed the international-security landscape. This "creeping proliferation" implies aggregate capabilities that exceed particular, often uncoordinated transactions by the relevant technology suppliers. Russian and North Korean assistance to Iran's ballistic missile development efforts is a clear case in point. Their individual efforts helped Iran "save years" in the research, development, testing, and evaluation process associated with the Shahab-3 MRBM, which was successfully tested in 1998.[29]

Tough calls. A third proliferation consideration relates to the tough calls, those concerning actors with the latent capability to pursue a weapons program but no evident intention to do so. As with Cuba and biological weapons, analytic difficulties rest in part with the uncertainties inherent in a leadership's plans or underlying intentions. Similarly, intelligence collection is becoming more difficult as dual-use technologies spread, the possibility of indigenous development of WMD and missiles increases, more secure communication modes (e.g., fiber optics) are installed, and additional denial techniques are implemented (see chapter 4).

Together, these developments have reduced the intelligence collection window and increased the margin of error for WMD-related threat assessment. Cuba's biotechnology sector, for instance, is known worldwide for its hepatitis B and meningitis vaccines and has attracted the attention of Western pharmaceutical corporations; yet the same technology can be harnessed for weapons-related applications.[30] Similarly, Japan's highly developed civilian nuclear facilities (and large stockpile of reprocessed plutonium), capable and extensive technical and manufacturing sectors, and space program suggest that it may be able to successfully establish a long-range nuclear weapons capability in a relatively short period of time.[31] And while Japan, or states similarly situated, may not have the intention of developing nuclear weapons today, changes in the regional security environment, the political leadership, national defense requirements, or other factors open the door for potential changes ahead.

Subnational WMD capabilities represent an even more acute analytic challenge. In this case the intention of particular actors appears clear: to acquire or develop and employ special weapons in pursuit of a defined political agenda.[32] Particularly following the tragedy of September 11, 2001, but also for several years prior to that, senior US officials and official government reports underscored the likelihood, over time, of terrorist organizations' coming into possession of unconventional materials and the prospect of their use against the United States homeland, US forward-deployed forces, or US friends and allies. The combination of an increasing availability of technology and expertise, the perception that particular terrorist organizations are motivated toward acts involving mass casualties, the impending end of a millennium, a spate of conventional attacks against US assets, and the widespread suspicion of terrorists seeking WMD all contributed to this general assessment.

Toward the end of the twentieth century this concern was heightened by, among other events, the Japanese cult Aum Shinrikyo's use of sarin in the Tokyo subway in 1995. While the group's attempts in the early 1990s to produce, weaponize, and disseminate anthrax and botulinum toxin in the early

1990s failed, it achieved at least qualified success with sarin: twelve fatalities and fifty-five hundred injured as a result of this attack.[33] Since then, al-Qaeda reportedly tried to develop such capabilities but was interrupted by military action in Afghanistan. More recently, the prospective linkage between terrorist organizations and state actors possessing WMD programs has become an acute security concern. As Secretary of Defense Donald Rumsfeld testified in May 2002, "We have to recognize that terrorist networks have relationships with terrorist states that have weapons of mass destruction, and that they inevitably are going to get their hands on them, and they would not hesitate one minute in using them. That's the world we live in."[34]

A National Counterproliferation Strategy

Counterproliferation was not created by the administration of President George W. Bush. The concept was developed in the final two years of the of George H. W. Bush administration, and it was systematically articulated under Clinton administration Secretary of Defense Les Aspin (see chapter 1). Indeed, in the view of Gilles Andréani, "one finds convincing signs of a gradual shift" toward counterproliferation in US national-security policy through the 1990s.[35]

While Andréani's general sense is undoubtedly accurate, counterproliferation achieved *national* stature with the administration of George W. Bush. While the DOD developed relevant counterproliferation capabilities, plans, and programs under Clinton, they remained subordinate to a larger national strategy predicated largely on nonproliferation measures, whether traditional measures such as export controls or more recent innovations such as cooperative threat reduction. While there were occasions when preemptive or preventive measures were actively contemplated against proliferant states, such as North Korea in 1993–94, the Clinton administration's sustained approach revolved around diplomatic dissuasion more than around military operations.

In comparison, Clinton's national-security strategy recognized prospective future requirements for "countering potential regional aggressors" and "confronting new threats," just as Bush's does.[36] But the two strategies differ fundamentally in their central policy approaches and specific prescriptions. Clinton defined "Arms Control and Nonproliferation," in a highly detailed, lengthy section, as the axis around which US response to WMD and missile proliferation centered, while measures relating to the "Department of Defense's Counterproliferation Initiative" drew just one short paragraph, supplemented by single paragraphs dedicated to deterrence, combating terrorism, and the role of nuclear weapons in the US security posture.[37] The Bush strategy gives continued importance to "strengthened" nonproliferation efforts but downgrades the prior treaties-and-regimes approach and elevates the status of both "proactive" counterproliferation efforts to deter and defend against WMD and missile threats and "effective" consequence management should such weapons be used.[38] The Bush administration also issued in December 2002 the first-ever companion *National Strategy to Combat Weapons of Mass Destruction*, an unclassified synopsis of National Security Presidential Directive 17.

The most striking aspect of the Bush administration's national-security strategy is the avowed determination that "we cannot let our enemies strike first," underscoring that in some cases the risk of inaction may outweigh the risk of action. Faced with a "looming" threat, a set of "new deadly challenges [that] have emerged from rogue states and terrorists," the United States "will, if necessary, act preemptively" to "forestall or prevent hostile acts by our adversaries."[39] While a decade ago discussion of preemption's potential future requirements, its prospective utility and potential liabilities, the requisite strategic and operational framework, and the military capabilities needed to enact such an approach nearly derailed the fledgling Defense Counterproliferation Initiative, issues relating to preemption have once again risen to the forefront of national strategy.[40]

The Bush Doctrine

"The gravest danger to freedom," said President Bush to an audience at West Point in June 2002, "lies at the crossroads of radicalism and technology. When the spread of chemical and biological and nuclear weapons, along with ballistic missile technology . . . occurs, even weak states and small groups could attain a catastrophic power to strike great nations."[41] Not surprisingly, this convergence of problem sets—the continuing prospect of terrorism against US interests and the continuing proliferation of nuclear, chemical, and biological weapons–related capabilities (e.g., materiel, technologies, expertise)—is central to the contemporary national-security approach. In the earliest "official" articulation of the Bush Doctrine, Vice President Dick Cheney declared, "We will hold those who harbor terrorists, those who provide sanctuary to terrorists, responsible for their acts."[42] Responding to the tragic events of September 11, 2001, senior officials in the Bush administration determined that the best defense against the proliferation-terror nexus would be a good offense against both terror organizations with global reach and rogue states that develop WMD and missile capabilities and sponsor terrorism.

Since then, the Bush Doctrine has arguably evolved, advancing at least five core propositions: (1) the highest priority of the armed forces and the US government as a whole is the safety and security of the US homeland; (2) states that support terrorists of "global reach" will be held accountable for any acts of terror propagated; (3) neutrality in the global war on terrorism is not an option; (4) the United States will oppose attempts by state sponsors of terrorism to acquire or develop WMD, by force of arms if necessary, including the possible preventive or preemptive use of military force; and (5) the United States will act on a multilateral or unilateral basis, as required, bringing to bear the full range of diplomatic, military, law enforcement, public health, and other relevant capabilities to maintain its security in light of manifest or developing proliferation and terrorism threats.

Effectively translating these propositions into practice will surely remain the central thrust of the Bush administration for the duration of the president's tenure in office. Indeed, given the scope of the challenge and the importance of the tasks at hand, these propositions are likely to remain front and center in US national-security policy for the foreseeable future. Prospects for ultimate success rest heavily on a sound understanding of the evolving threat, on the development of deterrent and defensive postures that diminish the likelihood of adversary WMD use, and on the ability of the United States to successfully meet key policy and planning challenges as they arise.[43]

At the end of the twentieth century the intelligence community assessed that "at least" sixteen states had active chemical weapons programs, "perhaps" a dozen pursued offensive biological weapons programs, and a growing number of states were actively seeking the relevant technologies or developing the indigenous capabilities necessary to produce increasingly capable ballistic and cruise missile delivery vehicles.[44] Compounding the problem are an accelerating diffusion of dual-use technologies; challenges posed by a growing network of secondary suppliers and by direct foreign assistance to aspiring proliferant states; the prospect of subnational or state-sponsored actors in the proliferation equation; and related considerations that suggest a trend in which, all things being equal, WMD-related concerns will likely continue to grow in the years ahead.[45]

Critics of the Bush administration's approach, such as G. John Ikenberry, have argued that an "American policy that leaves the United States alone to decide which states are threats and how best to deny them weapons of mass destruction will lead to a diminishment of multilateral mechanisms—most important of which is the nonproliferation regime." In Ikenberry's view, a "strategy of counterproliferation based on American willingness to use unilateral force to confront dangerous dictators" will be unlikely to "work" over the long term. Rather, he posits, "overwhelming American conventional military might, combined with a policy of preemptive strikes, could lead hostile states to accelerate programs to acquire their only possible deterrent to the United States: WMD." The "neo-imperialist" strategic vision articulated by the Bush administration, he concludes, "will leave the world more dangerous and divided—and the United States less secure."[46]

Yet the starting point of Ikenberry's analysis, at least in the proliferation arena, is fundamentally flawed, a point of departure rooted in an essential confusion of cause and effect. The implicit policy prescription advanced is both to seek enhancements to existing multilateral nonproliferation agreements and to diminish reliance on the more "proactive" approach taken since the 2001 attacks on the US homeland. But it is not clear whether international consensus on a substantially improved nonproliferation regime can be achieved or whether, in fact, such a regime would ultimately be capable of preventing the further proliferation of WMD or weapons-related technologies or expertise, let alone be capable of rolling back existing capabilities in key states of proliferation concern. Nor is it necessarily plausible that an inherently reactive rather than a proactive approach, a diplomacy-oriented rather than a military-operational one, or a multilateral more than a unilateral approach would diminish the possibility that a rogue state or terror cell would attack US interests. Rather than a recipe for further proliferation, the Bush national-security strategy is a direct outgrowth of an existing postproliferated and terror-prone security environment. It is both the logical culmination of more than a decade's worth of experience with recalcitrant proliferants in key regions and a sound premise on which to base US national-security planning in the years ahead.

Indeed, the Bush administration's counterproliferation posture is predicated on a series of critical analytic judgments: (1) that WMD-armed regional adversaries pose a clear and present danger to US national security; (2) that WMD capabilities have spread and will continue to do so in spite of extant nonproliferation regimes; (3) that particular actors who possess WMD or are likely to gain access to this weaponry are perhaps also likely to use it, potentially against both military and civilian targets, whether in overseas theaters of operation or against the US homeland; and (4) that the likelihood of strategic or tactical surprise is high, while the likelihood of advance warning of such strikes is low.[47]

In this context, successfully advancing US national security requires a sober appreciation of what George Tenet calls the "changing character of warfare." For adversaries "whose main goal is to cause the United States pain and suffering, rather than to achieve traditional military objectives," asymmetric capabilities—including WMD proliferation and terrorism—arguably afford powerful force multipliers. For this reason, and predicated on an assessed growing threat of chemical and biological weapons, Tenet concludes that there is a "significant risk within the next few years that we could confront an adversary—either terrorists or a rogue state—who possesses them."[48]

To effectively meet the challenge of a prolonged struggle to protect the United States from mass-destruction terrorism, nascent activities must build upon and extend the existing counterproliferation plans, programs, and policies that were systematically established in the aftermath of the Gulf War and have evolved since that time. Indeed, in order to enhance and sustain US efforts to counter security threats within the proliferation-terror nexus, policy officials must address at least five core challenges: confronting strategic actors, diminishing the prospects for and implications of surprise, building robust offensive capabilities, developing effective defense-in-depth, and determining the proliferation end game.

Confronting Strategic Actors

Preemption and prevention are not new to strategic deliberations within the US policy community. While recent discussion has been set in the context of military action against the Iraqi government of Saddam Hussein, the last time US officials contemplated preventive war was roughly a decade ago on the Korean Peninsula.[49] In that particular case Pyongyang's threatened withdrawal from the NPT in the context of reported intelligence assessments indicating that the state had already produced fissile material sufficient for at least one and possibly two nuclear devices led to policy and planning discussions about how best to prevent the DPRK from succeeding in its nuclear quest (see chapter 3).

The approach ultimately chosen privileged diplomacy over military action. Less than a decade later, however, this has proven to be a temporary fix, as the issue has reappeared with recent revelations of a continued nuclear weapons development program.[50] In response to the most recent nuclear challenge, it is likely that a diplomatic approach, whether principally cooperative or coercive, will again be pursued. But it is also possible that as in the second Gulf War, officials may ultimately choose to explore potential military options.

The need to develop cohesive options for preventive war, preemption, and other responses to North Korea and other tough proliferation cases will likely continue for as long as terrorism and WMD and missile proliferation jeopardize US security interests. It is unlikely that a one-size-fits-all approach will, or should, be applied equally in all cases, since regional political-military contexts, operational environments, and available options will likely vary. Tailored, actor-specific approaches will arguably have greater prospects for success.

Looking ahead, US officials will have to continue to balance between contending foreign-policy priorities. Rediscovering an old truth, single-issue policies tend over time to yield to the more complex mosaic of a state's aggregate foreign policy. For example, in the proliferation context there is a clear tension between potential legal requirements to impose sanctions against such strategic allies as Pakistan for their WMD or missile development (and export) activities, on the one hand, and identified strategic requirements and tactical imperatives to bolster a key regional ally, on the other. Similarly, states such as Yemen have forced US policymakers to find an appropriate balance between evidently conflicting objectives with respect to counterterrorism and counterproliferation. In December 2002 the Spanish military, at the request of the US government, successfully interdicted a North Korean freighter carrying Scud missiles bound for Yemen. But the shipment was soon released intact to Yemen, an avowed partner in the global war on terrorism, even though interdiction was viewed as a "critical part" of the US strategy to combat WMD proliferation.[51] In this case, at least, terrorism trumped proliferation in US policy implementation.

Nor are these difficult policy trade-offs limited to decisionmakers in the United States. If select UN Security Council members, or the international community as a whole, would prefer that the United States adopt alternative policies with respect to combating WMD proliferation—as the French, Russian, and other governments have publicly articulated—then they, specialized UN affiliates such as the IAEA, and the United Nations more broadly must demonstrate a sound ability to manage complex WMD-related issues as they arise, including appropriate enforcement of UN Security Council resolutions. If this proves beyond the pale, like-minded states should redouble their efforts on a bilateral or more limited multilateral basis to counter the continuing spread of WMD-related capabilities and to develop coordinated policy positions and security postures toward key regional proliferants. But while some tactical successes may ultimately result, these will not resolve the aggregate strategic or systemic problems posed by continued WMD proliferation.

If recent history is any guide, persistent political disunity within the United Nations, continued national disagreements that serve to constrain the performance of WMD-related treaties and regimes, and on the part of the most egregious proliferants a continued lack of will, interest, or capability to stem WMD-related transfers are more likely. While North Korea and Iran loom large today, in this postproliferated security arena there will clearly be other cases ahead.

Diminishing the Prospects for and Implications of Surprise

While tactical warnings of specific attack modes, timing, locations, and perpetrators will be difficult to come by, the intelligence community has provided credible strategic warning of the attempted development of, as well as the probable intent to employ, WMD against US interests by a range of potential actors at the state and subnational levels. While historically proliferation surprise has been most evident with respect to mistaken estimates of the nature or maturity of specific national programs, the potential exists for strategic surprise, such as the emergence of significant but unexpected proliferant states (e.g., allies or friends responding to regional proliferation developments), unknown capabilities (e.g., those acquired covertly from external sources), or unanticipated operational concepts for the employment of WMD. Particularly in nations or terror organizations hostile to the United States or its friends or allies, unexpected approaches to acquiring or developing WMD could have important political and military implications.[52] Indeed, the actors of greatest proliferation concern are also among the most challenging intelligence targets; their closed or restrictive political processes often make it difficult to obtain high-fidelity information on such sensitive issues. Information on adversary capabilities, plans, and intentions may not be available, may be fragmentary or misleading, or may change quickly.

At the same time, improving threat assessment is a difficult task but an important one if the prospect of strategic surprise is to be diminished. Retooling intelligence capabilities to deal more effectively with both enduring and emerging strategic challenges is a clear imperative. For example, the congressional joint inquiry into the September 2001 terrorist attacks found *systemic* weaknesses that hindered the intelligence community's counterterrorism efforts leading up to al-Qaeda's September 11, 2001, attacks against the United States, including the following:

- The intelligence community was "neither well-organized nor equipped, and did not adequately adapt, to meet the challenge posed by global terrorists focused on targets within the United States."
- Its "understanding of al-Qa'ida was hampered by insufficient analytic focus and quality, particularly in terms of strategic analysis. . . . There was a dearth of creative, aggressive analysis targeting Bin Laden and a persistent inability to comprehend the collective significance of individual pieces of intelligence. These analytic deficiencies seriously undercut the ability of U.S. policymakers to understand the full nature of the threat, and to make fully informed decisions."
- It was "not prepared to handle the challenge it faced in translating the volumes of foreign language counterintelligence it collected. Agencies within the Intelligence Community experienced backlogs in material awaiting translation, a shortage of language specialists and language-qualified field officers, and a readiness level of only 30% in the most critical terrorism-related languages used by terrorists."
- Its "ability to produce significant and timely signals intelligence on counterterrorism was limited by NSA's [the National Security Agency's] failure to address modern communications technology aggressively. . . . NSA continues to have mixed results in providing timely technical solutions to modern intelligence collection, analysis, and information sharing problems."
- It did "not effectively develop and use human sources to penetrate the al-Qa'ida inner circle. This lack of reliable and knowledgeable human sources significantly limited the Community's ability to acquire intelligence that could be acted upon before the September 11 attacks."
- It "depended heavily on foreign intelligence and law enforcement services for the collection of counterterrorism intelligence and the conduct of other counterterrorism activities. The results were mixed in terms of productive intelligence. . . . This reliance on foreign liaison services also resulted in a lack of focus on the development of unilateral human sources."

- It experienced an information-sharing breakdown, "not only between different Intelligence Community agencies, but also within individual agencies, and between the intelligence and the law enforcement agencies." The US government "does not presently bring together in one place all terrorism-related information from all sources."
- Its relations with the US military were sometimes strained. "Senior U.S. military officials were reluctant to use U.S. military assets to conduct offensive counterterrorism efforts in Afghanistan, or to support or participate in CIA operations directed against al-Qa'ida prior to September 11. At least part of this reluctance was driven by the military's view that the Intelligence Community was unable to provide the intelligence needed to support military operations."[53]

As many of the cases examined above suggest, the systemic weaknesses identified in the joint inquiry also generally apply to the intelligence community with respect to WMD and missile proliferation. Cogent and insightful assessments of nonstate actor WMD capabilities are a daunting task for these and other reasons. Credibly assessing the dynamic and evolutionary WMD problem set at the state level is further compounded by active deception and denial measures, the growing indigenization of production for many proliferants, the introduction of new technologies that further complicate the collection process, the analytic challenges inherent in discovering alternative weapon system acquisition pathways or production processes, and other salient issues discussed elsewhere in this book.

While perfect information will almost always be unobtainable, margins of error will at times be high, and performance will vary on a case-by-case basis, if intelligence disseminated is to help inform policy and to facilitate operations it must be viewed as credible by consumers. In the context of Iraq in 2002–3, for instance, both the "high confidence" judgments relating to Iraqi WMD capabilities and the "low confidence" judgments relating to that state's WMD-related plans and intentions articulated in an October 2002 NIE suggest the need both to reexamine and amplify established analytic approaches and to redouble collection efforts against hard proliferation targets.[54]

Moreover, using active diplomatic and operational measures to dissuade adversaries from employing and, where possible, developing WMD and long-range delivery vehicles is a principal task of national efforts to combat proliferation. At the same time, preparing for and mitigating the effects of surprise also means maintaining a robust counterproliferation science and technology base capable of supporting hedging strategies against emerging and to some degree unpredictable threat developments. Similarly, the more capable forces can operate in contaminated environments, the more resilient they will be in facing WMD surprise on the battlefield. Indeed, US military forces must prepare for a range of operating conditions and regional circumstances, unconstrained by rigidly "validated" threat information, which has frequently proven inaccurate and arguably counterproductive in the past. This capabilities-based approach, an effort to "anticipate the capabilities that an adversary might employ to coerce its neighbors, deter the United States from acting in defense of its allies and friends, or directly attack the United States or its deployed forces," is central to the 2001 *Quadrennial Defense Review*.[55] Finally, improvements to homeland security will further help devalue the attractiveness of WMD against "rear-area" targets.

Building Robust Offensive Capabilities

Just two days after the September 11 attacks, the search for appropriate offensive options for a prospective military engagement in Afghanistan rapidly unfolded. President Bush reportedly asked for "options on the table. . . . I don't want to put a million-dollar missile on a five-dollar tent."[56] With respect to offensive capabilities, the war in Afghanistan ultimately saw, among other things, the substantial use of SOF and the introduction of thermobaric munitions and other technologies. Yet, war on a battlefield characterized by adversary *threats* or actual *use* of nuclear, biological, or chemical weapons would clearly engender a somewhat different set of operational requirements.

Certainly, one clear lesson of the 1991 Gulf War was that an adversary need not have a highly effective tactical WMD capability to achieve important effects.[57] In that conflict, even conventionally armed ballistic missiles arguably had an impact at both the strategic and operational levels, at the former by altering the political dynamics of a coalition and at the latter by diverting military assets from their assigned wartime missions (see chapter 7). Indeed, the Gulf War exposed serious deficiencies in the US and coalition forces' ability to locate and target WMD and mobile targets. Coalition forces expended considerable resources in a largely unsuccessful effort to find and destroy Iraqi mobile missiles. While the coalition had considerable success targeting fixed sites associated with mobile missile operations and suppressing the overall missile rate of fire, the effort to target the mobile element of Iraqi missile operations was generally ineffective. Similarly, allied planners significantly underestimated the number, location, and type of Iraqi WMD assets; as a result, many important sites escaped attack and were not discovered until UN inspections took place.

Moreover, targeting WMD-related facilities raised an issue with acute political, legal, humanitarian, and operational implications: the potential for collateral, principally civilian, casualties resulting from the spread of toxic materials. The considerations were still critical seven years later, when the risk of inadvertently releasing chemical or biological materials led the United States and the United Kingdom to proscribe certain targets during Operation Desert Fox. The same considerations came into play again just five years later in Operation Iraqi Freedom, when core US campaign objectives included securing Iraq's WMD capabilities and overthrowing the regime of Saddam Hussein.

Within the counterproliferation context, research and development activities remain directed at developing strike capabilities that can achieve operational objectives while minimizing collateral effects and denying sanctuary to adversary assets located in hardened and/or buried targets. Given the significant policy and operational concerns regarding collateral effects, an important counterforce focus is to develop targeting support tools that integrate WMD effects phenomenology and target-specific information on critical nodes and WMD processes in countries of concern. A related technical challenge is to keep pace with adversary efforts to protect WMD assets through hardening and other forms of cover and concealment.

Yet, the counterproliferation program as a whole today remains defense-dominant. Most of the resources allocated go to either active or passive defense rather than to the development of improved counterforce or interdiction capabilities.[58] With available resources, trade-offs between competing priorities will arise; and without additional focus on improved offensive capabilities it will ultimately prove difficult to effectively implement the national counterproliferation strategy articulated by the Bush administration. To the extent that capabilities emerge over time that provide solutions to the long-identified challenges posed by fixed and mobile targets, whether nuclear or nonnuclear, US forces may become less constrained in their efforts to take offensive action against WMD assets, and the adversary's task in seeking to protect these assets will become increasingly difficult. As the US ability to credibly hold such targets at risk improves, some of the leverage associated with possessing WMD will arguably erode.

Developing Effective Defense-in-Depth

With respect to the proliferation-terror nexus, the Bush administration has argued persuasively that the best defense is a good offense. To this end, offensive capabilities are being developed or improved, plans are being crafted or revised, and government agencies from the DOD and the State Department to the Departments of Treasury and Justice are striving to proactively counter both manifest and emergent terrorism and proliferation threats. While necessary, a good offense alone is insufficient to meet emergent US national-security requirements. Offenses fall along a continuum of response measures ranging from preventive efforts, whether cooperative or forcible, to defensive measures to mitigating and restorative considerations.

On the premise that an ounce of prevention is worth a pound of cure, traditional nonproliferation measures, including export controls, sanctions, and nonproliferation accords, have long been considered the first line of defense against WMD and missile proliferation. More recently, considerably greater emphasis has been placed on expanding cooperative threat reduction programs with key former Soviet states. Such activities clearly remain in the national interest and have a place in the national strategy, but the balance of effort has shifted with the current administration, with much greater emphasis placed on measures intended to bolster deterrence and defense.[59]

As a result of the pervasive WMD threat, "we need new concepts of deterrence that rely on both offensive and defensive forces." Articulating one foundational counterproliferation precept, President Bush argued early in his term of office that "deterrence can no longer be based solely on the threat of nuclear retaliation. Defenses can strengthen deterrence by reducing the incentive for proliferation."[60] This is the essential logic of deterrence by denial, the ability to defeat, defend against, and operate in the context of WMD and, if needed, overcome the effects of WMD use. While the United States seeks to preserve its ability to deter by threat of overwhelming destruction, as during the Cold War, it also seeks to develop a more robust end-to-end response. An early indicator of the Bush administration's new approach to deterrence was the unilateral US withdrawal from the 1972 Antiballistic Missile Treaty in an effort to more rapidly field more capable defensive systems. The notion that offenses and defenses might work in concert to advance American interests is not new; presidents since Ronald Reagan recognized this possibility, and the limited deployment of theater missile defense assets on the Gulf War battlefield only reinforced this strategic concept. Yet, the Bush national-security team has endeavored to bolster denial capabilities in other areas. For example, anthrax and smallpox vaccinations were resumed for forces deploying to high-threat areas.

Nor have these defensive measures been limited to the US military. Following the September 11, 2001, and subsequent anthrax-by-mail attacks, the administration moved to improve the coordination and net performance of the many federal agencies having responsibilities related to homeland security. Moreover, key members of Congress, together with administration officials, joined in an effort to significantly improve the nation's response to bioterrorism, resulting in an aggregate budget increase of almost $6 billion for fiscal year 2003 alone.[61]

While initiatives designed to protect the homeland and preserve the military's ability to operate in WMD environments have improved over the past several years, much remains to be done. Indeed, to combat WMD-armed regional adversaries and successfully defend the homeland from WMD attack, a number of key enablers are required, including improved intelligence collection, analysis, and warning; more effective defenses against catastrophic threats; a robust science and technology research and development base geared toward improving our ability to respond to extant and developmental threats; appropriate bilateral and multilateral cooperation; the development of targeted strategies against particular state and subnational actors; and the protection of critical infrastructure both for military operations and for the defense of the homeland. Both forward-deployed and rear-area military and civilian personnel, US interests and those of our friends and allies, and US and allied homelands must be effectively protected for national security to be advanced in this era of acute asymmetric security challenges.

Ultimately, success will require new technologies, new procedures, and new organizational structures, as the creation of a White House Office of Homeland Security and then a Department of Homeland Security suggests. A cogent and well-implemented full-spectrum response, from preventive and offensive measures to defensive and restorative capabilities, will fundamentally enhance US national and homeland security both in the present environment and in the years ahead. Sustaining the momentum, building on senior leaders' interest, and properly resourcing all aspects of the layered defense strategy put in place early in the millennium are key challenges for the years ahead.

Determining the Proliferation End Game

Finally, important initiatives to counter WMD-related threats from state and nonstate actors have been undertaken in the first decade following the end of the Cold War. But the United States arguably has not yet come to terms with a fundamentally transformed security landscape.

On the one hand, the Bush administration's national-security strategy and the attendant *National Strategy to Combat Weapons of Mass Destruction* clearly acknowledge and operate within a postproliferated international-security environment. Yet, looking ahead, "success"—for the United States, for US friends and allies, and for the international community as a whole—is likely to equate more with learning to effectively cope with this persistent threat than with unambiguously defeating or rolling it back. While this suggests that improvements to counterproliferation and counterterrorism capabilities and operations are critical to advancing US national security, important policy and planning challenges must also be addressed. Indeed, even as the United States works with key partners on a bilateral or multilateral basis to combat manifest proliferation and terrorism threats, a number of key policy considerations arise. For example:

- How will the international community respond to the next significant use of nuclear, biological, or chemical weapons? The answer will set a precedent. When Iran and Iraq exchanged chemical weapons fire in the 1980s, the international community was virtually silent. To prevent further use, key states and international organizations will have to take appropriate punitive measures or risk an eradicated norm of nonuse in the years ahead.

- How relevant are prominent international organizations in combating WMD proliferation? The UN Security Council deadlocked in the context of Iraqi noncompliance. Clearly, the Iranian and North Korean nuclear challenges to the IAEA are clear test cases and will provide important data on the continued viability of concerted multilateral responses to proliferation. If the ultimate penalty for noncompliance with international accords and underlying norms is a round of sanctions that is ineffectively applied or quickly lifted, why should states not continue to acquire, develop, or export WMD? For many national governments, security competition, rather than trust in un-

enforced and unverifiable international restraint mechanisms, may
become the preferred alternative.

- Finally, to what extent can the United States, along with its friends
and allies, effectively reevaluate policy responses to intractable regional proliferants and determine the necessary additional or modified options? These should include solutions that neither reward nor
ignore those that seek WMD capabilities but, rather, seek to fundamentally alter the existing perceived incentives for potential adversaries to develop or employ unconventional capabilities.

Satisfactorily addressing these and related issues will help shape the future
security environment both in key regions and globally. The best defense
against both proliferant states and terrorist organizations is a robust offense
that places them on the defensive. Yet, an appropriate end-to-end strategy also
seeks to hedge against deterrence failure and to diminish the consequences of
any attack that may occur. For the foreseeable future there is no greater strategic imperative for the United States, like-minded friends and allies, and the international community as a whole.

Notes

Preface

1. Secretary of State Colin L. Powell, remarks to the UN Security Council, New York, 5 February 2003, www.state.gov/secretary/rm/2003/17300.htm, accessed February 2003.

2. George W. Bush, "Address to the United Nations General Assembly in New York City, September 12, 2002," *Weekly Compilation of Presidential Documents* 38, no. 37 (16 September 2002): 1532. See also White House, *A Decade of Deception and Defiance: Saddam Hussein's Defiance of the United Nations* (Washington, DC, 12 September 2002), www.whitehouse.gov/news/releases/2002/09/iraq/20020912.html, accessed September 2002.

3. White House, *The National Security Strategy of the United States of America* (Washington, DC: GPO, September 2002).

4. *Key Judgments (from October 2002 NIE): Iraq's Continuing Programs for Weapons of Mass Destruction*, www.washingtonpost.com/wp-srv/nation/nationalsecurity/documents /nie_iraq_wmd.pdf, accessed 2003, and *Written Statement from CIA Director Tenet* (August 2003), www.washingtonpost.com/ac2/wp-dyn?pagename=article&node=&contentId =A35443-2003Aug8&notFound=true, accessed 2003, both released to the public in August 2003, www.washingtonpost.com.

5. Mike Allen, "Cheney Says Failing to Attack Iraq Would Have Been 'Irresponsible,'" *Washington Post*, 25 July 2003, A1.

6. Hans Blix, "Briefing the Security Council: Inspections in Iraq and a Preliminary Assessment of Iraq's Weapons Declaration," New York, 19 December 2002, www.un.org /Depts/unmovic/new/pages/security_council_briefings.asp#2, accessed December 2002.

7. Hans Blix, "Briefing the Security Council: An Update on Inspections," New York, 27 January 2003, www.un.org/Depts/unmovic/new/pages/security_council_briefings .asp#5, accessed 2003.

8. Central Intelligence Agency (CIA) and Defense Intelligence Agency (DIA), *Iraqi Mobile Biological Warfare Agent Production Plants*, unclassified (Washington, DC, 28 May 2003), www.cia.gov/cia/reports/iraqi_mobile_plants/index.html, accessed May 2003.

9. David Kay, testimony before Senate Armed Services Committee, *Iraqi Weapons of Mass Destruction and Related Programs*, 108th Cong., 2nd sess., 29 January 2004. In this context British Prime Minister Tony Blair, for his part, acknowledged that the inspectors had "not found what I and many others including Dr. Kay confidently expected they would—actual weapons ready for immediate use." But he also proposed that "others accept that what they have found are laboratories, technology, diagrams, documents, teams of scientists told to conceal their work on biological, nuclear and chemical weapons capability, that in sum amounts to breaches of the United Nations Resolution" (see David

Stout, "Rumsfeld Rejects Criticism on Iraq Intelligence," *San Francisco Chronicle,* 5 February 2004, A12).

10. For Kay's views as outgoing head of the Iraq Survey Group see Kay, testimony before Senate Armed Services Committee, 29 January 2004; James Risen, "Ex-Inspector Says C.I.A. Missed Disarray in Iraqi Arms Program," *New York Times,* 26 January 2004, 1; and Iraq Survey Group chief David Kay, interview by Jane Corbin, *Frontline,* PBS, 22 January 2004, www.pbs.org/wgbh/pages/frontline/shows/wmd/.

11. Joseph Cirincione, Jessica T. Matthews, and George Perkovich, *WMD in Iraq: Evidence and Implications* (Washington, DC: Carnegie Endowment for International Peace, January 2004); David Isenberg and Ian Davis, *Unraveling the Known Unknowns: Why No Weapons of Mass Destruction Have Been Found in Iraq,* BASIC Special Report 2004.1 (Washington, DC: British American Security Information Council, January 2004); former State Department Bureau of Intelligence and Research official Greg Thielmann, interview, *Frontline,* PBS, 22 January 2004, www.pbs.org/wgbh/pages/frontline/shows/truth/why/selective.html. For extensive treatment of the prewar US and UK assessments, see Anthony H. Cordesman, *Intelligence, Iraq, and Weapons of Mass Destruction: Main Report and Supporting Annex,* 1st working draft (Washington, DC: Center for Strategic and International Studies, 26 January 2004).

12. Senator Carl Levin (D-MI) suggested the need for an independent commission to review the data: "Although the issue of Iraq's weapons of mass destruction intentions or ambitions and program-related activities is a serious issue, it is not why we went to war. The case for war was Iraq's possession, production, deployment and stockpiling of weapons of mass destruction. A different case for war against Iraq can be made, but the case which the administration made to the American people was the presence of actual weapons of mass destruction. When lives are at stake and our military is going to be placed in harm's way—in other words, when we decide to go to war—it is totally unacceptable to have intelligence that is this far off or to exaggerate or shape the intelligence for any purpose by anybody" (statement before Senate Armed Services Committee, *Iraqi Weapons of Mass Destruction and Related Programs,* 108th Cong., 2nd sess., 29 January 2004). Similarly, former British foreign secretary Robin Cook, for instance, pressed for an inquiry to take place as soon as possible: "I see no reason why the people of Britain should have to wait until next year to hear a report on why it was we committed British troops to war on the basis of intelligence which turned out to be wrong, on the claim of a threat that wasn't there when we could have let the U.N. weapons inspectors finish the job and find out there were no weapons without fighting a war to prove it" (see Patrick E. Tyler, "Following U.S. Lead, Blair May Start Weapons Inquiry," *New York Times,* 2 February 2004).

13. Despite allegations of politicized intelligence, Director of Central Intelligence George Tenet clearly states that with respect to the October 2002 NIE, "No one told us what to say or how to say it" (see "Remarks as prepared for delivery by Director of Central Intelligence George J. Tenet at Georgetown University," 5 February 2004, www.odci.gov/cia/public_affairs/speeches/2004/tenet_georgetownspeech_02052004.html. See also the press release of Stu Cohen, who was acting National Intelligence Council (NIC) chairman when the October 2002 NIE was prepared: "Iraq's WMD Programs: Culling Hard Facts from Soft Myths," 28 November 2003, www.odci.gov/cia/public_affairs/press_release/2003/pr11282003.html).

14. Kay, testimony before Senate Armed Services Committee, 29 January 2004.

15. Dana Priest and Walter Pincus, "Hill Probers Fault Iraq Intelligence," *Washington Post*, 30 January 2004, A1. Representative Porter Goss (R-FL), who led the House study, concluded that "they just kept turning the page"; if "it was true yesterday, it must be true today." See also Bruce Berkowitz, "We Collected a Little and Assumed a Lot," ibid., 1 February 2004, B1.

16. Dana Priest, "No Evidence CIA Slanted Iraq Data," ibid., 31 January 2004, A1. Also in January, a judicial inquiry cleared British Prime Minister Tony Blair from charges that he had exaggerated intelligence claims to make the case for war (see Glenn Frankel, "Top Judge Absolves Britain's Tony Blair," *San Francisco Chronicle*, 29 January 2004, A1).

17. Kay, testimony before Senate Armed Services Committee, 29 January 2004.

18. Former UNMOVIC executive chairman Hans Blix, interview by Jane Corbin, *Frontline*, PBS, 22 January 2004, www.pbs.org/wgbh/pages/frontline/shows/wmd/.

19. Senate Armed Services Committee, *Iraqi Weapons of Mass Destruction and Related Programs*, 108th Cong., 2nd sess., 29 January 2004.

20. Glenn Kessler, "Powell Says New Data May Have Affected War Decision," *Washington Post*, 3 February 2004, A1.

21. While a number of journal articles or book chapters briefly cover the intersection of WMD proliferation and intelligence-policy considerations, only a few examine it at length. See, e.g., John C. Gannon, "The US Intelligence Community and the Challenge of BCW," in *The New Terror: Facing the Threat of Biological and Chemical Weapons*, ed. Sidney D. Drell, Abraham D. Sofaer, and George D. Wilson (Stanford, CA: Hoover Institution Press, 1999), 123–27; Gordon Oehler, "Warning and Detection," in ibid., 138–51; Loch K. Johnson, "Strategic Intelligence and Weapons Proliferation," *Monitor* 1, no. 2 (1995): 5–31; Henry Sokolski, "Fighting Proliferation with Intelligence," in *Fighting Proliferation: New Concerns for the Nineties*, ed. Henry Sokolski (Maxwell AFB, AL: Air University Press, 1996), 227–98; and Jeffrey T. Richelson, "Can the Intelligence Community Keep Pace with the Threat?" in *Nuclear Proliferation after the Cold War*, ed. Mitchell Reiss and Robert S. Litwak (Washington, DC: Woodrow Wilson Center Press, 1994), 291–308; and Robert D. Blackwill and Ashton B. Carter, "The Role of Intelligence," in *New Nuclear Nations: Consequences for U.S. Policy*, ed. Robert D. Blackwill and Albert Carnesale (New York: Council on Foreign Relations, 1993), 216–50.

ONE: Proliferation 101

1. The phrase *weapons of mass destruction* is commonly used to refer to nuclear, biological, and chemical weapons and by statute (Public Law 103-160) also encompasses conventional high explosives and radiological dispersal devices. However, given the range of effects, the means of delivery, and other criteria for such weapons, *weapons of mass destruction* is clearly a misnomer: while the term retains evident political salience, substantially different operational effects result from the spread of nuclear, chemical, and biological weapons, and they have very different strategic implications. Nevertheless, for the reader's convenience the phrase will be used to describe these weapons throughout.

2. See, e.g., George W. Bush, "Remarks at the National Defense University, May 1, 2001," *Public Papers of the Presidents of the United States: George W. Bush, 2001* (Washington, DC: GPO, 2003), 1:471–72; Donald H. Rumsfeld, statement before the Senate Armed Services Committee, 11 January 2001, *Nominations before the Senate armed Services Committee*, 107th Cong., 1st sess., 2001, 13–20; Office of the Secretary of Defense, *Quadren-*

nial Defense Review Report (Washington, DC: Department of Defense [DOD], 30 September 2001), 6–7, 41.

3. White House, *National Strategy to Combat Weapons of Mass Destruction* (Washington, DC: GPO, December 2002).

4. While the precise definitions have evolved over time, *nonproliferation* refers to the more traditional measures undertaken to restrain supply (e.g., export controls, sanctions) in an effort to prevent, halt, or roll back proliferation, as well as to the more recent measures designed to diminish existing capabilities (e.g., cooperative threat reduction); and *counterproliferation* refers to the "full range of military preparations and activities to reduce, and protect against, the threat posed by nuclear, biological, and chemical weapons and their associated delivery means," key elements including, but not limited to, active and passive defenses, counterforce, and consequence-management capabilities (see Office of the Secretary of Defense, *Proliferation: Threat and Response* [Washington, DC: GPO, January 2001], 77–109, quotation on 78; and White House, *National Strategy to Combat Weapons of Mass Destruction*, 2–5). Together nonproliferation and counterproliferation encompass a continuum of prevention and protection activities, several facets of which are addressed in the chapters that follow.

5. William Webster, statement before the Senate Armed Services Committee, 23 January 1990, *Threat Assessment, Military Strategy, and Operations Requirements*, 101st Cong., 2nd sess., 1990, 60–61.

6. Office of the Deputy Secretary of Defense, *Report on Nonproliferation and Counterproliferation Activities and Programs* (Washington, DC: DOD, May 1994), 2.

7. John A. Lauder, unclassified statement for the record on the Worldwide WMD threat to the Commission to Assess the Organization of the Federal Government to Combat the Proliferation of Weapons of Mass Destruction (as prepared for delivery), 29 April 1999, www.cia.gov/cia/public_affairs/speeches/1999/lauder_speech_042999.htm, accessed 26 January 2001, pp. 1, 3.

8. Donald H. Rumsfeld, testimony before the Senate Armed Services Committee, 24 September 1998, *Ballistic Missile Defense Programs*, 105th Cong., 2nd sess., 1998, 4. See also Thomas R. Wilson, statement for the record, Senate Select Committee on Intelligence, 19 March 2002, *Current and Projected National Security Threats to the United States*, 107th Cong., 2nd sess., 2002, 66–67, 73–74.

9. Office of the Secretary of Defense, *Report of the Quadrennial Defense Review* (Washington, DC: DOD, May 1997). See also idem, *Proliferation: Threat and Response*, 1; Center for Counterproliferation Research, *The NBC Threat in 2025: Concepts and Strategies for Adversarial Use of Nuclear, Biological and Chemical Weapons* (Washington, DC: National Defense University, 1997), i–v; Counterproliferation Program Review Committee, *Report on Activities and Programs for Countering Proliferation and NBC Terrorism* (Washington, DC: DOD, May 1998), 3-1.

10. DCI George J. Tenet testified as early as March 2000 that "terrorist groups worldwide continue to explore how rapidly evolving and spreading technologies might enhance the lethality of their operations" and that "we are aware of several instances in which terrorists have contemplated using" chemical, biological, radiological, or nuclear agents. Tenet singled out both Osama bin Laden's organization, for its "strong interest in chemical weapons" and whose operatives "have trained to conduct attacks with toxic chemicals or biological toxins," and Hamas, which is "also pursuing a capability to conduct attacks with toxic chemicals" (see George J. Tenet, testimony before the Senate Se-

lect Committee on Intelligence, 21 March 2000, *Current and Projected National Security Threats to the United States*, 106th Cong., 2nd sess., 2000, 13).

11. George J. Tenet, statement for the record, Senate Select Committee on Intelligence, 6 February 2002, *Current and Projected National Security Threats to the United States*, 107th Cong., 2nd sess., 2002, 7.

12. See, e.g., Mark M. Lowenthal, *Intelligence: From Secrets to Policy* (Washington, DC: CQ Press, 2000), 40–52; Arthur S. Hulnick, "The Intelligence Producer-Policy Consumer Linkage: A Theoretical Approach," *Intelligence and National Security* 1, no. 2 (1986): 217–18; and Jeffrey T. Richelson, *The U.S. Intelligence Community*, 4th ed. (Boulder, CO: Westview Press, 1999), 3–4.

13. Traditionally, the intelligence community, led by the DCI, has comprised thirteen agencies that carry out the intelligence activities of the US government: the CIA, the National Security Agency, the DIA, the National Imagery and Mapping Agency, the National Reconnaissance Office, the military service intelligence agencies, the Federal Bureau of Investigation, the Department of the Treasury, the Department of Energy, and the Department of State. The 2002 creation of a Department of Homeland Security adds a "new" consumer and possibly a new producer (through the Coast Guard) of intelligence.

14. The intelligence community uses a wide array of methods to collect intelligence data, referred to as "collection disciplines" or, more simply, as "INTs." These INTs include imagery intelligence (IMINT), signals intelligence (SIGINT), measurement and signature intelligence (MASINT), human intelligence (HUMINT), and open-source intelligence (OSINT), among others. For a general discussion of the INTs, their advantages, and their limitations, see Lowenthal, *Intelligence*, 61–71; and Richelson, *U.S. Intelligence Community*.

15. See, e.g., Lowenthal, *Intelligence*, 49; Mark M. Lowenthal, "Tribal Tongues: Intelligence Consumers, Intelligence Producers," *Washington Quarterly* 15, no. 1 (1992): 162–63; Hulnick, "Intelligence Producer-Policy Consumer Linkage," 213–14; *Combating Proliferation of Weapons of Mass Destruction: Report from the Commission to Assess the Organization of the Federal Government to Combat the Proliferation of Weapons of Mass Destruction, Pursuant to Public Law 293*, 104th Cong., 2nd sess., 1999, 67–68; *Report of the Commission to Assess the Ballistic Missile Threat to the United States, Executive Summary, Pursuant to Public Law 201*, 104th Cong., 1st sess., 1998, 22 (hereafter cited as Rumsfeld Report); Gordon Oehler, testimony before the Senate Foreign Relations Committee, 11 June 1998, *Chinese Missile Proliferation*, 105th Cong., 2nd sess., 1998, 4–5; John C. Gannon, "The US Intelligence Community and the Challenge of BCW," in *The New Terror: Facing the Threat of Biological and Chemical Weapons*, ed. Sidney D. Drell, Abraham D. Sofaer, and George D. Wilson (Stanford, CA: Hoover Institution Press, 1999), 134–36; Gordon Oehler, "Warning and Detection," in ibid., 141–47; Robert Gates, "The CIA and American Foreign Policy," *Foreign Affairs* 66, no. 2 (1997–98): 225–29; Richard K. Betts, "Analysis, War, and Decision: Why Intelligence Failures Are Inevitable," *World Politics* 31, no. 1 (1978): 67–72; idem, "Policy-Makers and Intelligence Analysts: Love, Hate, or Indifference?" *Intelligence and National Security* 3, no. 1 (1988): 184–89; and House Permanent Select Committee on Intelligence, *IC21: Intelligence Community in the Twenty-first Century* (Washington, DC: GPO, 1996).

16. According to voluntary disclosures made by George Tenet, in 1997 and 1998 the budgets for intelligence were $26.6 billion and $26.7 billion, respectively. Reportedly, funding for the intelligence community rose to approximately $35 billion after the tragedies of September 11, 2001 (see Dana Priest, "Panel Favors Intelligence Czar," *Wash-*

ington Post, 8 December 2002, A8; John Diamond, "Panel Details Intelligence Slip on Terror Suspect," *USA Today,* 12 December 2002, 18A; Vernon Loeb, "Intelligence Budget Can Be Secret, Judge Rules," *Washington Post,* 23 November 1999, A4; Tim Weiner, "Voluntarily, CIA Director Reveals Intelligence Budget," *New York Times,* 21 March 1998, A11; "CIA Releases Intelligence Budget," *Washington Post,* 21 March 1998, A6; and Bryan Bender, "Tenet Declassifies Intelligence Budget Figure: $26.6 Billion," *Defense Daily,* 16 October 1997, 1).

17. Sherman Kent, *Strategic Intelligence for American World Policy* (Princeton, NJ: Princeton University Press, 1949), 195, 198, 201; Lowenthal, *Intelligence,* 3–4; Betts, "Policy-Makers and Intelligence Analysts," 187–88; Duncan L. Clarke, *American Defense and Foreign Policy Institutions: Toward a Sound Foundation* (New York: Harper & Row, 1989), 141–44; Gates, "CIA and American Foreign Policy," 225, 228–29.

18. Kent, *Strategic Intelligence,* 200–201; Lowenthal, *Intelligence,* 3, 49–50; Gates, "CIA and American Foreign Policy," 223–25; Abram N. Shulsky, *Silent Warfare: Understanding the World of Intelligence,* 2nd ed., rev. Gary J. Schmitt (Washington, DC: Brassey's, 1993), 183, 186–87; Clarke, *American Defense and Foreign Policy Institutions,* 138–40; Hulnick, "Intelligence Producer-Policy Consumer Linkage," 213–16.

19. Intelligence community official, interview by Jason Ellis, Washington, DC, July 1998.

20. David A. Kay, "Denial and Deception Practices of WMD Proliferators: Iraq and Beyond," *Washington Quarterly* 18, no. 1 (1995): 100; David L. Marcus, "US Intelligence Missed Signs of India Tests: Neighbor's Warnings, Hindu Party's Pledge Were Unheeded in Washington," *Boston Globe,* 13 May 1998, A19; Rumsfeld Report, 22; Michael Moodie, "Beyond Proliferation: The Challenge of Technology Diffusion," *Washington Quarterly* 18, no. 2 (1995): 183–202; Khidhir Hamza, "Inside Saddam's Secret Nuclear Program," *Bulletin of the Atomic Scientists* 54, no. 5 (1998): 26–33.

21. Joseph Cirincione, "Assessing the Assessment: The 1999 National Intelligence Estimate of the Ballistic Missile Threat," *Nonproliferation Review* 7, no. 1 (2000): 127. This conclusion is substantively similar to that of a 1993 NIE, 93-17: "Only China and the CIS [Commonwealth of Independent States] strategic forces . . . currently have the ability to strike the continental United States . . . with land-based ballistic missiles. Analysis of available information shows the probability is low that any other country will acquire this capability during the next 15 years" (ibid.).

22. General Accounting Office, *Foreign Missile Threats: Analytic Soundness of National Intelligence Estimate 95-19,* GAO/T-NSIAD-97-53 (Washington, DC, 4 December 1996). See also Senate Select Committee on Intelligence, *Hearing on Intelligence Analysis on the Long-Range Missile Threat to the United States,* 104th Cong., 2nd sess., 4 December 1996; and Robert Gates, chairman, "NIE 95-19: Independent Panel Review of 'Emerging Missile Threats to North America during the Next 15 Years,'" CIA, OCA 96-1908, 23 December 1996, www.fas.org/irp/threat/missile/oca961908.htm, accessed 2001.

23. Rumsfeld Report, 5–6.

24. Ibid., 26.

25. NIC, *Foreign Missile Developments and the Ballistic Missile Threat through 2015,* unclassified summary, September 1999 (Washington, DC, 2000), 46, www.odci.gov/nic /other_missilethreat1999.html.

26. NIC, *Foreign Missile Developments and the Ballistic Missile Threat through 2015,* unclassified summary, December 2001 (Washington, DC, 2003), 5, 19, www.odci.gov/nic /other_missilethreat2001.html.

27. William J. Broad, "Spy Photos of Korea Missile Site Bring Dispute," *New York Times*, 11 January 2000, A8. See also John Donnelly, "Satellite Images For Sale," *Boston Globe*, 16 March 2000, 2; Alexander Calhoun, "Top-Secret Kodak Moment In Space Shakes Global Security," *Christian Science Monitor*, 21 March 2000, 2; Massimo Calabresi, "Quick, Hide The Tanks!" *Time*, 15 May 2000, 60; and William J. Broad, "Snooping's Not Just for Spies Any More," *New York Times*, 23 April 2000, A6.

28. *Combating Proliferation of Weapons of Mass Destruction*, 68. The commission's warning is in stark contrast to *Washington Times* reporter Bill Gertz's declared justification for publishing *Betrayal: How the Clinton Administration Undermined American Security* (Washington, DC: Regnery, 1999): "This betrayal of American national security so angered some intelligence, defense, and foreign policy officials that they responded in the only way they knew how: by disclosing to the press some of the nation's most secret intelligence" (5).

29. Office of the Secretary of Defense, *Proliferation: Threat and Response*, 39; *Iraq Weapons of Mass Destruction*, US government white paper, 13 February 1998, www.state .gov/www/regions/nea/iraq_white_paper.html, accessed 2 November 2000; International Atomic Energy Agency (IAEA), "Fourth Consolidated Report of the Director General of the International Atomic Energy Agency under paragraph 16 of Security Council Resolution 1051 (1996)," S/1997/779, 8 October 1997, www.iaea.org/worldatom/Programmes /ActionTeam/reports/s_1997_779.pdf, accessed 2001; Richard Butler, *Report to the Security Council on the Status of Disarmament and Monitoring*, S/1999/94, 29 January 1999, www.un.org/Depts/unscom/s99-94.htm.

30. See Bruce Carey, "U.S. Begins 'Counter-Proliferation' against Mass Destruction Weapons," United States Information Agency press release, 7 December 1993, www.fas .org/news/usa/1993/45215398-45219581.html, accessed 2001; Les Aspin, remarks to the National Academy of Sciences Committee on International Security and Arms Control, 7 December 1993, www.fas.org/irp/offdocs/pdd18.htm, accessed 2001.

31. Butler, *Report to the Security Council on the Status of Disarmament and Monitoring*.

32. Ibid.; Office of the Secretary of Defense, *Proliferation: Threat and Response*, 38–39; Richard Butler, *The Greatest Threat: Iraq, Weapons of Mass Destruction, and the Crisis of Global Security* (New York: Public Affairs, 2000), 218; Charles Duelfer, testimony before the House International Relations Committee, Subcommittee on the Middle East and South Asia, 4 October 2001, *U.S. Policy toward Iraq*, 107th Cong., 1st sess., 2001, 13–17.

33. Tom Mangold and Jeff Goldberg, *Plague Wars: The Terrifying Reality of Biological Warfare* (New York: St. Martin's, 1999), 91–105, 177–95; Ken Alibek with Stephen Handelman, *Biohazard: The Chilling True Story of the Largest Covert Biological Weapons Program in the World—Told from the Inside by the Man Who Ran It* (New York: Random House, 1999), 150, 262; Office of the Secretary of Defense, *Proliferation: Threat and Response*, 56.

34. Alibek with Handelman, *Biohazard*, 263–64.

35. Article 1 of the Biological and Toxin Weapons Convention prohibits signatories from developing, producing, stockpiling, or otherwise acquiring or retaining "microbial or other biological agents, or toxins whatever their origin or method of production, of types and in quantities that have no justification for prophylactic, protective or other peaceful purposes." However, the treaty does not specify exactly what the latter three purposes encompass.

36. Chandré Gould and Peter I. Folb, "The South African Chemical and Biological Warfare Program: An Overview," *Nonproliferation Review* 7, no. 3 (2000): 10–23; Zondi

Masiza, "A Chronology of South Africa's Nuclear Program," ibid. 1, no. 1 (1993): 34–53; Stephen Burgess and Helen Purkitt, *The Rollback of South Africa's Chemical and Biological Warfare Program* (Maxwell AFB, AL: USAF Counterproliferation Center, April 2001).

37. Marcus, "US Intelligence Missed Signs of India Tests"; "India BJP," Voice of America Report, 3 February 1998; CIA, Office of Public Affairs, Jeremiah News Conference, 2 June 1998, www.cia.gov/cia/public_affairs/press_release/archives/1998/jeremiah.html.

38. Stephen Engelberg and Michael R. Gordon, "Intelligence Study Says North Korea Has Nuclear Bomb," *New York Times*, 26 December 1993, A1; R. James Woolsey, testimony before the House Committee on Foreign Affairs, Subcommittee on International Security, International Organizations, and Human Rights, 28 July 1993, *U.S. Security Policy toward Rogue Regimes*, 103rd Cong., 1st sess., 1993, 5–15.

39. Jason D. Ellis, *Defense by Other Means: The Politics of US-NIS Threat Reduction and Nuclear Security Cooperation* (Westport, CT: Praeger, 2001), 35–36.

40. John F. Sopko and Alan Edleman, "Staff Report—Global Proliferation of Weapons of Mass Destruction: A Case Study on the Aum Shinrikyo," Senate Committee on Governmental Affairs, Permanent Subcommittee on Investigations, *Global Proliferation of Weapons of Mass Destruction, Part I*, 104th Cong., 1st sess., 1995, 49.

41. Jason D. Ellis, "Beyond Nonproliferation: Secondary Supply, Proliferation Management, and U.S. Foreign Policy," *Comparative Strategy* 20, no. 1 (2001): 4–6.

42. See, e.g., Celine Tng and Kate Yu Juan, "A Case of Sino-US Ties Riding on Choppy Waters," *Straits Times* (Singapore), 12 September 1993, 8; Patrick E. Tyler, "No Chemical Arms Aboard China Ship," *New York Times*, 6 September 1993, A4; Sid Balman Jr., "U.S. Intelligence: Chinese Shipped Chemical Weapons," United Press International, 7 September 1993.

43. Karl Vick, "U.S., Sudan Trade Claims on Factory; Washington Cites Toxin in Soil Sample," *Washington Post*, 25 August 1998, A1; Vernon Loeb, "Employees Dispute Charge That Plant Made Nerve Agent," ibid., 26 August 1998, A15; "U.S. Reveals More Details on Airstrike; Defending the Attack on Sudan, the Clinton Administration Has Offered Some of the Evidence behind the Strike," *Minneapolis Star Tribune*, 24 August 1998, 1A; James Risen, "U.S. Says It Has Strong Evidence of Threat Justifying the Retaliation," *New York Times*, 21 August 1998, A1.

44. See, e.g., Former Defense Secretary William Cohen's statement regarding the fact that US and UK forces did not target chemical or biological facilities during the Desert Fox strikes: "We're not going to take a chance and try to target any facility that would release any kind of horrific damage to innocent people" (quoted in Steven Lee Myers, "The Targets; Jets Said to Avoid Poison Gas Sites," *New York Times*, 18 December 1998, A1).

45. White House, *The National Security Strategy of the United States of America* (Washington, DC: GPO, September 2002), 1. This section draws significantly on Jason D. Ellis, "The Best Defense: Counterproliferation and U.S. National Security," *Washington Quarterly* 26, no. 2 (2003): 115–33; and idem, "The Gravest Danger: Proliferation, Terrorism, and the Bush Doctrine," *Monitor* 9, no. 1 (2003): 5–9.

46. White House, *National Security Strategy of the United States of America*, 5.

47. Ibid., 13.

48. Ibid., 13–15.

49. Ibid., 6. See also Secretary of Defense Donald H. Rumsfeld, *Annual Report to the President and the Congress* (Washington, DC: GPO, August 2002), 30.

50. National Defense University Center for Counterproliferation Research, *The Counterproliferation Imperative: Meeting Tomorrow's Challenges* (Washington, DC: National Defense University, 2001), 2–7.

51. Dan Balz and Bob Woodward, "America's Chaotic Road to War," *Washington Post,* 27 January 2002, A1.

52. George W. Bush, "Address before a Joint Session of the Congress on the United States Response to the Terrorist Attacks of September 11," *Weekly Compilation of Presidential Documents* 37, no. 38 (24 September 2001): 1348.

53. George W. Bush, "Address before a Joint Session of the Congress on the State of the Union," ibid. 38, no. 5 (4 February 2002): 135.

54. Secretary of Defense Donald H. Rumsfeld, remarks delivered at National Defense University, Washington, DC, 31 January 2002.

55. White House, *National Security Strategy of the United States of America,* 15.

56. Joby Warrick, "Iran Given Deadline to Lay Bare Nuclear Program," *Washington Post,* 13 September 2003, A1.

57. *Secondary proliferation* refers to exports of WMD or missile delivery systems, their constituent enabling or production technologies, or the requisite material or expertise necessary to their development or production undertaken by nontraditional suppliers (e.g., DPRK–Iranian–Pakistani collusion in MRBM development). *Foreign assistance* refers to the transfer or cooperative development of technologies, material, or expertise with possible weapons-related applications (e.g., PRC support to the Pakistani missile or nuclear weapons programs) (see Ellis, "Beyond Nonproliferation," 1–2).

58. *The Biological and Chemical Warfare Threat,* rev. ed. (Washington, DC: GPO, 1999), 32. On *novichoks,* see Office of the Secretary of Defense, *Proliferation: Threat and Response,* 4.

59. Office of the Secretary of Defense, *Proliferation: Threat and Response,* 4.

60. *The Worldwide Biological Warfare Weapons Threat* (Washington, DC: GPO, 2001), 1.

61. Butler, *Report to the Security Council on the Status of Disarmament and Monitoring,* app. 3.

62. Central Intelligence Agency (CIA) and Defense Intelligence Agency (DIA), *Iraqi Mobile Biological Warfare Agent Production Plants,* unclassified (Washington, DC, 28 May 2003), www.cia.gov/cia/reports/iraqi_mobile_plants/index.html, accessed May 2003.

63. White House, *National Security Strategy of the United States of America,* 13–14.

64. Office of Homeland Security, *National Strategy for Homeland Security* (Washington, DC: GPO, July 2002), vii, ix. According to this strategy document, an important point of departure is the increased availability of mass-casualty capabilities, which "have never been more accessible and the trends are not in our favor" (9).

65. White House, *National Security Strategy of the United States of America,* 15.

66. Tenet, testimony before the Senate Select Committee on Intelligence, 21 March 2000.

67. Ibid.

68. National Defense University Center for Counterproliferation Research, *Counterproliferation Imperative,* 27.

69. Ibid., 5–11. See also John F. Reichart, "Adversary Use of NBC Weapons: A Neglected Challenge," *Strategic Forum,* no. 187 (Washington, DC: National Defense University, December 2001); and Peter R. Lavoy, Scott D. Sagan, and James J. Wirtz, eds., *Planning the Unthinkable: How New Powers Will Use Nuclear, Biological, and Chemical Weapons* (Ithaca, NY: Cornell University Press, 2000).

70. Office of the Secretary of Defense, *Quadrennial Defense Review Report,* 13–14. Capabilities-based planning focuses more on *how* an adversary might fight than on *who* particular adversaries are or *where* conflict might occur.

71. Donald H. Rumsfeld, testimony before the House Armed Services Committee, 18 September 2002, *United States Policy toward Iraq,* 107th Cong., 2nd sess., 2002, 80–81.

T W O : Standards of Evidence

1. With respect to Pakistan's development of nuclear weapons, Paul Leventhal argues that "looking the other way" in the context of Soviet military activity in Afghanistan "provides a striking case history of what happens to non-proliferation policy when it comes up against a competing foreign policy interest. It loses, badly." Similarly, Joseph Nye concludes that unsuccessful efforts to restrain the Pakistani nuclear program represent a "chronic failure of American policy" (see House Committee on Foreign Affairs, *Hearing on Pakistan and United States Nuclear Nonproliferation Policy,* 100th Cong., 1st sess., 22 October 1987, 89; and Joseph S. Nye Jr., "A Cat-and-Mouse Game by U.S. and Pakistan over the Atomic Bomb," *Toronto Star,* 16 November 1986, D4). The parallels regarding unsuccessful US policy with respect to the PRC's 1990s-era transfer of ballistic missiles, missile components, and key production technology for their manufacture are striking (see below).

2. House Committee on Foreign Affairs, *Hearing on Pakistan and United States Nuclear Nonproliferation Policy,* 6–7.

3. Leonard S. Spector with Jacqueline R. Smith, *Nuclear Ambitions: The Spread of Nuclear Weapons, 1989–1990* (Boulder, CO: Westview Press, 1990), esp. chaps. 4 and 7; Seymour M. Hersh, "On the Nuclear Edge," *New Yorker,* 29 March 1993, 69–73. See also Zia Mian, *Pakistan's Atomic Bomb and the Search for Security* (Islamabad: Sustainable Development Policy Institute, 1995); and Ashok Kapur, *Pakistan's Nuclear Development* (London: Croon Helm, 1987).

4. R. Bates Gill, *Chinese Arms Transfers: Purposes, Patterns, and Prospects in the New World Order* (Westport, CT: Praeger, 1992), 150–51.

5. Zachary S. Davis, "China's Nonproliferation and Export Control Policies: Boom or Bust for the NPT Regime?" *Asian Survey* 35, no. 6 (1995): 589–90; Gary Milhollin, testimony before the Senate Governmental Affairs Committee, Subcommittee on International Security, Proliferation, and Federal Services, *Hearing on Weapons Proliferation in China,* 104th Cong., 2nd sess., 10 April 1997, 3; Majority report of the Senate Governmental Affairs Committee, Subcommittee on International Security, Proliferation, and Federal Services, *The Proliferation Primer* (Washington, DC: GPO, January 1998), 4.

6. US Department of State, "The Pakistani Nuclear Program," 23 June 1983, quoted in Rodney W. Jones and Mark G. McDonough with Toby F. Dalton and Gregory D. Koblentz, *Tracking Nuclear Proliferation: A Guide in Maps and Charts, 1998* (Washington, DC: Carnegie Endowment for International Peace, 1998), 131.

7. Hedrick Smith, "A Bomb Ticks in Pakistan," *New York Times Magazine,* 6 March 1988, 38; Bob Woodward and Don Oberdorfer, "Pakistan A-Project Upsets Superpowers," *Washington Post,* 15 July 1986, A1; Gerald M. Boyd, "Pakistan Denies Developing Bomb," *New York Times,* 17 July 1986, A9; Bob Woodward, "Pakistan Reported Near Atom Arms Production," *Washington Post,* 4 November 1986, A1.

8. Hersh, "On the Nuclear Edge," 56. See also David Albright and Mark Hibbs, "Pakistan's Bomb: Out of the Closet," *Bulletin of the Atomic Scientists* 48, no. 6 (1992): 32.

9. George Perkovich, *India's Nuclear Bomb: The Impact on Global Proliferation* (Berkeley and Los Angeles: University of California Press, 1999), 308.

10. Hersh, "On the Nuclear Edge," 65.

11. Ibid., 56–68. See also Devin T. Hagerty, "Nuclear Deterrence in South Asia: The 1990 Indo-Pakistani Crisis," *International Security* 20, no. 3 (1995–96): 79–114; Kanti Bajpal et al., *Brass Tacks and Beyond: Perception and Management of Crises in South Asia* (Columbia, MO: South Asia Books, 1995). Although there is a consensus that the events of early 1990 were indeed a crisis, there is some dissension with regard to the nuclear aspects, especially as reported in the media. For example, George Perkovich asserts that the "conventional wisdom" on the crisis, based largely on journalist Seymour Hersh's account of events in 1993, contains "serious factual and interpretive flaws" (*India's Nuclear Bomb*, 306). See also Stephen P. Cohen, P. R. Chari, and Pervaiz Iqbal Cheema, "The Compound Crisis of 1990: Perception, Politics, and Insecurity," Arms Control, Disarmament and International Security (ACDIS) Research Report, University of Illinois at Urbana-Champaign, 10 August 2000; Douglas Jehl, "Did India and Pakistan Face Atomic War? Claim Is Debated," *New York Times*, 23 March 1993, A3; and Michael Krepon and Mishi Faruqee, eds., *Conflict Prevention and Confidence-Building Measures in South Asia: The 1990 Crisis*, Occasional Paper 17 (Washington, DC: Stimson Center, 1994).

12. Jack C. Miklos, "South Asia: U.S. Policy toward Afghanistan and Pakistan," *Department of State Bulletin* 78 (October 1979): 56.

13. *Department of State Bulletin* 80 (March 1980): 65–66.

14. Ibid. 81 (November 1981): 84–85. This approach was not limited to Pakistan. While under President Carter's export directive the transfer of arms was an "exceptional" component of foreign policy, under President Reagan this became "indispensable," an "essential element" of America's global defense posture (see Duncan L. Clarke, Daniel B. O'Connor, and Jason D. Ellis, *Send Guns and Money: Security Assistance and U.S. Foreign Policy* [Westport, CT: Praeger, 1997], 72–81).

15. *Congressional Record*, 98th Cong., 2nd sess., 130 (21 June 1984): H17735.

16. Ibid., H17737-38.

17. Ibid. 130 (3 October 1984): S28880, S28887.

18. Ibid., S28881-82.

19. Ibid., S28884-85.

20. John Elliott, "China and Pakistan Sign Nuclear Agreement," *Financial Times* (London), 16 September 1986, 3; "China Denies Plan to Aid Pakistan on Nuclear Arms," United Press International, 25 September 1986; Simon Henderson, "China May Help Build Pakistan's N-Bomb," *Financial Times*, 29 September 1986, 3.

21. Smith, "Bomb Ticks in Pakistan," 38; Spector with Smith, *Nuclear Ambitions*, 92–93.

22. Leslie H. Gelb, "Pakistan Tie Imperils U.S.-China Nuclear Pact," *New York Times*, 22 June 1984, A1; idem, "Peking Said to Balk at Nuclear Pledges," ibid., 23 June 1984, A3.

23. Spector with Smith, *Nuclear Ambitions*, 93–94.

24. Ibid., 95.

25. Richard W. Murphy, "Pakistan and the Nuclear Issue," *Department of State Bulletin* 87 (October 1987): 53–54. See also Robert A. Peck, "FY 1987 Assistance Requests for South Asia," ibid. 86 (July 1986): 82–84; and Michael H. Armacost, "South Asia and the United States: An Evolving Partnership," ibid. 87 (July 1987): 75–80.

26. Philip Revzin, "Nuclear Project Bedevils Aid for Pakistan," *Wall Street Journal,* 8 December 1987, 32.

27. "White House Statement on the Continuation of Military Aid to Pakistan, January 15, 1988," in *Public Papers of the Presidents of the United States: Ronald Reagan, 1988* (Washington, DC: GPO, 1990), 1:46.

28. Compounding this issue was the State Department's interpretation of what constituted possession of a nuclear explosive device, a view evident in a 5 March 1987 letter from its legal adviser to a subcommittee of the House Committee on Foreign Affairs: "A state may possess a nuclear explosive device, and yet maintain it in an unassembled form for safety reasons or to maintain effective command and control over its use or for other purposes. The fact that a state does not have an assembled device would not, therefore, necessarily mean that it does not possess a device under the statutory standard" (see Spector with Smith, *Nuclear Ambitions,* 102, 340n73).

29. Spector with Smith, *Nuclear Ambitions,* 101. See also, "White House Statement on the Continuation of Military Aid to Pakistan, 15 January 1988," in *Public Papers of the Presidents of the United States: Ronald Reagan, 1988* (Washington, DC: GPO, 1990), 1:46.

30. Senate Governmental Affairs Committee, *Hearing on Nuclear Proliferation,* 101st Cong., 1st sess., 18 May 1989. Similarly, Pakistan's foreign secretary, Shahryar Khan, formally acknowledged during a 1992 visit to Washington that "there was a capability in 1989" (See Paul Lewis, "Pakistan Tells of Its A-Bomb Capacity," *New York Times,* 8 February 1992, 5).

31. Stephen Engelberg, "U.S. Sees Pakistan Moving an A-Arms," *New York Times,* 11 June 1989, sec. 1, 5; William Beecher, "Pakistan Will Halt Nuclear Arms Work to Keep U.S. Aid," *Minneapolis Star-Tribune,* 14 June 1989.

32. *Congressional Record,* 104th Cong., 1st sess., 141 (20 September 1995): S13956.

33. Spector with Smith, *Nuclear Ambitions,* 108.

34. Jones and McDonough with Dalton and Koblentz, *Tracking Nuclear Proliferation,* 132.

35. *Congressional Record,* 104th Cong., 1st sess., 141 (20 September 1995): S13958.

36. Lewis, "Pakistan Tells of Its A-Bomb Capacity."

37. James A. Baker III, testimony before the Senate Foreign Relations Committee, 5 February 1992, *Foreign Policy Overview,* 102nd Cong., 2nd sess., 1992, 31.

38. Michael Matheson, statement before the Senate Foreign Relations Committee, 30 July 1992, *Interpreting the Pressler Amendment: Commercial Military Sales to Pakistan,* 102nd Cong., 2nd sess., 1992, 28.

39. Ibid., 4.

40. Ibid., 5.

41. Ibid., 64.

42. Ibid., 28, 30. The State Department also responded to written questions posed by Senator Claiborne Pell, reiterating that "the Department did not attempt to conceal its interpretation . . . but acted in good faith through what we regarded as the normal channels for communicating such matters to the Congress and the public" (90).

43. Ibid., 60.

44. Ballistic missiles are generally defined according to their respective ranges. SRBMs are those having a range of less than 1,000 km; MRBMs are those having a range of 1,000 to 3,000 km; IRBMs have a range of 3,000 to 5,500 km; and intercontinental ballistic missiles have a range greater than 5,500 km (see Office of the Secretary of Defense, *Proliferation: Threat and Response* [Washington, DC: GPO, January 2001], 115).

45. Information Office of the State Council of the People's Republic of China, "China: Arms Control and Disarmament," white paper, November 1995, www.china.org .cn/e-white/army/index.htm, accessed 2000, 2, 3, 8. See also Li Daoyu, "Foreign Policy and Arms Control: The View from China," *Arms Control Today* 23, no. 10 (1993): 9–11; Sha Zukang, "Some Thoughts on Non-Proliferation" (remarks delivered at the 7th Carnegie International Non-proliferation Conference, Washington, DC, 11–12 January 1999), www.ceip.org/files/events/Conf99Sha.asp?p=8&EventID=156, accessed 2001. In July 1998 the PRC reiterated this basic stance: "Necessary measures should be adopted to apply effective international control to the transfer of sensitive materials and technologies in order to prevent the proliferation of weapons of mass destruction and their carriers. However, at the same time, China holds that international efforts to prevent such proliferation should follow the principle of fairness and rationality, and opposes a double standard whereby anti-proliferation is used as a pretext to infringe upon the sovereignty of other countries and harm normal international cooperation and exchanges in the fields of economy, trade, science and technology" (see Information Office of the State Council of the People's Republic of China, "China's National Defense," white paper, July 1998, 5, www.china.org.cn/e-white/5/, accessed 2000).

46. Senate Governmental Affairs Committee, Subcommittee on International Security, Proliferation, and Federal Services, *Hearing on Weapons Proliferation in China*, 10 April 1997. See also Koro Bessho, *Identities and Security in East Asia*, Adelphi Paper 325 (London: International Institute for Strategic Studies, 1999), esp. 27–37.

47. Mitchell B. Wallerstein, "China and Proliferation: A Path Not Taken?" *Survival* 38, no. 3 (1996): 58–61, 64–65. For a discussion of the commercial motivations for PRC conventional arms transfers, see Eden Y. Woon, "Chinese Arms Sales and U.S.-China Military Relations," *Asian Survey* 29, no. 6 (1989): 601–18; Richard A. Bitzinger, "Arms to Go: Chinese Arms Sales to the Third World," *International Security* 17, no. 2 (1992): 84–111; and Karl W. Eikenberry, *Explaining and Influencing Chinese Arms Transfers*, McNair Paper 36 (Washington, DC: National Defense University, February 1995).

48. Bates Gill, "Chinese Arms Exports to Iran," *Middle East Review of International Affairs* 2, no. 2 (1998): 1–4.

49. Senate Foreign Relations Committee, *Hearing on the Proliferation of Chinese Missiles*, 105th Cong., 2nd sess., 11 June 1998. See also Ming Zhang, *China's Changing Nuclear Posture: Reactions to the South Asian Nuclear Tests* (Washington, DC: Carnegie Endowment for International Peace, 1998), 9–17; Office of the Secretary of Defense, *Proliferation: Threat and Response* (Washington, DC: GPO, November 1997), 12.

50. Daniel Byman and Roger Cliff, *China's Arms Sales: Motivations and Implications*, MR-1110-AF (Santa Monica, CA: RAND Corporation, 1999), x–xi, 7–30. See also Frank J. Gaffney Jr., "China Arms the Rogues," *Middle East Quarterly* 4, no. 3 (1997): 39; and J. Mohan Malik, "China and the Nuclear Non-Proliferation Regime," *Contemporary Southeast Asia* 22, no. 3 (December 2000): 452–53.

51. Joseph S. Bermudez Jr., "DPRK-Pakistan Ghauri Missile Cooperation," 21 May 1998, www.fas.org/news/pakistan/1998/05/ghauri2.htm, accessed 2001.

52. Barbara Crosette, "Pakistan Claims Major Gains In Developing Its Own Arms," *New York Times*, 6 February 1989, A6.

53. Government of Pakistan, "Pakistan Test Fires Ghauri Missile: A Landmark in Country's Defence History," press release, 6 April 1998; Bermudez, "DPRK-Pakistan Ghauri Missile Cooperation"; David C. Wright, "An Analysis of the Pakistani Ghauri Mis-

sile Test of 6 April 1998," 12 May 1998, www.fas.org/news /pakistan/1998/04/980423-pak-m.htm, accessed 2001; Federation of American Scientists, "Ghauri [Hatf-5]" and "Pakistan," www.fas.org; *Report of the Commission to Assess the Ballistic Missile Threat to the United States, Executive Summary, Pursuant to Public Law 201,* 104th Cong., 1st sess., 1998, 16 (hereafter cited as Rumsfeld Report).

54. Jason D. Ellis, "Beyond Nonproliferation: Secondary Supply, Proliferation Management, and U.S. Foreign Policy," *Comparative Strategy* 20, no. 1 (2001): 1–2.

55. Bermudez, "DPRK-Pakistan Ghauri Missile Cooperation." While most analysts seem to agree that the Ghauri is based largely on the DPRK's Nodong, Mohan Malik suggests that the Ghauri may in fact be more closely related to the PRC's CSS-2 (DF-3) and CSS-5 (DF-21) ballistic missiles ("China and the Nuclear Non-Proliferation Regime," 457). See also Wright, "Analysis of the Pakistani Ghauri Missile Test of 6 April 1998"; and Fred Wiener, "U.S. Says North Korea Helped Develop New Pakistani Missile," *New York Times,* 11 April 1998, A3.

56. Malik, "China and the Nuclear Non-Proliferation Regime," 452.

57. The expanded guidelines as well as the material and technical annex can be found at www.fas.org/nuke/control/mtcr/text/index.html.

58. Malik, "China and the Nuclear Non-Proliferation Regime," 452.

59. See, e.g., Majority report of the Senate Governmental Affairs Committee, Subcommittee on International Security, Proliferation, and Federal Services, *Proliferation Primer,* 3–4; Office of the Secretary of Defense, *Proliferation: Threat and Response* (January 2001), 17–18; Rumsfeld Report, 10–11; Director of Central Intelligence (DCI), "Unclassified Report to Congress on the Acquisition of Technology Relating to Weapons of Mass Destruction and Advanced Conventional Munitions, 1 July through 31 December 2000," 7 September 2001, www.cia.gov/cia/reports/721_reports/july_dec2000.htm, accessed 2001 (see also previous reports, archived at www.cia.gov/cia/reports/index.html); Ellis, "Beyond Nonproliferation," 6–10.

60. Center for Counterproliferation Research, *The Counterproliferation Imperative: Meeting Tomorrow's Challenges* (Washington, DC: National Defense University, 2001), 2, 6, 12.

61. White House Press Office, "President Bush Announces Plan to Bolster Nonproliferation Efforts," 13 July 1992, www.fas.org/irp/news/1992/75958047-75961150.htm.

62. Arms Control Association, "The Missile Technology Control Regime at a Glance," www.armscontrol.org/factsheets/mtcr.asp, accessed 2001; Wyn Q. Bowen, "U.S. Policy on Ballistic Missile Proliferation: The MTCR's First Decade (1987–1997)," *Nonproliferation Review* 5, no. 1 (1997): 27.

63. R. Jeffrey Smith, "Chinese Missile Launchers Sighted in Pakistan," *Washington Post,* 6 April 1991, A17; James Gerstenzang and David Lauter, "Bush Bars U.S. Export to China of Satellite Gear," *Los Angeles Times,* 1 May 1991, A1. Previous reports had suggested the presence of "training" versions of the M-11 missile and launcher in Pakistan.

64. Gerstenzang and Lauter, "Bush Bars U.S. Export to China."

65. Ibid.

66. Raymond Whitaker, "Pakistan Bought Chinese Missiles," *Independent* (London), 21 June 1991, 11.

67. James L. Tyson, "Chinese Vow Tested By Leader's Visit to Biggest Arms Buyers," *Christian Science Monitor,* 1 November 1991, 7.

68. "Comments on Missile Control, GATT, Korea," *Zhongguo Xinwen She* (Beijing), 21

November 1991, FBIS-CHI-91-225, 1; Thomas L. Friedman, "Baker's China Trip Fails to Produce Pledge on Rights," *New York Times,* 18 November 1991, A1.

69. Friedman, "Baker's China Trip Fails to Produce Pledge on Rights."

70. Elaine Sciolino and Eric Schmitt, "China Said to Sell Parts for Missiles," *New York Times,* 31 January 1992, A1.

71. R. Jeffrey Smith, "U.S. Lifts Sanctions against Chinese Firms; Biden Seeks Session on Reported Violations," *Washington Post,* 22 February 1992, A15.

72. Ibid.; Guy Gugliotta, "Senate Backs China Trade Conditions; Reports of Arms Sales to the Middle East Debated," *Washington Post,* 26 February 1992, A19.

73. Gugliotta, "Senate Backs China Trade Conditions"; "Senate Rebuffs China on Trade," *St. Louis Post-Dispatch,* 26 February 1992, 10A; William J. Eaton, "Congress Approves Stiffer Terms on Trade with China; Diplomacy: Final Vote Follows a Secret Senate Session on Missile Sales; A Veto by Bush Is Likely," *Los Angeles Times,* 26 February 1992, A1. The vote on the legislation in the Senate was split along party lines, and although the legislation passed in both houses, it lacked sufficient votes to override a presidential veto.

74. "Senate Rebuffs China on Trade."

75. Smith, "U.S. Lifts Sanctions against Chinese Firms"; "Taking China's Word on Arms Sales, U.S. Allows Export of High Technology," *Atlanta Journal and Constitution,* 22 February 1992, A14.

76. R. Jeffrey Smith, "China Said to Sell Arms to Pakistan; M-11 Missile Shipment may Break Vow to U.S.," *Washington Post,* 4 December 1992, A10; Michael Chugani, "US Acts over China Arms Sales," *South China Morning Post,* 6 December 1992, 1; Jim Mann, "China Said to Sell Pakistan Dangerous New Missiles," *Los Angeles Times,* 4 December 1992, A1.

77. Mann, "China Said to Sell Pakistan Dangerous New Missiles"; Chugani, "US Acts over China Arms Sales."

78. R. Jeffrey Smith and Dan Southerland, "U.S. Plans to Let China Purchase Jet Technology; Proposed Sale Disputed Inside Administration," *Washington Post,* 12 December 1992, A4; Chugani, "US Acts over China Arms Sales."

79. Lena H. Sun, "China Works to Improve U.S. Relations; Rhetoric Toned Down as Trade Status Is Viewed at Risk under Clinton," *Washington Post,* 2 January 1993, A1.

80. Gary Milhollin and Meg Dennison, "China's Cynical Calculation," *New York Times,* 24 April 1995, A17.

81. Douglas Jehl, "China Breaking Missile Pledge, U.S. Aides Say," ibid., 6 May 1993, A1; Ann Devroy and R. Jeffrey Smith, "U.S. Evidence 'Suggests' China Breaks Arms Pact; Report Comes on Eve of Trade Status Debate," *Washington Post,* A9.

82. Devroy and Smith, "U.S. Evidence 'Suggests' China Breaks Arms Pact."

83. Jehl, "China Breaking Missile Pledge."

84. Michael McCurry, Department of State Daily Press Briefing, 25 August 1993.

85. Category II sanctions are applied when a suspected violator has transferred certain missile components and related equipment and technology, while the more stringent Category I sanctions are applied when a gross violation of the MTCR occurs, such as the transfer of a complete missile system (see Department of State, "Missile Technology Control Regime," fact sheet, www.state.gov/t/ac/trty/5073.htm).

86. McCurry, Department of State Daily Press Briefing, 25 August 1993.

87. Rone Tempest, "Flourishing U.S. Satellite Business May Be Grounded by Curbs on

China," *Los Angeles Times*, 27 August 1993, A10. See also Norman Kempster and Rone Tempest, "U.S. Imposes Sanctions on China, Pakistan over Missile Deal; Arms Technology: Export of Satellite Gear to Beijing Is Banned; Both Asian Nations Deny Violating Controls," ibid., 26 August 1993, A8.

88. Kempster and Tempest, "U.S. Imposes Sanctions on China, Pakistan over Missile Deal."

89. Tempest, "Flourishing U.S. Satellite Business May Be Grounded by Curbs on China."

90. Earl Lane, "Satellite Sanctions on China May Ease," *Chicago Sun-Times*, 14 November 1993, 41.

91. Daniel Williams and Peter Behr, "U.S. Moves to Punish China over Textiles; Beijing Said to Let Exporters Skirt Quotas; Progress Reported on Missile Proliferation Issue," *Washington Post*, 7 January 1994, A8.

92. Lane, "Satellite Sanctions on China May Ease."

93. See "U.S., China Sign Non Proliferation Pact; Clinton Administration to Lift Sanctions Barring Delivery of Satellite Technology," *Minneapolis Star Tribune*, 5 October 1994, 2A; Elaine Sciolino, "U.S. and Chinese Resolve Dispute on Missile Sales; Clinton Eases Sanctions," *New York Times*, 5 October 1994, A1; and Robert S. Greenberger, "U.S. and China Reach Accord on M-11 Missile," *Wall Street Journal*, 5 October 1994, A18.

94. "U.S., China Sign Non Proliferation Pact."

95. Warren Christopher, remarks with PRC Vice Premier and Foreign Minister Qian Qichen following the signing of joint US-PRC Statement on missile proliferation and joint US-PRC statement on stopping production of fissile materials for nuclear weapons, 4 October 1994, dosfan.lib.uic.edu/ERC/briefing/dossec/1994/9410/941004dossec.html, accessed 2001.

96. Ibid.

97. R. Jeffrey Smith and David B. Ottaway, "Spy Photos Suggest China Missile Trade; Pressure for Sanctions Builds over Evidence That Pakistan Has M-11s," *Washington Post*, 3 July 1995, A1.

98. Ibid.

99. Steve Holland, "China Risks US Sanctions after Missile Report," *Guardian* (London), 23 June 1995, 13. Part of the difficulty in obtaining "firm, conclusionary evidence" stemmed from the steps taken by the PRC and Pakistan to conceal some of their dealings from American eavesdropping. Bill Gertz cites an intercept detailing conversations between PRC and Pakistani nuclear officials discussing methods of concealing information from US intelligence agencies, including the use of falsified end-user documentation and the diplomatic pouch (see Bill Gertz, *Betrayal: How the Clinton Administration Undermined American Security* [Washington, DC: Regnery, 1999], 266–67).

100. Holland, "China Risks US Sanctions after Missile Report."

101. Ibid.

102. Ibid.

103. Ibid.

104. Smith and Ottaway, "Spy Photos Suggest China Missile Trade."

105. R. Jeffrey Smith, "Helms Pressures Administration to Punish China," *Washington Post*, 9 February 1996, A25.

106. Ibid.

107. R. Jeffrey Smith, "Proliferation Concerns May Delay U.S. Arms Shipment to Pakistan," *Washington Post*, 15 February 1996, A23.

108. Gordon Oehler, testimony before the Senate Foreign Relations Committee, 11 June 1998, *Chinese Missile Proliferation*, 105th Cong., 2nd sess., 1998. See also Richard W. Stevenson, "U.S. Debates Whether to Punish Pakistan and China on Missiles," *New York Times*, 13 June 1996, A5; and R. Jeffrey Smith, "Report Cites China-Pakistan Missile Links," *Washington Post*, 13 June 1996, A19.

109. Gordon Oehler, testimony before the Senate Foreign Relations Committee, 11 June 1998.

110. Gertz, *Betrayal*, 161; R. Jeffrey Smith, "China Linked to Pakistani Missile Plant; Secret Project Could Renew Sanctions Issue," *Washington Post*, 25 August 1996, A1.

111. Gordon Oehler, testimony before the Senate Foreign Relations Committee, 11 June 1998. In addition to this report on the missiles, another document was leaked at this time, a purported "statement of fact" declaring that Pakistan and the PRC had taken part in a "conspiracy to transfer M-11s" in deliberate defiance of U.S. nonproliferation laws and international regimes (see Bill Gertz, "Missile Sanctions on China Vowed; Sale to Pakistan Spurs U.S. Probe," *Washington Times*, 13 June 1996, A1; and idem, "Pakistan Deploys Chinese Missiles; But State Dept. Opposes Sanctions," ibid., 12 June 1996, A1).

112. Smith, "China Linked to Pakistani Missile Plant."

113. Smith, "Report Cites China-Pakistan Missile Links"; Stevenson, "U.S. Debates Whether to Punish Pakistan and China on Missiles"; Smith, "China Linked to Pakistani Missile Plant"; Gertz, "Missile Sanctions on China Vowed."

114. Smith, "China Linked to Pakistani Missile Plant"; Gertz, "Missile Sanctions on China Vowed"; and Gertz, "Pakistan Deploys Chinese Missiles."

115. Gertz, *Betrayal*, 158.

116. Smith, "China Linked to Pakistani Missile Plant."

117. Ibid.

118. "China Praised for Non-Proliferation Work," United Press International Release, 9 October 1996.

119. Elaine Sciolino, "Clinton Argues for 'Flexibility' over Sanctions," *New York Times*, 28 April 1998, A1.

120. Andrea Stone, "Albright: Sanctions Have Hindered Foreign Policy," *USA Today*, 15 June 1998, 10A.

121. Ibid.

122. Milhollin, testimony before Senate Governmental Affairs Committee, Subcommittee on International Security, Proliferation, and Federal Services, 10 April 1997.

123. James B. Foley, Department of State Daily Press Briefing, 14 September 1999, secretary.state.gov/www/briefings/9909/990914db.html.

124. Oehler, testimony before the Senate Foreign Relations Committee, 11 June 1998.

125. Ibid.

126. Gertz, *Betrayal*, 135.

127. Senate Governmental Affairs Committee, Subcommittee on International Security, Proliferation, and Federal Services, *Hearing on Weapons Proliferation in China*, 10 April 1997. Interestingly, on the day after the hearing the State Department recalled the testimony of its witness, Acting Assistant Secretary of State for Nonproliferation Robert Einhorn, and reportedly revised his testimony to remove a reference to Iran's chemical weapons program that would have suggested PRC contributions to Iran's efforts in this area (see Rowan Scarborough, "State Dept. Revises Report on China's Arms Sales to Iran," *Washington Times*, 15 April 1997, A3).

128. Senate Governmental Affairs Committee, Subcommittee on International Security, Proliferation, and Federal Services, *Hearing on Weapons Proliferation in China,* 10 April 1997.

129. Senate Foreign Relations Committee, 11 June 1998, *Chinese Missile Proliferation,* 105th Cong., 2nd sess., 1998.

130. Bill Gertz, "U.S. May Help China on Missiles; But Beijing Must Halt Tech Exports," *Washington Times,* 18 March 1998, A1.

131. Bill Gertz, "Clinton Arms Official Cites Secrecy, Refuses Comment on Missile Deal; Leaked Memo Urges U.S. Backing for China to Join Pact," ibid., 19 March 1998, A3.

132. Ibid.

133. John Mintz, "NSC Papers Trace Concerns on Export Waivers for China," *Washington Post,* 11 June 1998, A10.

134. Milhollin, testimony before Senate Governmental Affairs Committee, Subcommittee on International Security, Proliferation, and Federal Services, 10 April 1997.

135. NIC, *Foreign Missile Developments and the Ballistic Missile Threat through 2015,* unclassified summary, September 1999 (Washington, DC, 2000), 46, www.odci.gov/nic/other_missilethreat1999.html.

136. Foley, Department of State Daily Press Briefing, 14 September 1999.

137. Ibid.

138. Bob Drogin, "U.S. Seeks to Curb Asian Missile Sales," *Los Angeles Times,* 8 July 2000, A9.

139. Erik Eckholm, "U.S.-China Talks Don't Resolve Issue of Pakistan Missile Aid," *New York Times,* 9 July 2000, 4.

140. Ibid.

141. Karl Inderfurth, testimony before the Senate Foreign Relations Committee, Subcommittee on Near Eastern and South Asian Affairs, 13 July 1998, *Crisis in South Asia: India's Nuclear Tests; Pakistan's Nuclear Tests; India and Pakistan: What Next?* 105th Cong., 2nd sess., 1998, 99.

142. United States Information Service, "Transcript: Senate Vote Eases Sanctions against Pakistan and India," 10 July 1998, www.mtholyoke.edu/acad/intrel/easesanc.htm, accessed January 2001.

143. Barbara Leitch LePoer, *India-Pakistan Nuclear Tests and U.S. Response,* CRS Report 98-570 F (Washington, DC: Congressional Research Service, 24 November 1998), 35.

144. William J. Clinton, "Statement on Signing the Agriculture Export Relief Act of 1998, July 15, 1998," *Public Papers of the Presidents of the United States, William J. Clinton, 1998* (Washington, DC: GPO, 2000), 1:1238.

145. Ibid. The Brownback amendment eventually became part of the Omnibus Consolidated and Emergency Supplemental Appropriations Act of 1999 (Public Law 105-277).

146. Senator Sam Brownback, statement in committee, Senate Foreign Relations Committee, Subcommittee on Near Eastern and South Asian Affairs, *Hearing on Nuclear Proliferation in India and Pakistan,* 13 July 1998.

147. Andrew Ward and Richard Wolffe, "Bush to Press China over Missile Sales," *Financial Times,* 21 February 2002, 11; Alan Sipress, "U.S. Lists Conditions for Lifting Sanctions," *Washington Post,* 2 September 2001, A19; idem, "Chinese Firm Faces U.S. Sanctions; Technology Allegedly Passed to Pakistan," ibid., 1 September 2001, A1; John Pomfret, "U.S. Protests Exports of Missiles by China; Beijing Denies Sales; Powell to Raise Issue on Visit," ibid., 27 July 2001, A21.

THREE: Through a Glass Darkly

1. Joseph S. Nye Jr., "Peering into the Future," *Foreign Affairs* 73, no. 4 (1994): 86.

2. John C. Gannon, "The US Intelligence Community and the Challenge of BCW," in *The New Terror: Facing the Threat of Biological and Chemical Weapons*, ed. Sidney D. Drell, Abraham D. Sofaer, and George D. Wilson (Stanford, CA: Hoover Institution Press, 1999), 134.

3. Nye, "Peering into the Future," 83.

4. Sherman Kent, *Strategic Intelligence for American World Policy* (Princeton, NJ: Princeton University Press, 1949), 60.

5. Mark M. Lowenthal, "Tribal Tongues: Intelligence Consumers, Intelligence Producers," *Washington Quarterly* 15, no. 1 (1992): 160. See also Paula L. Scalingi, "Proliferation and Arms Control," *Intelligence and National Security* 10, no. 4 (1995): 153.

6. *Combating Proliferation of Weapons of Mass Destruction: Report from the Commission to Assess the Organization of the Federal Government to Combat the Proliferation of Weapons of Mass Destruction, Pursuant to Public Law 293*, 104th Cong., 2nd sess., 1999, 68.

7. See, e.g., Michael J. Mazarr, *North Korea and the Bomb: A Case Study in Nonproliferation* (New York: St. Martin's, 1995), 15–34; Joseph S. Bermudez Jr., "North Korea's Nuclear Programme," *Jane's Intelligence Review* 3, no. 9 (1991): 404–11; Michael J. Mazarr, "Going Just a Little Nuclear: Nonproliferation Lessons from North Korea," *International Security* 20, no. 2 (1995): 93–94; Alexandre Y. Mansourov, "The Origins, Evolution, and Current Politics of the North Korean Nuclear Program," *Nonproliferation Review* 2, no. 3 (1995): 25–28; and Tai Sung An, "The Rise and Decline of North Korea's Nuclear Weapons Program," *Korea and World Affairs* 16, no. 4 (1992): 674–76.

8. Robert Carlin, "North Korea," in *Nuclear Proliferation after the Cold War*, ed. Mitchell Reiss and Robert S. Litwak (Washington, DC: Woodrow Wilson Center Press, 1994), 129.

9. See, e.g., Joseph S. Bermudez Jr., "Exposing North Korea's Secret Nuclear Infrastructure—Part One," *Jane's Intelligence Review* 11, no. 7 (1999): 36–40; and idem, "Exposing North Korea's Secret Nuclear Infrastructure—Part Two," ibid. 11, no. 8 (1999): 41–45. See also Mazarr, *North Korea and the Bomb*, 35–54; and Rodney W. Jones and Mark G. McDonough with Toby F. Dalton and Gregory D. Koblentz, *Tracking Nuclear Proliferation: A Guide in Maps and Charts, 1998* (Washington, DC: Carnegie Endowment for International Peace, 1998), 158–59.

10. Bermudez, "North Korea's Nuclear Programme," 406; idem, "Exposing North Korea's Secret Nuclear Infrastructure—Part One," 41.

11. IAEA inspectors who visited the facility—the second largest of its kind in the world—in 1992 reported that it was "a reprocessing plant in the terminology of the industrial world" (Sheryl WuDunn, "North Korea Site Has A-Bomb Hints," *New York Times*, 17 May 1992, A1; Mazarr, *North Korea and the Bomb*, 44; Bermudez, "Exposing North Korea's Secret Nuclear Infrastructure—Part Two," 43; T. R. Reid, "N. Korean Plutonium Plant Cited; Pyongyang Building Reprocessing Facility," *Washington Post*, 17 May 1992, A25).

12. Bermudez, "Exposing North Korea's Secret Nuclear Infrastructure—Part One," 41.

13. Such signatures would include the presence of power generation and transmission equipment, which was notably lacking at Yongbyon when IAEA inspectors arrived

in 1992 (Mazarr, *North Korea and the Bomb,* 39, 84; Bermudez, "North Korea's Nuclear Programme," 408).

14. Mazarr, *North Korea and the Bomb,* 44.

15. See Bermudez, "Exposing North Korea's Secret Nuclear Infrastructure—Part One," 41, 43; idem, "Exposing North Korea's Secret Nuclear Infrastructure—Part Two," 43; Mazarr, *North Korea and the Bomb,* 44; David Albright, Frans Berkhout, and William Walker, *World Inventory of Plutonium and Highly Enriched Uranium, 1992* (New York: Oxford University Press, 1993), 174; and Larry A. Niksch, *North Korea's Nuclear Weapons Program,* CRS Report 91-141 (Washington, DC: Congressional Research Service, Library of Congress, 12 December 1996), www.fas.org/spp/starwars/crs/91-141.htm, accessed 21 December 2000.

16. Mitchell Reiss, *Bridled Ambition: Why Countries Constrain Their Nuclear Capabilities* (Washington, DC: Woodrow Wilson Center Press, 1995), 242; Bermudez, "Exposing North Korea's Secret Nuclear Infrastructure—Part Two," 43. The IAEA gradually uncovered evidence that challenged the DPRK's declaration, however, stimulating speculation that the DPRK might have produced more than 90 grams of plutonium (see IAEA, "Report by the Director General of the International Atomic Energy Agency on Behalf of the Board of Governors to all Members of the Agency on the Non-Compliance of the Democratic People's Republic of Korea for the Application of Safeguards in Connection with the Treaty on the Non-Proliferation of Nuclear Weapons [INFCIRC/403] and on the Agency's Inability to Verify the Non-Diversion of Material Required to be Safeguarded," Information Circular 419, 8 April 1993; David Albright, "How Much Plutonium Does North Korea Have?" *Bulletin of the Atomic Scientists* 50, no. 5 [1994]: 47; and David E. Sanger, "West Knew of North Korea Nuclear Development," *New York Times,* 13 March 1993, A3).

17. Niksch, *North Korea's Nuclear Weapons Program;* WuDunn, "North Korea Site Has A-Bomb Hints"; Stephen Engelberg and Michael R. Gordon, "Intelligence Study Says North Korea Has Nuclear Bomb," *New York Times,* 26 December 1993, A1; Albright, Berkhout, and Walker, *World Inventory of Plutonium and Highly Enriched Uranium, 1992,* 175; Margaret Shapiro, "1990 KGB Document Concluded North Korea Had 'Nuclear Device,'" *Washington Post,* 25 June 1994, A17. Interestingly, the PRC allegedly put forth the position that the DPRK had abandoned its attempt to build nuclear weapons in the late 1980s and that the DPRK had been bluffing since that time in order to win concession from the United States (see "The Bomb Bluffers?" *Economist,* 16 May 1992, 41).

18. Niksch, *North Korea's Nuclear Weapons Program;* WuDunn, "North Korea Site Has A-Bomb Hints"; Engelberg and Gordon, "Intelligence Study Says North Korea Has Nuclear Bomb."

19. The IAEA estimated that 8 kilograms of plutonium would be needed to produce one nuclear weapon (see Niksch, *North Korea's Nuclear Weapons Program*).

20. Engelberg and Gordon, "Intelligence Study Says North Korea Has Nuclear Bomb."

21. David E. Sanger, "Defense Chief Says North Korea Could Soon Build 4 A-Bombs," *New York Times,* 21 April 1994, A7; idem, "North Korea Moves to Use Fuel for Bomb," ibid., 22 April 1994, A3.

22. David E. Sanger, "North Koreans Say Nuclear Fuel Rods Are Being Removed," ibid., 15 May 1994, A1.

23. Mark Thompson, "Well, Maybe a Nuke or Two," *Time,* 11 April 1994, 58.

24. Marc Dean Millot, "Facing the Emerging Reality of Regional Nuclear Adversaries," *Washington Quarterly* 17, no. 3 (1994): 47.

25. Thompson, "Well, Maybe a Nuke or Two," emphasis added.

26. William Perry, testimony before the Senate Armed Services Committee, 26 January 1995, *Security Implications of the Nuclear Non-proliferation Agreement with North Korea*, 104th Cong., 1st sess., 1995, 40.

27. Ibid. As Andrew Mack observed, "It is by definition impossible to hit unknown targets" (Andrew Mack, "A Nuclear North Korea: The Choices Are Narrowing," *World Policy Journal* 11, no. 2 [1994]: 33; Robert Manning, "The Enigma of the North," *Wilson Quarterly* 23, no. 3 [1999]: 80).

29. Manning, "Enigma of the North," 80; DIA, *North Korea: The Foundations of Military Strength* (Washington, DC: October 1991), 57; John M. Collins, *Korean Crisis, 1994: Military Geography, Military Balance, Military Options*, CRS Issue Brief 94-311S (Washington, DC: Congressional Research Service, Library of Congress, 11 April 1994).

30. Mazarr, *North Korea and the Bomb*, 214; Robert Gallucci and Christine Shelly, Department of State Daily Press Briefing, 17 June 1994; Greg J. Gerardi and James A. Plotts, "North Korea—To The Brink and Back," in *Jane's Intelligence Review Yearbook: The World in Conflict, 1994/95* (Coulsdon, Surrey, UK: Jane's Information Group, 1995), 131.

31. Collins, *Korean Crisis, 1994.*

32. General Gary Luck, testimony before the Senate Armed Services Committee, *Hearing on the Security Implications of the Nuclear Agreement with North Korea*, 26 January 1995.

33. Peter Lewis Young, "The Threat of War on the Korean Peninsula," *Jane's Intelligence Review* 7, no. 9 (1995): 419.

34. Perry, testimony before the Senate Armed Services Committee, 26 January 1995, 38.

35. Ibid.; Sanger, "North Koreans Say Nuclear Fuel Rods Are Being Removed."

36. Young, "Threat of War on the Korean Peninsula," 419.

37. "Agreed Framework between the United States of America and the Democratic People's Republic of Korea," 21 October 1994, www.fas.org/news/dprk/1994/941021-D415 .htm.

38. Robert Gallucci and Christine Shelly, Department of State Daily Press Briefing, 25 October 1994.

39. Perry, testimony before the Senate Armed Service Committee, 26 January 1995.

40. Robert Gallucci, testimony before the House International Relations Committee, Subcommittee on International Economic Policy and Trade and Subcommittee on Asian and Pacific Affairs, 23 February 1995, *North Korean Military and Nuclear Proliferation Threat*, 104th Cong., 1st sess., 1995.

41. William J. Clinton, "Memorandum of Certification of North Korea," *Weekly Compilation of Presidential Documents* 33, no. 12 (24 May 1997): 382. This certification is required by Public Law 104-208.

42. Rust Deming, testimony before the Senate Foreign Relations Committee, Subcommittee on East Asian and Pacific Affairs, 14 July 1998, *KEDO and the Korean Agreed Nuclear Framework: Problems and Prospects*, 105th Cong., 2nd sess., 1998, 4.

43. Charles Kartman, testimony before the House International Relations Committee, 24 September 1998, *U.S. Policy toward North Korea*, 105th Cong., 2nd sess., 1998, 4.

44. Perry, testimony before the Senate Armed Services Committee, 26 January 1995.

45. Gary Milhollin, testimony before the Senate Armed Services Committee, 26 January 1995, *Security Implications of the Nuclear Non-proliferation Agreement with North Korea*, 104th Cong., 1st sess., 1995, Wisconsin Project on Nuclear Arms Control, www .wisconsinproject.org/pubs/testimonies/1995/1-26.html.

46. Ibid.

47. North Korea Advisory Group, "Report to the Speaker, U.S. House of Representatives," November 1999, www.fas.org/nuke/guide/dprk/nkag-report.htm.

48. Ashton Carter, testimony before the Senate Armed Services Committee, 26 January 1995, *Security Implications of the Nuclear Non-proliferation Agreement with North Korea,* 104th Cong., 1st sess., 1995.

49. William Perry, "Review of United States Policy toward North Korea: Findings and Recommendations," 12 October 1999, www.state.gov/www/regions/eap /991012 _northkorea_rpt.html, accessed 2001.

50. Ibid.

51. Rep. Dan Burton, statement made to witness before the House International Relations Committee, Subcommittee on International Economic Policy and Trade and Subcommittee on Asian and Pacific Affairs, 23 February 1995, *North Korean Military and Nuclear Proliferation Threat,* 104th Cong., 1st sess., 1995.

52. Mack, "A Nuclear North Korea," 33.

53. James Risen, "Ferreting Out North Korea's Nuclear Secrets: U.S. Intelligence Experts at Odds," *New York Times,* 5 August 2000, A4.

54. David E. Sanger, "North Korea Site an A-Bomb Plant, U.S. Agencies Say," ibid., 17 August 1998, A1; "North Korea's Nuclear Ambitions," ibid., 19 August 1998, A30; William Perry, testimony before the Senate Foreign Relations Committee, Subcommittee on East Asian and Pacific Affairs, 12 October 1999, 106th Cong., 1st sess., www.state .gov/www/policy_remarks/1999/991012_perry_nkorea.html.

55. See Risen, "Ferreting Out North Korea's Nuclear Secrets"; Steven Mufson, "N. Korean Site Passes A Test; U.S. Finds No Evidence of Nuclear Weapons Development," *Washington Post,* 29 May 1999, A24; Philip Shenon, "Suspected North Korean Atom Site Is Empty, U.S. Finds," *New York Times,* 28 May 1999, A3; and Associated Press, "U.S. Inspects North Korean Military Site," ibid., 31 May 2000, A14.

56. Consider Hans Heymann's remark that "administrations have often found that intelligence analyses appear at times and in various ways unhelpful to the pursuit of policies on which they had embarked" (Hans Heymann, "Intelligence/Policy Relationships," in *Intelligence: Policy and Process,* ed. Alfred C. Maurer, Marion D. Tunstall, and James M. Keagle [Boulder, CO: Westview Press, 1985], 63).

57. Robert A. Manning, "Time Bomb: Have We Really Contained North Korea?" *New Republic,* 30 November 1998, 30; Risen, "Ferreting Out North Korea's Nuclear Secrets."

58. Risen, "Ferreting Out North Korea's Nuclear Secrets."

59. Joseph S. Bermudez Jr., "Lifting the Lid on Kim's Nuclear Workshop," *Jane's Defence Weekly* 38, no. 22 (2002): 21; Peter Slavin and Karen DeYoung, "N. Korea Admits Having Secret Nuclear Arms; Stunned U.S. Ponders Next Steps," *Washington Post,* 17 October 2002, A1; David S. Cloud, "North Korea Has Nuclear Program," *Wall Street Journal,* 17 October 2002, A3; Barbara Slavin, "N. Korea Admits Nuclear Program," *USA Today,* 17 October 2002, 1A; David E. Sanger, "North Korea Says It Has a Program on Nuclear Arms," *New York Times,* 17 October 2002, A1.

60. David E. Sanger, "In North Korea and Pakistan, Deep Roots of Nuclear Barter," *New York Times,* 24 November 2002, A1.

61. Robert Harris and Jeremy Paxman, *A Higher Form of Killing: The Secret Story of Chemical and Biological Warfare* (New York: Hill & Wang, 1982), 140.

62. Tom Mangold and Jeff Goldberg, *Plague Wars: The Terrifying Reality of Biological Warfare* (New York: St. Martin's, 1999), 49.

63. H arris and Paxman, *Higher Form of Killing*, 142. Ken Alibek offers some corroboration of this intelligence, noting that Soviet bioweaponeers driven out of their initial bases in Leningrad and at Solovetsky Island by the advancing German army had made their way to Vozrozhdeniya (Rebirth) Island (see Ken Alibek with Stephen Handelman, *Biohazard: The Chilling True Story of the Largest Covert Biological Weapons Program in the World—Told from the Inside by the Man Who Ran It* [New York: Random House, 1999], 36).

64. Harris and Paxman, *Higher Form of Killing*, 142.

65. Alibek with Handelman, *Biohazard*, 36–37.

66. Mangold and Goldberg, *Plague Wars*, 49.

67. Harris and Paxman, *Higher Form of Killing*, 143.

68. According to Mark M. Lowenthal, mirror imaging is "assuming that other states or individuals will act just the way we do," an analytic trap that can undermine objective intelligence analyses (see Lowenthal's *Intelligence: From Secrets to Policy* [Washington, DC: CQ Press, 2000], 7).

69. Gary Crocker, interview for "Plague War," *Frontline*, PBS, 13 October 1998, www.pbs.org/wgbh/pages/frontline/shows/plague/interviews/crocker.html.

70. Alibek with Handelman, *Biohazard*, 22, 297.

71. House Committee on Appropriations, Subcommittee on Department of Defense Appropriations, *Hearing on Department of Defense Appropriations for 1963*, 87th Cong., 2nd sess., 1962, pt. 6, 184.

72. D. E. Viney, "Research Policy—Soviet Union," in *CBW: Chemical and Biological Warfare*, ed. Steven Rose (London: George G. Harrap, 1968), 131–32.

73. Convention on the Prohibition of the Development, Production, and Stockpiling of Bacteriological (Biological) and Toxin Weapons and on Their Destruction, article 1.

74. Harris and Paxman, *Higher Form of Killing*, 219.

75. William Beecher, "Soviets Feared Violating Germ Weapon Ban; Photographic Evidence Cited," *Boston Globe*, 28 September 1975, 1. The three facilities referred to were the Zagorsk Virology Institute and the Sverdlovsk Institute of Military Technical Problems, both run by the Ministry of Defense, and the Omutninsk Science and Production Base, which was under the jurisdiction of Biopreparat. See also Alibek with Handelman, *Biohazard*, 299–300.

76. Beecher, "Soviets Feared Violating Germ Weapon Ban," 1.

77. Harris and Paxman, *Higher Form of Killing*, 220–21; Mangold and Goldberg, *Plague Wars*, 72, 75; Milton Leitenberg, "Anthrax in Sverdlovsk: New Pieces to the Puzzle," *Arms Control Today* 22, no. 3 (1992): 11.

78. R. Jeffrey Smith, "Soviets Offer Account of '79 Anthrax Outbreak; U.S. Tied Incident to Biological Weapons," *Washington Post*, 9 October 1986, A24.

79. See Harris and Paxman, *Higher Form of Killing*, 263n; and Beecher, "Soviets Feared Violating Germ Weapon Ban," 20.

80. Eliot Marshall, "Sverdlovsk: Anthrax Capital?" *Science*, 22 April 1988, 383. See also Leitenberg, "Anthrax in Sverdlovsk," 11; and Matthew S. Meselson, "The Biological Weapons Convention and the Sverdlovsk Anthrax Outbreak of 1979," *Public Interest Report* 41, no. 7 (1988): 6.

81. Smith, "Soviets Offer Account of '79 Anthrax Outbreak."

82. Mangold and Goldberg, *Plague Wars,* 81.

83. Judith Miller, Stephen Engelberg, and William Broad, *Germs: Biological Weapons and America's Secret War* (New York: Simon & Schuster, 2001), 143.

84. John Barry, Daniel Pedersen, and Tom Post, "Planning a Plague?" *Newsweek,* 1 February 1993, 40.

85. Mangold and Goldberg, *Plague Wars,* 92; Mark Urban, "The Cold War's Deadliest Secret," *Spectator,* 23 January 1993, 9.

86. "Concerns Renewed about Russia's Bio Weapons Program," *CBW Chronicle* 2, no. 4 (1998): 1; David Hoffman, "Russia Challenged to Disclose Status of Biological Weapons," *Washington Post,* 26 February 1998, A17; Mangold and Goldberg, *Plague Wars,* 92; Urban, "Cold War's Deadliest Secret," 10.

87. Urban, "Cold War's Deadliest Secret," 9; Barry, Pedersen, and Post, "Planning a Plague?"; Bill Gertz, "Russia Has Biological Weapons, Defector Says," *Washington Times,* 22 January 1993, A9; "Concerns Renewed about Russia's Bio Weapons Program," 2.

88. Frank Malinoski, interview for "Plague War," *Frontline,* PBS, 13 October 1998, www.pbs.org/wgbh/pages/frontline/shows/plague/interviews/malinoski.html.

89. Jonathan B. Tucker, "Biological Weapons in the Former Soviet Union: An Interview with Dr. Kenneth Alibek," *Nonproliferation Review* 6, no. 3 (1999): 4.

90. Alibek with Handelman, *Biohazard,* 22.

91. Tucker, "Biological Weapons in the Former Soviet Union," 4.

92. Alibek with Handelman, *Biohazard,* 172, 301–2.

93. According to Alibek, Soviet doctrine divided biological weapons into three categories: strategic, for attacks on adversary homelands; operational, for attacks on military targets 100–150 km behind front lines; and strategic-operational, for use against both target sets (Tucker, "Biological Weapons in the Former Soviet Union," 2; Kenneth Alibek, testimony before US Congress, Joint Economic Committee, 20 May 1998, *Terrorism and Intelligence Operations,* 105th Cong., 2nd sess., 1998, 52–53.

94. Tucker, "Biological Weapons in the Former Soviet Union," 2–3; Alibek with Handelman, *Biohazard,* 5; Al J. Venter, "Spectre of Biowar Remains," *Jane's Defence Weekly* 31, no. 17 (1999): 23; Alibek, testimony before Joint Economic Committee, 20 May 1998.

95. See Tucker, "Biological Weapons in the Former Soviet Union," 2; Alibek, testimony before Joint Economic Committee, 20 May 1998; and Dr. Kanatjan Alibekov, interview for "Plague War," *Frontline,* PBS, 13 October 1998, www.pbs.org/wgbh/pages/frontline/shows/plague/interviews/alibekov.html.

96. General Accounting Office, *Biological Weapons: Effort to Reduce Former Soviet Threat Offers Benefits, Poses New Risks,* NSIAD-00-138 (Washington, DC: April 2000), 27.

97. Sergei Popov, interview for "Bioterror," *Nova,* PBS, 13 November 2001, www.pbs.org/wgbh/nova/bioterror/biow_popov.html.

98. Alibek with Handelman, *Biohazard,* 154, 159.

99. Miller, Engelberg, and Broad, *Germs,* 302–3; Alibek with Handelman, *Biohazard,* 163–64; Popov, interview for "Bioterror."

100. Miller, Engelberg, and Broad, *Germs,* 302.

101. Ibid., 303; Popov, interview for "Bioterror."

102. Miller, Engelberg, and Broad, *Germs,* 304.

103. Ronald J. Jackson, Alistair J. Ramsey, Carina D. Christensen, Sandra Beaton, Diana F. Hall, and Ian A. Ramshaw, "Expression of Mouse Interleukin-4 by a Recombi-

nant Ectromelia Virus Suppresses Cytolytic Lymphocyte Responses and Overcomes Genetic Resistance to Mousepox," *Journal of Virology* 75, no. 3 (2001): 1205–10.

104. Consider the titles of the following articles, which appeared after the Australian announcement: Rachel Nowak, "Disaster in the Making," *New Scientist*, 13 January 2001, 4–5; Lois Ember, "Bioengineering Work Gone Wrong," *Chemical & Engineering News* 79, no. 5 (2001): 13; "Killer Virus Accidentally Made in Lab," *Current Science*, 6 March 2001, 12.

105. Malinoski, interview for "Plague War."

106. Tucker, "Biological Weapons in the Former Soviet Union," 7.

107. Christopher Davis, interview for "Plague War," *Frontline*, PBS, 13 October 1998, www.pbs.org/wgbh/pages/frontline/shows/plague/interviews/davis.html.

108. Mangold and Goldberg, *Plague Wars*, 127.

109. Ibid., 134; Malinoski, interview for "Plague War." The other WHO-approved repository was the Centers for Disease Control and Prevention in Atlanta, Georgia.

110. Mangold and Goldberg, *Plague Wars*, 138–39. See also Davis, interview for "Plague War"; and Malinoski, interview for "Plague War."

111. It was this inspection tour that provided the catalyst for Alibek's defection. The evidence he had seen contradicted assertions by the KGB and the GRU, the Soviet military intelligence directorate, of an active U.S. offensive program. Nevertheless, the inspection team's report claimed that the United States continued to run an offensive program. Shortly thereafter Alibek resigned from Biopreparat; his defection to the United States followed several months later (Alibek with Handelman, *Biohazard*, 238, 242–43; see also Alibekov, interview for "Plague War").

112. Michael R. Gordon, "Russia and West Reach Accord on Monitoring Germ-Weapon Ban," *New York Times*, 15 September 1992, A6; John-Thor Dahlburg, "Russia Admits It Violated Pact on Biological Warfare," *Los Angeles Times*, 15 September 1992, A1; "Concerns Renewed about Russia's Bio Weapons Program," 1.

113. Mangold and Goldberg, *Plague Wars*, 173–74.

114. Ibid., 210–11.

115. Dahlburg, "Russia Admits It Violated Pact on Biological Warfare"; "Concerns Renewed about Russia's Bio Weapons Program," 1; Anthony Rimmington, "Invisible Weapons of Mass Destruction: The Soviet Union's BW Programme and Its Implications for Contemporary Arms Control," *Journal of Slavic Military Studies* 13, no. 3 (2000): 27; Hoffman, "Russia Challenged to Disclose Status of Biological Weapons"; "Russia Claims Full Compliance with Biological Weapons Convention," *International Defense Review* 25, no. 10 (1992): 933.

116. Dahlburg, "Russia Admits It Violated Pact on Biological Warfare"; Gordon, "Russia and West Reach Accord on Monitoring Germ-Weapon Ban."

117. Mangold and Goldberg, *Plague Wars*, 161, 165.

118. Judith Miller, "U.S. Aid Diverted to Germ Warfare, Russian Scientists Say," *New York Times*, 25 January 2000, A6.

119. "Russia Denies It Is Building Germ Weapons," *Washington Post*, 1 September 1992, A14; R. Jeffrey Smith, "Russia Fails to Detail Germ Arms; U.S. and Britain Fear Program Continues in Violation of Treaty," ibid., 31 August 1992, A1.

120. Rimmington, "Invisible Weapons of Mass Destruction," 28. See also John Donnelly, "CIA Worried about Russian Chem-Bio Programs," *Defense Week*, 14 September 1998, 1; David Fairhall, "Russia 'Continues to Develop New Germ Weapons,'" *Guardian*

(London), 26 February 1998, 12; Hoffman, "Russia Challenged to Disclose Status of Biological Weapons."

121. Among other claims, Tulykin asserted that in 1994 the facility's commander, Major General Anatoli Kharechko, announced a plan to rebuild and modernize the facilities and condemned Gorbachev's decision to convert the plant into a production center for vaccines. He stated that in 1997 "they [the Russian military] reconstructed compartmentalized sectors in the labs to handle dangerous biological agents and prevent leaks like the one in 1979" and that Kharechko declared in 1998 that the renovation would continue ("Concerns Renewed about Russia's Bio Weapons Program," 2).

122. Alibek with Handelman, *Biohazard,* 153–67.

123. On the subject of Iraq's aflatoxin bombs UNSCOM inspector Richard Spertzel commented that "the toxicity [of aflatoxin] is such that it would be easier to kill a person by hitting him with the bomb" (Christopher Dickey, "Plagues in the Making," *Newsweek,* 9 October 1995, 50; see also Nigel Hawkes, "Trail that Led to the Poisonous Arsenal," *Times* [London], 11 November 1997; and Philip Shenon, "Report Faults Pentagon's Gulf War Studies," *New York Times,* 15 June 1997, sec. 1, 4).

124. Office of the Secretary of Defense, *Proliferation: Threat and Response* (Washington, DC: GPO, January 2001), 4.

125. Center for Counterproliferation Research, *Toward a National Biodefense Strategy: Challenges and Opportunities* (Washington, DC: National Defense University, 2003), 9–10.

126. Richard Butler, *Report to the Security Council on the Status of Disarmament and Monitoring,* S/1999/94, 29 January 1999, app. 3, www.un.org/Depts/unscom/s99-94.htm.

127. John R. Bolton, remarks at the Fifth Biological Weapons Convention RevCon Meeting, Geneva, Switzerland, 19 November 2001.

128. Jason D. Ellis, *Defense by Other Means: The Politics of US-NIS Threat Reduction and Nuclear Security Cooperation* (Westport, CT: Praeger, 2001), 149–51, 163; General Accounting Office, *Biological Weapons,* 6, 14–16, 30; Miller, "U.S. Aid Diverted to Germ Warfare."

FOUR: Intelligence Surprise

1. *Report of the Commission to Assess the Ballistic Missile Threat to the United States, Executive Summary, Pursuant to Public Law 104–201,* 104th Cong., 1st sess., 1998, 22 (hereafter cited as Rumsfeld Report).

2. George J. Tenet, testimony before the Senate Select Committee on Intelligence, 21 March 2000, *Current and Projected National Security Threats to the United States,* 106th Cong., 2nd sess., 2000.

3. Ibid.

4. George Perkovich, *India's Nuclear Bomb: The Impact on Global Proliferation* (Berkeley and Los Angeles: University of California Press, 1999), 368; "A Bomb Test in the Desert? There Better Not Be One, Washington Tells New Delhi," *Asiaweek,* 5 January 1996, 31; John F. Burns, "India Denies Atom-Test Plans but Then Turns Ambiguous," *New York Times,* 16 December 1995, A4; Tim Weiner, "US Suspects India Prepares to Conduct Nuclear Test," *New York Times,* 15 December 1995, A9.

5. Robin Wright, "U.S. Intelligence Failed to Warn of India's Atom Test," *Los Angeles Times,* 13 May 1998, 1.

6. Mark M. Lowenthal, *Intelligence: From Secrets to Policy* (Washington, DC: CQ Press, 2000), 7.

7. CIA, Office of Public Affairs, Jeremiah News Conference, 2 June 1998 (hereafter cited as Jeremiah News Conference),www.cia.gov/cia/public_affairs/press_release/archives /1998/jeremiah.html.

8. "The CIA's Failure of Imagination," *Boston Globe,* 19 June 1998, A30; David L. Marcus, "US Intelligence Missed Signs of India Tests: Neighbors' Warnings, Hindu Party's Pledge Were Unheeded in Washington," ibid., 13 May 1998, A19.

9. "India BJP," Voice of America Report, 3 February 1998; "17 Days in May: Chronology of Indian Nuclear Weapons Tests," www.fas.org/nuke/guide/india/nuke/chron.htm.

10. See, e.g., "India N-option Put On Hold, Says Fernandes," *The Hindu,* 20 March 1998; John F. Burns, "Hindu Party Says It Will Reconsider Its Nuclear Policy," *New York Times,* 19 March 1998, A1; and Perkovich, *India's Nuclear Bomb,* 407.

11. Jeremiah News Conference; "Spies Need a Shake-Up," *Los Angeles Times,* 5 June 1998, B8; "Jeremiah's Jeremiad," *Washington Post,* 15 Jun 1998, A22; Carla Anne Robbins, "Failure to Predict India's Test Is Tied to Systemwide Intelligence Breakdown," *Wall Street Journal,* 3 June 1998, A8; "Somnambulant Spies," *New York Times,* 4 June 1998, A26; Jeffrey T. Richelson, "Examining U.S. Intelligence Failures," *Jane's Intelligence Review* 12, no. 9 (1999): 42–43.

12. James Risen, Steven Lee Myers, and Tim Weiner, "U.S. May Have Helped India Hide Its Nuclear Activity," *New York Times,* 25 May 1998, A3; James Risen, "India's A-Tests Prompt C.I.A. to Review Its Warning System," ibid., 4 July 1998, A3; Bruce D. Berkowitz, "The CIA Needs to Get Smart," *Wall Street Journal,* 1 March 1999, A22.

13. Perkovich, *India's Nuclear Bomb,* 408; Tim Weiner, "U.S. Blundered on Intelligence, Officials Admit," *New York Times,* 13 May 1998, A1. For example, Defense Minister George Fernandes stated at the time that "through a first ever strategic defence review we will examine our security and threat perceptions and in light of that decide on induction of nuclear weapons" (Perkovich, *India's Nuclear Bomb,* 408).

14. See, e.g., "What If . . . ," *Economist,* 24 February 1996, 36–37; Emily McFarquhar, "India's Born-Again Archnationalists," *U.S. News & World Report,* 27 May 1996, 60; Miriam Jordan, "BJP Stance on Kashmir, Nuclear Arms Could Raise Temperature in South Asia," *Wall Street Journal,* 16 May 1996, A10; "Indian Party Vows to Take Power, May Go for Nuclear Weapons," Agence France Presse, 7 April 1996; Mahesh Uniyal, "Disarmament—India: Nuclear Bomb An Election Issue," Inter Press Service, 21 April 1996; and Christopher Lockwood, "Kashmir May be Nuclear Flashpoint," *Daily Telegraph,* 30 April 1996, 16.

15. Perkovich, *India's Nuclear Bomb,* 374.

16. Ibid., 375; Kenneth J. Cooper, "Premier of India Sought Tests in '96: Vajpayee's Government Fell before Preparations Could Be Completed," *Washington Post,* 13 May 1998, A25.

17. "CIA's Failure of Imagination."

18. Weiner, "U.S. Blundered on Intelligence." See also Wyn Q. Bowen, "Open-Source Intel: A Valuable National Security Resource," *Jane's Intelligence Review* 11, no. 11 (1999): 50; and Elaine Sciolino, "Scooped on Tests, U.S. Scorns a Sikh Journal," *New York Times,* 16 May 1998, A5.

19. Sciolino, "Scooped on Tests." The Pakistani ambassador to the United States delivered a copy of the newsletter to Assistant Secretary of State Karl Inderfuth and sardonically inquired how the small newsletter had managed to get it right on the tests, when the United States had failed to do so.

20. Lowenthal, *Intelligence,* 70; Bowen, "Open-Source Intel," 50; Mark M. Lowenthal, "Open Source Intelligence: New Myths, New Realities," November 1998, www.defensedaily.com/reports/osintmyths.htm.

21. David A. Kay, "Denial and Deception Practices of WMD Proliferators: Iraq and Beyond," *Washington Quarterly* 18, no. 1 (1995): 86; James F. Dunnigan and Albert A. Nofi, *Victory and Deceit: Dirty Tricks at War* (New York: William Morrow, 1995), 7–9.

22. Jeremiah News Conference.

23. Sam Brownback, opening statement, 13 May 1998, Senate Foreign Relations Committee, Subcommittee on Near Eastern and South Asian Affairs, *Crisis in South Asia: India's Nuclear Tests; Pakistan's Nuclear Tests; India and Pakistan: What Next?* 105th Cong., 2nd sess., 1998, 1.

24. Ashok Sharma, "New Delhi Nuclear Expert Says Tests Were Easy to Hide," *Buffalo News,* 16 May 1998, 3A. See also "CIA Searching for Answers behind Its India-Nuclear Failure," Associated Press, 16 May 1998.

25. See, e.g., Marcus, "US Intelligence Missed Signs of India Tests"; Risen, Myers, and Weiner, "U.S. May Have Helped India Hide Its Nuclear Activity"; Weiner, "U.S. Blundered on Intelligence"; and R. Jeffrey Smith, "CIA Missed Signs of Tests, U.S. Officials Say," *Washington Post,* 13 May 1998, A1.

26. Kay, "Denial and Deception Practices of WMD Proliferators," 100.

27. Perkovich, *India's Nuclear Bomb,* 368; "A Bomb Test in the Desert?" 31; Burns, "India Denies Atom-Test Plans"; Weiner, "US Suspects India Prepares to Conduct Nuclear Test."

28. See, e.g., "A CIA Warning," *Boston Globe,* 6 July 1998, A14; Risen, Myers, and Weiner, "U.S. May Have Helped India Hide Its Nuclear Activity"; and David L. Marcus, "U.S. Checking If Leak Let India Cloak Its Testing," *Boston Globe,* 14 May 1998, A28.

29. "United States: Don't Blame the CIA," *Economist,* 23 May 1998, 26.

30. Richelson, "Examining U.S. Intelligence Failures," 43.

31. Kay, "Denial and Deception Practices of WMD Proliferators," 100.

32. Marcus, "U.S. Checking If Leak Let India Cloak Its Testing."

33. ". . . As Nuclear Test Preparations Avoid Detection," *Jane's Defence Weekly* 29, no. 20 (1998): 3.

34. Sharma, "New Delhi Nuclear Expert Says Tests Were Easy to Hide."

35. See, e.g., www.heavens-above.com, which seeks to provide a "wealth" of spaceflight and astronomical information.

36. Perkovich, *India's Nuclear Bomb,* 413.

37. Howard Diamond, "After BJP Election, Leaders Soften Line on Nuclear Weapons," *Arms Control Today* 28, no. 2 (1998): 25.

38. Ibid. Perkovich argues that Fernandes was actually unaware of the new government's stance on nuclear weapons since the prime minister had not briefed him on nuclear policy (*India's Nuclear Bomb,* 408).

39. Risen, Myers, and Weiner, "U.S. May Have Helped India Hide Its Nuclear Activity"; Diamond, "After BJP Election."

40. Risen, Myers, and Weiner, "U.S. May Have Helped India Hide Its Nuclear Activity"; Perkovich, *India's Nuclear Bomb,* 408; Diamond, "After BJP Election."

41. White House Press Office, "Press Briefing by National Security Advisor Samuel Berger," 13 May 1998, clinton6.nara.gov/1998/05/1998-05-13-press-briefing-by-sandyberger.html.

42. James P. Rubin, Department of State Daily Press Briefing, 14 May 1998.

43. Shiv S. Mukherjee, Embassy of India Press Release, 18 May 1998.

44. Perkovich, *India's Nuclear Bomb,* 415.

45. Jeremiah News Conference; Tim Weiner, "C.I.A. Study Details Failures; Scouring of System Is Urged," *New York Times,* 3 June 1998, A1; Risen, Myers, and Weiner, "U.S. May Have Helped India Hide Its Nuclear Activity"; Lawrence B. Sulc, "Can the CIA Be Fixed?" *World & I* 13, no. 9 (1998): 88.

46. Weiner, "C.I.A. Study Details Failures."

47. Barbara Slavin, "CIA Failed on India, Study Says," *USA Today,* 3 June 1998, 1A; Sulc, "Can the CIA Be Fixed?" 88.

48. Lowenthal, *Intelligence,* 67–68.

49. Ibid., 68.

50. "Spies Need a Shake Up," B5; Robbins, "Failure to Predict India's Test Is Tied to Systemwide Intelligence Breakdown"; Walter Pincus, "Spy Agencies Faulted for Missing Indian Tests; Wide Range of Failures Cited by Review Panel, but No Firings Recommended," *Washington Post,* 3 June 1998, A18.

51. Jeremiah News Conference.

52. Weiner, "U.S. Blundered on Intelligence"; Milton A. Bearden, "Don't Blame the CIA for Bad Policy," *Los Angeles Times,* 31 May 1998, 2; Douglas Waller, "Why the Sky Spies Missed the Desert Blasts," *Time,* 25 May 1998, 40; Craig Covault, "Eavesdropping Satellite Parked on Crisis Zone," *Aviation Week and Space Technology,* 18 May 1998, 30.

53. Walter Pincus, "CIA Chief Cited Loss of Agency's Capabilities; Remarks Preceded Indian Bomb," *Washington Post,* 25 May 1998, A4.

54. Tenet, testimony before the Senate Select Committee on Intelligence, 21 March 2000.

55. Senate Foreign Relations Committee, *Crisis in South Asia,* 31.

56. Bill Gertz, "N. Korean Missile Seen as Posing Risk to U.S.; Rocket Might Reach Alaska, Hawaii," *Washington Times,* 16 September 1998, A1.

57. Frank Wolfe, "Intelligence a Success on Latest Missile Launch, DoD Says," *Defense Daily,* 1 September 1998, 1.

58. Joseph S. Bermudez Jr., "North Koreans Test Two-Stage IRBM over Japan," *Jane's Defence Weekly* 30, no. 10 (1998): 26. See also "North Korea 'Preparing to Test Taepo Dong 1,'" 21 August 1998, www.cdiss.org/98aug2.htm.

59. David A. Fulghum, "U.S. Doubts Korean Space Launch Claim," *Aviation Week and Space Technology,* 14 September 1998, 58; Wolfe, "Intelligence a Success on Latest Missile Launch."

60. Wolfe, "Intelligence a Success on Latest Missile Launch"; Robert Bell, Ted Warner, Gary Samore, and Debra Cagan, NSC, DOD, State Briefing, 1 September 1998, usembassy-australia.state.gov/hyper/WF980901/epf202.htm, accessed 2001. See also Bermudez, "North Koreans Test Two-Stage IRBM over Japan"; Sandra Sugawara, "N. Korea Fires Ballistic Missile toward Japan, Tokyo Reports; Pentagon Confirms Firing, Calls It 'Serious Development,'" *Washington Post,* 31 August 1998, A17; Sheryl WuDunn, "North Korea Fires Missile over Japanese Territory," *New York Times,* 1 September 1998, A6; and Robert S. Greenberger, "North Koreans Launch Missile, Stirring Call to Halt U.S. Funds," *Wall Street Journal,* 1 September 1998, A14.

61. Korean Central News Agency, "Successful Launch of First Satellite in DPRK," 4 September 1998, www.kcna.co.jp/item/1998/9809/news09/04.html#1, accessed 2001.

62. David Wright suggested prior to the August launch that these mock-ups were actually fabrications to deceive US intelligence (see "Taepodong Missile 'Does Not Make Technical Sense,'" *Jane's Missiles and Rockets* 2, no. 5 [1998]: 2; and David Wright, "An Analysis of the North Korean Missile Program," in Rumsfeld Report, 351).

63. Greg Gerardi and Joseph S. Bermudez Jr., "An Analysis of North Korean Ballistic Missile Testing," *Jane's Intelligence Review* 7, no. 4 (1995): 186.

64. Joseph S. Bermudez Jr., "Taepo-dong Launch Brings DPRK Missiles Back into the Spotlight," ibid. 10, no. 10 (1998): 32; idem, "The Rise and Rise of North Korea's ICBMs," ibid. 32, no. 7 (July 1999): 60; Tim McCarthy and Holly Porteous, "Ballistic Missile Shadow Lengthens," *International Defense Review Extra* 2, no. 2 (1997): n.p.

65. Art Pine, "CIA Reports New Korean Missiles," *Los Angeles Times*, 18 March 1994, A5; "New N. Korean Missiles 'Can Hit S-E Asia,'" *Straits Times* (Singapore), 19 March 1994; R. Jeffrey Smith, "CIA Confirms North Korea's New Missiles," *Washington Post*, 18 March 1994, A24; "U.S. Says North Korea Is Making New Missiles," *New York Times*, 18 March 1994, A12; Bill Gertz, "N. Korea Builds New Missiles," *Washington Times*, 19 March 1994, A3.

66. Bermudez, "North Koreans Test Two-Stage IRBM over Japan."

67. Office of the Secretary of Defense, *Proliferation: Threat and Response* (Washington, DC: GPO, November 1997), 8. See also Selig S. Harrison, "Missile Capabilities in Northeast Asia: Japan, South Korea, and North Korea," in Rumsfeld Report, 166.

68. "Taepodong Missile 'Does Not Make Technical Sense.'" See also David Wright and Timur Kadyshev, "The North Korean Missile Program: How Advanced Is It?" *Arms Control Today* 24, no. 3 (1994): 11.

69. Rumsfeld Report, 12. With respect to the Nodong, the commission judged that it had been "operationally deployed long before the U.S. government recognized that fact."

70. George J. Tenet, "Letter to Congress Regarding the Rumsfeld Commission's Report," 15 July 1998, www.cia.gov/cia/public_affairs/press_release/archives/1998/pr071598.html.

71. Ibid.

72. Robert D. Walpole, "Remarks on the Ballistic Missile Threat to the United States Given at the Carnegie Endowment for International Peace," 17 September 1998, www.ceip.org/programs/npp/walpole.htm. See also idem, "North Korea's Taepo Dong Launch and Some Implications on the Ballistic Missile Threat to the United States," remarks at the Center for Strategic and International Studies, 8 December 1998, www.cia.gov/cia/public_affairs/speeches/archives/1998/walpole_speech_120898.html.

73. Korean Central News Agency, "Successful Launch of First Satellite in DPRK."

74. Kenneth Bacon, DOD News Briefing, 15 September 1998. See also Frank Umbach, "World Gets Wise to P'yongyang's Nuclear Blackmail," *Jane's Intelligence Review* 11, no. 9 (1999): 36.

75. Steven Lee Myers, "U.S. Calls North Korean Rocket a Failed Satellite," *New York Times*, 15 September 1998, A6; Robert S. Greenberger and Carla Anne Robbins, "U.S. Analysis Finds North Korea Nearer Development of Long-Range Missiles," *Wall Street Journal*, 15 September 1998, A6.

76. Bermudez, "Rise and Rise of North Korea's ICBMs," 60; Myers, "U.S. Calls North Korean Rocket a Failed Satellite."

77. Greg Seigle, "North Korea's Failed Satellite Bid Verified," *Jane's Defence Weekly* 30, no. 12 (1998): 5.

78. Wright, "Analysis of the North Korean Missile Program," 348.

79. Bill Gertz, "The North Korea Missile Threat," *Air Force Magazine* 83, no. 1 (2000): 43.

80. George J. Tenet, "Dangers and Threats to the U.S.," *Vital Speeches of the Day*, 1 March 1999, 294.

81. Robert Karniol, "Details Emerge of Taepo Dong 1," *Jane's Defence Weekly* 32, no. 12 (1999): 19.

82. Bermudez, "Rise and Rise of North Korea's ICBMs," 57; Karniol, "Details Emerge of Taepo Dong 1." According to the Rumsfeld Commission, the Nodong itself relied on a "scaled up Scud engine" (see Rumsfeld Report, 11). Bermudez, "Rise and Rise of North Korea's ICBMs," 60.

84. Ibid. Bermudez posits that the Kwangmyongsong satellite program received, and possibly continues to receive, considerable assistance from the Chinese Academy of Launch Technology. Other sources postulate that the Kwangmyongsong 1 was a virtual copy of the Dong Fang Hong 1, the PRC's first satellite (see, e.g., Mark Wade's *Encyclopedia Astronautica*, s.v. "Kwangmyongsong," www.astronatuix.com/craft/kwangsong.htm).

85. Bermudez, "Rise and Rise of North Korea's ICBMs," 60; Bermudez, "Taepo-dong Launch Brings DPRK Missiles Back into the Spotlight," 32.

86. See Nicholas D. Krystof, "North Korean Missile Parts Said to Be from Japan," *New York Times*, 9 July 1999, A4; Norihiko Shirouzu, "Exports to North Korea Worry Japanese," *Wall Street Journal*, 8 July 1999, A14.

87. DCI, "Unclassified Report to Congress on the Acquisition of Technology Relating to Weapons of Mass Destruction and Advanced Conventional Weapons, 1 July through 31 December 2000," 7 September 2001, www.cia.gov/cia/reports/721_reports /july _dec2000.htm, accessed 2001. These assessments largely echo those reported since the original semiannual report bearing this title mandated by Congress in 1997.

88. Wright and Kadyshev, "North Korean Missile Program," 9; Gerardi and Bermudez, "Analysis of North Korean Ballistic Missile Testing," 184.

89. Thomas E. Ricks and Jackie Calmes, "Report That China Aided North Korea on Missiles Complicates Trade Issue," *Wall Street Journal*, 15 March 1994, A3. See also "China Denies a Transfer of Data to North Korea," ibid., 18 March 1994, A7.

90. Bermudez, "Rise and Rise of North Korea's ICBMs," 60.

91. Bill Gertz, "China Still Shipping Arms Despite Pledges," *Washington Times*, 15 April 1999, A1.

92. Bill Gertz, "Missile Parts Sent to North Korea by Chinese Companies; Response to Embassy Bombing Seen," ibid., 20 July 1999, A1.

93. Bill Gertz, "China Breaks Vow, Sends N. Korea Missile Materials; Pentagon Report Tells of Latest Deal," ibid., 6 January 2000, A1; Peter Grier, "Missile Help for North Korea?" *Air Force Magazine* 83, no. 3 (2000): 16.

94. See, e.g., DCI, "Unclassified Report to Congress," 7 September 2001.

95. Jim Mann, "N. Korean Missiles Have Russian Roots, Explosive Theory Suggests," *Los Angeles Times*, 6 September 2000, 5.

96. Steven Zaloga, "Russian Reports," *Armed Forces Journal International*, April 1993, 17.

97. Mann, "N. Korean Missiles Have Russian Roots," 5. Ibid.

99. Rowan Scarborough, "N. Korea Missiles Can Improve, Experts Warn; Russia, Iran Likely Share Technology," *Washington Times*, 4 September 1998, A6.

100. NIC, *Foreign Missile Developments and the Ballistic Missile Threat through 2015*, unclassified summary, December 2001 (Washington, DC, 2003), www.odci.gov/nic /other _missilethreat2001.html.

101. Jason D. Ellis, "Beyond Nonproliferation: Secondary Supply, Proliferation Management, and U.S. Foreign Policy," *Comparative Strategy* 20, no. 1 (2001): 11.

102. Rumsfeld Report, 18.

103. Ibid., 7.

104. Ibid., 18.

105. Lim Eul-chul, "North Korea's Missile Program: Assessment and Future Outlook," *Korea Focus* 7, no. 5 (1999): 3.

106. Gerardi and Bermudez, "Analysis of North Korean Ballistic Missile Testing," 188–89.

107. Umbach, "World Gets Wise to P'yongyang's Nuclear Blackmail," 33.

108. See, e.g., Ben Sheppard, "Pakistan Tests 'Chinese/North Korean-based Missiles,'" *Jane's Intelligence Review* 11, no. 5 (1999): 3; Pravin K. Swahney, "Pakistan Scores over India in Ballistic Missile Race," ibid. 12, no. 11 (2000): 31–35; and Mark Hewish, "The Ballistic Missile Threat Evolves," *Jane's International Defense Review* 33, no. 10 (2000): 39–41.

109. Ellis, "Beyond Nonproliferation," 10–13. See also NIC, *Foreign Missile Developments and the Ballistic Missile Threat through 2015,* unclassified summary, December 2001.

110. Bermudez, "Rise and Rise of North Korea's ICBMs," 61. For instance, it was reported that Pakistani and Iranian observers were present for the August 1998 launch and that the Iranian crew brought along telemetry equipment (ibid.).

111. David A. Fulghum, "North Korea Space Attempt Verified," *Aviation Week and Space Technology,* 21 September 1998, 32.

112. Rumsfeld Report, 6–7.

113. Frank Wolfe, "NIE: Countries May Not Require Missile Flight Tests," *Defense Daily,* 10 February 2000, 1.

114. James Oberg, "Missiles for All: The New Global Threat," *IEEE Spectrum* 36, no. 3 (1999): 28. Oberg presents a chart outlining the links between the Soviet Scud missile and various other missile programs around the world. The Rumsfeld Commission also noted that the "basis for most missile developments by emerging ballistic missile powers is the Soviet Scud missile and its derivatives" (11).

115. "Nodong-1 Missiles 'May Soon Be Deployed,'" Seoul KBS-1 Radio, 1 September 1994, FBIS-EAS-94-170, 33; Son Tae-kyu, "North to Deploy Nodong Missiles by 'End of 1996,'" *Hanguk Ilbo,* 10 October 1995, FBIS-EAS-95-195, 61; Barbara Starr, "CIA Expects Nodong Deployment Next Year," *Jane's Defence Weekly* 24, no. 19 (1995): 16; Paul Beaver, "Ten Nodongs Fielded but Accuracy Is Low, Says USA," ibid. 27, no. 21 (1997): 4; Jim Lea, "Report: NK Rodong-1 Missile Battalions in Place," *Stars and Stripes* (Pacific Edition), 26 October 1999, 3; "At Least 10 No-Dongs Deployed in North Korea," CDISS Current Missile News, 9 July 1999, www.cdiss.org/99july7.htm.

116. See, e.g., DOD news briefing by William Cohen and South Korean Defense Minister Chun Yong-Taek, 9 July 1998. Cohen stated, "What we can say is that North Korea has completed its development of the No Dong missile, but I am not in a position to comment in terms of when or where or how there has been a deployment of the missile itself." See also Bill Gertz, "The North Korean Missile Threat," *Air Force Magazine* 83, no. 1 (2000): 42, where Gertz states, "Officially, the Pentagon won't say if they consider the No Dong deployed and threatening."

117. Rumsfeld Report, 12.

118. Bermudez, "Rise and Rise of North Korea's ICBMs," 59; Jung-Hoon Lee and Il Hyun Cho, "The North Korean Missiles: A Military Threat or a Survival Kit?" *Korean Jour-*

nal of Defense Analysis 12, no. 1 (2000): 138; "ROKG Official Cites US Sources: DPRK Deploys 100 Nodong-1 Missiles since 1998," *Chosun Ilbo* (Seoul), Internet Version, 2 March 2001, FBIS, KPP20010302000010; "North Korea Doubles Rodong-1 Missile Deployment: Report," Agence France Presse, 2 March 2001. See also Lim, "North Korea's Missile Program," 3, which suggests that the DPRK has produced and deployed seven Nodong missiles since the end of 1996.

119. Umbach, "World Gets Wise to P'yongyang's Nuclear Blackmail," 34; Bermudez, "Rise and Rise of North Korea's ICBMs," 61. Bermudez hypothesizes that a long-range missile under development in Pakistan referred to as the Ghaznavi missile may in fact be a TD-1.

120. Umbach, "World Gets Wise to P'yongyang's Nuclear Blackmail," 35.

121. Vernon Loeb, "Rumsfeld Armed With Know-How to Take On Defense," *Washington Post,* 22 January 2001, washingtonpost.com/wp-dyn/nation/columns/intelligencia/A18982-2001Jan19.html.

122. NIC, *Foreign Missile Developments and the Ballistic Missile Threat to the United States through 2015,* unclassified summary, September 1999 (Washington, DC, 2000), 46, www.odci.gov/nic/other_missilethreat1999.html. For excerpts from the 1995 NIE see Joseph Cirincione, "Assessing the Assessment: The 1999 National Intelligence Estimate of the Ballistic Missile Threat," *Nonproliferation Review* 7, no. 1 (2000): 127.

123. William Schneider Jr., testimony before the Senate Governmental Affairs Committee, Subcommittee on International Security, Proliferation, and Federal Services, 9 February 2000, *The National Intelligence Estimate on the Ballistic Missile Threat to the United States,* 106th Cong., 2nd sess., 2000, 68.

124. Ibid., 9. See also Office of the Secretary of Defense, *Quadrennial Defense Review Report* (Washington, DC: DOD, 30 September 2001), 13–14.

125. See, e.g., Jeremiah News Conference; *Combating Proliferation of Weapons of Mass Destruction: Report from the Commission to Assess the Organization of the Federal Government to Combat the Proliferation of Weapons of Mass Destruction, Pursuant to Public Law 293,* 104th Cong., 2nd sess., 1999, 66–71; House Permanent Select Committee on Intelligence, *IC21: Intelligence Community in the Twenty-first Century* (Washington, DC: GPO, 1996); Donald H. Rumsfeld, statement before the Senate Armed Services Committee, 11 January 2001, *Nominations before the Senate Armed Services Committee,* 107th Cong., 1st sess., 2001; Rumsfeld Report; U.S. Commission on National Security in the Twenty-first Century, *Road Map for National Security: Imperative for Change* (Washington, DC: GPO, 15 March 2001), 82–86.

FIVE: Intelligence Sharing

1. *Combating Proliferation of Weapons of Mass Destruction: Report from the Commission to Assess the Organization of the Federal Government to Combat the Proliferation of Weapons of Mass Destruction, Pursuant to Public Law 293,* 104th Cong., 2nd sess., 1999, 34–35.

2. Gregory F. Giles, "The Islamic Republic of Iran and Nuclear, Biological, and Chemical Weapons," in *Planning the Unthinkable: How New Powers Will Use Nuclear, Biological, and Chemical Weapons,* ed. Peter R. Lavoy, Scott D. Sagan, and James J. Wirtz (Ithaca, NY: Cornell University Press, 2000), 79–103; Anthony Cordesman, *Iran's Military Forces in Transition: Conventional Threats and Weapons of Mass Destruction* (Westport, CT: Praeger, 1999), 294–328, 362–98; Michael Eisenstadt, *Iranian Military Power: Capabilities and In-*

tentions (Washington, DC: Washington Institute for Near East Policy, 1996), 9–34, 103–12; Paula A. DeSutter, *Denial and Jeopardy: Deterring Iranian Use of NBC Weapons* (Washington, DC: National Defense University Press, 1997), 47–56; Andrew Koch and Jeanette Wolf, "Iran's Nuclear Procurement Program: How Close to the Bomb?" *Nonproliferation Review* 5, no. 1 (1997): 123–35; Aaron Karp, "The Spread of Ballistic Missiles and the Transformation of Global Security," ibid. 7, no. 3 (2000): 113–14.

3. See, e.g., "India Says It Gave U.S. Secret Data," *Washington Times,* 17 September 2001, A13; David R. Sands, "U.S. Wary as Offers to Assist Flood In; Some Want to Advance Own Agendas," ibid., 16 September 2001, A9; Michael Evans, "World's Agents Pool Intelligence," *Times* (London), 15 September 2001; Bill Nichols, "Intelligence Help from Russia May Be Crucial," *USA Today,* 19 September 2001, 8A; Gopal Ratnam, "Logistics, Intel Help Likely from Gulf Allies," *Defense News,* 24–30 September 2001, 4; Michele Orecklin, "Sharing Secrets," *Time,* 12 November 2001, 36; Norman Kempster, "Bush Critics Warn of Going Too Far to Attract Allies," *Los Angeles Times,* 27 September 2001; and Bob Woodward, "50 Countries Detain 360 Suspects at CIA's Behest," *Washington Post,* 22 November 2001, A1.

4. Jason D. Ellis, *Defense by Other Means: The Politics of US-NIS Threat Reduction and Nuclear Security Cooperation* (Westport, CT: Praeger, 2001), 1–8, 34–37; Graham Allison, Ashton B. Carter, Steven E. Miller, and Philip Zelikow, eds., *Cooperative Denuclearization: From Pledges to Deeds,* CSIA Studies in International Security 2 (Cambridge, MA: Center for Science and International Affairs, 1993), 4–12; James A. Baker III with Thomas M. Defrank, *The Politics of Diplomacy: Revolution, War, and Peace, 1989–1992* (New York: G. P. Putnam's Sons, 1995), esp. 614–16; Glenn E. Schweitzer, *Moscow DMZ: The Story of the International Effort to Convert Russian Weapons Science to Peaceful Purposes* (Armonk, NY: M. E. Sharpe, 1996), 16–18; Kurt M. Campbell, Ashton B. Carter, Steven E. Miller, and Charles A. Zraket, eds., *Soviet Nuclear Fission: Control of the Nuclear Arsenal in a Disintegrating Soviet Union,* CSIA Studies in International Security 1 (Cambridge, MA: Center for Science and International Affairs, 1991), 65–92, 107–16; Michael R. Beschloss and Strobe Talbott, *At the Highest Levels: The Inside Story of the End of the Cold War* (Boston: Little, Brown, 1993).

5. NIC, *Foreign Missile Developments and the Ballistic Missile Threat to the United States through 2015,* unclassified summary, September 1999 (Washington, DC, 2000), 9, www.odci.gov/nic/other_missilethreat1999.html; Office of the Secretary of Defense, *Proliferation: Threat and Response* (Washington, DC: GPO, January 2001), 34–38; Kori Schake and Judith Yaphe, *The Strategic Implications of a Nuclear-Armed Iran,* McNair Paper 64 (Washington, DC: National Defense University Press, 2001), 18–22.

6. Thomas W. Lippman, "U.S. Keeps After Russia to Halt Flow of Missile Technology to Iran," *Washington Post,* 18 January 1998, A9.

7. Jason D. Ellis, "Beyond Nonproliferation: Secondary Supply, Proliferation Management, and U.S. Foreign Policy," *Comparative Strategy* 20, no. 1 (2001): 3–6; Fred Wehling, "Russian Nuclear and Missile Exports to Iran," *Nonproliferation Review* 6, no. 2 (1999): 134, 141–42; Michael Dobbs, "A Story of Iran's Quest for Power; A Scientist Details the Role of Russia," *Washington Post,* 13 January 2002, A1; idem, "How Politics Helped Redefine the Threat," ibid., 14 January 2002, A1.

8. Robert Gallucci, remarks delivered at the 7th Carnegie International Nonproliferation Conference, Washington, DC, 11–12 January 1999, www.ceip.org/programs/npp/gallucci.htm.

9. According to Kenneth Timmerman, the RSA received more than $140 million per year, in addition to technical expertise, in assistance from the United States (see Timmerman, "Missile Threat from Iran," *Reader's Digest,* January 1998, 91).

10. "Russia also remained a key supplier for civilian nuclear programs in Iran, primarily focused on the Bushehr Nuclear Power Plant project. With respect to Iran's nuclear infrastructure, Russian assistance enhances Iran's ability to support a nuclear weapons development effort, even though the ostensible purpose of most of this assistance is for civilian applications" (DCI, "Unclassified Report to Congress on the Acquisition of Technology Related to Weapons of Mass Destruction and Advanced Conventional Munitions, 1 January through 30 June 2001," 30 January 2002, www.cia.gov/cia/reports/721_reports/jan_jun2002.html, accessed 2002).

11. "Russia Will Deliver Reactors to Iran—Ministry Staffer," *ITAR-TASS,* 14 April 1995.

12. Patrick E. Tyler, "Russian's Links to Iran Offer a Case Study in Arms Leaks," *New York Times,* 10 May 2000, A6.

13. Gallucci, remarks delivered at the 7th Carnegie International Non-proliferation Conference, 11–12 January 1999.

14. Ellis, "Beyond Nonproliferation," 5.

15. Bill Gertz, "U.S. May Punish Russia for Iran Sales; But White House Opposes New Laws," *Washington Times,* 16 October 1997, A1.

16. Henry Sokolski, testimony before the House Committee on Science, Subcommittee on Space and Aeronautics, 13 July 1999, *Iran Nonproliferation Act of 1999,* 106th Cong., 1st sess., 1999, 146–47.

17. "U.S.-Russian Commission on Economic and Technological Cooperation," www.usia.gov/regional/bnc/usrussia/gcchead.htm.

18. Timmerman, "Missile Threat from Iran," 89.

19. Alan Philps, "US Fails to Prevent Sale of Reactors to Iran," *Daily Telegraph,* 11 May 1995, 12. See also Judy Keen, "Yeltsin, Clinton Remain Divided; Russia Agrees to Scrap Part of Iran Nuke Deal," *USA Today,* 11 May 1995, 6A; Elizabeth Sullivan, "Clinton Yeltsin Fail to Make Any Major Deals," *Cleveland Plain Dealer,* 11 May 1995, 1A; "Yeltsin Backs Down on Iran Nuclear Sale," *Jerusalem Post,* 11 May 1995, 1.

20. Jeffrey T. Richelson, *The U.S. Intelligence Community,* 4th ed. (Boulder, CO: Westview Press, 1999), 291–314.

21. Steven Erlanger, "U.S. Telling Russia to Bar Aid to Iran by Arms Experts," *New York Times,* 22 August 1997, A1.

22. Michael S. Lelyveld, "When Trade Meets Foreign Policy: A Collision on Iran Missile Sales over Iran Arms Sales," *Journal of Commerce,* 27 February 1998, 1A.

23. Jim Hoagland, "Fallout from Russia: Lethal Human Skills," *Sacramento Bee,* 10 January 1998, B7.

24. Bill Gertz, "Russia Disregards Pledge to Curb Iranian Missile Output; Tehran, Moscow Sign Pacts for Additional Support," *Washington Times,* 22 May 1997, A3. See also idem, *Betrayal: How the Clinton Administration Undermined American Security* (Washington, DC: Regnery, 1999), 180–81.

25. Gertz, *Betrayal,* 180–81. Gertz references a purported National Security Agency cable from May 1997 outlining information that "revealed a deeper cooperation that was previously known between Iran's Defense Industries Organization (DIO) and several Russian firms on the production of liquid-fueled ballistic missiles."

26. Mark Dennis and Patrick Cockburn, "Israeli Spies' Cover Blown; Key Intelligence

Sources Have Been Exposed Along with Russia's Missile Aid to Iran," *Independent* (London), 2 November 1997, 13. See also Gertz, *Betrayal,* 173–74.

27. Dennis and Cockburn, "Israeli Spies' Cover Blown," 13.

28. Kenneth Timmerman, "Time to End Iran's Russian Connection," *Wall Street Journal,* 28 April 1998, A18.

29. Timmerman, "Missile Threat from Iran," 89; Gertz, *Betrayal,* 175–76.

30. K. Petrov, "More and More Work for Counterintelligence: Spies and Terrorists Unabated," *Krasnaya Zvezda,* 18 November 1997, 3; A. Sashin, "Fewer and Fewer Iranians in Russia," *Kommersant-Daily,* 18 November 1997, 7; "Russia Does Not Encourage the Collaboration of its Enterprises with Iran in the Missile Field," *Eksport Obychnykh Vooruzheniy* 10–11 (1997): 6; and "A Citizen of Iran Wanted to Buy the Secrets of Russian Missiles," *Segodnya,* 15 November 1997, 1—all cited and discussed in Ivan Safranchuk, "Scientific Notes No. 8: The Nuclear and Missile Programs of Iran and Russian Security—The Framework of Russian-Iranian Collaboration," FBIS, 5 May 1999, 21, 41–42. RSA chief Yuri Koptev acknowledges contacts between "certain organizations" in Russia and Iranian representatives but declares that "all attempts" to supply Tehran with Russian missile technologies "were cut short by the state" (see "Russia Refuses to Acknowledge the Fact of Having Supplied Missile Technologies to Iran," *Segodnya,* translated in *Defense and Security,* 28 January 1998; see also Wehling, "Russian Nuclear and Missile Exports to Iran," 139).

31. Michael R. Gordon and Eric Schmidt, "Washington Queries Moscow Crackdown on Iran," *Moscow Times,* 28 April 1998, 4.

32. Steven Erlanger, "U.S. Gets Russia's Firm Vow to Halt Missile Aid to Iran," *New York Times,* 16 January 1998, A8.

33. Gallucci, remarks delivered at the 7th Carnegie International Non-proliferation Conference, 11–12 January 1999.

34. Erlanger, "U.S. Telling Russia to Bar Aid to Iran by Arms Experts."

35. Michael Beck, "Russia and Efforts to Establish Export Controls," Center for International Trade and Security, University of Georgia, n.d., 1–11, www.uga.edu/cits /documents/html/nat_eval_russia.htm, accessed 2001; Michael H. Newlin, "Export Controls and the CTR Program," in *Dismantling the Cold War: U.S. and NIS Perspectives on the Nunn-Lugar Cooperative Threat Reduction Program,* ed. John M. Shields and William C. Potter, CSIA Studies in International Security (Cambridge, MA:, MIT Press for Center for Science and International Affairs, 1997), 293.

36. Vladimir A. Orlov, "Export Controls in Russia: Policies and Practices," *Nonproliferation Review* 6, no. 4 (1999): 143; Scott Parrish and Tamara Robinson, "Efforts to Strengthen Export Controls and Combat Illicit Trafficking and Brain Drain," ibid. 7, no. 1 (2000): 118.

37. Orlov, "Export Controls in Russia," 144; Parrish and Robinson, "Efforts to Strengthen Export Controls and Combat Illicit Trafficking and Brain Drain," 118.

38. David Filipov, "What US calls Arms Proliferation, Russia Firm Calls Business as Usual," *Boston Globe,* 19 August 1998, A1.

39. Center for Nonproliferation Studies, "Institutions Suspected by the Russian Government of Violating Export Control Legislation," Center for Nonproliferation Studies, cns.miis.edu/research/summit/9firms.htm.

40. Wehling, "Russian Nuclear and Missile Exports to Iran," 140.

41. Nikolai Kuchin, "Russian Firms Say U.S. Sanction Unfounded," *Kommersant* (Moscow), 26 February 1999, 2, FBIS FTS19990226000759.

42. Ibid.

43. Wehling, "Russian Nuclear and Missile Exports to Iran," 140; Parrish and Robinson, "Efforts to Strengthen Export Controls and Combat Illicit Trafficking and Brain Drain," 112; Tyler, "Russian's Links to Iran Offer a Case Study in Arms Leaks," A6. According to the rector of the Baltic State Technical University, the investigation "reached the conclusion that Baltic State was not teaching anything related to rocket construction."

44. Tyler, "Russian's Links to Iran Offer a Case Study in Arms Leaks," A6; Wehling, "Russian Nuclear and Missile Exports to Iran," 140.

45. Wehling, "Russian Nuclear and Missile Exports to Iran," 140.

46. Judith Miller, "U.S. Asks Putin Not to Sell Iran a Laser System," *New York Times*, 19 September 2000, A1.

47. Michael Dobbs, "U.S., Russia at Odds on Iranian Deal; Bush to Raise Atomic Issues at Summit," *Washington Post*, 15 June 2001, A1; Alex Wagner, "Moscow Puts Hold on Transfer of Laser Isotope Separator to Iran," *Arms Control Today* 30, no. 8 (2000): 28.

48. Dobbs, "U.S., Russia at Odds on Iranian Deal."

49. "The Regime Was Not Being Violated," *Rossiyskaya Gazeta*, 26 February 1998, 2, quoted in Safranchuk, "Scientific Notes No. 8."

50. "Q&A: 'Partners . . . Should Respect Each Other," *Washington Post*, 25 July 1999, B4.

51. R. James Woolsey testimony before the House International Relations Committee, *Hearing on Russian Weapons Sales to Rogue Nations*, 106th Cong., 1st sess., 25 March 1999.

52. DCI, "Unclassified Report to Congress on the Acquisition of Technology Relating to Weapons of Mass Destruction and Advanced Conventional Munitions, 1 July through 31 December 1998," 9.

53. Stephen Blank, "Proliferation and Counterproliferation in Russian Strategy," *Korean Journal of Defense Analysis* 11, no. 2 (1999): 148–89.

54. "Primakov Reassures Netanyahu on Technology Exports to Iran," *Interfax*, BBC Summary of World Broadcasts, 23 March 1999.

55. Viktor Mizin, remarks delivered at the 7th Carnegie International Non-proliferation Conference, Washington, DC, 11–12 January 1999, www.ceip.org/files/events/Conf99Mizin.asp?p=8&EventID=156, accessed 2001.

56. Ibid. Alternatively, Anthony Cordesman argues that "private and state-owned firms may not be fully honoring the agreements of the Russian government" (Cordesman, *Iran's Military Forces*, 377).

57. Tyler, "Russian's Links to Iran Offer a Case Study in Arms Leaks," A6. Savelyev's program was later shut down at the insistence of the Clinton administration, and he was threatened with dismissal by the Ministry of Education for "concealing the educational program" he had organized.

58. Simon Saradzhyan, "Maslyukov Says U.S. Right on Iran Leaks," *Moscow Times*, 22 January 1999.

59. Michael D. Beck, "Lids for Nuclear Leaks," ibid., 9 March 1999; Daniel Williams, "U.S., Russia Trade Gibes over Iran; Kremlin Vows 'Tough' Reply to American Sanctions, Threats," *Washington Post*, 15 January 1999, A23; Vladimir Isachenkov, "Russian Spy Service Says U.S. Counterparts Didn't Do Their Homework," Associated Press, 14 January 1999.

60. Vladimir Moskvin, "The Russian-Iranian Conundrum and Proliferation Concerns," *Monitor* 5, nos. 1–2 (1999): 11.

61. Vladimir Orlov, "Russia, Iran, Iraq, and Export Controls: Facts and Conclusions," ibid. 4, nos. 2–3 (1998): 31.

62. Williams, "U.S., Russia Trade Gibes over Iran."

63. Kenneth R. Timmerman, testimony before the House Committee on Science, Subcommittee on Space and Aeronautics, 13 July 1999, *Iran Nonproliferation Act of 1999*, 106th Cong., 1st sess., 1999.

64. Gertz, *Betrayal*, 184.

65. Timmerman, "Time to End Iran's Russian Connection."

66. Kenneth Timmerman, "Iran's Deadly Missile Potential," *Washington Times*, 16 July 1999, A16.

67. Kuchin, "Russian Firms Say U.S. Sanctions Unfounded," 2.

68. Dennis and Cockburn, "Israeli Spies' Cover Blown," 13.

69. Ibid.

70. "Russia Reaffirms Nuclear Aid Commitment to Iran," *Arms Control Today* 30, no. 1 (2000): 27; "Russia, Iran Vow to Strengthen Nuclear Bond," *Washington Post*, 19 May 1998, A16.

71. John M. Broder, "Russia Ending Deal on Arms Negotiated by Gore," *New York Times*, 23 November 2000, A1.

72. Susan B. Glasser, "Russia, Iran Renew Alliance Meant to Boost Arms Trade; Tehran Seeking Advanced Technology; U.S. Is Concerned," *Washington Post*, 13 March 2001, A14.

73. DCI, "Unclassified Report to Congress," 30 January 2002. See also Alan Sipress, "Israel Emphasizes Iranian Threat," *Washington Post*, 7 February 2002, A22.

74. Paul Mann, "Russia-Iran Link Fuels Nuke/Missile Threat," *Aviation Week and Space Technology*, 18 January 1999, 22.

75. W ehling, "Russian Nuclear and Missile Exports to Iran," 141.

76. Bill Gertz, "U.S. Sanctions 3 Russian Institutes for Aiding Iran's Nuclear Arms," *Washington Times*, 13 January 1999, A3; Isachenkov, "Russian Spy Service Says U.S. Counterparts Didn't Do Their Homework."

77. Williams, "U.S., Russia Trade Gibes over Iran."

78. "The US Promises to Unilaterally Cancel the US-Russian Program for Satellite Launches If Moscow Sells Its Technology to Iran," *Defense and Security*, 18 January 1999, 2.

79. Bill Gertz, "Russia Warned on Deals with Iran; Nuclear Suppliers Face U.S. Sanctions," *Washington Times*, 15 December 1998, A1. See also Erlanger, "U.S. Telling Russia to Bar Aid to Iran by Arms Experts."

80. Timmerman, testimony before the House Committee on Science, 13 July 1999.

81. Ibid., 15, 146.

82. Wehling, "Russian Nuclear and Missile Exports to Iran," 142.

83. Gallucci, remarks delivered at the 7th Carnegie International Non-proliferation Conference, 11–12 January 1999. See also Ellis, "Beyond Nonproliferation," 5–6.

84. Kenneth Katzman, "Iraq's Long Range Missile Capabilities," in *Report of the Commission to Assess the Ballistic Missile Threat to the United States, Pursuant to Public Law 201, Appendix III: Unclassified Working Papers*, 104th Cong. (Washington, DC: GPO, 1998), 214–15.

85. James Bruce, "Playing Hide and Seek with Saddam," *Jane's Defence Weekly* 25, no. 1 (1996): 15–19; David A. Kay, "Denial and Deception Practices of WMD Proliferators: Iraq and Beyond," *Washington Quarterly* 18, no. 1 (1995): 87–88.

86. A minority view that is not well substantiated maintains that Iraq may have used some chemical weapons. For a review of the allegation, see Jonathan B. Tucker, "Evidence Iraq Used Chemical Weapons during the 1991 Persian Gulf War," *Nonproliferation Review* 4, no. 3 (1997): 114–22.

87. Stephen Black, "Verification under Duress: The Case of UNSCOM," in *Verification Yearbook 2000*, ed. Trevor Findlay (London: VERTIC, 2000), 116; Graham S. Pearson, *The UNSCOM Saga: Chemical and Biological Weapons Non-Proliferation* (New York: St. Martin's, 1999), table 4.1.

88. Kay, "Denial and Deception Practices of WMD Proliferators," 86. Kay does not explain the discrepancy between the number of missiles and the number of warheads; most likely, there was one warhead that was not mated to a missile. UNSCOM historian Stephen Black states that Iraq initially declared sixty-two missiles (Black, "Verification under Duress," 116).

89. Pearson, *UNSCOM Saga*, 127; Rolf Ekeus, "UN Biological Inspections in Iraq," in *The New Terror: Facing the Threat of Biological and Chemical Weapons*, ed. Sidney D. Drell, Abraham D. Sofaer, and George D. Wilson (Stanford, CA: Hoover Institution Press, 1999), 240; Tom Mangold and Jeff Goldberg, *Plague Wars: The Terrifying Reality of Biological Warfare* (New York: St. Martin's, 1999), 292.

90. Kay, "Denial and Deception Practices of WMD Proliferators," 86.

91. David Kay, an IAEA inspector, estimated that Iraq had spent approximately $10 billion in developing its nuclear infrastructure and pursuing various methods of enriching uranium in pursuit of nuclear weapons (see Kay, "Denial and Deception Practices of WMD Proliferators," 85). Khidhir Hamza, former head of Iraq's nuclear program, generally agrees with this figure (see Khidhir Hamza with Jeff Stein, *Saddam's Bombmaker: The Terrifying Inside Story of the Iraqi Nuclear and Biological Weapons Agenda* [New York: Scribner, 2000], 334).

92. Kay, "Denial and Deception Practices of WMD Proliferators," 86.

93. UNSCOM distributed the initial Iraqi declaration to several dozen states, some of which provided additional WMD-related information not contained in the formal documentation (see John Molander, "The United Nations Elimination of Iraq's Weapons of Mass Destruction," in *From Versailles to Baghdad: Post-War Armament Control of Defeated States*, ed. Fred Tanner [New York: United Nations Press, 1992], 147).

94. For example, when UNSCOM inspectors eventually arrived at Salman Pak, a suspected BW site, they found that the facility had been thoroughly cleaned two weeks before their arrival, with all equipment removed and the ruins razed and buried (see Ekeus, "UN Biological Inspections in Iraq," 240; and Karen Jansen, "Biological Weapons Proliferation," in *Multilateral Verification and the Post-Gulf Environment: Learning from the UNSCOM Experience*, ed. Steven Mateija and J. Marshall Beier [Toronto: York University Centre for International and Strategic Studies, December 1992], 113).

95. Kay, "Denial and Deception Practices of WMD Proliferators," 92. Scott Ritter, interview for "Spying on Saddam," *Frontline*, PBS, 27 April 1999, www.pbs.org/wgbh/pages/frontline/shows/unscom/interviews/ritter.html. See also Jonathan B. Tucker, "Monitoring and Verification in a Noncooperative Environment: Lessons from the U.N. Experience in Iraq," *Nonproliferation Review* 3, no. 3 (1996): 1–14.

97. Pearson, *UNSCOM Saga*, 22. See also Rolf Ekeus, *Fifth Report of the Executive Chairman of the Special Commission under Resolution 687*, S/25977, 21 June 1993, app. 5, www.un.org/Depts/unscom/sres25977.htm, accessed 2001.

98. Black, "Verification under Duress," 117.

99. Barton Gellman, "Arms Inspectors 'Shake the Tree'; UNSCOM Adds Covert Tactics," *Washington Post*, 12 October 1998, A1.

100. Richard Butler, *The Greatest Threat: Iraq, Weapons of Mass Destruction, and the Cri-*

sis of Global Security (New York: Public Affairs, 2000), 181; Barton Gellman, "Israel Gave Key Help to U.N. Team in Iraq; U-2 Photos among Intelligence Shared," *Washington Post,* 29 September 1998, A1.

101. Arms Control Association, "Ambassador Rolf Ekeus: Leaving Behind the UNSCOM Legacy in Iraq," *Arms Control Today* 27, no. 4 (1997): 6.

102. Kay, "Denial and Deception Practices of WMD Proliferators," 99.

103. Black, "Verification under Duress," 117. Although the United States retained ownership of the aircraft, the plane carried UN markings, and the pilot carried documentation stating that he was flying UN missions (see Butler, *Greatest Threat,* 66).

104. Black, "Verification under Duress," 117; Rolf Ekeus, *Sixth Report of the Executive Chairman of the Special Commission under Resolution 699,* S/26910, 21 December 1993, www.un.org/Depts/unscom/sres26910.htm.

105. Butler, *Greatest Threat,* 66.

106. Ekeus, *Fifth Report.*

107. Butler, *Greatest Threat,* 66.

108. Pearson, *UNSCOM Saga,* 25. According to Scott Ritter, UNSCOM proposed sharing U-2 film with the Israelis in December 1994 in order to make use of their skilled photographic interpreters. Beginning in July 1995, with US government approval, he personally carried film to Israel, where Israeli photographic interpreters assisted him in analyzing the aerial photographs (see Ritter, interview for PBS, "Spying on Saddam").

109. Butler, *Greatest Threat,* 66; Ekeus, *Fifth Report;* idem, *Sixth Report;* Pearson, *UNSCOM Saga,* 25.

110. Tucker, "Monitoring and Verification in a Noncooperative Environment," 4–5.

111. "'Good Overall Picture' Provided of Military Weapons Capabilities," *UN Chronicle* 32, no. 2 (1995): 46; Black, "Verification under Duress," 121.

112. Rolf Ekeus, *Ninth Report of the Executive Chairman of the Special Commission under Resolution 687,* S/1994/494, 20 June 1995, www.un.org/Depts/unscom/Semiannual /srep95-494.htm.

113. Pearson, *UNSCOM Saga,* 96–97.

114. Black, "Verification under Duress," 121; Butler, *Greatest Threat,* 123. Butler refutes Iraqi Foreign Minister Tariq Aziz's mistaken claim that UNSCOM was on the brink of declaring Iraq disarmed, paving the way for the lifting of sanctions.

115. IAEA, "Fourth Consolidated Report of the Director General of the International Atomic Energy Agency under paragraph 16 of Security Council Resolution 1051 (1996)," S/1997/779, 8 October 1997, www.iaea.org/worldatom/Programmes/ActionTeam /reports/s_1997_779.pdf, accessed 2001. See also Hamza with Stein, *Saddam's Bombmaker.*

116. Tucker, "Monitoring and Verification in a Noncooperative Environment," 8–10; Alan J. Mohr, "Biological Samples and Analysis Procedures for the United Nations Special Commission (UNSCOM) in Iraq," *Politics and the Life Sciences* 14, no. 2 (1995): 242; Black, "Verification under Duress," 120; Barbara Crossette, "Iraq Hides Biological Warfare Effort Report Says," *New York Times,* 12 April 1995, A4.

117. Pearson, *UNSCOM Saga,* 141; Tucker, "Monitoring and Verification in a Noncooperative Environment," 5.

118. UN Doc S/1995/284, 20; Rolf Ekeus, *Seventh Report of the Executive Chairman of the Special Commission Under Resolution 715,* S/1995/284, 10 April 1995, www.un.org /Depts/unscom/Semiannual/srep95-284.htm, accessed 2001; Crossette, "Iraq Hides Biological Weapons Effort."

119. Black, "Verification under Duress," 120–21; Pearson, *UNSCOM Saga,* 139–43.

120. Black, "Verification under Duress," 121; see also Mangold and Goldberg, *Plague Wars,* 293. So great was the impact of Kamal's defection and its aftermath that Iraqi Foreign Minister Tariq Aziz referred to Kamal as the "idiot" who upset the applecart that could have led to an UNSCOM declaration of total disarmament (see Butler, *Greatest Threat,* 123).

121. Black, "Verification under Duress," 122; Pearson, *UNSCOM Saga,* 31; Scott Ritter, *Endgame: Solving the Iraq Problem Once and For All* (New York: Simon & Schuster, 1999), 47. Black states that "about 680,000 pages" were recovered ("Verification under Duress," 122). Pearson agrees with this estimate, stating that "well over half a million pages" were recovered (*UNSCOM Saga,* 106). Ritter, however, says that Ekeus's team recovered "some 1.5 million pages of documents" (*Endgame,* 47), and Mangold and Goldberg give an even larger figure, stating that Iraqi officials released more than 2 million pages (*Plague Wars,* 293). See also Rolf Ekeus, *Eighth Report of the Executive Chairman of the Special Commission under Resolution 715,* 11 October 1995, S/1995/864, www.un.org/Depts/unscom /sres95-864.htm.

122. Black, "Verification Under Distress," 122.

123. Pearson, *UNSCOM Saga,* 107.

124. Ibid., 108; Evan S. Medeiros, "Report Says Iraqi Weapons Programs Were More Advanced Than Admitted," *Arms Control Today* 25, no. 9 (1995): 21.

125. Mangold and Goldberg, *Plague Wars,* 294.

126. Medeiros, "Report Says Iraqi Weapons Programs Were More Advanced Than Admitted," 21.

127. Rolf Ekeus, *First Report of the Executive Chairman of the Special Commission under Resolution 687,* 25 October 1991, S23165, cited in Black, "Verification under Duress," 119.

128. Black, "Verification under Duress," 118.

129. Ritter, *Endgame,* 49; Black, "Verification under Duress," 122.

130. Ritter, *Endgame,* 49.

131. Gellman, "Arms Inspectors 'Shake the Tree.'"

132. Thomas W. Lippman and Barton Gellman, "U.S. Says It Collected Iraq Intelligence via UNSCOM," *Washington Post,* 8 January 1999, A1; Colum Lynch, "US Used UN to Spy on Iraq, Aides Say; Focus on Hussein Seen," *Boston Globe,* 6 January 1999, A1.

133. B arton Gellman, "What It Took," interview for "Spying on Saddam," *Frontline,* PBS, 27 April 1999, www.pbs.org/wgbh/pages/frontline/shows/unscom/etc/what.html.

134. Ibid.; see also Ritter, *Endgame,* 136.

135. Lynch, "US Used UN to Spy on Iraq, Aides Say."

136. Richard Butler, "The Lessons and Legacy of UNSCOM: An Interview with Ambassador Richard Butler," *Arms Control Today* 29, no. 4 (1999): 7–8.

137. Thomas Pickering, testimony before the Senate Foreign Relations Committee and the Senate Energy and Natural Resources Committee, 21 May 1998, *Iraq: Are Sanctions Collapsing?* 105th Cong., 2nd sess., 1998, 9.

138. Jason Vest and Wayne Madsen, "A Most Unusual Collection Agency," *Village Voice,* 2 March 1999, 46.

139. Barton Gellman, "U.S. Spied on Iraqi Military via U.N.; Arms Control Team Had No Knowledge of Eavesdropping," *Washington Post,* 2 March 1999, A1.

140. Thomas W. Lippman and Barton Gellman, "'Spying' by UNSCOM Denied; U.S. Calls Intelligence-Sharing a Byproduct of Arms Inspections," ibid., 7 January 1999, A18.

141. Gellman, "U.S. Spied on Iraqi Military via U.N." Gellman cites a "knowledge-able U.S. official" who stated, "We did not want to rely on a multinational body that might or might not continue to operate as it was operating."

142. James P. Rubin, Department of State Daily Press Briefing, 6 January 1999.

143. Butler, *Greatest Threat*, 184.

144. Butler, "Lessons and Legacy of UNSCOM," 7–8.

145. Barton Gellman, "U.S. Tried to Halt Several Searches; Intervention Began Last Fall," *Washington Post*, 27 August 1998, A1.

146. Bruce B. Auster, "Inspecting the Inspectors," *U.S. News & World Report*, 18 January 1999, 31. Auster quotes a US official lamenting after the March standoff that resulted in Iraq backing down, "Damn it, we had won. UNSCOM got to the sites we wanted. But we were looking for a way not to have to do this again in three months."

147. Ibid.; Ritter, *Endgame*, 192. Auster cites an anonymous US official who commented, "We didn't want UNSCOM in charge of when to use the world's greatest military." In Scott Ritter's view, "actions by the U.S. in the Persian Gulf over the past seven years had almost always been taken in response to UNSCOM-initiated confrontation with Iraq, which meant in effect that UNSCOM held the lever that could launch American military forces into combat" (*Endgame*, 192).

148. Gellman, "U.S. Tried to Halt Several Searches."

149. Ibid.

150. Butler, *Greatest Threat*, 95–97.

151. Ibid., 206; Black, "Verification under Duress," 126.

152. Richard Butler, *Report to the Security Council on the Status of Disarmament and Monitoring*, S/1999/94, 29 January 1999, www.un.org/Depts/unscom/s99-94.htm. In contrast to the majority opinion expressed by Ekeus, Butler, and others, Scott Ritter voices the minority opinion that as of 1997 "it was possible to determine . . . from a qualitative standpoint, that Iraq had been disarmed" (see Scott Ritter, "The Case for Iraq's Qualitative Disarmament," *Arms Control Today* 30, no. 5 [2000]: 8).

153. Butler, *Report to the Security Council on the Status of Disarmament and Monitoring*. Separately, Butler refers to the Iraqi BW program as a "black hole" (idem, *Greatest Threat*, 81).

154. CIA, "Unclassified Report to Congress on the Acquisition of Technology Relating to Weapons of Mass Destruction and Advanced Conventional Munitions, 1 January through 30 June 2000," February 2001,www.cia.gov/cia/reports/721_reports/jan_jun2000 .htm, accessed 2001.

155. Office of the Secretary of Defense, *Proliferation: Threat and Response*, 38–39.

156. Butler, *Greatest Threat*, 218. See also Jonathan S. Landay, "Is Iraq Building Weapons Again?" *Christian Science Monitor*, 30 August 1999, 1; Bill Gertz, "Saddam Secretly Making Weapons," *Washington Times*, 2 September 1999, A1; Richard Lardner, "Iraq Has Rebuilt Military, Weapons Sites Destroyed During Desert Fox," *Inside the Air Force*, 3 March 2000, 3. For views to the contrary, see Karen DeYoung, "Baghdad Weapons Programs Dormant," *Washington Post*, 15 July 1999, A15; and Robert Burns, "Unseen by U.N. Inspectors, Has Iraq Advanced Weapons Programs?" Associated Press, 8 August 1999.

157. Carla Anne Robbins, "Pressure on Iraq Puts Swedish Ex-Diplomat in a Harsh Spotlight," *Wall Street Journal*, 21 February 2002, A1.

158. Barton Gellman, "Iraq Inspections, Embargo in Danger at U.N. Council; U.S. Fights to Save Sanctions, UNSCOM," *Washington Post*, 22 December 1998, A25; Robert Kagan, "Saddam Wins—Again," *Weekly Standard* 4–11 January 1999, 14.

159. Robbins, "Pressure on Iraq Puts Swedish Ex-Diplomat in a Harsh Spotlight"; "Lawmakers Criticize Iraq Inspection Plan," *Washington Times,* 2 March 2002, 7; Colum Lynch, "New U.N. Arms Monitor Seeks Calmer Relations with Iraq," *Washington Post,* 2 March 2000, A5; Barbara Crossette, "U.S. Is Trying to Put Teeth in Inspections of Iraq Arms," *New York Times,* 11 December 1999, A6.

160. Arms Control Association, "Anticipating Inspections: UNMOVIC Readies Itself for Iraq," *Arms Control Today* 30, no. 6 (2000): 5.

161. Karen DeYoung, "Inspectors Await Data on Iraq; U.S. to Hold Onto Intelligence Until after Regime's Report," *Washington Post,* 7 December 2002, A15; Karen DeYoung and Walter Pincus, "U.S. Is Preparing to Share Intelligence with U.N. Team; Data to Include Possible Iraqi Weapons Sites, Scientists' Names," ibid., 21 December 2002, A18.

162. Julia Preston, "Weapons Inspector Asks U.S. to Share Secret Iraq Data," *New York Times,* 7 December 2002, A1.

163. David E. Sanger and Julia Preston, "U.S. Is to Release Spy Data on Iraq to Aid Inspectors," ibid., 21 December 2002, A1.

164. Karen DeYoung and Walter Pincus, "U.S. Is Sharing Data with Blix; Intelligence Reports Aid Inspections, Powell Says," *Washington Post,* 9 January 2003, A1.

165. Secretary of State Colin L. Powell, remarks to the UN Security Council, New York, 5 February 2003, www.state.gov/secretary/rm/2003/17300.htm, accessed February 2003.

166. According to State Department spokesman James Rubin, "The Iraq case was a unique case in history. UNSCOM never has been seen as a precedent, nor need be seen as a precedent, for other nonproliferation efforts around the world" (see Gellman, "U.S. Spied on Iraqi Military via U.N.").

SIX: Military Support

1. "White House Statement on Weapons of Mass Destruction, March 7, 1991," in *Public Papers of the Presidents of the United States: George Bush, 1991* (Washington, DC: GPO, 1992), 1:223. See also "White House Fact Sheet on the Middle East Arms Control Initiative, May 29, 1991," in ibid., 1:579.

2. Les Aspin, remarks to the National Academy of Sciences Committee on International Security and Arms Control, 7 December 1993.

3. Jon B. Wolfstahl, "Aspin Outlines Pentagon's New Counterproliferation Initiative," *Arms Control Today* 24, no. 1 (1994): 27.

4. William J. Clinton, "Remarks on the 50th Anniversary of the Central Intelligence Agency in Langley, Virginia, September 16, 1997," *Public Papers of the Presidents of the United States, William J. Clinton, 1997* (Washington, DC: GPO, 1999), 2:1169.

5. Aspin, remarks to the National Academy of Sciences, 7 December 1993.

6. Ibid.

7. Brad Roberts, "Strategies of Denial," in *Countering the Proliferation and Use of Weapons of Mass Destruction,* ed. Peter L. Hays, Vincent J. Jodoin, and Alan R. Van Tassel (New York: McGraw-Hill, 1998), 77.

8. Allison Kaplan, "U.S. Fears Israeli Attack on Scud Ship to Syria; Report: North Korean Vessel Being Tracked," *Jerusalem Post,* 11 October 1991; Alon Pinkas, "Defense Ministry: Israel Not Monitoring N. Korea Ship," ibid., 15 October 1991; Bill Gertz and Warren Strobel, "Israeli Strike on Arms Ship Feared," *Washington Times,* 10 October 1991, A11.

9. Kaplan, "U.S. Fears Israeli Attack on Scud Ship to Syria"; Gertz and Strobel, "Israeli Strike on Arms Ship Feared."

10. Bill Gertz, "Threat Forces N. Korea Ship to Return Home with Scuds," *Washington Times*, 24 January 1992, A3; Allison Kaplan, "Korean Ship Fails to Deliver Scuds to Syria," *Jerusalem Post*, 16 January 1992; C. Fenyvesi, "Slow Boat," *U.S. News & World Report*, 11 November 1991, 30; Alon Pinkas, "Ship Carrying Scuds Changes Its Course," *Jerusalem Post*, 12 November 1991; Bill Gertz, "Ship with Scud Cargo for Syria Alters Course," *Washington Times*, 9 November 1991, A6.

11. R. Jeffrey Smith, "U.S. Orders North Korea to Stop Scud Shipment," *Washington Post*, 22 February 1992, A15; Elaine Sciolino, "U.S. Tracks a Korean Ship Taking Missile to Syria," *New York Times*, 21 February 1992, A9; "North Korean Freighter Watched for Transport of Scuds to Syria," *Atlanta Journal and Constitution*, 21 February 1992, A2.

12. Smith, "U.S. Orders North Korea to Stop Scud Shipment." See also Sciolino, "U.S. Tracks a Korean Ship Taking Missile to Syria"; Raymond Whitaker, "'Scud Ship' Sails under Watchful Eye," *Independent* (London), 22 February 1992, 11; "North Korean Freighter Watched for Transport of Scuds to Syria"; and Allison Kaplan, "U.S. Warns N. Korea to Stop Scud Deliveries to Syria," *Jerusalem Post*, 23 February 1992.

13. "Senate Resolution 266—Relating to the Arms Cargo of the North Korean Merchant Ship 'Dae Hung Ho,'" S266, 102nd Cong., 2nd sess., *Congressional Record* 138, no. 30 (5 March 1992): S2931.

14. Patrick E. Tyler, "U.S. Weighs Boarding Korea Arms Ships," *New York Times*, 6 March 1992, A10.

15. Dian McDonald, "U.S. Express Concern about North Korean Ship," U.S. Information Agency Report, 8 March 1992, www.fas.org/news/dprk/1992/26578232-26579936 .htm, accessed 2001. See also Melissa Healy and James Gerstenzang, "U.S. May Halt N. Korean Ship for Arms Check," *Los Angeles Times*, 8 March 1992, A1; and Barton Gellman, "U.S. Failed to Detect Ship; General Tells of Intense Search for N. Koreans," *Washington Post*, 12 March 1992, A1.

16. Susanne M. Shafer, "'Scud' Freighter Reaches Iran Port," *Chicago Sun-Times*, 10 March 1992, 3; Jacquelyn S. Porth, "U.S. Ship Intercepts Focus on Cargoes Destined for Iraq," U.S. Information Agency Report, 10 March 1992, www.fas.org/news/iran/1992 /920310-218992.htm, accessed 2001; Patrick E. Tyler, "North Korea Cargo Ship Said to Elude U.S. Force," *New York Times*, 11 March 1992, A1; "Scud Ship at Iran Port, U.S. Reports," *Houston Chronicle*, 11 March 1992, A14; John Lancaster, "Suspected Scud Shipment Reaches Iran; Pentagon Plays Down Attempt to Intercept N. Korean Vessel," *Washington Post*, 11 March 1992, A11.

17. "Middle East Briefly," *Orange County Register*, 12 March 1992, A25; "Korean Ship Unloads Big Containers in Iran," *New York Times*, 12 March 1992, A10.

18. Tyler, "North Korea Cargo Ship Said to Elude U.S. Force"; "Scud Ship at Iran Port"; Lancaster, "Suspected Scud Shipment Reaches Iran."

19. Gellman, "U.S. Failed to Detect Ship"; Lancaster, "Suspected Scud Shipment Reaches Iran"; "N. Korean Ship Eludes Navy, Reaches Iran," *St. Louis Post-Dispatch*, 11 March 1992, 1A.

20. General Hoar attributed surveillance units' losing track of the ship to a shift in the search pattern (Gellman, "U.S. Failed to Detect Ship"; Melissa Healy, "General Takes Blame for Ship That Got Away; Gulf: U.S. Commander in Region Tells How His Forces

Lost Track of Vessel Suspected of Carrying Scud Missiles to Iran," *Los Angeles Times*, 12 March 1992, A4).

21. George Lardner Jr., "Probe Ordered in Failure to Track N. Korean Ship," *Washington Post*, 14 March 1992, A17.

22. Jonathan C. Randal, "Assad Criticizes Israel, U.S. in N. Korean Freighter Affair," ibid., 13 March 1992, A18; "N. Korean Vice President Denies Scuds Were on Ship," ibid.; "Assad Denounces U.S. over N. Korean Ship," *St. Louis Post-Dispatch*, 13 March 1992, 14A.

23. Barbara Rudolph, "The Mysterious Stealth Ship," *Time*, 23 March 1992, 34.

24. White House, Office of the President, "President to Nominate Carter for Nuclear Security Post," press release, 13 April 1993, clinton6.nara.gov/1993/04/1993-04-13-president-to-nominate-carter-for-nuclear-security-post.html.

25. R. Jeffrey Smith, "Mideast Allies Frustrate Ship Inspection by U.S.; Prohibited Chemicals May Be Bound for Iran," *Washington Post*, 10 August 1993, A6.

26. This was not the first time the United States had caught India shipping dual-use chemicals to suspected proliferants and demanded that India tighten its export controls. India admitted selling thionyl chloride to Iran in 1989, was caught selling trimethyl phosphate to Syria in 1992, and had also sold chemicals to Iraq and Egypt (see Sanjoy Hazarika, "India Says It Sold Iran a Chemical Used in Poison Gas," *New York Times*, 1 July 1989, A1; "No Move to Seize Alleged Poison Gas Cargo," *St. Louis Post-Dispatch*, 2 July 1989, 11D; Jackson Diehl, "India to Investigate Chemical Shipment; Material Used for Making Poison Gas Was Bound for Syria," *Washington Post*, 22 September 1992, A17; and Michael R. Gordon, "U.S. Accuses India on Chemical Arms," *New York Times*, 21 September 1992, A1).

27. The route runs from Xingang to Shanghai, Hong Kong, Singapore, Jakarta, Dubai, Dhahran, and Kuwait (see "U.S. Tracks Iran-Bound Chinese Ship, Refuses to Reveal Plans," Agence France Presse, 13 August 1993; and "Chinese Foreign Ministry Official on 'Yinhe' Incident," Xinhua General Overseas News Service, 13 August 1993).

28. Celine Tng and Kate Yu Juan, "Case of Sino-US Ties Riding on Choppy Waters," *Straits Times* (Singapore), 12 September 1993, 8. See also Office of the Secretary of Defense, *Proliferation: Threat and Response* (Washington, DC: GPO, April 1996), 10, 13.

29. Thiodiglycol is a chemical precursor used in the manufacture of mustard agents, but it has numerous commercial applications, including "making preservatives, insecticides, herbicide, dyestuff for cotton textiles, and [ballpoint] pen ink." Thionyl chloride, a chemical that can be used to manufacture nerve agents, has commercial applications primarily in batteries but is also used in the manufacture of "organic synthetics, dyestuff, agricultural drugs, and other medicines" (Liu Yegang, "The Whole Story of the Yinhe Incident," Xinhua Domestic Service [Beijing], 5 September 1993, FBIS-CHI-93-173).

30. Chen Wenru, "Findings Report on Yinhe Freighter," *Liaowang* (Hong Kong), 13 September 1993, overseas edition, 4–5, FBIS-CHI-93-177. When the inspections finally began, American investigators asked to see these containers first. However, no containers with these serials numbers appeared on the ship's manifest or any associated bills of lading. It should also be noted that the United States never publicly revealed any details of the information that led to the *Yin He* incident, so the Chinese account has not been confirmed by U.S. sources.

31. Jim Mann, "No Chemicals on Chinese Vessel, State Dept. Says," *Los Angeles Times*, 5 September 1993, A1; Nicholas D. Kristoff, "China Says U.S. Is Harassing Ship Suspected of Taking Arms to Iran," *New York Times*, 9 August 1993, A6.

32. "Chinese Foreign Ministry Official on 'Yinhe' Incident."

33. Ibid.; "U.S. Tracks Iran-Bound Chinese Ship"; Tng and Yu Juan, "Case of Sino-US Ties Riding on Choppy Waters," 8. While the United States alleged that the *Yin He* was sailing to the Iranian port of Bandar Abbas to unload the twenty-four suspicious containers, Chinese critics used the fact that the *Yin He*'s regular route did not run to Bandar Abbas, along with that port's lack of container terminals, to undermine the U.S. allegations.

34. "Chinese Foreign Ministry Official on 'Yinhe' Incident."

35. Ibid.

36. Chris Dobson, "'Blockade' Ship's Case Call," *South China Morning Post,* 15 August 1993, 5.

37. Ian Brodie, "China Defies U.S. over Ship," *Times* (London), 16 August 1993; "China Says Cargo Ship Will Anchor off Oman," *New York Times,* 15 August 1993, A7; "U.S. Tracks Iran-Bound Chinese Ship"; "Christopher Says Ship Will Be Inspected," Associated Press, 13 August 1993; Charles Richards, "US Thwarts 'Suspicious' Cargo Ship; Washington Is Acting to Allay Fears about Chemical Weapons in Iran," *Independent,* 17 August 1993, 10; "To Board or Not to Board; International Law and Complex Chinese Cargo," *Times* (London), 21 August 1993.

38. Lan Ching, "True Colors of Power Politics as Viewed from the 'Yinhe' Incident," *Ta Kung Pao* (Hong Kong), 27 August 1993, 7, FBIS-CHI-93-186.

39. "Response to Charges of Shipping Chemicals to Iran; VOA Interviews Official," Xinhua Domestic Service (Beijing), 13 August 1993, FBIS-CHI-93-156; "Chinese Foreign Ministry Official on 'Yinhe' Incident."

40. "Response to Charges of Shipping Chemicals to Iran"; "Chinese Foreign Ministry Official on 'Yinhe' Incident."

41. The stopping and searching of foreign merchant ships in peacetime is governed by the Convention on the High Seas of 1958, which was reaffirmed by the UN Convention on the Law of the Sea of 10 December 1982 (UNCLOS III). According to article 22 of the 1958 High Seas Convention, there is no justification, barring such powers conferred by treaties, for stopping and searching a foreign merchant ship unless there is reasonable ground for suspecting that the ship in question is engaged in piracy, is engaged in the slave trade, or is of the same nationality as the stopping ship even though the merchant ship may be flying a foreign flag or no flag at all. The 1982 UN Convention contains similar verbiage but adds two additional justifications covering unauthorized radio broadcasting and ships without nationality. Also, according to article 6 of the 1958 convention and article 92 of the 1982 convention, ships are subject to the exclusive jurisdiction of the state whose flag they fly, barring exceptional cases due to treaty powers (see Ian Brownlie, *Principles of Public International Law,* 4th ed. [Oxford: Clarendon, 1990], 243–44; and I. A. Shearer, *Starke's International Law,* 11th ed. [Salem, NH: Butterworth Legal Publishers, 1994], 246). The CWC allows challenge inspections of any facility or location in the territory of any state that is party to the CWC or in any other place under the jurisdiction or control of such states, but it was not in effect at the time of the *Yin He* incident.

42. Jim Mann, "Saudis May Inspect Chinese Cargo Due in Iran; Diplomacy: Under the Proposed Plan, Ship Would Dock at Saudi Port; U.S. Thinks It Is Carrying Deadly Chemicals," *Los Angeles Times,* 24 August 1993, A4.

43. "Foreign Ministry on 'Yinhe' Incident," *Beijing Review,* 13–19 September 1993, 4; "Official Statements Issued on 'Yinhe' Incident," *Renmin Ribao* (Beijing), 5 September 1993, 1, FBIS-CHI-93-171.

44. "Foreign Ministry on 'Yinhe' Incident."

45. Ibid.; Rone Tempest, "China Demands U.S. Apology; Search of Ship Fails to Find Warfare Chemicals," *Chicago Sun-Times,* 6 September 1993, 10; "COSCO Demands Public Apology and Compensation from U.S.," Xinhua General Overseas News Service, 10 September 1993.

46. Chris Yeung, "Washington Told to Learn from Yinhe," *South China Morning Post,* 9 September 1993, 8.

47. Ibid.

48. Michael McCurry, Department of State Daily Press Briefing, 7 September 1993.

49. Mann, "No Chemicals on Chinese Vessel"; Willy Wo-Lap Lam, "Ties Worsen over Ship Row; Beijing, US Head for Crisis," *South China Morning Post,* 6 September 1993, 1.

50. Mann, "No Chemicals on Chinese Vessel."

51. Patrick E. Tyler, "No Chemical Arms Aboard China Ship," *New York Times,* 6 September 1993, A4.

52. McCurry, Department of State Daily Press Briefing, 7 September 1993.

53. Sid Balman Jr., "U.S. Intelligence: Chinese Shipped Chemical Weapons," United Press International, 7 September 1993.

54. Ibid. See also Mann, "No Chemicals on Chinese Vessel"; and Celes Eckerman, "Inspection of Chinese Cargo Ship Yields No Evidence of Chemicals," *Arms Control Today* 23, no. 8 (1993): 19. Yet, this view was not universally accepted (see "Yinhe Incident Shrouded in Mystery," Agence France Presse, 7 September 1993; and Asad Laif, "US Action against Yin He: Whither New World Order?" *Straits Times,* 11 September 1993, 35).

55. Eckerman, "Inspection of Chinese Cargo Ship Yields No Evidence of Chemicals"; Tng and Yu Juan, "Case of Sino-US Ties Riding on Choppy Waters," 8. Perhaps lending support to the first theory was a report in the *Far Eastern Economic Review* that the CIA had confirmed the presence of the chemicals on board the ship when it stopped in Singapore (see "Intelligence: Chemical Leak," *Far Eastern Economic Review,* 9 September 1993, 9). There were some allegations that PRC intelligence had been behind the reports of the chemicals and that this had been an operation to discredit the United States (see, e.g., Tng and Yu Juan, "Case of Sino-US Ties Riding on Choppy Waters," 8).

56. McCurry, Department of State Daily Press Briefing, 7 September 1993.

57. Ibid.

58. See, e.g., Tempest, "China Demands U.S. Apology," 10; and Ching, "True Colors of Power Politics as Viewed from the 'Yinhe' Incident," 7.

59. The 1990s revealed a persistent pattern of PRC assistance and transfers to Iran's chemical weapons program. In 1997 the United States imposed sanctions on seven PRC entities for such transfers and assistance (DCI, "Unclassified Report to Congress on the Acquisition of Technology Relating to Weapons of Mass Destruction and Advanced Conventional Munitions, 1 January through 30 June 2001," 30 January 2002, www.cia.gov /cia/reports/721_reports/jan_jun2000.htm, accessed 2001).

60. Ibid.

61. Center for Counterproliferation Research, *The Counterproliferation Imperative: Meeting Tomorrow's Challenges* (Washington, DC: National Defense University, 2001), 2, 14–15,

29; Barry R. Schneider, *Future War and Counterproliferation: U.S. Military Responses to NBC Proliferation Threats* (Westport, CT: Praeger, 1999), 50–51; Office of the Secretary of Defense, *Proliferation: Threat and Response* (Washington, DC: GPO, January 2001), 69.

62. Michael Barletta, "Chemical Weapons in the Sudan: Allegations and Evidence," *Nonproliferation Review* 6, no. 1 (1998): 116, 130.

63. Karl Vick, "Six More Die in Kenya, Raising Death Toll in Africa Bombings to 263," *Washington Post*, 21 August 1998, A20; Vernon Loeb, "Trial of 4 in Alleged Bin Laden Bomb Plot Set to Begin," ibid., 31 December 2000, A6.

64. Michael Grunwald, "Tanzania Detains 2 Bombing Suspects; Momentum Grows in Probe of Attacks on U.S. Embassies," ibid., 6 September 1998, A1; idem, "Ex-Aide to Bin Laden Held in Bomb Probe; U.S. Details Links to Terror Group," ibid., 18 September 1998, A1; Madeleine Albright and Samuel Berger, Press Briefing, 20 August 1998, secretary.state.gov/www/statements/1998/980820.html, accessed 2001.

65. William J. Clinton, "Address to the Nation on Military Action against Terrorist Sites in Afghanistan and Sudan, August 20, 1998," *Public Papers of the Presidents of the United States, William J. Clinton, 1998* (Washington, DC: GPO, 2000), 2:1460.

66. "Bin Laden Denies Role in Bombings," *Washington Post*, 25 December 1998, A4.

67. Albright and Berger, Press Briefing, 20 August 1998.

68. Steven Lee Myers, "U.S. Offers More Details on Attack in the Sudan," *New York Times*, 24 August 1998, A6.

69. Michael Grunwald, "CIA Halted Plot to Bomb U.S. Embassy in Uganda," *Washington Post*, 25 September 1998, A27.

70. Ibid.

71. Clinton, "Address to the Nation on Military Action against Terrorist Sites in Afghanistan and Sudan, August 20, 1998."

72. "Transcript: Pickering on US Sudan, Afghanistan Strikes," USIS Washington File, 26 August 1998, usembassy-australia.state.gov/hyper/WF980826/epf303.htm, accessed 2001.

73. Madeline Albright and William Cohen, remarks at Press Stake-out on Capitol Hill, 21 August 1998, secretary.state.gov/www/statements/1998/9800821a.html, accessed 2001.

74. The intelligence community had been concerned about what it saw as a growing interest among terrorist groups in nuclear, biological, and chemical weapons. Seven months before the cruise missile strikes, George Tenet testified that "growing indications of terrorist interests in acquiring chemical, biological and nuclear weapons" were "most worrisome," although he did not mention bin Laden by name (see George J. Tenet, testimony before the Senate Select Intelligence Committee, 28 January 1998, *Current and Projected National Security Threats to the United States*, 105th Cong., 2nd sess., 1998, 14).

75. Barletta, "Chemical Weapons in the Sudan," 126–28.

76. Robert Pear, "Sudan Rebels Say They Are Victims of Poison Gas," *New York Times*, 10 January 1989, A12; Paul Mann, "Sudan Alleged WMD User," *Aviation Week and Space Technology*, 31 August 1998, 34.

77. Mann, "Sudan Alleged WMD User," 34.

78. Pear, Sudan Rebels Say They Are Victims of Poison Gas"; Mann, "Sudan Alleged WMD User," 34. See also Office of the Secretary of Defense, *Proliferation: Threat and Response* (January 2001), 49: "Sudan acceded to the CWC in 1999, although allegations of Sudanese chemical warfare use against rebels in southern Sudan have persisted. These, and prior allegations of chemical warfare use, have not been confirmed."

79. "Sudan's Weapons," *World Press Review* 36, no. 2 (1989): 41; Mann, "Sudan Alleged WMD User," 34.

80. James B. Foley, Department of State Daily Press Briefing, 26 August 1998; Office of the Coordinator for Counterterrorism, U.S. Department of State, *Patterns of Global Terrorism* (Washington, DC: GPO, 20 April 2001).

81. Jane Perlez, "Iraqi Deal With Sudan on Nerve Gas Is Reported," *New York Times,* 26 August 1998, A8. According to James Foley, "We are concerned about the possibility that Iraq may have made an agreement with Sudan to allow it to continue its pursuit of chemical weapons without being subject to the scrutiny of UN weapons inspectors" (Department of State Daily Press Briefing, 26 August 1998).

82. Perlez, "Iraqi Deal With Sudan on Nerve Gas Is Reported."

83. Foley, Department of State Daily Press Briefing, 26 August 1998.

84. In various open-source accounts the enterprise is also referred to as the "Military Industrialization Organization" or the "War Industrialization Project."

85. Shadiyah Hamid, "Sudanese Alliance Forces Leader Interviewed," *Al-Majallah* (London), 5–11 January 1997, FBIS, FTS19970317001393.

86. Ibid.; "Khartoum Striving to Acquire Chemical and Biological Weapons" [in Arabic], *al-Diyar* (Beirut), 14 January 1998, 14, FBIS 19980115001140.

87. DOD, Background Briefing on Terrorist Camp Strikes, 20 August 1998, www.defenselink.mil/news/Aug1998/x08201998_x820bomb.html, accessed 2001.

88. Ibid.; James Risen, "U.S. Says It Has Strong Evidence of Threat Justifying the Retaliation," *New York Times,* 21 August 1998, A1.

89. DOD, Background Briefing on Terrorist Camp Strikes, 20 August 1998.

90. Ibid.

91. Karl Vick, "U.S., Sudan Trade Claims on Factory; Washington Cites Toxin in Soil Sample," *Washington Post,* 25 August 1998, A1; Vernon Loeb, "Employees Dispute Charge That Plant Made Nerve Agent," ibid., 26 August 1998, A15; "U.S. Reveals More Details on Airstrike; Defending the Attack on Sudan, the Clinton Administration Has Offered Some of the Evidence behind the Strike," *Minneapolis Star Tribune,* 24 August 1998, 1A; Steven Lee Myers, "U.S. Says Iraq Aided Production of Chemical Weapons in Sudan," *New York Times,* 25 August 1998, A1.

92. Myers, "U.S. Says Iraq Aided Production of Chemical Weapons in Sudan."

93. "Transcript: Pickering on US Sudan, Afghanistan Strikes." See also Myers, "U.S. Says Iraq Aided Production of Chemical Weapons in Sudan"; and Perlez, "Iraqi Deal With Sudan on Nerve Gas Is Reported."

94. DOD, Background Briefing on Terrorist Camp Strikes, 20 August 1998.

95. Albright and Berger, Press Briefing, 20 August 1998.

96. DOD, Background Briefing on Terrorist Camp Strikes, 20 August 1998.

97. Samuel Berger and Mike McCurry, Press Briefing, 21 August 1998, www.fas.org/man/dod-101/ops/docs/980821-wh-pm.htm, accessed 20 November 2000.

98. Seymour M. Hersh, "The Missiles of August," *New Yorker,* 12 October 1998, 35–37.

99. Tim Weiner and James Risen, "Decision to Strike Factory in Sudan Based on Surmise Inferred from Evidence," *New York Times,* 21 September 1998, A1; Hersh, "Missiles of August," 34.

100. Weiner and Risen, "Decision to Strike Factory in Sudan Based on Surmise Inferred from Evidence."

101. Hersh, "Missiles of August," 34; Tim Weiner and Steven Lee Myers, "Flaws in U.S. Account Raise Questions on Strike in Sudan," *New York Times,* 29 August 1998, A1.

102. Weiner and Myers, "Flaws in U.S. Account Raise Questions on Strike in Sudan."

103. "Joint Chiefs Left Out of Planning for Raids; Secrecy before Afghan, Sudan Strikes Defended," *Chicago Sun-Times,* 6 October 1998, 21.

104. Hersh, "Missiles of August," 36.

105. Ibid.; Martin Kettle, "US Cruise Attacks 'Ignored Warnings,'" *Guardian* (London), 6 October 1998, 16. However, when queried on the subject, the Department of Justice declined the opportunity to comment on these allegations (see "Joint Chiefs Left Out of Planning for Raids").

106. A spokesman for Army Chief of Staff Dennis Reimer stated, "Our leadership was not uncomfortable with the level of notification they received" (see "Joint Chiefs Left Out of Planning for Raids"; and Hersh, "Missiles of August," 36).

107. "Joint Chiefs Left Out of Planning for Raids."

108. Hersh, "Missiles of August," 36.

109. David Hirst, "The Missing Evidence: The 'Secret' Chemical Factory That No One Tried to Hide," *Observer* (London), 23 August 1998, 14; Vick, "U.S., Sudan Trade Claims on Factory."

110. Tim Weiner and Steven Lee Myers, "U.S. Notes Gaps in Data about Drug Plant but Defends Attack; Sudan Envoy Is Angry," *New York Times,* 3 September 1998, A6.

111. Vick, "U.S., Sudan Trade Claims on Factory."

112. Actually, US officials never revealed the precise location of the sample's extraction. Various accounts in the media place it within the gates of the factory, a stone's throw away, from an effluent discharge pipe, or some other location relatively near the factory (see, e.g., Lucy Howard and Paul O'Donnell, "Making a Case," *Newsweek,* 28 September 1998, 6 [sample taken "from a discharge pipe"]; Paul Richter, "Sudan Attack Claims Faulty, U.S. Admits," *Los Angeles Times,* 1 September 1998, A1 ["soil sample secretly collected from just outside the facility"]; James Risen, "To Bomb Sudan Plant, or Not: A Year Later, Debates Rankle," *New York Times,* 27 October 1998, A1 ["In December 1997 an agent working for the C.I.A. collected a soil sample about 60 feet from Al Shifa, directly across an access road from the main entrance. . . . The sample was taken from land that does not appear to have been owned by Al Shifa"]; and Weiner and Myers, "U.S. Notes Gaps in Data about Drug Plant but Defends Attack" ["an agent stole a soil sample from inside the plant's gates, a few yards from the building"]).

113. Vernon Loeb and Bradley Graham, "Sudan Plant Was Probed Months before Attack," *Washington Post,* 1 September 1998, A14; Vick, "U.S., Sudan Trade Claims on Factory."

114. Loeb and Graham, "Sudan Plant Was Probed Months before Attack," A14.

115. Ibid.; Richter, "Sudan Attack Claims Faulty."

116. "U.S. Claims Proof of Deadly Chemical at Sudan Plant; Soil Sample at Site Shows VX Element, Official Says; Clinton Is Called a 'War Criminal,'" *St. Louis Post-Dispatch,* 25 August 1998, A1.

117. MASINT is officially defined as "technically derived intelligence (excluding signals intelligence and traditional imagery intelligence) that, when collected, processed, and analyzed results in intelligence that locates, tracks, identifies, or describes the signatures (distinctive characteristics) of fixed or dynamic target sources" (Office of the Assistant Secretary of Defense for Command, Control, Communications, and Intelligence,

DOD Instruction 5105.58, "Management of Measurement and Signature Intelligence (MASINT)," 9 February 1993, www.dtic.mil/whs/directives/corres/pdf/i510558_020993 /i510558.pdf, accessed 2001.

118. Jeffrey T. Richelson, "MASINT: The New Kid in Town," *International Journal of Intelligence and Counterintelligence* 14, no. 2 (2001): 152.

119. Weiner and Myers, "Flaws in U.S. Account Raise Questions on Strike in Sudan."

120. Richter, "Sudan Attack Claims Faulty."

121. "U.S. Claims More Evidence Linking Sudanese Plant to Chemical Weapons," 1 September 1998, www.cnn.com/WORLD/africa/9809/01/sudan.plant/.

122. Perlez, "Iraqi Deal With Sudan on Nerve Gas Is Reported."

123. Loeb, "Employees Dispute Charge That Plant Made Nerve Agent."

124. Ian Brodie, "America Insists Factory Was Gas Producer," *Times*, 3 September 1998.

125. Mahdi Ibrahim Mohamed, News Conference on U.S. Military Strikes in Khartoum, 24 September 1998. Critics of the US attack also pointed out that the plant was producing Shifazole, a veterinary antiworm medicine, for Iraq under the auspices of the oil-for-food program and that on the night before the strike workers on the night shift had been working late to fill this order for Iraq (see Daniel Pearl, "In Sudanese Bombing, 'Evidence' Depends on Who Is Viewing It," *Wall Street Journal*, 28 October 1998, A10; and Perlez, "Iraqi Deal With Sudan on Nerve Gas Is Reported").

126. Hirst, "Missing Evidence."

127. Richter, "Sudan Attack Claims Faulty."

128. "U.S. Claims Proof of Deadly Chemical at Sudan Plant."

129. Hassan Ibrahim, Martin Bright, Shyam Bhatia and Ed Vulliamy, "The Missiles, the Bungling Pentagon, and the Nerve Gas Factory That Never Was; the US Engineer Who Drew Up the Plans for the al-Shifa Plant Has Shaken American Claims That It Was Producing Chemical Weapons," *Observer* (London), 31 August 1998, 4.

130. Loeb, "Employees Dispute Charge That Plant Made Nerve Agent"; Steven Lee Myers and Tim Weiner, "Possible Benign Use Is Seen for Chemical at Factory in Sudan," *New York Times*, 27 August 1998, A1; Weiner and Myers, "Flaws in U.S. Account Raise Questions on Strike in Sudan."

131. Ibrahim et al., "The Missiles, the Bungling Pentagon," 4.

132. Loeb, "Employees Dispute Charge That Plant Made Nerve Agent."

133. Gary Younge, "Agency Queries US Labeling of Sudan Chemical," *Guardian*, 28 August 1998, 14; Myers and Weiner, "Possible Benign Use Is Seen for Chemical at Factory in Sudan"; Weiner and Myers, "U.S. Notes Gaps in Data about Drug Plant but Defends Attack."

134. Myers and Weiner, "Possible Benign Use Is Seen for Chemical at Factory in Sudan"; Younge, "Agency Queries US Labeling of Sudan Chemical."

135. Loeb and Graham, "Sudan Plant Was Probed Months before Attack."

136. "U.S. State Dept. Says Soil Showed VX-Sudan Link," Reuters, 26 August 1998.

137. Weiner and Myers, "Flaws in U.S. Accounts Raise Questions on Strike in the Sudan"; Gregory Koblenz, "Countering Dual-Use Facilities: Lessons from Iraq and Sudan," *Jane's Intelligence Review* 11, no. 3 (1999): 50.

138. Hersh, "Missiles of August," 40.

139. Myers and Weiner, "Possible Benign Use Is Seen for Chemical at Factory in Sudan."

140. Ibid. See also Weiner and Myers, "Flaws in U.S. Account Raise Questions on Strike in Sudan."

141. Myers and Weiner, "Possible Benign Use is Seen for Chemical at Factory in Sudan"; Hersh, "Missiles Of August," 40; Barletta, "Chemical Weapons in the Sudan," 124–25.

142. DOD, Background Briefing on Terrorist Camp Strikes, 20 August 1998.

143. John Ellis, "The Ugly Truth about Attack in Sudan," *Boston Globe,* 13 May 1999, A21.

144. Hersh, "Missiles of August," 35.

145. Myers and Weiner, "Possible Benign Use Is Seen for Chemical at Factory in Sudan."

146. Karl Vick, "Many in Sudan Dispute Plant's Ties with Bomber," *Washington Post,* 22 October 1998, A29.

147. Ellis, "Ugly Truth about Attack in Sudan"; Tim Weiner and James Reisen, "Small Group Decision; Questions Well Up after Sudan Attack," *Minneapolis Star Tribune,* 21 September 1998, 5A.

148. Loeb and Graham, "Sudan Plant Was Probed Months before Attack."

149. Koblenz, "Countering Dual-Use Facilities," 50.

150. Vick, "Many in Sudan Dispute Plant's Tie with Bomber," A29.

151. James Risen and David Johnston, "Experts Find No Arms Chemical at Bombed Sudan Plant," *New York Times,* 9 February 1999, A3.

152. Ibid.

153. Vernon Loeb, "Plant Owner to Sue U.S. to Free Frozen Assets; Saudi-Owned Factory Destroyed in Sudan Raid," *Washington Post,* 26 February 1999, A3; idem, "A Dirty Business," ibid., 25 July 1999, F1.

154. Loeb, "Dirty Business."

155. Bruce D. Berkowitz, "Facing the Consequences; As El Shifa Shows, It Takes More Than Intelligence to Make Smart Decisions," ibid., 5 September 1999, B1. See also Seymour M. Hersh, "The Target Is Destroyed," *Atlantic Monthly,* September 1986, 46–69.

156. Berkowitz, "Facing the Consequences."

157. National Defense University, Center for Counterproliferation Research, *Counterproliferation Imperative,* 2–3; Jason D. Ellis, "Beyond Nonproliferation: Secondary Supply, Proliferation Management, and U.S. Foreign Policy," *Comparative Strategy* 20, no. 1 (2001): 16; Office of the Secretary of Defense, *Proliferation: Threat and Response* (January 2001), 69–70.

SEVEN: Warfighting in a WMD Context

1. *Gulf War Air Power Survey,* vol. 1, pt. 1, *Planning and Command and Control* (Washington, DC: GPO, 1993), 84.

2. Ibid.

3. Ibid.

4. US officials reportedly believed that Iraq was capable of employing mustard and nerve agents, including sarin, soman, and VX, in the chemical domain and anthrax and botulinum toxin in the biological arena but had not yet successfully completed its nuclear weapons program. British officials apparently believed that Iraq was capable of using nerve, blister, and blood agents in the chemical area and anthrax, botulinum toxin,

and plague in the biological area. French officials reportedly did not identify a biological threat from Iraq, and no specific information is available on the French assessment of the Iraqi chemical threat (General Accounting Office, *Coalition Warfare: Gulf War Allies Differed in Chemical and Biological Threats Identified and in Use of Defensive Measures*, GAO-01-13, [Washington, DC, April 2001], 5–7; Graham S. Pearson, *The UNSCOM Saga: Chemical and Biological Weapons Non-Proliferation* [New York: St. Martin's, 1999]; James Bruce, "Playing Hide and Seek with Saddam," *Jane's Defence Weekly* 25, no. 1 [1996]: 15–19; Timothy V. McCarthy and Jonathan B. Tucker, "Saddam's Toxic Arsenal: Chemical and Biological Weapons in the Gulf Wars," in *Planning the Unthinkable: How New Powers Will Use Nuclear, Biological, and Chemical Weapons*, ed. Peter R. Lavoy, Scott D. Sagan, and James J. Wirtz [Ithaca, NY: Cornell University Press, 2000], 52–56; Judith Miller, Stephen Engelberg, and William Broad, *Germs: Biological Weapons and America's Secret War* [New York: Simon & Schuster, 2001], 102).

5. Charles A. Horner and Barry R. Schneider, "Counterforce," in *Countering the Proliferation and Use of Weapons of Mass Destruction*, ed. Peter J. Hays, Vincent J. Jodoin, and Alan R. Van Tassel (New York: McGraw-Hill, 1998), 241.

6. *Gulf War Air Power Survey*, 1, pt. 1: 200. The *Gulf War Air Power Survey* does not identify the CENTCOM-and CENTAF-identified targets.

7. Ibid., 212–13.

8. US Central Command, "Iraq's Chemical and Biological Weapons Program," September 1990, 2, www.gulflink.osd.mil/cgi-bin/display_full_document.pl?af&19970211&970207 _aadbc_.

9. *Gulf War Air Power Survey*, vol. 2, pt. 2, *Operations and Effects and Effectiveness* (Washington, DC: GPO, 1993), 322; DOD, *Final Report to Congress on the Conduct of the Persian Gulf War Pursuant to Title V of the Persian Gulf Conflict Supplemental Authorization and Personnel Benefits Act of 1991 (Public Law 102-25)* (Washington, DC: GPO, April 1992), 159.

10. DOD, *Final Report to Congress on the Conduct of the Persian Gulf War*, 154–55. The report also indicates that much of the Iraqi nuclear infrastructure was unknown at the time of Desert Storm.

11. Gregory Koblenz, "Countering Dual-Use Facilities: Lessons from Iraq and Sudan," *Jane's Intelligence Review* 11, no. 3 (1999): 50.

12. *Gulf War Air Power Survey*, 2, pt. 2: 316–17; David A. Kay, "Denial and Deception Practices of WMD Proliferators: Iraq and Beyond," *Washington Quarterly* 18, no. 1 (1995): 85–86; Williamson Murray and Wayne W. Thompson, *Air War in the Persian Gulf* (Baltimore: Nautical and Aviation Publishing Company of America, 1995), 209.

13. Horner and Schneider, "Counterforce," 241.

14. *Gulf War Air Power Survey*, 1, pt. 1: 217. See also Thomas A. Keaney, "Surveying Gulf War Airpower," *Joint Force Quarterly*, no. 2 (1993): 29.

15. *Gulf War Air Power Survey*, 2, pt. 2: 327.

16. Ibid., 330.

17. Ibid., 326.

18. *Gulf War Air Power Survey*, 1, pt. 1: 219.

19. Ibid., 220.

20. Richard Butler, *Report to the Security Council on the Status of Disarmament and Monitoring*, S/1999/94, 29 January 1999, www.un.org/Depts/unscom/s99-94.htm.

21. Janne E. Nolan notes, "By traditional measures of utility, most ballistic missiles in third world arsenals are of limited military significance. The systems are generally too

inaccurate to strike at military targets effectively or to give aggressors confidence that such attacks could result in decisive military gains" (*Trappings of Power: Ballistic Missiles in the Third World* [Washington, DC: Brookings Institution, 1991], 95. See also Center for Counterproliferation Research, *The Counterproliferation Imperative: Meeting Tomorrow's Challenges* [Washington, DC: National Defense University, 2001], 6, 32).

22. *Gulf War Air Power Survey*, 1, pt. 1: 101.

23. Michael R. Gordon and Bernard E. Trainor, *The Generals' War: The Inside Story of the Conflict in the Gulf* (Boston: Little, Brown, 1995), 230.

24. DOD, *Final Report to Congress on the Conduct of the Persian Gulf War*, 97; *Gulf War Air Power Survey*, 2, pt. 2: 330.

25. *Gulf War Air Power Survey*, 1, pt. 1: 165–67; Tim Ripley, "Scud Hunting: Counterforce Operations against Theatre Ballistic Missiles," Bailrigg Memorandum 18 (Lancaster, UK: CDISS, 1996), 8.

26. *Gulf War Air Power Survey*, 1, pt. 1: 166; Ripley, "Scud Hunting," 8.

27. Murray and Thompson, *Air War in the Persian Gulf*, 166. According to Murray, DIA analysts believed that these deployments might have occurred as early as August 1990.

28. Michael Gordon and Bernard Trainor describe several tense days as US officials attempted to persuade the Israelis not to launch counterattacks against Iraq (*Generals' War*, 230–33). They also discuss difficulties in getting CENTCOM commanders and forces to be more accommodating of Israeli demands for action against the Scuds even though Israel was out of CENTCOM's area of responsibility and the CENTCOM commander continued to insist that the Scuds were not militarily significant weapons (ibid., 235. See also H. Norman Schwartzkopf, *It Doesn't Take a Hero* [New York: Bantam Books, 1992], 416–18).

29. DOD, *Final Report to Congress on the Conduct of the Persian Gulf War*, 167.

30. See Gordon and Trainor, *Generals' War*, 237; Ripley, "Scud Hunting," 10–11; Stewart M. Powell, "Scud War, Round Two," *Air Force Magazine* 75, no. 4 (1992): 50; Daniel P. Bolger, *Death Ground: Today's American Infantry in Battle* (Novata, CA: Presidio Press, 1999), 167–69; and Gordon and Trainor, *Generals' War*, 241–48.

31. Ripley, "Scud Hunting," 10.

32. Mark Hewish and Joris Janssen Lok, "Stopping the Scud Threat: Engaging Theater Ballistic Missiles on the Ground," *Jane's International Defense Review* 30, no. 6 (June 1997): 40.

33. *Gulf War Air Power Survey*, 2, pt. 2: 331; David Eshel, "In Search of an Effective Defence," *Jane's Defence Weekly* 31, no. 10 (1999): 71.

34. Gordon and Trainor, *Generals' War*, 238.

35. John M. Clearwater, "Scud Hunting: Theater Missile Defense and SOF," *Special Warfare* 12, no. 2 (1999): 27.

36. Ripley, "Scud Hunting," 9.

37. *Gulf War Air Power Survey*, 2, pt. 2: 330–31; Eshel, "In Search of an Effective Defence," 71; Gordon and Trainor, *Generals' War*, 245. Of these, between seventy and eighty suspected TELs were destroyed by smart bombs and another seven to twenty-nine TELs were destroyed by SOF acting in conjunction with aircraft. All of these later turned out to be decoys.

38. *Gulf War Air Power Survey*, 2, pt. 2: 340. Similarly, the DOD's *Final Report to Congress on the Conduct of the Persian Gulf War* observed that "by early February, the counter-Scud effort seemed to be having an effect, although no destruction of mobile launchers had been confirmed" (168).

39. Gordon and Trainor, *Generals' War*, 247; Powell, "Scud War, Round Two," 51; Bolger, *Death Ground*, 169.

40. Walter E. Boomer, John J. Yeosock, Stanley R. Arthur, and Charles A. Horner, "Ten Years After," *Proceedings* (US Naval Institute) 127, no. 1 (2001): 65.

41. David A. Fulghum, "Key Military Officials Criticize Intelligence Handling in Gulf War," *Aviation Week and Space Technology*, 24 June 1991, 83.

42. See Jonathan B. Tucker, "Evidence Iraq Used Chemical Weapons during the 1991 Persian Gulf War," *Nonproliferation Review* 4, no. 3 (1997): 114–22.

43. This hypothesis is put forward in many of the reports released by the Office of the Special Assistant to the Deputy Secretary of Defense for Gulf War Illness (see, e.g., the "Methodology" section of DOD, Special Assistant for Gulf War Illnesses, *Possible Mustard Release at Ukhaydir Ammunition Storage Depot* [Washington, DC: GPO, 16 June 2000], www.gulflink.osd.mil/ukhaydir/, accessed April 2001).

44. In addition to these two sites, the Muhammadiyat Ammunition Storage Site and Al Muthanna were examined for possible connections to Gulf War Illness (see DOD, *Chemical Warfare Agent Release at Muhammadiyat Ammunition Storage Site*, 22 March 2001, www.gulflink.osd.mil/muhammadiyat/, accessed 11 April 2001; idem, *The Gulf War Air Campaign—Possible Chemical Warfare Agent Release at Al Muthanna, February 8, 1991*, 19 March 2001, www.gulflink.osd.mil/al_muth/, accessed March 2001; and CIA, Office of Weapons, Technology and Proliferation, *Report on Intelligence Related to Gulf War Illnesses*, 2 August 1996, www.gulflink.osd.mil/cia_report/102496_war.htm, accessed 12 April 2001).

45. Deborah Funk, "Second Iraqi Ammo Depot Studied," *Army Times*, 18 August 1997, 6.

46. DOD, Special Assistant for Gulf War Illnesses, *Possible Mustard Release at Ukhaydir Ammunition Storage Depot*.

47. Ibid.

48. Persian Gulf War Illness Task Force, "Update on Potential Mustard Release at Ukhaydir Ammunition Storage Depot," 4 September 1997, 2, www.gulflink.osd.mil /ukhaydir_ii/ukhaydir_ii_refs/n56en021/7287_023_0000011.htm, accessed April 2001.

49. DOD, Special Assistant for Gulf War Illnesses, *Possible Mustard Release at Ukhaydir Ammunition Depot*, Tab D. The models used in this ensemble approach were the Global Data Assimilation System (GDAS), the Naval Operational Global Atmospheric Prediction System (NOGAPS), the Coupled Ocean-Atmosphere Mesoscale Prediction System (COAMPS), and the Operational Multiscale Environment Model with Grid Adaptivity (OMEGA). In addition, DOD modelers used the Second-Order Closure Integrated Puff (SCIPUFF) and Vapor, Liquid, and Solid Tracking (VLSTRACK) transport/diffusion models to determine how the released agent would disperse under those conditions.

50. Ibid.

51. Ibid. The DOD report points out that the CIA's reassessment "did not specifically address how the empty, green rounds from UNSCOM's inspection at the Fallujah Proving Ground might have leaked."

52. George C. Wilson, "Missed Signal at Khamisiyah," *Navy Times*, 10 March 1997, 16.

53. Ibid.

54. Persian Gulf War Illness Task Force, "Khamisiyah: A Historical Perspective on Related Intelligence" (Washington, DC: GPO, 9 April 1997), 8; Wilson, "Missed Signal at Khamisiyah." Originally stored in the open near the Khamisiyah depot, the mustard shells were apparently transferred to another storage depot during the air campaign.

55. Wilson, "Missed Signal at Khamisiyah"; Patrick Pexton and Jack Weible, "CIA Admits It Knew of Chemical Weapons at Khamisiyah," *Army Times,* 21 April 1997, 26.

56. DOD, *U.S. Demolition Operations at Khamisiyah,* 7 December 2000, www.gulflink .osd.mil/khamisiyah_ii/, accessed 13 April 2001 The chemical agent was assessed by modelers to be 50 percent pure.

57. Ibid.

58. Dana Priest and Bill McAllister, "Gulf War's Depot of Distrust; Pentagon Lagged in Noting Possible Chemical Exposure," *Washington Post,* 10 November 1998, A1; Pexton and Weible, "CIA Admits It Knew of Chemical Weapons at Khamisiyah"; Wilson, "Missed Signal at Khamisyah."

59. DOD, *U.S. Demolition Operations at Khamisiyah;* Philip Shenon, "U.N. Reveals New Evidence of Gas from 2d Iraqi Depot," *New York Times,* 30 July 1997, A14.

60. Butler, *Report to the Security Council on the Status of Disarmament and Monitoring.*

61. William S. Cohen, General Hugh Shelton, Vice Admiral Scott A. Fry, and Rear Admiral Thomas R. Wilson, DOD News Briefing on Operation Desert Fox, 19 December 1998, www.defenselink.mil/news/Dec1998/t12191998_t1219fox.html, accessed 23 February 2001; William S. Cohen, General Hugh Shelton, and Rear Admiral Thomas Wilson, DOD news briefing on Operation Desert Fox, 18 December 1998, www.defenselink .mil/news/Dec1998/ t12181998_t1218sd.html.

62. G eneral Zinni made these remarks in early 1999 before a scandal erupted over allegations that the U.S. used UNSCOM to spy on Iraq. General Anthony Zinni, DoD news briefing on Operation Desert Fox and Iraq, 8 January 1999, www.defenselink .mil/news/Jan1999/t01081999_t0108znn.html.

63. Jonathan B. Tucker, "Perspectives on the Iraqi Crisis; The First Nonproliferation War?" *Los Angeles Times,* 15 November 1998, M5.

64. William M. Arkin, "Desert Fox Delivery; Precision Undermined Its Purpose," *Washington Post,* 17 January 1999, B1; Ralph Peters, "Operation Desert Fox Showed Our Powerlessness," *Army Times,* 22 February 1999, 39; Romesh Ratnesar, "What Good Did It Do?" *Time,* 28 December 1998, 68; Fred Kaplan, "Strikes Didn't Finish Job US Set Out to Do," *Boston Globe,* 21 December 1998, www.fas.org/news/iraq/1998/12/21 /finish_job.html.

65. William J. Clinton, "Address to the Nation Announcing Military Strikes on Iraq, December 16, 1998," *Public Papers of the Presidents of the United States, William J. Clinton, 1998* (Washington, DC: GPO, 2000), 2:2182.

66. Al Sava Airfield was reportedly targeted because of an Iraqi program to convert L-29 trainer aircraft at the base into unmanned aircraft capable of delivering biological agents including anthrax via spray tanks. See Cohen, Shelton, and Wilson, DOD news briefing on Operation Desert Fox, 18 December 1998.

67. Arkin, "Desert Fox Delivery."

68. Steven Lee Myers, "The Targets; Jets Said to Avoid Poison Gas Sites," *New York Times,* 18 December 1998, A1.

69. Terence P. Jeffrey, "U.S. Didn't Target Saddam's Chemical, Biological Weapons," *Human Events,* 12 February 1999, 7.

70. Myers, "Targets."

71. Ripley, "Scud Hunting," 15; David A. Fulghum, "Scud Hunting May Drop under 10-Minute Mark," *Aviation Week and Space Technology,* 21 February 1994, 90; idem, "New Intelligence Link Speeds Mobile Scud Hunt," ibid., 1 May 1995, 23; Hewish and Lok, "Stopping the Scud Threat," 40.

72. Counterproliferation Program Review Committee (CPRC), *Report on Activities and Programs for Countering Proliferation and NBC Terrorism* (Washington, DC: DOD, May 1998), 5-26, 5-27.

73. Arkin, "Desert Fox Delivery"; Ratnesar, "What Good Did It Do?" 68.

74. Cohen, Shelton, and Wilson, DOD news briefing on Operation Desert Fox, 19 December 1998.

75. Arkin, "Desert Fox Delivery." Arkin claims that it was this stricture, rather than concern over collateral damage, that led to CW and BW production facilities' being left off the target list.

76. Richard J. Newman, Kevin Whitelaw, Thomas Omestad, and Bruce B. Auster, "Bombs over Baghdad," *U.S. News & World Report,* 28 December 1998, 32; Kaplan, "Strikes Didn't Finish Job US Set Out to Do."

77. Jeffrey, "U.S. Didn't Target Saddam's Chemical, Biological Weapons," 7.

78. William Cohen, DOD News Briefing, 19 December 1998,www.defenselink.mil /news/Dec1998/t12201998_t1219coh.html.

79. Newman et al., "Bombs over Baghdad," 32.

80. Office of the Deputy Secretary of Defense, *Report on Nonproliferation and Counterproliferation Activities and Programs* (Washington, DC: DOD, May 1994), 29.

81. CPRC, *Report on Activities and Programs for Countering Proliferation and NBC Terrorism,* 5-10, 5-26, 5-27.

82. See, e.g., Thomas Ricks, "US Military Mulls Weapons That Disable Bunkers, Spare People," *Wall Street Journal,* 1 July 1999, A1. Bryan Bender describes the Air Force's "Colt 45" test, which featured a 2,000-pound bomb filled with solid rocket propellant to be used as an incendiary to destroy agents ("Contamination Fears in the War against WMD," *Jane's Defence Weekly* 29, no. 8 [1998]: 8).

83. Bryan Bender, "USA Planning Warhead to Hit CB Weapons," *Jane's Defence Weekly* 31, no. 12 (1999): 6.

84. David Atkinson, "Agent Defeat Warhead Proposals Insufficient," *Defense Daily,* 27 May 1999, 1; "Empty Handed," *Aviation Week and Space Technology,* 31 May 1999, 17.

85. The program is formally known as Optimal Dual Delivery and involves dropping aerial bombs so close together that the first one blasts a path for the second to penetrate deeper into the target (Andrew Koch, "Dual Delivery Is Key to Buried Targets," *Jane's Defence Weekly* 33, no. 10 [2000]: 11).

86. See, e.g., Andrew C. Revkin, "U.S. Making Weapons to Blast Underground Hide-Outs," *New York Times,* 3 December 2001, B4; Peter Baker and Susan B. Glasser, "U.S. and Afghan Forces Attack Al Qaeda Refuge; One American Dies in Heavy Fighting," *Washington Post,* 2 March 2002, A1; "Hunt for Bin Laden Will Enter a New Phase with Use of 'Thermobaric' Bombs in Caves," *St. Louis Post-Dispatch,* 22 December 2001, 5A; and Richard Sisk, "Cave-Buster Bombs Are Ace in Hole," *New York Daily News,* 27 December 2001, 2.

87. Bender, "Contamination Fears in the War against WMD."

88. DOD, *Report to Congress: Kosovo/Operation Allied Force After-Action Report* (Washington, DC: GPO, 31 January 2000), 62.

89. Estimates of Yugoslav forces present in Kosovo at the beginning of Allied Force were 300–350 tanks, 430–50 armored personnel carriers, 750 artillery/mortar pieces, and an undetermined number of other military vehicles (see John A. Tirpak and Peter Grier, "Survey Shows NATO Close on Serb Damage Estimates," *Air Force Magazine* 82, no. 11 [1999]: 13; David A. Fulghum, "Report Tallies Damage, Lists U.S. Weaknesses," *Aviation Week and Space Technology,* 14 February 2000, 34; and DOD, *Report to Congress: Kosovo/*

Operation Allied Force After-Action Report, 86, www.defenselink.mil/pubs/kaar02072000
.pdf, accessed 2002).

90. David A. Fulghum, "Pentagon Dissecting Kosovo Combat Data," *Aviation Week and Space Technology,* 26 July 1999, 68; Mike Blanchfield, "Forces Mum on Jets' Hit Rate: DND Won't Say if CF-18s Destroyed Serb Tanks," *Ottawa Citizen,* 9 July 1999, A12.

91. DOD, *Report to Congress: Kosovo/Operation Allied Force After-Action Report,* 85. Confirmed strikes were as follows: 93 tanks, 153 armored personnel carriers, 389 artillery/mortars, and 339 other military vehicles.

92. Ibid., 62.

EIGHT: Combating Proliferation

1. John R. Bolton, "Beyond the Axis of Evil," remarks Made at the Heritage Foundation, 6 May 2002, www.state.gov/t/us/rm/9962.htm, accessed 16 May 2002.

2. Joseph D. Douglass Jr. and Neil C. Livingstone, *America the Vulnerable: The Threat of Chemical and Biological Warfare* (Lexington, MA: Lexington Books, 1987). While the authors state that there were reports from "émigrés, defectors and captured Cuban soldiers" that authenticate Cuba's effort to develop toxin weapons, they provide no references to supporting documentation.

3. Senate Governmental Affairs Committee, Permanent Subcommittee on Investigations, *Global Spread of Chemical and Biological Weapons,* 101st Cong., 1st sess., 1990, 57.

4. W. Seth Carus, *The Poor Man's Atomic Bomb? Biological Weapons in the Middle East,* Policy Paper 23 (Washington, DC: Washington Institute for Near East Policy, 1991), 27.

5. The report, based on criteria developed by Elisa Harris, defined "possible" as "those countries reported by Western government officials, generally off the record, as seeking to acquire [biological] weapons or a production capability, or as being suspected of possessing [biological] weapons" (House Armed Services Committee, *Countering the Chemical and Biological Weapons Threat in the Post-Soviet World: Report of the Special Inquiry into the Chemical and Biological Threat,* 102nd Cong., 2nd sess., 1993, 12–13).

6. DIA, "The Cuban Threat to U.S. National Security," 6 May 1998, www.defenselink .mil/pubs/cubarpt.htm, accessed 23 May 2002. No reference is made to Cuba in Office of the Secretary of Defense, *Proliferation: Threat and Response* (Washington, DC: GPO, January 2001).

7. David Gonzalez, "Carter and Powell Cast Doubt on Bioarms in Cuba," *New York Times,* 14 May 2002, A3; Mark Fineman, "Carter Doubts Claim of Cuban Bioterror," *Los Angeles Times,* 14 May 2002, A1; Kevin Sullivan, "Carter Says He Was Told U.S. Had No Proof Cuba Shared Bioweapons Data; State Dept. Official's Claim Contradicted," *Washington Post,* 14 May 2002, A14.

8. Gonzalez, "Carter and Powell Cast Doubt on Bioarms in Cuba."

9. Carl Ford Jr., testimony before the Senate Foreign Relations Committee, Subcommittee on Western Hemisphere, Peace Corps, and Narcotics Affairs, 107th Cong., 2nd sess., 5 June 2002.

10. Tim Johnson, "Talk of Germ Weapons in Cuba Jolts Congress," *Miami Herald,* 8 May 2002.

11. Judith Miller, "Washington Accuses Cuba of Germ-Warfare Research," *New York Times,* 7 May 2002, A6.

12. "More Doubt Is Cast on Cuba Bioweapons," *Washington Post,* 25 May 2002, A24.

13. John Hall, "Cuba: Threat or Not?" *Washington Times*, 10 May 2002, 21.

14. Gonzalez, "Carter and Powell Cast Doubt on Bioarms in Cuba."

15. See, e.g., Joseph Cirincione, Jon B. Wolfsthal, and Miriam Rajkumar, *Deadly Arsenals: Tracking Weapons of Mass Destruction* (Washington, DC: Carnegie Endowment for International Peace, 2002); Stephen Burgess and Helen Purkitt, *The Rollback of South Africa's Chemical and Biological Warfare Program* (Maxwell AFB, AL: USAF Counterproliferation Center, April 2001); Leonard S. Spector with Jacqueline R. Smith, *Nuclear Ambitions: The Spread of Nuclear Weapons, 1989–1990* (Boulder, CO: Westview Press, 1990); Leonard S. Spector, *The New Nuclear Nations* (New York: Vintage Books, 1985); Julio C. Carasales, "The Argentine-Brazilian Nuclear Rapprochement," *Nonproliferation Review 2*, no. 3 (1995): 39–48; David Albright and Corey Gay, "Taiwan: Nuclear Nightmare Averted," *Bulletin of the Atomic Scientists 54*, no. 1 (1998): 54–60; and Andrew Mack, "Potential, Not Proliferation," ibid. 53, no. 4 (July/August 1997): 48–53.

16. George W. Bush, "Address before a Joint Session of the Congress on the State of the Union," *Weekly Compilation of Presidential Documents 38*, no. 5 (4 February 2002): 135.

17. Office of the Secretary of Defense, *Proliferation: Threat and Response*, 21–30, 33–50; Bolton, "Beyond the Axis of Evil." See also Cirincione et al., *Deadly Arsenals*, 191–205, 207–19, 221–36, 305–11.

18. Office of the Secretary of Defense, *Proliferation: Threat and Response*, 34–42; Kori N. Schake and Judith S. Yaphe, *The Strategic Implications of a Nuclear-Armed Iran*, McNair Paper 64 (Washington, DC: National Defense University Press, 2001), 9–11; Anthony H. Cordesman, *Iran's Military Forces in Transition: Conventional Threats and Weapons of Mass Destruction* (Westport, CT: Praeger, 1999), esp. chaps. 18–20; Mike Eisenstadt, *"The Sword of the Arabs": Iraq's Strategic Weapons*, Policy Paper 21 (Washington, DC: Washington Institute for Near East Policy, 1990).

19. Office of the Secretary of Defense, *Proliferation: Threat and Response*, 9, 18; Howard W. French, "North Korean Radio Asserts Country Has Nuclear Arms," *New York Times*, 19 November 2002, A12; idem, "North Korea Clarifies Statement on A-Bomb," ibid., A16; Doug Struck, "North Korea Says It Will Renew Work at Reactors," *Washington Post*, A1; Richard W. Stevenson, "North Korea Begins to Reopen Plant for Processing Plutonium," *New York Times*, 24 December 2002, A1; Seth Mydans, "North Korea Says It Is Withdrawing from Arms Treaty," ibid., 10 January 2003, A1.

20. George Perkovich, *India's Nuclear Bomb: The Impact on Global Proliferation* (Berkeley and Los Angeles: University of California Press, 1999); D. K. Palit and P. K. S. Namboodiri, *Pakistan's Islamic Bomb* (New Delhi: Vikas, 1979); Office of the Secretary of Defense, *Proliferation: Threat and Response*, 21–30.

21. IAEA, "Fourth Consolidated Report of the Director General of the International Atomic Energy Agency under paragraph 16 of Security Council Resolution 1051 (1996)," S/1997/779, 8 October 1997, www.iaea.org/worldatom/Programmes/ActionTeam/reports/s_1997_779.pdf, accessed 2001. See also Khidhir Hamza with Jeff Stein, *Saddam's Bombmaker: The Terrifying Inside Story of the Iraqi Nuclear and Biological Weapons Agenda* (New York: Scribner, 2000); and David Albright and Khidhir Hamza, "Iraq's Reconstitution of Its Nuclear Weapons Program," *Arms Control Today 28*, no. 7 (1998): 9–15.

22. Avner Cohen, *Israel and the Bomb* (New York: Columbia University Press, 1998), esp. 299–303.

23. Jason D. Ellis, "Beyond Nonproliferation: Secondary Supply, Proliferation Management, and U.S. Foreign Policy," *Comparative Strategy 20*, no. 1 (2001): 6–10, 13–14.

24. This has also been a longstanding rationale for U.S. security assistance and arms transfers to foreign countries (see Duncan L. Clarke, Daniel B. O'Connor, and Jason D. Ellis, *Send Guns and Money: Security Assistance and U.S. Foreign Policy* [Westport, CT: Praeger, 1997], esp. ch. 5).

25. Stephen Blank, "Yevgeny Primakov and Russia's Proliferation Strategy: What We Should Expect," *Monitor* 4, no. 4 (1998): 9. Russian Foreign Minister Andrei Kozyrev also underscored this view in 1995, arguing that "we must be sure that we are really taking into account all the circumstances. We must implement only projects that meet our long-term interests. This means that the economic situation should not make us lean to this side or that" (see "Kozyrev Rejects US Attempts to Pressure Russia," *ITAR-TASS*, 4 April 1995).

26. "Primakov Reassures Netanyahu on Technology Exports to Iran," *Interfax*, BBC Summary of World Broadcasts, 23 March 1999.

27. Ellis, "Beyond Nonproliferation," 3–6, 13–14.

28. Aaron Karp, "Lessons of the Iranian Missile Program for U.S. Nonproliferation Policy," *Nonproliferation Review* 5, no. 3 (1998): 23. See also Robert J. Einhorn and Gary Samore, "Ending Russian Assistance to Iran's Nuclear Bomb," *Survival* 44, no. 2 (2002): 51–70.

29. George J. Tenet, statement prepared for delivery to the Senate Armed Services Committee, *Worldwide Threats*, 106th Cong., 1st sess., 2000, 7–9; *Report of the Commission to Assess the Ballistic Missile Threat to the United States, Executive Summary, Pursuant to Public Law 201*, 104th Cong., 1998, 12.

30. Patty Reinert and Michael Hedges, "U.S. Rebuts Remarks by Carter in Havana; Cuba's Biotechnology 'Sharing' at Issue," *Houston Chronicle*, 14 May 2002, A1; Johnson, "Talk of Germ Weapons in Cuba Jolts Congress."

31. Michael J. Mazarr, ed., *Nuclear Weapons in a Transformed World: The Challenge of Virtual Nuclear Arsenals* (New York: St. Martin's, 1997); Michael J. Mazarr, "Virtual Nuclear Arsenals," *Survival* 37, no. 3 (1995): 7–26; Marc Erikson, "Japan Could 'Go Nuclear' in Months," *Asia Times Online*, 14 January 2003, http://www.atimes.com/atimes/Japan /EA14Dh01.html, accessed 14 January 2003; Charles Krauthammer, "The Japan Card," *Washington Post*, 3 January 2003, A19; Ching Cheong, "Is Japan Going Nuclear?" *Strait Times* (Singapore), 25 June 2002.

32. Center for Counterproliferation Research, *CBRN Terrorism: An Annotated Bibliography* (Washington, DC: National Defense University, 2001), 1–12. See also Jonathan B. Tucker, ed., *Toxic Terror: Assessing Terrorist Use of Chemical and Biological Weapons* (Cambridge: MIT Press, 2000); Brad Roberts, ed., *Terrorism with Chemical and Biological Weapons: Calibrating Risks and Responses* (Washington, DC: Chemical and Biological Arms Control Institute, 1997); and Sidney D. Drell, Abraham D. Sofaer, and George D. Wilson, eds., *The New Terror: Facing the Threat of Biological and Chemical Weapons* (Stanford, CA: Hoover Institution Press, 1999).

33. David E. Kaplan and Andrew Marshall, *The Cult at the End of the World: The Terrifying Story of the Aum Doomsday Cult, from the Subways of Tokyo to the Nuclear Arsenals of Russia* (New York: Crown, 1996), 251; John F. Sopko and Alan Edleman, "Staff Report—Global Proliferation of Weapons of Mass Destruction: A Case Study on the Aum Shinrikyo," Senate Committee on Governmental Affairs, Permanent Subcommittee on Investigations, *Global Proliferation of Weapons of Mass Destruction, Part I*, 104th Cong., 1st sess., 1995, 24.

34. Senate Committee on Appropriations, *Hearing on Fiscal Year '03 Defense Department Appropriations*, 110th Cong., 2nd sess., 21 May 2002.

35. Gilles Andréani, "The Disarray of US Non-Proliferation Policy," *Survival* 41, no. 4 (1999–2000): 43. See also Brad Roberts, "Proliferation and Nonproliferation in the 1990s: Looking for the Right Lessons," *Nonproliferation Review* 6, no. 4 (1999): 70–82.

36. White House, *A National Security Strategy for a Global Age* (Washington, DC: GPO, December 2000), 2–3.

37. Ibid., 16–18.

38. White House, *The National Security Strategy of the United States of America* (Washington, DC: GPO, September 2002), 14. See also White House, *National Strategy to Combat Weapons of Mass Destruction* (Washington, DC: GPO, December 2002).

39. Ibid., 13–15.

40. Robert S. Litwak, "The New Calculus of Pre-emption," *Survival* 44, no. 4 (2002–3): 54–60; Harald Muller and Mitchell Reiss, "Counterproliferation: Putting New Wine in Old Bottles," *Washington Quarterly* 18, no. 2 (1996): 145–49.

41. George W. Bush, "Commencement Address at the United States Military Academy in West Point, New York, June 1, 2002," *Weekly Compilation of Presidential Documents* 38, no. 23 (10 June 2002): 946.

42. See Richard B. Cheney, remarks to the U.S. Chamber of Commerce, November 14, 2001, www.whitehouse.gov/vicepresident/news-speeches/speeches/vp20011114-1 .html, accessed 2003.

43. Jason D. Ellis, "'The Gravest Danger': Proliferation, Terrorism, and the Bush Doctrine," *Monitor* (2003).

44. John A. Lauder, unclassified statement for the record on the Worldwide WMD threat to the Commission to Assess the Organization of the Federal Government to Combat the Proliferation of Weapons of Mass Destruction (as prepared for delivery), 29 April 1999, www.cia.gov/cia/public_affairs/speeches/1999/lauder_speech_042999.htm, accessed 26 January 2001, pp. 1, 3.

45. See George J. Tenet, statement for the record, Senate Select Committee on Intelligence, 6 February 2002, *Current and Projected National Security Threats to the United States*, 107th Cong., 2nd sess., 2002, 15–19; Thomas R. Wilson, statement for the record, Senate Select Committee on Intelligence, 19 March 2002, *Current and Projected National Security Threats to the United States*, 107th Cong., 2nd sess., 2002, 73–74.

46. G. John Ikenberry, "America's Imperial Ambition," *Foreign Affairs* 81, no. 3 (2002): 56–60. See also Litwak, "New Calculus of Pre-emption," 54–60.

47. Jason D. Ellis, "The Best Defense: Counterproliferation and U.S. National Security," *Washington Quarterly* 26, no. 2 (2003): 115–33.

48. Tenet, statement for the record, Senate Select Committee on Intelligence, 6 February 2002, 7.

49. While these terms are often conflated, for the purposes of this discussion a *preventive* attack would be one undertaken in order to preclude a given actor from achieving a particular weapons capability, whereas a *preemptive* attack would be one undertaken to degrade or destroy an existing capability.

50. David E. Sanger, "In North Korea and Pakistan, Deep Roots of Nuclear Barter," *New York Times*, 24 November 2002, A1.

51. Thom Shanker with Terence Neilan, "Yemen Protests Seizure of North Korean Ship; Says Scuds Were Bound for Its Army," *New York Times*, 11 December 2002, www.nytimes .com/2002/12/11/international/12CND-MISS.html, accessed December 2002; Thomas E.

Ricks and Peter Slevin, "Intercepted Missile Shipment Released to Yemen," *Washington Post*, 11 December 2002, www.washingtonpost.com/ac2/wp-dyn/A39775-2002Dec11 ?language=printer, accessed December 2002. National Security Presidential Directive 17 underscores that interdiction is a "critical part of the U.S. strategy to combat" the proliferation of WMD and their attendant delivery means (see White House, *National Strategy to Combat Weapons of Mass Destruction*, 2).

52. Center for Counterproliferation Research, *The Counterproliferation Imperative: Meeting Tomorrow's Challenges* (Washington, DC: National Defense University, 2001), 8–11.

53. Senate Select Committee on Intelligence and House Permanent Select Committee on Intelligence, *Joint Inquiry into Intelligence Community Activities Before and After the Terrorist Attacks of September 11, 2001*, 107th Cong., 2nd sess., 2002, S. Rep. 107-351 and H. Rep. 107-792, xv–xviii.

54. *Key Judgments (from October 2000 NIE): Iraq's Continuing Programs for Weapons of Mass Destruction*, www.washingtonpost.com/wp-srv/nation/nationalsecurity/documents /nie_iraq_wmd.pdf, accessed 2003, and *Written Statement from CIA Director Tenet* (August 2003), www.washingtonpost.com/ac2/wp-dyn?pagename=article&node=&contentId =A35443-2003Aug8&notFound=true, accessed 2003, both released to the public in August 2003, www.washingtonpost.com.

55. Office of the Secretary of Defense, *Quadrennial Defense Review Report* (Washington, DC: DOD, 30 September 2001), 14.

56. Dan Balz, Bob Woodward, and Jeff Himmelman, "Afghan Campaign's Blueprint Emerges," *Washington Post*, 29 January 2002, A1.

57. National Defense University Center for Counterproliferation Research, *Counterproliferation Imperative*, 28–31. See also *Gulf War Air Power Survey*, vol. 1, pt. 1, *Planning and Command and Control* (Washington, DC: GPO, 1993); and DOD, *Final Report to Congress on the Conduct of the Persian Gulf War Pursuant to Title V of the Persian Gulf Conflict Supplemental Authorization and Personnel Benefits Act of 1991 (Public Law 102-25)* (Washington, DC: GPO, April 1992).

58. Traditionally, about two-thirds of all funds appropriated for counterproliferation within the DOD have gone toward missile defense (see Counterproliferation Program Review Committee [CPRC], *Report on Activities and Programs for Countering Proliferation and NBC Terrorism* [Washington, DC: DOD, May 1998], ES2-7). Note that 1998 information remains the most recent data publicly available. While the executive summaries of subsequent annual reports are unclassified, the full reports, including data on funds allocated by area for capability enhancement, are not. According to the General Accounting Office, the DOD planned to spend approximately $7.3 billion on committee-related activities in fiscal year 2001, roughly $5.3 billion (or almost 73 percent) of which would be allocated for missile defense. Typically, about $1 billion annually has gone to the Chemical and Biological Defense Program, which focuses on passive defense activities. Together, these funds would constitute 86 percent of all dedicated DOD research, development, and acquisition resources associated with the CPRC (see General Accounting Office, *Weapons of Mass Destruction: DOD's Actions to Combat Weapons Use Should Be More Integrated and Focused*, NSIAD-00-97 (Washington, DC, May 2000), 20; and DOD, *Chemical and Biological Defense Program Annual Report to Congress* [Washington, DC: GPO, 2000]).

59. White House, *National Security Strategy of the United States of America*, 1–6.

60. President George W. Bush, remarks to the students and faculty at National Defense University, 1 May 2001.

61. See Center for Counterproliferation Research, *Anthrax in America: A Chronology and Analysis of the Fall 2001 Attacks* (Washington, DC: National Defense University, 2002), 1–13. See also President George W. Bush, *Securing the Homeland, Strengthening the Nation* (Washington, DC: White House, February 2002), www.whitehouse.gov/homeland /homeland_security_book.pdf, accessed February 2002; and U.S. Congress, *Public Health Security and Bioterrorism Preparedness Act of 2002*, Public Law 107-188, 107th Cong., 2nd sess. (12 June 2002).

Index

About the Authors

Jason Ellis is senior director for asymmetric strategies at Hicks & Associates, Inc., in McLean, Virginia. From May 1999 through June 2003 Dr. Ellis was senior research professor at the National Defense University, a member of the professional staff at the university's Center for Counterproliferation Research, and on the faculty of the National War College. Dr. Ellis was previously a senior analyst with the Commission to Assess the Organization of the Federal Government to Combat the Proliferation of Weapons of Mass Destruction (chaired by John Deutch), a postdoctoral research fellow at the Belfer Center for Science and International Affairs, Harvard University, and on the faculty of American University's School of International Service. He has published widely on American defense and foreign policy, including *Defense by Other Means: The Politics of U.S.-NIS Threat Reduction and Nuclear Security Cooperation* (2001) and *Send Guns and Money: Security Assistance and U.S. Foreign Policy* (1997).

Geoffrey Kiefer joined the staff of the Center for Counterproliferation Research, National Defense University, as a research support specialist in July 2000. In this capacity Mr. Kiefer conducts research on projects relating to the security implications of proliferation, including consequence management, the restoration of operations following chemical or biological weapons attacks, and the evolution of national policy to combat the spread of weapons of mass destruction. Mr. Kiefer completed his undergraduate studies at Saint Louis University in 1997 and received his master's degree from the Defense and Strategic Studies Program at Southwest Missouri State University.

Printed in the United States
134155LV00005B/15/A

9 780801 886263